Praise for
Essentials of Practice-Based Coaching

"For too long the early care and education field has sidelined the importance of early childhood educators' competent practice. Given the expanding knowledge base about children's early learning and the exponential growth of professional development opportunities, this book could not be more timely."
—**Stacie G. Goffin, Ed.D.,** Principal,
Goffin Strategy Group, LLC, and author of *Early Childhood
Education For A New Era: Leading For Our Profession*

"Written by the premier experts on the subject, this book is a must-have for anyone using or supporting practice-based coaching in early childhood settings. Filled with countless tips and strategies, this book will be an incredibly useful tool for both new and experienced practice-based coaches—and everyone in between."
—**Rob Corso, Ph.D.,** Senior Researcher,
Vanderbilt University

"What a gift! Snyder, Hemmeter, and Fox provide us with a thorough grounding in the theory and research undergirding practice-based coaching. Then, they offer practical steps and guides for implementing the approach. This is an indispensable resource for understanding and implementing practice-based coaching."
—**Susan R. Sandall, Ph.D.,** Professor Emeritus,
University of Washington

"A thorough description of effective supports for promoting best practices with infants, toddlers, and preschoolers. The coaching model is compelling, and the case examples and implementation resources are especially rich."
—**Douglas R. Powell, Ph.D.,** Distinguished Professor Emeritus,
Department of Human Development and Family Studies, Purdue University

"A thoroughly researched and thoughtfully designed description of practice-based coaching that integrates evidence and recommended practice with the implementation strategies and procedures for early childhood educators to apply the model in their programs. The book capitalizes on the authors' excellence in research and extensive experience in professional development and coaching to produce a highly readable guide with accompanying field-tested resources ready for use."
—**Juliann J. Woods, Ph.D.,** SLP-CCC, Professor Emeritus,
School of Communication Science and Disorders,
Communication and Early Childhood Research and
Practice Center, Florida State University

"An essential book on one of the most important education and policy issues of our time—supporting teacher quality through coaching. Snyder, Hemmeter, and Fox, internationally renowned experts in coaching, artfully and clearly synthesize the empirical evidence supporting the effectiveness of practice-based coaching. This book will be used as the 'gold standard' for implementing evidenced-based coaching in early childhood classrooms."
—**Barbara A. Wasik, Ph.D.,** PNC Endowed Chair in Early Childhood Education,
College of Education and Human Development, Temple University

"The quintessential resource for new and experienced coaches alike. Readers will appreciate the authors' detailing of the theoretical foundations and professional applications of practice-based coaching."
—**Alexandra Stoerger,** University of Miami,
Early Steps program

Essentials of Practice-Based Coaching

Essentials of Practice-Based Coaching

Supporting Effective Practices in Early Childhood

by

Patricia Snyder, Ph.D.
Distinguished Professor and David Lawrence Jr. Endowed Chair
University of Florida
Gainesville

Mary Louise Hemmeter, Ph.D.
Professor, Vanderbilt University
Nashville, Tennessee

and

Lise Fox, Ph.D.
Professor, University of South Florida
Tampa

with invited contributors

Baltimore • London • Sydney

Paul H. Brookes Publishing Co.
Post Office Box 10624
Baltimore, Maryland 21285-0624
USA

www.brookespublishing.com

Typeset by Absolute Service, Inc., Towson, Maryland.
Manufactured in the United States of America by Sheridan Books, Inc., Chelsea, Michigan.

All examples in this book are composites. Any similarity to actual individuals or circumstances is coincidental, and no implications should be inferred.

Library of Congress Cataloging-in-Publication Data

Names: Snyder, Patricia, 1955 July 13- author. | Hemmeter, Mary Louise,
   author. | Fox, Lise, author.
Title: Essentials of Practice-Based Coaching: Supporting Effective
Practices in Early Childhood/by Patricia Snyder, Mary
   Louise Hemmeter and Lise Fox; with invited contributors.
Description: Baltimore: Paul H. Brookes Publishing Co., [2022] | Includes
   bibliographical references and index.
Identifiers: LCCN 2021023523 (print) | LCCN 2021023524 (ebook) | ISBN
   9781681253817 (paperback) | ISBN 9781681253824 (epub) | ISBN
   9781681253831 (pdf)
Subjects: LCSH: Early childhood teachers—Training of. | Early childhood
   teachers—In-service training. | Mentoring in education. |
   Employees—Coaching of. | BISAC: EDUCATION / Professional Development |
   EDUCATION / Teacher Training & Certification
Classification: LCC LB1775.6 .S68 2022 (print) | LCC LB1775.6 (ebook) |
   DDC 372.21—dc23
LC record available at https://lccn.loc.gov/2021023523
LC ebook record available at https://lccn.loc.gov/2021023524

British Library Cataloguing in Publication data are available from the British Library.

2025   2024

10   9   8   7   6   5   4   3

Contents

About the Downloads

Purchasers of this book may download, print, and/or photocopy appendices for professional and educational use.

To access the materials that come with this book:

1. Go to the Brookes Download Hub: http://downloads.brookespublishing.com

2. Register to create an account (or log in with an existing account).

3. Filter or search for the book title *Essentials of Practice-Based Coaching*.

About the Editors

Patricia Snyder, Ph.D., Distinguished Professor and David Lawrence Jr. Endowed Chair, University of Florida, Gainesville

Dr. Patricia Snyder is the inaugural occupant of the University of Florida's (UF) David Lawrence Jr. Endowed Chair in Early Childhood Studies. She is a UF Distinguished Professor of Special Education and Early Childhood Studies and an affiliate professor of pediatrics. She is the founding director of the UF Anita Zucker Center for Excellence in Early Childhood Studies. Dr. Snyder has worked for more than four decades in community-based and academic settings with an emphasis on advancing transdisciplinary approaches to practice, research, and policy in early childhood. She has been a direct service provider, an early learning program administrator, and a faculty member, researcher, and higher education administrator. She has been actively involved at local, state, and national levels in early childhood systems development and integration, including serving as a gubernatorial appointee to the Children's Trust of Alachua County. Dr. Snyder served as the editor of the *Journal of Early Intervention* from 2002 to 2007. She has been a principal investigator/co-principal investigator for numerous studies and projects funded by the Institute of Education Sciences and the Office of Special Education Programs. She has authored more than 130 refereed journal articles, book chapters, monographs, and books focused on early intervention and early learning with a particular focus on young children with or at risk for disabilities, their families, and the personnel who support them. Dr. Snyder has received a number of awards for her teaching, service, and research activities. Among these awards are the Division for Early Childhood Mary McEvoy Service to the Field Award, Merle B. Karnes Service to the Division Award, and the DEC Award for Mentoring. Dr. Snyder received the Kauffman-Hallahan-Pullen Distinguished Researcher Award from the Division for Research, Council for Exceptional Children. She and her colleagues have been conducting research on practice-based coaching and its application in a variety of early childhood contexts for the past 16 years.

Mary Louise Hemmeter, Ph.D., Professor, Vanderbilt University, Nashville, Tennessee

Dr. Mary Louise Hemmeter is a professor of special education at Vanderbilt University. Her research focuses on effective instruction, supporting social-emotional development and addressing challenging behavior, and coaching teachers. She has directed numerous projects funded by the U.S. Departments of Education and Health and Human Services. Through her work on the national Center on the Social and Emotional Foundations for Early Learning and Institute of Education Sciences–funded research projects, she was involved in the development of the Pyramid Model for Supporting Social Emotional Competence in Young Children and the practice-based coaching model. She is a co-author on the Connect4Learning Early Childhood Curriculum and the Teaching Pyramid Observation Tool. She was co-editor of the *Journal of Early Intervention* and president of the Council for Exceptional Children's Division for Early Childhood. She received the Merle B. Karnes Service to the Division Award and the Mary McEvoy Service to the Field Award.

Lise Fox, Ph.D., Professor, University of South Florida, Tampa

Dr. Lise Fox is a professor in the Department of Child and Family Studies at the University of South Florida in Tampa, Florida, and the co-director of the Florida Center for Inclusive Communities: A University Center for Excellence in Developmental Disabilities. Dr. Fox was one of the developers of the Pyramid Model for Promoting the Social Emotional Competence in Infants and Young Children and has authored 95 books, book chapters, and articles. She has developed and managed numerous technical assistance, research, model demonstration, and personnel preparation projects in the areas of early childhood special education, state capacity building, implementation of the Pyramid Model, preventing and addressing challenging behavior, and positive behavior support.

About the Contributors

Kathleen Artman-Meeker, Ph.D., Associate Professor, University of Washington, Seattle

Dr. Artman-Meeker is an associate professor of early childhood special education at the University of Washington (UW) and the director of research at the UW Haring Center for Inclusive Education. She maintains an active research agenda and community partnerships focused on professional development for early educators, particularly around young children's social-emotional development. Dr. Artman-Meeker's research, teaching, and writing focus on personalized, efficient, and effective coaching across early childhood settings.

Crystal Bishop, Ph.D., Assistant Research Scientist, Anita Zucker Center for Excellence in Early Childhood Studies, University of Florida, Gainesville

Dr. Bishop is an assistant research scientist at the University of Florida Anita Zucker Center for Excellence in Early Childhood Studies. Dr. Bishop and her colleagues collaborate to study, develop, and provide evidence-based professional development that supports the use of practice-based coaching in a variety of early learning environments.

Jolenea Ferro, Ph.D., BCBA-Doctoral, Associate Professor, University of South Florida, Tampa

Dr. Ferro is associate professor in the Florida Center for Inclusive Communities: A University Center for Excellence in Developmental Disabilities at the University of South Florida. Her research primarily focuses on individualized interventions and preventing challenging behaviors, addressing all age groups and abilities. Her current focus is on young children. Dr. Ferro provides training and technical assistance to states, program teams, and coaches to support implementation of the Pyramid Model, young children's social-emotional development, and the reduction of challenging behavior.

Jessica K. Hardy, Ph.D., Assistant Professor, University of Illinois at Urbana–Champaign

Dr. Hardy received her doctorate in early childhood special education from Vanderbilt University and her M.Ed. and B.A. from the University of Florida. She taught in Portland, Oregon, as a Head Start teacher and an early childhood special education teacher. Dr. Hardy's primary research interests are evidence-based instructional practices and early childhood coaching and professional development.

Kiersten A. Kinder, Ph.D., Research Associate, Vanderbilt University, Nashville, Tennessee

Dr. Kinder is a research associate at Vanderbilt University in Nashville, Tennessee. She coordinates a variety of research studies focused on the Pyramid Model and practice-based coaching. Dr. Kinder has worked for more than 15 years in public and lab school settings in a variety of roles including associate director, coach, and teacher. Her professional interests include inclusive education, embedded instruction, building collaborative partnerships, and supporting coaches in the field.

Tara McLaughlin, Ph.D., Senior Lecturer, Massey University, New Zealand

Dr. McLaughlin is a senior lecturer in the Institute of Education at Massey University. Her research interests focus on professional learning and development to support effective teaching, curriculum implementation, assessment and evaluation in early childhood education, and early intervention. Dr. McLaughlin has worked with teachers, children, and families in inclusive learning settings in the United States and in New Zealand. She leads the Massey University Early Years Research Lab.

Ragan H. McLeod, Ph.D., Assistant Professor, University of Alabama, Tuscaloosa

Dr. McLeod has coached preservice and in-service teachers to implement effective practices in early childhood classrooms. She currently develops materials and provides training and technical assistance related to practice-based coaching for the Head Start National Center on Early Childhood Development, Teaching, and Learning. Dr. McLeod is an assistant professor and coordinator of the early childhood special education program at the University of Alabama. Her research interests include language and literacy interventions for young children and professional development to support teachers to implement evidence-based practices.

Chelsea T. Morris, Ph.D., Assistant Professor, Faculty Director, University of West Georgia, Carrollton

Dr. Morris was a teacher in a children's hospital and later, in a public early childhood special education classroom. She recently completed a fellowship with the National Center for Pyramid Model Innovations under the mentorship of Mary Louise Hemmeter. Dr. Morris is founder and faculty director of the Early Learning Center at the College of Education at the University of West Georgia. In each of these endeavors, Dr. Morris has committed to building resilience in young children, their communities, and their families through inclusive practices, positive relationships, and meaningful engagement.

Denise Perez Binder, M.A., Learning and Development Facilitator, National Center for Pyramid Model Innovations, The University of South Florida, Tampa

Denise Perez Binder has been on the faculty at the University of South Florida for more than 18 years. She has provided training, technical assistance, and coaching on Pyramid Model practices for several different technical assistance centers. Currently, she is a technical assistance specialist for the National Center for Pyramid Model Innovations and the Early Childhood Technical Assistance Center.

Darbianne Shannon, Ph.D., Assistant Research Scientist, Anita Zucker Center for Excellence in Early Childhood Studies, University of Florida, Gainesville

Dr. Shannon is an assistant research scientist at the University of Florida in the Anita Zucker Center for Excellence in Early Childhood Studies. She has been working in the field of early childhood studies for more than 15 years, teaching in school- and center-based inclusive early childhood programs and providing professional development and coaching to teachers, coaches, and administrators in public, private, and Head Start settings.

Meghan von der Embse, Ed.S., Learning and Development Facilitator, University of South Florida, Tampa

Meghan von der Embse is a learning and development facilitator with the Florida Center for Inclusive Communities at the University of South Florida and staff member at the National Center for Pyramid Model Innovations. She provides training, technical assistance, and ongoing coaching supports for early childhood programs to build capacity implementing and sustaining Pyramid Model supports. She has practiced as a K–12 school psychologist and behavior specialist, and she has expertise in providing training and technical assistance with multi-tiered systems of support.

Anna Winneker, Ph.D., Assistant Professor, University of South Florida, Tampa

Dr. Winneker is an assistant professor in the College of Behavioral and Community Sciences at the University of South Florida (USF). She serves as project director of the Program-Wide Positive Behavior Support project at USF. Dr. Winneker has extensive experience working with children, families, and teachers to implement a multi-tiered approach to supporting the social-emotional development of young children. Her focus is on supporting educators to implement evidence-based practices to effectively meet the needs of all children.

Foreword

I know when I've read a book that I will go back to again and again. It's a book that causes me to say, "I wish I had known this sooner." *Essentials of Practice-Based Coaching: Supporting Effective Practices in Early Childhood,* written and edited by Patricia Snyder, Ph.D., Mary Louise Hemmeter, Ph.D., and Lise Fox, Ph.D., is one of those comprehensive classics.

As I read the book, cover to cover, I reflected on my early career when I had decent content knowledge but little to no process information about coaching—let alone practice-based coaching. These were early days when it was not standard practice to observe staff and provide feedback. Nevertheless, as a newly minted Ph.D., I found myself sitting in a community-based group home in rural North Carolina. I was there to provide support and feedback after observing new staff interacting with the teens referred to the program through the county's social services system, and at least I knew enough to first recognize all the great work they were doing. Then I launched into a constructive mini-lecture that apparently went on and on and on. As tears ran down the cheeks of one of the staff, I realized that maybe this wasn't going well! I apologized and asked her what was wrong. She said, "You just went on too long." Decades later that scene is still vivid. The conversation might have gone better had I'd known how to initiate a coaching relationship, the importance of growing a partnership through shared goals and buy-in, the importance of using reflective questions, and so much more. Our small staff engaged in a lot of trial and learning loops, and we eventually arrived at some decent practice-based coaching routines. It's just too bad that so many staff had to suffer through our learning curve.

I have had the privilege of being professionally associated with the authors of *Essentials of Practice-Based Coaching* for the last 14 years and have been consistently impressed with their dedication to research and to exemplary services for young children, their families, and caregivers. As always, the authors' goals are ambitious and worthwhile. In this current work, they set out to provide readers with essential information, materials, and resources to implement practice-based coaching. A goal that has been achieved admirably!

There are so many noteworthy aspects to this book: its organization, clarity, usefulness, and systems approach. A broad audience will benefit from three noteworthy and unique aspects. First, the information, materials, and resources are grounded in implementation science and best practices. Second, coaching practices and routines are articulated as core functions rather than as a prescribed form. Third, the book brings to life the coaching practices and offers examples, inspiration, and practical tools for creating the infrastructure to develop, sustain, and improve a practice-based system of coaching.

Grounded in Implementation Science. It's been exhilarating to have spent my last 20 years focused on implementation science and translating that science into implementation best practices that can be used in the field. The authors and invited contributors of *Essentials of Practice-Based Coaching* have helped advance implementation science and relied on it in crafting their approach to practice-based coaching. The literature reviews are comprehensive, yet focused, so that the reader can have confidence in the content, the array of tools, the coaching skills, and the recommended infrastructure to support a coaching system. And finally, they offer clear guidance, based on implementation science, on how to develop a practice-based coaching system that is teachable and able to be evaluated, improved, and sustained. You will learn a great deal from their reliance on and organization of the implementation and coaching literature.

Focus on Core Functions of Practice-Based Coaching. As I have coached at both systems and practice levels, I've grown used to my partners initial concerns about creating and sustaining core functions (e.g., "We don't have money for full-time coaches." "We don't have a state leadership team with those people on it."). This book tackles these concerns by focusing on the functions of each core element while allowing the forms to vary, so long as they support the necessary functions. The authors and invited contributors keep the focus on functions by clearly defining the required operations and simultaneously providing diverse examples of the functions in action. For example, Chapter 5 highlights the important core functions of conducting and using practitioner strength and needs assessments (e.g., identify strengths, set goals, create action plans). The authors also offer various forms of assessments (e.g., document analysis, observation of practices, interviews) that will support those functions.

The second benefit of this focus on functions, is the ability of the authors to cogently define and discuss the parallel processes that need to occur for coaches, so that they too receive the kind of support, training, coaching, and fidelity information to grow and develop. This focus on function is a gift to the field and one that makes this book useful not only for early childhood programs but for any well-defined human service program or set of practices.

Practice-Based Coaching Comes to Life. As important as it is to cite the literature and define the functions of practice-based coaching, it is also essential to make the information accessible and useful to a broad audience of practitioners, coaches, supervisors, and organizational leaders at multiple levels. The transition from big ideas to practical application is not an easy one, but the authors have done this so well. Two primary translation mechanisms are the use of case stories and the provision of job aids, tools, and measures in the Appendices.

The three diverse case stories illustrate the use of skills, practices, and systems changes through running narratives that are integrated within each chapter. These stories of practitioners and coaches engagingly demonstrate how practice-based coaching can play out in the real world. The stories maintain the focus on functions because of the diversity of application across the three stories. And importantly, the case stories provide realistic examples that will encourage readers to move forward in developing their own practice-based coaching system. You will be engaged and interested in the professional development of Lynn, Sam, Maureen, and Maria and the practice-based coaching offered by their coaches, Sirena, Kenya, and Elley.

It is noteworthy that the Appendices comprise roughly 30% of the book's text. The tools, checklists, instruments, assessments, and guidance documents are targeted to each chapter that focuses on coaching processes and skills. In addition, there is plenty of starter dough for those ready to systematically develop coaches' skills and a coaching system (e.g., outline of training programs, recommendations regarding coaching fidelity) for their early childhood programs. Like the case stories, the materials in the Appendices help readers understand what to create, do, say, analyze, and improve to ensure that practice-based coaching comes to life and is maintained with fidelity over time and across coaches and practitioners.

In short, this book is a comprehensive classic. The field of early childhood, and indeed, the field of human services owes a debt of gratitude to the authors and invited contributors of this grounded, thoughtful, engaging, well-organized, and useful book. A pleasure to have it for future use. Grateful.

Karen A. Blase, Ph.D.
Director, Active Implementation Research Network

Acknowledgments

We thank our colleagues, current and former students, and the program leaders, training and technical assistance specialists, coaches, practitioners, and families who have supported the development, implementation, and evaluation of practice-based coaching (PBC). Our collaborative and sustained partnerships have informed and strengthened our insights about the essentials of PBC. We look forward to working with existing and future partners to continue to advance PBC research and practice.

1

Overview of Practice-Based Coaching

Theoretical, Empirical, and Practice-Based Rationales

Patricia Snyder, Mary Louise Hemmeter, and Lise Fox

INTRODUCTION

Practice-Based Coaching (PBC) is an empirically based coaching framework designed to support practitioners' or caregivers' implementation of evidence-based or recommended practices that lead to positive developmental and learning outcomes for infants, toddlers, and preschoolers (Snyder et al., 2015). As shown in Figure 1.1, the PBC framework has three key components: 1) shared goals and action planning, 2) focused observation, and 3) reflection and feedback. These components occur in the context of a collaborative coaching partnership, which is focused explicitly on supporting implementation of evidence-based or recommended practices.

Each component of PBC and the essential elements needed to implement it as intended, or with fidelity, are the focus of this book. In this chapter, we set the context for the chapters that follow by providing background information about PBC and the theoretical, empirical, and practice-based rationales that support it.

The term *evidence-based practices* refers to effective practices that, when implemented as intended, have been demonstrated through empirical research to support children's development and learning. *Recommended practices* refer to practices that are informed by the best available research evidence, the knowledge and wisdom gained through experiences applying practices in authentic contexts, and the values of an organization or field of practice. Examples of recommended practices are the Division for Early Childhood Recommended Practices in Early Intervention/Early Childhood Special Education (Division for Early Childhood, 2014). Throughout the book, the term *effective practices* will be used to encompass both types of practices. Chapter 5 provides information about how the term *practice* is defined within the PBC framework.

BACKGROUND FOR PRACTICE-BASED COACHING

PBC was initially developed, validated, and evaluated for efficacy as part of an Institute of Education Sciences (IES)–funded research project. The project was focused on evaluating the effects of professional development, which included what is now known as PBC, on preschool

Figure 1.1. Practice-Based Coaching framework. Snyder, P. A., Hemmeter, M. L., & Fox, L. (2015). Supporting implementation of evidence-based practices through practice-based coaching. *Topics in Early Childhood Special Education, 35*(3), 133–143. https://doi .org/10.1177/0271121415594925; reprinted by permission.

teachers' use of embedded instruction practices. This work began in 2007 and continues to the present time (e.g., Snyder, Hemmeter, et al., 2018).

PBC was subsequently used in other IES-funded projects conducted by the editors and contributors to this text. In addition to embedded instruction, these projects have included the use of PBC along with workshops and other implementation aids to support practitioners' use of social, emotional, and behavioral practices reflected in the Pyramid Model (e.g., Hemmeter et al., 2016; Hemmeter et al., 2021). PBC was the coaching framework used as part of the Head Start National Center on Quality Teaching and Learning (Head Start/ECLKC: Early Childhood Learning and Knowledge Center, n.d.). PBC is recognized as a critical professional development approach for the implementation of the Pyramid Model (von der Embse et al., 2019). It is also being used to support practitioners' and caregivers' implementation of evidence-based practices in early intervention, early childhood special education, and early care and education contexts (e.g., Fox, 2017; National Center for Pyramid Model Innovations, 2020; Snyder, Woods, et al., 2018).

Beyond projects in which contributors to this book have developed, validated, implemented, and evaluated PBC, many professional development providers, faculty in practitioner preparation programs, researchers, training and technical assistance personnel, coaches, program leaders, and practitioners are using PBC. For example, PBC has been used in studies focused on the BEST in CLASS intervention. BEST in CLASS is a Tier 2 intervention designed to address the needs of children (preschool to second grade) who demonstrate persistent and intensive challenging behaviors in classroom settings, which place them at future risk for developing social-emotional learning difficulties (e.g., Conroy et al., 2019). In addition, the most recent Head Start Program Performance Standards require that programs implement a research-based coordinated coaching strategy for education staff (Training and Professional Development, 2016). PBC is recognized as a research-based coordinated coaching strategy.

Given the widespread use of PBC in early childhood settings, we determined a need existed for a book that contains practical and evidence-informed information on the essentials of PBC. In this book, we provide detailed information about the PBC framework and each component of the framework, case story application examples, and resources to support fidelity of PBC implementation. After spending more than 16 years developing, refining, and evaluating PBC, we are committed to disseminating more widely this research-based coaching approach to support those who coach, those who are being coached, and those who oversee the implementation of professional development, including coaching.

Throughout the book, when appropriate, we refer to those who are being coached as *coachees* and those who are coaching as *coaches*. Coachees are practitioners in early childhood programs such as early care and education programs; state-funded preschool programs; Early Head Start/Head Start programs; inclusive infant, toddler, and preschool programs; home-visiting programs; and early intervention programs. Coachees can also be caregivers (e.g., parent, grandparent, family care provider). Coaches are individuals with a designated role as a coach or caregiver coach. Coaches can be internal to the program or external to the program as professional development or training and technical assistance providers.

Essentials of Practice-Based Coaching provides guidance on the use of PBC and the evaluation of how PBC is being implemented and whether it is being implemented as intended or with fidelity. A focus on implementation fidelity is particularly important for those adopting PBC. Promising findings related to practitioners' and caregivers' fidelity of implementation of effective practices following receipt of professional development that includes PBC, and associated positive child outcomes, are unlikely to be realized outside controlled research studies without attention to fidelity. This latter assertion is particularly important given that consensus has not been reached about how coaching should be defined and how components of coaching should be implemented across various early childhood sectors and contexts (Artman-Meeker et al., 2015; O'Keefe, 2017).

Practice-Based Coaching and Other Coaching Frameworks

Several coaching definitions have been offered in early childhood and related literatures, and the number of coaching frameworks or models appears to be growing. This growth is likely the result of multiple reviews and meta-analyses that have highlighted the promise of coaching as a job-embedded professional development strategy in early childhood and Kindergarten through Grade 12 (K–12) contexts (e.g., Artman-Meeker et al., 2015; Kraft et al., 2018; Lloyd & Modlin, 2012).

Table 1.1 shows key elements from coaching definitions or frameworks commonly used in early childhood or K–12 education. The coaching definitions in Table 1.1 are from the National Association for the Education of Young Children and the National Association of Child Care Resource and Referral Agencies (2012) and Cusumano and Preston (2018). In addition to PBC, frameworks included in Table 1.1 are an early childhood coaching framework (Rush & Shelden, 2020) and an instructional coaching framework (Knight, 2007). Although variations exist, commonalities are evident. Comparing the key elements of PBC to the definitions and other frameworks shown in Table 1.1 helps identify the common or distinct elements of PBC.

Each definition or framework identifies coaching as a relationship, partnership, or collaboration. In PBC, we distinguish a collaborative partnership from a relationship. A relationship is a broader term used to describe connections, often emotional, between two or more people. In PBC, a collaborative partnership focuses on connections to achieve goals. In PBC, the partnership is formed so the coach can support the coachees' practice-focused goals. All aspects of PBC—conducting practice-focused strengths and needs assessment, goal setting and

Table 1.1. Comparing key elements from coaching definitions or coaching frameworks

Key elements from definition	Sources for definitions and coaching frameworks				
	Coaching definition NAEYC/NACCRRA (2012)	Coaching definition Cusumano & Preston (2018)	Early childhood coaching Rush & Shelden (2020)	Instructional coaching Knight (2007)	Practice-based coaching Snyder et al. (2015)
Partnership or relationship	Relationship-based process	Collaborative effort	Collaborative coach–coachee relationship	Partnership through collaboration	Collaborative partnership
Coach	Expert with specialized and adult learning knowledge and skills	Content knowledge about practice or program is critical coach selection criteria	Expert based	Individuals who are full-time professional developers on-site in schools	Individual with specialized knowledge, dispositions, and skills in coaching and in the practices that are the focus of coaching
Purpose or desired outcome	Build [coachee] capacity	Support and transfer skills gained during professional development to use with fidelity in practice context. Improve precision, fluency, and use across settings, recipients, and time while maintaining fidelity of practice implementation	Coachee competence and confidence to engage in self-reflection, self-correction, and generalization of new skills and strategies to other situations	Work with teachers to help them incorporate research-based instructional practices	Support practitioners or caregivers to implement effective practices with fidelity during use in practice contexts
Coaching focus	Specific professional dispositions, skills, or behaviors	Specific skills gained during professional development. Behaviors that support performance feedback, behavior change, and use of skills in job-embedded settings	Acknowledge and improve existing knowledge and practices, develop new skills, and promote continuous self-assessment and learning on the part of the coachee	Engage in partnership communications with teachers to support them to identify goals so coach can help teachers create a plan for realizing their professional goals	Support acquisition, fluency, maintenance, and generalization of practice implementation
Components explicitly included	Goal setting	Prompting Performance feedback Creating an enabling and collaborative context Data use Application of content knowledge Continuum of supports Scaffolding	Joint planning Observation Action/Practice Reflection Feedback	Enroll Identify Explain Model Observe Explore Support Reflect	Strengths and needs assessment Shared goals and action planning Focused observation Reflection and feedback Collaborative partnerships
Delivery method	Face to face, distance (technology based), hybrid	Not explicitly specified	Not explicitly specified although descriptions and examples are face to face	Face to face, with model lessons delivered by instructional coaches	Face to face, distance (technology based), hybrid
Duration	One time or series of sessions, dependent on achievement of goal	Never ends, but fades over time with a continuum of support tied to data related to use of skills (i.e., fidelity data)	Short term or long term depending on the complexity of the innovation learned and its application to the work setting and the number of different formal learning opportunities that occur	Series of sessions depending on the teacher's stage of change	Coaching cycles: Number of cycles depends on fidelity of practice implementation and number of practices
Theoretical model or approach undergirding	—	Implementation science and implementation research (Fixsen & Blase, 2008; Fixsen et al., 2005)	Contextual model (Stober & Grant, 2006a, 2006b)	Partnership approach (Knight, 1999)	Science of human behavior/ Organizational behavior management (Crow & Snyder, 1998) Behavioral coaching (Seniuk et al., 2013) Implementation science and implementation research/Active Implementation Frameworks (Fixsen & Blase, 2008; Fixsen et al., 2005)

Key: NAEYC, National Association for the Education of Young Children; NACCRRA, National Association of Child Care Resource and Referral Agencies.

action planning, focused observation, and reflection and feedback—occur in the context of a collaborative partnership.

Across definitions and frameworks, coaches are identified as individuals with expertise in professional development, coaching, and adult learning principles. In PBC, we include these areas of expertise as well as explicitly acknowledging that coaches need specialized knowledge and skills in the practices that will be the focus of coaching (Snyder et al., 2015). The purposes or desired outcomes of coaching are to build coachees' capacity, to strengthen their practice-focused competence and confidence, and to support them to implement effective practices with fidelity. In PBC, we specifically identify fidelity of practice implementation as the desired coaching outcome.

A focus on enhancing knowledge, skills, or practices is evident across the definitions and frameworks. In PBC, the focus is on coachees' acquisition, fluency, maintenance, and generalization of practices. We define a *practice* as an observable or measurable action or behavior of a coachee. PBC guides practice implementation and supports contextual adaptation while ensuring practice integrity (Cusumano & Preston, 2018).

Components of coaching differ somewhat across the definitions and frameworks. The National Association for the Education of Young Children (NAEYC)/National Association of Child Care Resource and Referral Agencies (NACCRRA) definition only specifies a goal-setting component. Cusumano and Preston (2018) identify seven components in their coaching profile. In PBC, instructional coaching, and early childhood coaching, common components include setting goals, action planning, observation, and reflection. Feedback is included as a component in early childhood coaching, Cusumano and Preston's coaching profile, and PBC. PBC distinguishes supportive and constructive feedback. PBC includes practice-focused strengths and needs assessment as part of goal setting and action planning, which is a distinct component.

As shown in Table 1.1, face-to-face interactions between the coach and coachee are recognized as a delivery method. In addition, NAEYC/NACCRRA and PBC include distance- or technology-based or hybrid delivery methods (e.g., live observations, distance reflection and feedback meetings). The duration of coaching is noted to range from one session to a series of sessions, depending on the number of practices and the coachees' stage of change or fidelity of practice implementation.

Consensus and converging evidence suggest that coaching should include planning, observation, action, reflection, feedback, and alliance building or collaborative partnerships (Kraft et al., 2018; Kunemund et al., 2021; Snyder et al., 2015). PBC includes each of these components as part: goal setting and action planning, focused observation, and reflection and feedback. In PBC, these components occur in the context of a collaborative partnership and are guided by practice-focused strengths and needs assessments.

Theoretical Foundations of Practice-Based Coaching

The coaching definitions and frameworks shown in Table 1.1 have been influenced by other models or frameworks. For example, Rush and Shelden (2020) used the contextual model for coaching described by Stober and Grant (2006a) to inform the coaching processes used in their early childhood coaching framework. Knight's instructional coaching model has its conceptual roots in a partnership approach (Knight, 1999, 2007). Cusumano and Preston's Practice Profile for Coaching (2018) is based in the active implementation science frameworks and implementation research.

PBC has been influenced by principles from the science of human behavior and a related discipline known as organizational behavior management (OBM; Crow & Snyder, 1998). PBC is aligned with behavioral coaching approaches based on the science of

PBC Theoretical Influences

- Principles from the science of human behavior
- Organizational behavior management principles and practices
- Implementation science and implementation research

human behavior and OBM (Seniuk et al., 2013) and how coaching is described as a competency driver in active implementation science frameworks (Cusumano & Preston, 2018; Fixsen & Blase, 2008).

Science of Human Behavior, Organizational Behavior Management, and Behavioral Coaching Influences These PBC theoretical influences focus on applying principles from the science of human behavior to human performance. In PBC, performance is related to both fidelity of coaching implementation and fidelity of practice implementation in job-embedded early childhood contexts ("organizations"), such as classrooms or homes. Applying OBM principles to PBC, Snyder et al. (2012) described four major functions of coaching: provide support, analyze application, offer feedback, and adapt results.

Using principles from the science of human behavior, Seniuk et al. (2013) identified six characteristics of effective behavioral coaching initially developed by Martin and Hrycaiko (1983). These characteristics were based on dimensions from the science of human behavior initially described by Baer et al. (1968). Table 1.2 shows these characteristics and how they have been applied in PBC for both coaches and coachees. Many structural and process features of PBC are based on these six characteristics.

PBC has an explicit focus on coachees' actions or behaviors and emphasizes repeated, job-embedded learning opportunities to prompt, practice, reflect on, and receive feedback about implementation, which is supported by OBM principles (Crow & Snyder, 1998). PBC acknowledges that adult learners are both autonomous and collaborative. A collaborative partnership provides opportunities for those being coached to implement practices independently and with the support of a coach. When coachees are implementing newly learned actions or behaviors, having a collaborative partnership with a coach who provides effective prompts and explicit feedback about practice implementation helps shape successive approximations toward fidelity of practice implementation. In addition to helping support fidelity of practice implementation, the provision of implementation supports and resources has been identified by coachees as an important motivator for practice implementation and for building and sustaining a collaborative coaching partnership (Shannon et al., 2015; Shannon, Snyder, et al., 2021). Strengths and needs assessments are important for gathering data about learners' current practices and determining priorities and motivations for enhancement, refinement, or change (Snyder & Wolfe, 2008).

Consistent with principles from OBM and behavioral coaching, setting performance-based practice goals supports data-informed decision making and accountability. Goals based on individual priorities, strengths, and needs are important when coaching for behavior change. Action plans are accountability plans tailored to the coachees' priorities and their stage and pace of practice learning. Chapter 6 details how to write SMA^{2}R^{2}T (specific, measurable, action-oriented/achievable, realistic/relevant, and time sensitive) goals and action plans. Focused observation likely helps motivate the practitioner to use a practice or practices (Kretlow & Bartholomew, 2010). Chapter 7 describes how to conduct observations focused on fidelity of practice implementation. With respect to reflection, asking open-ended questions and providing reflective comments are strategies that can eventually lead to self-reflection, autonomy, and self-efficacy (Frates et al., 2011). The provision of feedback based on implementation (also known as performance-based feedback) has been demonstrated to support fidelity of implementation of effective practices (Barton et al., 2011; Fallon et al., 2015). Practitioners have also reported that they find performance feedback to be useful and acceptable (Shannon et al., 2015; Shannon, Snyder, et al., 2021). Chapter 8 includes resources for supporting reflection and providing feedback within the PBC framework.

Implementation Science and Research Implementation has been defined as a specified set of activities designed to put into use practices or programs with known dimensions (Fixsen et al., 2005). Implementation science refers to understanding processes and procedures that promote or impede the transfer, adoption, and use of evidence-based intervention practices in real-world

Table 1.2. Principles from science of human behavior and behavioral coaching as applied in practice-based coaching for coaches and coachees

Principle	Applied in PBC for coaches	Applied in PBC for coachees
Measurement of performance is specific, detailed, and frequent.	Measurement of PBC implementation (e.g., dose, coaching strategies used, coaching component fidelity indicators) by using a coaching log for every coaching session	Measurement of practice implementation using content-aligned practice fidelity assessments (e.g., Teaching Pyramid Observation Tool, Hemmeter et al., 2014;Embedded Instruction Observation System, Snyder et al., 2009), at regular intervals
Clear distinction between the development and maintenance of behavior and positive procedures are emphasized for both.	Initial professional development and measures of knowledge and skill for coaches on coaching behaviors and practices that are the focus of coaching with ongoing supportive and constructive feedback provided Ongoing measures of coaching and practice fidelity with supportive and constructive feedback provided	Initial professional development and coaching for acquisition of knowledge and skills related to practice implementation focus with supportive and constructive feedback provided Ongoing coaching and other forms of professional development to build practice fluency, generalization, and maintenance with supportive and constructive feedback provided
Improvement is measured with respect to own performance.	Fidelity of coaching is measured and feedback is provided about each coach's performance using criterion-based thresholds rather than relative to other coaches' performance. Self-monitoring and self-evaluation of coaching in relation to coaching fidelity feedback received from others Provision of supportive and constructive feedback	Fidelity of practice implementation is measured and feedback is provided about each coachee's performance using criterion-based thresholds rather than relative to other coachees' performance. Self-monitoring and self-evaluation of action plan goals and steps with reciprocal verbal reflections between coach and coachee Provision of supportive and constructive feedback
Emphasis is on coaching as a science rather than as an art.	Coaches use data-based approaches to inform coaching practices implementation and to examine coaching fidelity and coachee and child or family outcomes.	Coachee, with support from coach, uses data-based approaches to inform practice implementation and to examine intervention fidelity and child or family outcomes.
Science of human behavior tactics are used to nudge and boost[a] behavior.	Coach self-assesses and discusses with lead coach strengths and needs relative to PBC and practice implementation Coach uses strategies from science of human behavior to support change in coachee's behavior in desired directions (e.g., supportive feedback, constructive feedback, consideration of motivators and prompts to set occasion for behavior). Lead coach uses strategies to support change in coach's behavior in desired directions (e.g., supportive feedback, constructive feedback, consideration of motivators, prompts to set occasion for behavior). Coach uses data or video to demonstrate change in coaching behavior.	Coachee self-assesses and discusses with coach strengths and needs relative to practice implementation. Coachee identifies preferred coaching strategies and processes throughout coaching with support from coach. Coachee uses data or video from coach and self to demonstrate practice (behavior) change.
Social validity	Social validity data about PBC structural and process features and practices that are the focus of PBC are gathered from coaches to examine feasibility, acceptability, utility, response-costs, and satisfaction.	Social validity data about PBC structural and process features and practices that are the focus of PBC are gathered from coachees to examine feasibility, acceptability, utility, response-costs, and satisfaction.

[a]Nudges and boosts for behavior refer to simplified four-term contingencies associated with human behavior (i.e., motivating operations, antecedent stimuli, behavior, consequences) as described in Crow (2017). (*Key:* PBC, practice-based coaching).

contexts (Kelly & Perkins, 2014). Implementation research focuses on the scientific study of methods to promote the systematic uptake of evidence-based practices into routine practice (Eccles et al., 2009). In their literature synthesis focused on implementation research, Fixsen and colleagues (2005) identified coaching as a core component or driver of successful implementation of evidence-based practices and programs. Along with staff selection and training (i.e., professional development), coaching is depicted in the active implementation science drivers framework as a key competency driver (Fixsen & Blase, 2008; see Figure 1.2).

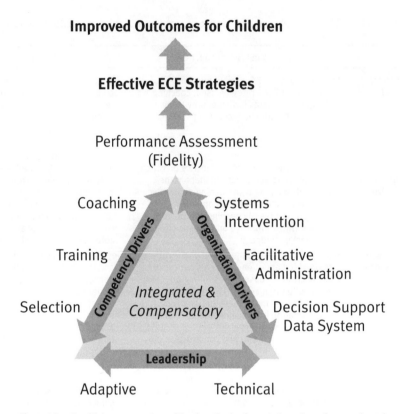

Figure 1.2. Coaching as a competency driver in active implementation science frameworks and research. From Fixsen, D. L., & Blase, K. A. (2008, June). *Effective applications of innovations* [Paper presentation]. OASAS Meetings, New York, NY. (*Key:* ECE, early childhood education.)

PBC is theoretically and operationally aligned with coaching as depicted in the Fixsen and Blase framework and with the Practice Profile for Coaching (Cusumano & Preston, 2018), which was developed as part of the State Implementation and Scale-Up of Evidence-Based Practices Center. Coaching is defined in the Practice Profile as a process that supports and transfers skills acquired during professional development to use in practice contexts. Coaching shapes newly learned skills with a focus on improving precision, fluency, and use of practices across settings, recipients, and time, while maintaining fidelity of practice implementation. According to Cusumano and Preston, coaching should be informed by data that document fidelity of coaching implementation, fidelity of practice implementation, the intensity of coaching support, and outcomes. Essential components of coaching, which are also reflected in PBC, are prompting for practice implementation and for reflection and feedback, the provision of performance feedback, creating an enabling and collaborative context, data use, application of content knowledge, continuum of supports for coaches and coachees, and scaffolding for practice learning and implementation.

Theory of Change for Practice-Based Coaching

Based on theoretical and empirical foundations, an abbreviated theory of change for PBC is shown in Figure 1.3. Professional development that includes PBC, when implemented with fidelity, is associated with fidelity of practice implementation (i.e., effective early childhood practices). Implementation of these practices, in turn, is associated with improved or

IMPLEMENTATION SUPPORTS	COACHEE KNOWLEDGE, DISPOSITIONS, & SKILLS	CHILD/FAMILY OUTCOMES

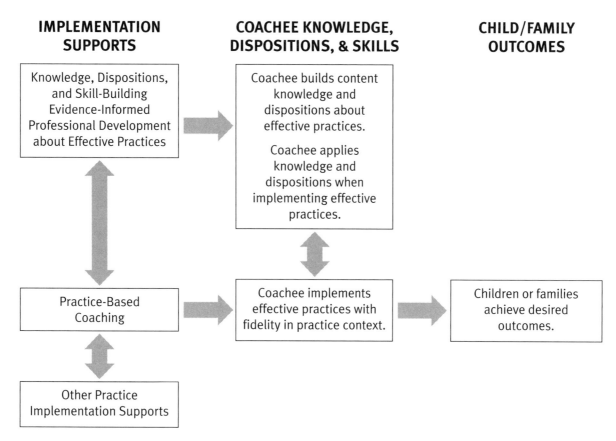

Figure 1.3.   Abbreviated theory of change for practice-based coaching.

desired child developmental and learning or family outcomes. This theory of change has been used to guide research on PBC and its use in training and technical assistance contexts (e.g., Conroy et al., 2015; Hemmeter et al., 2016; Hemmeter et al., 2020; Snyder, Hemmeter et al., 2018; Sutherland et al., 2018).

Empirical Foundation for Structural, Content, and Process Features of Practice-Based Coaching

Literature reviews, systematic reviews, and meta-analyses have identified key structural, content, and process features of coaching that support fidelity of practice or intervention implementation (Artman-Meeker et al., 2015; Kraft et al., 2018; Kretlow & Bartholomew, 2010; Lloyd & Modlin, 2012; Powell & Diamond, 2013; Snyder et al. 2012). These features align with those identified for professional development when the desired outcome is fidelity of coachees' practice implementation in job-embedded contexts and associated positive outcomes for children or their families (e.g., Zaslow et al., 2010). A description of these structural, content, and process features and their relation to PBC follows.

Coaching should be coherent and sustained versus episodic. It should be job-embedded, and it should focus on a set of high-leverage (Ball & Forzani, 2011) effective practices relevant for the coachees' practice context. Multiple exemplars of the practices should be available through both modeling and video modeling. Contextual fit, defined as the alignment between the practices that are the focus of coaching and their relevance for the coachees' practice context, particularly alignment with curricula or practices already being used, should be explicitly emphasized. Embedded opportunities for practice implementation with reflection and feedback are essential. Explicit linkages between practice implementation and child learning outcomes should be emphasized. Strategies used by coaches should be defined, and the use of these strategies during coaching should be documented. Coaches should receive professional development to ensure fidelity of coaching and practice implementation (Snyder et al., 2015).

Key Features of PBC

- Coherent and sustained
- Job-embedded
- Focused on high-leverage and effective practices
- Multiple examples of the practices that are the content focus of PBC through modeling and video modeling
- Emphasis on contextual fit between the practices that are the focus of PBC and the coachees' practice context
- Embedded opportunities for practice implementation in context
- Reflection and feedback about practice implementation
- Use of effective coaching strategies
- Collaborative partnerships between coach and coachee
- Documentation of coaching dose, dose formats, and coaching strategies
- Coaches receive professional development to ensure fidelity of PBC and practice implementation

---

In their meta-analysis of coaching, Kraft et al. (2018) reported findings from 60 studies, 31 of which were conducted in early childhood contexts. These authors identified essential features of coaching, which were used to frame their meta-analysis: (a) *individualized*, coaching sessions are one-on-one; (b) *time intensive*, coaches and coachees interact at least every few weeks; (c) *sustained*, coachees receive coaching over a semester or year(s); (d) *context specific*, coaching occurs in job-embedded contexts; and (e) *focused*, coaches work with coachees to engage in implementation of specific evidence-based practices. These features align with those of PBC.

Kraft et al. (2018) found that coaching in 91% of the 60 studies was combined with other forms of professional development, including workshops, professional learning communities, or training events designed to support teachers' knowledge, dispositions, and skill development. Specific to early childhood, Snyder et al. (2012) analyzed 256 studies as part of a descriptive systematic review focused on early childhood professional development. These authors found coaching with performance feedback was provided in follow-up to other forms of professional development in 51.6% of the reviewed studies. Schachter (2015) conducted an analytic study of professional development research in early childhood education and found that 54.8% (40 of 73) of the studies reviewed included coaching as well as other forms of professional development.

Exploratory analyses from the Kraft et al. (2018) meta-analysis examined select features of coaching structures and processes. Studies that paired coaching with other forms of professional development (e.g., group training) had larger effects on teacher instructional practices. The authors suggested coachees might benefit from professional development designed to build their knowledge and application skills before they engage in coaching. As shown in Table 1.3, in the studies conducted to date that have used PBC, other forms of professional development, in addition to PBC, occurred in every study.

Twenty-two of the 60 studies reviewed by Kraft et al. (2018) provided teachers with instructional content materials such as curriculum, lesson plans, guidebooks, or practice guides. Studies that included these materials had larger effects on teachers' instructional practices. Most studies conducted to date with PBC provide teachers with these types of materials or practice implementation aides (see Table 1.3).

Fourteen of the studies supplemented coaching with a video library that teachers could access to observe other teachers implementing the practices that were the focus of coaching.

(text continued on page 17)

Table 1.3. Characteristics and outcomes of studies using practice-based coaching

					Group experimental design studies (N = 10)							
Study	N practitioners	N children	Practice context	Practice focus	Experimental conditions	PD dose	PBC delivery format	PBC dose	Coach training and protocol	PBC coach fidelity	Practitioner outcomes	Child outcomes
Artman-Meeker et al. (2014)	33 teachers (16 exp, 17 con)	N/A	Head Start classrooms in one state	Pyramid Model	Workshop, PBC, practice guides, materials Workshop only	1 workshop (6 hr)	Distance PBC through e-mail using video observations collected in classroom (Individual)	Planned: 8 sessions over 12 wk Delivered: M = 6 sessions (range 1–8)	External coach (first author) trained by senior authors	M = 99% (range= 77.8%–100%)	Workshop training + distance coaching associated with small improvements in emotional, organizational, and instructional classroom interactions based on differential participation in distance PBC	NR
Conroy et al. (2015)	53 teachers (26 exp, 27 con)	130 children at risk for EBD	Head Start and state-funded preschool classrooms in 2 states	6 BiC practices (rules, BSP, OTR, PC, IF, CF)	Workshop, teacher manual, PBC BAU	1 workshop (6 hr)	On-site PBC (Individual)	14 weeks; 1× per week; 90-min focused observation, 30-min debrief	8 external coaches trained by senior authors and followed written protocol	NR	Teachers in BIC condition increased use of rules, BSP, PC, IF, and CF relative to teachers in BAU	Higher levels of child engagement; less disruptive, aggressive, or defiant behavior; and more positive social interactions than children with teachers in BAU
Conroy et al. (2018)	185 teachers (92 exp, 93 con)	462 children at risk for EBD	Early childhood classrooms across 5 school districts and 3 Head Start agencies	6 BiC practices (rules, BSP, OTR, PC, IF, CF)	Workshop, resource manual, PBC BAU	1 workshop (6 hr)	On-site PBC (Individual)	14 weeks; 1× per week; 90-min focused observation, 30-min debrief	NR	NR	Adherence differences on BiC practices across BiC and BAU teachers	Reduced number of children in the clinical or borderline range for social skills and problem behaviors in BiC vs. BAU
Conroy et al. (2019)	186 teachers (92 exp, 94 con)	NA	Early childhood classrooms across 5 school districts and 3 Head Start agencies	6 BiC practices (rules, BSP, OTR, PC, IF, CF)	Workshop, resource manual, PBC BAU	1 workshop (6 hr)	On-site PBC (Individual)	14 weeks, 1× per week; 90-min focused observation, 30-min debrief	2-d PBC and BiC training, 6-step checkout process and followed written protocol	M = 85% (range 81.24%–100%)	Teachers in BiC increased use of all BiC practices relative to teachers in BAU	NR

(continued)

Table 1.3. *(continued)*

					Group experimental design studies ($N = 10$)							
Study	N practitioners	N children	Practice context	Practice focus	Experimental conditions	PD dose	PBC delivery format	PBC dose	Coach training and protocol	PBC coach fidelity	Practitioner outcomes	Child outcomes
Greenwood et al. (2017)	20 teachers (10 exp, 10 con)	297 children	Half-day pre-K programs, reverse inclusion	10 literacy practices	Literacy 3D workshop, PBC Wait list control (received PD Year 2)	Six 2-hr workshops (12 hr)	On-site (Individual)	3 coaching cycles for school year, 19–20 hr total	NR	NR	Literacy practice implementation increased Quality of literacy implementation increased	No significant effects on child literacy outcomes, but correlation ($r = .79$) between teacher literacy focus and child literacy engagement
Hemmeter et al. (2016)	40 teachers (20 exp, 18 con)	494 children, 104 focal children at risk for SE and behavior delays	Public preschool classrooms	Pyramid Model practices	Pyramid Model workshops, PBC, guides and materials BAU PD	Three 6.5-hr workshops (19.5 hr)	On-site (Individual)	$M = 13.4$ (7–17) sessions per teacher over 6 mo $M_o = 105$-min observation (range 30–305 min) $M_d = 44$-min debrief (range 10–135)	3 coaches affiliated with research project, trained by study authors and followed written PBC coaching protocol	$M = 87.4\%$ (range 45%–100%)	Differences in Pyramid Model teachers' practice implementation relative to BAU PD as measured by Teaching Pyramid Observation Tool (TPOT)	Children (all children and focal children) in Pyramid Model classrooms had higher social skills and less problem behavior than children in BAU classrooms Focal children in Pyramid Model classrooms had more social interactions than children in BAU classrooms
Hemmeter et al. (2021)	92 teachers (45 exp, 47 con)	995 children, 250 focal children at risk for SE and behavior delays	Public preschool classrooms	Pyramid Model practices	Pyramid Model workshops, PBC, guides and materials BAU PD	Three 6.5-hr workshops (19.5 hr)	On-site (Individual)	$M = 16.5$ (16–17) coaching sessions per teacher over 6 mo $M_o = 91.3$-min observation ($SD = 25.1$) $M_d = 33.3$ debrief ($SD = 12.7$)	11 coaches affiliated with research project, trained by study authors and followed written PBC coaching protocol	$M = 97.7\%$ (range 40%–100%)	Differences in Pyramid Model teachers' practice implementation relative to BAU PD as measured by TPOT	Nonfocal and focal children had higher social skills and less problem behavior Focal children had higher social skills and less problem behavior Focal children had more social interactions

Table 1.3. (continued)

Study	Sample (teachers)	Sample (children)	Setting	Content	Intervention components	Orientation/Training	Delivery format	Dosage	Coach/Interventionist	Fidelity	Teacher outcomes	Child outcomes
McCollum et al. (2011)	13 teachers (7 exp, 6 con)	NR (4-yr-old children)	State-funded preschool programs	Emergent literacy practices (18 strategies organized under A, B, C clusters)	Workshops, PBC, guides and materials Waitlist control	Orientation group meeting (2 d, 10 hr), 3 additional group meetings (1.5 hr each), biweekly (14.5 hr total)	On-site (Individual)	Biweekly, 15 total sessions (5 per each of 3 literacy strategy clusters)	4 researchers, 3 with doctorates in EC, 2 worked as emergent literacy coaches in a previous project, trained on observation checklists	NR	Differences in implementation of literacy strategies for Cluster B and C practices Differences on ELLCO language and literacy environment scores, including LEC, LLC, and LARS	NR
Snyder, Hemmeter, et al. (2018)	36 teachers (12 exp1, 12 exp2, 12 con)	106 children with disabilities	Public school preschool classrooms in 3 states	Embedded instruction for early learning	Workshops, on-site coaching, practice guides, materials, web site Workshops, self-coaching, practice guides, materials, web site BAU PD	Four ~3.5-hr workshops (14.9 hr total) for on-site and self-coaching conditions	On-site (Individual) Web-based self-coaching (Individual)	16 weekly coaching sessions per teacher over 4–5 mo $M_o = 73.9$-min observation ($SD = 19.5$ min) $M_d = 39.3$-min debrief ($SD = 12.1$ min) 16 weekly e-mail reminders to self coach	4 external coaches in on-site condition trained by senior authors and followed written PBC protocol Project staff who delivered self-coaching prompts trained by senior authors and followed written PBC protocol	$M = 95\%$ (range 78%–100%) $M = 99\%$ (range 97%–100%)	Higher quality embedded instruction learning targets for on-site and self-coaching relative to BAU as measured by Learning Targets Rating Scale (LTRS; Snyder et al., 2009). More accurate implementation of embedded instruction learning trials for on-site relative to self-coaching and BAU as measured by the Embedded Instruction Observation System (EIOS; Snyder et al., 2009)	Children whose teachers in on-site coaching acquired more skills and behaviors specified in embedded instruction learning targets than children whose teachers in self-coaching or BAU Children whose teachers in on-site and self-coaching showed noteworthy improvements on standardized assessments of early literacy, receptive language, pre-academic and social skills compared to children whose teachers in BAU

(continued)

Table 1.3. *(continued)*

					Group experimental design studies (N = 10)							
Study	N practitioners	N children	Practice context	Practice focus	Experimental conditions	PD dose	PBC delivery format	PBC dose	Coach training and protocol	PBC coach fidelity	Practitioner outcomes	Child outcomes
Snyder, Hemmeter, Algina et al. (2021)	111 teachers (36 exp1, 38 exp2, 37 con)	327 children with disabilities	Public school preschool classrooms in 2 states	Embedded instruction for early learning	Workshops, on-site coaching, practice guides, materials, web site Workshops, self-coaching, practice guides, materials, web site BAU PD	Four 4-hr workshops (16 hr total) for on-site and self-coaching conditions	On-site (Individual) Web-based self-coaching (Individual)	16 weekly coaching sessions per teacher over 4–5 mo M_o = 60.6-min observation (SD = 7.4 min) M_d = 46.7-min debrief (SD = 13.9 min) 16 weekly e-mail reminders to self-coach	11 external coaches in on-site condition trained by senior authors and followed written PBC protocol Project staff who delivered self-coaching prompts trained by senior authors and followed written protocol	M = 90.6% (range 71%–100%) M = 99.4% (96.2%–100%)	Higher quality embedded instruction learning targets for on-site coaching teachers relative to teachers in self-coaching or BAU conditions as measured by the LTRS More and more accurate implementation of embedded instruction learning trials for on-site coaching teachers relative to teachers in self-coaching or BAU conditions as measured by EIOS	Children whose teachers in on-site coaching acquired more skills and behaviors specified in embedded instruction learning targets than children whose teachers in self-coaching or BAU Children whose teachers received on-site coaching showed noteworthy improvements on a preacademic composite measure constructed of standardized early literacy, language, and school readiness assessments compared to children whose teachers were in BAU.

Single-Case Experimental Design Studies (N = 6)

Study	N practitioners	N children	Practice context	Practice focus	Design	PD	PBC delivery format	PBC dose	Coach training and protocol	Coach fidelity	Practitioner outcomes	Child (family) outcomes
Artman-Meeker & Hemmeter (2012)	4 (2 teaching teams)	2	University-based inclusive child care	Transition preparations, rule reminders, social-emotional teaching strategies from Pyramid Model	Multiple baseline across practices and teaching teams	Three 1-hr trainings over ~27 d (3 hr total) Materials and resources	E-mail	9–11 e-mails per participant	NR	96%–100%	Team 1 and Team 2 increased use of transition preparation strategies, rule reminders, and social-emotional practices relative to baseline (Replication across strategies and teams)	Child 1: Effects on challenging behavior were variable, but level of challenging behavior was lower during transitions, rule reminders, and social-emotional strategies than during baseline Child 2: Effects on challenging behavior were variable, but level of challenging behavior was lower during transitions relative to baseline
Bishop et al. (2015)	3 teachers	3 children at risk for learning challenges	University-based early care and education center	Embedded instruction on 3 learning targets	Combined multi-element and multiple probes across participants	2-hr training Videos and materials	Self-coaching (self-monitoring) with feedback from coach (Individual)	Session 1 35–40 min 2–8 coaching sessions per participant 10–20 min	NR	97% (range 87%–100%)	All teachers increased their implementation of embedded instruction learning trial implementation over baseline	One child mastered 2/3 embedded instruction learning targets, one child mastered 3/3 embedded instruction learning targets One child did not master learning target
Fox et al. (2011)	3 early childhood special education teachers	N/A	Inclusive public school classrooms	Pyramid Model practices	Multiple-probe across participants	3-d training (hours NR)	On site (Individual)	6–14 PBC coaching sessions per participant	Master's level coach trained in PBC	NR	2/3 teachers met criterion of 80% implementation of Pyramid Model practices and <1 red flag, 1 teacher did not meet criterion but improved her percentage of implemented Pyramid Model practices and reduced number of red flags, but not to criterion	N/A

(continued)

Table 1.3. *(continued)*

Single-Case Experimental Design Studies (N = 6)

Study	N practitioners	N children	Practice context	Practice focus	Design	PD	PBC delivery format	PBC dose	Coach training and protocol	Coach fidelity	Practitioner outcomes	Child (family) outcomes
Hemmeter et al. (2011)	Four preschool teachers	79 children	Inclusive preschool classrooms (3 Head Start, 1 child care)	Descriptive praise	Multiple-probe across participants	One 30-min training	E-mail (Individual)	5–7 PBC e-mails per participant	Doctoral students in early childhood special education	E-mail fidelity 100%	All 4 teachers increased percentage of intervals of descriptive praise, 2 teachers required additional supports	3 /4 classrooms had reductions in percentage of intervals with challenging behavior, slight increases in child engagement
Hemmeter et al. (2015)	3 teachers from control group of previous Pyramid Model study	NR	Inclusive preschool classrooms	Pyramid Model practices	Multiple probe-across sets of practices, replicated across teachers	One 30- to 60-min training, four guides, One 30- to 60-min booster training due to 2-wk break	Live or e-mail (Individual)	3× per wk On-site: 16–26 sessions E-mail: 8–10 e-mails per participant	NR	Live coaching: 99.43% (range 90.9%–100%) E-mail fidelity: 100%	All three teachers increased use of Pyramid Model practices to criterion levels (>80%)	2/3 classrooms had reductions in classwide challenging behavior
Hsieh et al. (2009)	5 full-time early childhood teachers	NR	Public pre-K classrooms, 3 child care centers	18 emergent literacy teaching strategies	Multiple baseline across teaching strategies replicated with 5 teachers	NA	On site (Individual)	2–3 coaching sessions per wk, 6 wk, 8 to 12 PBC sessions per participant	NR	100%	All 5 teachers increased their use of emergent literacy strategies above baseline levels, 4 teachers required booster sessions to reach higher levels	Statistically significant changes in mean picture naming, alliteration, rhyming, print knowledge from pre-test to post-test

Key: BAU, business as usual; BIC, BEST in CLASS; BSP, behavior-specific praise; con, control, comparison or BAU condition; CF, corrective feedback; d, day; mo, month; yr, year; EBD, emotional and behavioral disorders; ELLCO, Early Language and Literacy Classroom Observation Tool (ELLCO-PreK; Smith et al., 2008); exp1, experimental condition 1; exp2, experimental condition 2; IF, instructive feedback; N/A, not applicable for study; exp, experimental condition; LAR, Learning Activities Rating Scale; LEC, Literacy Environment Checklist; LLC, language, literacy, and curriculum; M_d (SD), mean intensity and standard deviation of reflection and feedback (debrief); M_o (SD), mean intensity and standard deviation of focused observation; NR, not reported; OTR, opportunities to respond; PBC, practice-based coaching; PC, precorrection; PD, professional development; SE, social-emotional; practice focus, practices that were the content focus of PD and PBC; TPOT, Teaching Pyramid Observation Tool (Hemmeter et al., 2014).

Although the sample size was limited to 14 studies, less robust effects were shown in these studies. What is not reported by Kraft et al. (2018) is the extent to which teachers accessed or were shown the available video models during coaching.

No differences were found for coaching delivered face-to-face or virtually, although the number of virtual coaching studies was 13, compared to 47 conducted face-to-face. Table 1.3 shows the delivery format for PBC studies conducted to date. Chapter 2 describes different PBC delivery formats and Chapter 10 describes how to use technology supports for delivering PBC virtually or in a hybrid format.

Dose of coaching was somewhat difficult to quantify based on information reported in the studies. In the 44 studies that reported dose, 16 reported dosages of 10 hr or less, 14 reported 21 hr or more, 6 reported 21–30 hr, and 8 reported 30 hr or more. Kraft et al. did not find any evidence to support that coaching had to be delivered at a higher dose to be effective. This finding should be interpreted with caution, however, given information about dose and particularly dose formats (e.g., dose and type of observation, dose and type of feedback or reflection) often are not reported in the literature. As Kraft et al. noted, "The lack of evidence supporting dosage effects suggests that the quality and focus of coaching may be more important than the actual number of contact hours" (p. 565). In addition, the dose and dose formats of coaching needed to support fidelity of practice implementation are also likely affected by motivational and learning characteristics of coachees and coaches, the number and type of practices that are the focus of coaching, coachees' current practice knowledge and skills, the collaborative partnership, and contextual factors that facilitate or hinder practice implementation (Snyder et al., 2015). In Chapter 9, we provide resources for coaching implementation that include coaching logs to record dose, dose formats, and other PBC content and process features.

In addition to the key coaching features described by Kraft et al. (2018), Lloyd and Modlin (2012) emphasized the importance of building partnerships with coachees; observing, modeling, and advising in the practice context; discussing practices; providing support and feedback; assisting with problem-solving challenges; and reviewing and documenting progress toward identified practice goals. As these authors noted, ". . . [coachees] are more likely to follow through and consistently apply the skills they have learned when they have continued support [partnerships]" (p. 3). Collaborative partnerships are an important part of PBC, and strategies for building and maintaining these partnerships are described in Chapter 3.

In their 2012 descriptive systematic review of early childhood professional development studies published between 1970 and 2011, Snyder et al. examined which coaching strategies (e.g., performance feedback, goal setting, modeling) were used in the 159 studies that included follow-up support (including coaching) as part of professional development. Although Snyder et al. reported the number and type of follow-up strategies used in these studies, they did not analyze whether these strategies were used separately or in combination, or whether use of particular strategies or combinations of strategies were differentially effective in supporting fidelity of practice implementation.

Artman-Meeker et al. (2015) reviewed 49 studies that focused on coaching early childhood professionals to implement intervention practices in job-embedded settings. In addition to examining the characteristics of learners and coaches, preparation and supports offered to coaches, and the rigor and quality of the studies, these authors identified coaching strategies used in the reviewed studies from a list of 12 strategies. The most commonly used strategies, occurring in 30% or more of the reviewed studies, were performance feedback (85.7%), intentional planning for practice between sessions (55.1%), use of a coaching manual (53.1%), collaborative progress monitoring (38.8%), ongoing use of an action plan (32.7%), and practice of new skills (30.6%). Less frequently used strategies were live modeling (26.5%), help with instructional materials (20.4%), video models (16.3%), video self-reflection (14.3%), intentional focus on relationships (12.2%), and role play (4.1%). Of note, only 2 of 49 studies included in the review described a comprehensive coaching model like PBC with a focus on partnerships, goal setting and action planning, focused observation, reflection and feedback, and action in the early childhood setting. More than half of the studies included four of these five features but did not describe an emphasis on the collaborative partnership, which is an essential component of PBC. Less than one third of the studies reported providing training or follow-up support to coaches on the effective practices that were the focus of coaching. This is a key feature of PBC, which emphasizes the importance of professional development for coaches, including ongoing support for fidelity, on both PBC and the practices that are the focus of PBC. Chapter 9 details essential supports for coaches.

Findings from Snyder et al. (2012) and Artman-Meeker et al. (2015) about coaching strategies were used to inform the identification of and operational definitions for the coaching strategies included in the PBC framework. Subsequent empirical studies conducted using PBC (see Table 1.3), which have examined further the use of these strategies, have resulted in the identification of essential and enhancement coaching strategies. Both classes of strategies are defined and illustrated in detail in Chapter 4. In addition, Chapter 5 defines what is meant by a practice and provides resources for conducting practice-focused strengths and needs assessments. Chapter 9 describes supports for PBC implementation, including coaching logs that list essential and enhancement coaching strategies. Chapter 10 provides information about how technology can be used to support PBC implementation and how essential and enhancement coaching strategies can be included.

Empirical Support for Practice-Based Coaching

As shown in Table 1.3, there is growing empirical support for PBC and its promise for improving coachees' implementation of evidence-based practices and child outcomes. Both group experimental ($N = 10$) and single-case design experimental studies ($N = 6$) have been conducted. Across these 16 studies, 605 practitioners were included. For the 12 studies that examined both practitioner and child outcomes, 2,895 children were included.

As shown in Table 1.3, the practice focus for PBC in the 16 studies was social-emotional practices, including the Pyramid Model (e.g., Hemmeter et al., 2016); targeted social, emotional, and behavioral teaching practices for young children at elevated risk for emotional and behavioral disabilities (BEST in CLASS; e.g., Conroy et al., 2015); early literacy practices (e.g., Greenwood et al., 2017; Hsieh et al., 2009); and embedded instruction (e.g., Snyder et al., 2018). To date, practice contexts have included Head Start, state-funded pre-Kindergarten programs, preschool classrooms in public schools serving children with disabilities, and early care and education settings. The use of practice-based coaching is currently being examined in early intervention programs serving infants and toddlers with disabilities and their families (e.g., Bigelow et al., 2020; Woods et al., 2018).

In all but one study shown in Table 1.3, knowledge-, dispositional-, or skill-building forms of professional development (e.g., workshop series, brief trainings, online video exemplars, case stories, web-based modules, implementation guides, materials) were provided to coachees in addition to PBC. PBC was provided as follow-up support for fidelity of practice implementation in the coachees' job-embedded context. This approach is consistent with evidence that shows knowledge- dispositional-, and skills-building forms of professional development are necessary, but not sufficient, for supporting practice implementation in job-embedded contexts (Joyce & Showers, 2002; Kraft et al., 2018). The dose of the professional development varied as a function of the number of practices and ranged from one 30-min training in a study focused on supporting teachers' implementation of a single practice (i.e., descriptive praise; Hemmeter et al., 2011) to 19.5 hr in a study focused on supporting teachers' implementation of Pyramid Model practices (Hemmeter et al., 2016; Hemmeter et al., 2020).

PBC was primarily provided face-to-face, although two studies examined the effects of distance coaching via e-mail on providers' implementation of Pyramid Model practices (Artman-Meeker & Hemmeter, 2012; Artman-Meeker et al., 2014), and three studies examined effects of self-coaching, including self-monitoring (Bishop et al., 2015; Snyder, Hemmeter, et al., 2018;

Snyder, Hemmeter, Algina et al., 2021). Those providing coaching were a) study authors with expertise in both PBC and the practices that were the focus of coaching, b) study personnel who were experienced providers of professional development or technical assistance and received additional training and support to reach and maintain fidelity in PBC implementation and the practices, or c) graduate students or research assistants who received training and ongoing support to reach and maintain fidelity in PBC implementation and the practices. Dose of coaching in the group experimental design studies ranged from 6 to 16.5 coaching sessions with variability in the duration and length of sessions. In the single-case experimental design studies, dose varied as a function of the number and type of practices and the delivery format for the coaching.

Improved reporting about coaching dose and dose formats is needed in both research and practice (Kraft, 2018). As Artman et al. (2015) noted, these data are important to increase understanding and decision making, both in research and in practice, about what dose (intensity, frequency, duration) and dose formats (e.g., expert/peer/self/group; on site/distance/hybrid) are needed for which coachees and under what conditions (e.g., PBC to support implementation of six instructional practices versus a comprehensive framework such as the Pyramid Model).

Research to date has illuminated the importance of preparing coaches to implement PBC and to ensure they have knowledge and skills in the practices that are the content focus of coaching. In addition, coaches need ongoing professional development to maintain fidelity of PBC implementation, including opportunities to discuss coaching successes and challenges with other coaches, to have focused observations of their coaching implementation, and to reflect and receive feedback about coaching implementation. Professional development supports provided to coaches should mirror the components of the PBC provided to coachees (i.e., coaching strengths and needs assessment, coaching goal setting and action planning, focused observation of coaching, reflection and feedback about coaching implementation). The professional development supports should be provided in the context of a collaborative partnership with other coaches, including lead coaches who are internal or might be external to the program as part of technical assistance or professional development systems at programmatic, local, regional, state, or national levels.

In 11 of 16 studies, data were reported about the fidelity with which PBC was implemented. Fidelity data often were obtained from coaching protocols, including coaching logs and action plans. Data on the fidelity of PBC implementation are important to enable data-informed decision making about relationships among coaching structures, content, and processes (i.e., coaching efforts); practice implementation; and desired outcomes (i.e., coaching effects) as shown in Figure 1.3.

The group experimental design studies show increases in practitioners' fidelity of practice implementation relative to those who did not receive professional development and PBC. The data reported in these studies represent average practice implementation for participants based on the experimental condition to which they were assigned. For the single-case design studies, all practitioners showed increases in their fidelity of practice implementation relative to their baseline implementation of practices. Seven of the 10 group experimental design studies examined child outcomes. On average, children in practitioners' classrooms who received professional development and PBC had better development and learning outcomes relative to children in practitioners' classrooms who did not receive professional development and PBC. More detailed information about each of the studies shown in Table 1.3 can be found in the original research reports, which are referenced with asterisks in the reference list.

SUMMARY

In this chapter, we have provided background about PBC and its common and distinct features. The theoretical foundations for PBC, including how PBC relates to coaching as a competency driver in the active implementation science frameworks, and an abbreviated theory of change for PBC has been described and illustrated. The empirical foundations for the structural, content, and process features of PBC have been described along with a summary of the existing empirical evidence for PBC. Chapter 2 provides additional information about PBC, including an overview of professional development, PBC in the context of professional development, PBC components, and PBC delivery formats and modalities. Three case stories are introduced at the end of Chapter 2 that will be used throughout the remaining chapters. Following Chapter 2, each chapter provides detailed information about the structural and process features of PBC. Supplemental materials and resources to support implementation of PBC are included in these chapters, and the case stories are used to illustrate how these materials and resources are used. Our goal is to provide readers with essential information, materials, and resources to implement PBC.

2

Introduction to the Practice-Based Coaching Framework

Patricia Snyder, Mary Louise Hemmeter, Lise Fox, and Crystal Bishop

INTRODUCTION TO THE PRACTICE-BASED COACHING FRAMEWORK

In Chapter 1, we described the theoretical, empirical, and practice-based rationales for practice-based coaching (PBC). In this chapter, we introduce the PBC framework by situating it within the larger context of professional development. We describe the key components of the PBC framework to set the stage for subsequent chapters that provide essential information and resources about how to implement PBC with fidelity. Different PBC delivery formats and modalities are discussed, including how the key components of PBC are reflected in these various formats and modalities. The chapter ends with three case stories that illustrate how PBC can be applied in diverse early childhood contexts. We return to these case stories throughout the text to illustrate application of the essential elements of PBC.

Defining and Describing Professional Development

Professional development has been identified as an important mechanism or driver to support the competence and confidence with which coachees' implement effective practices with fidelity to advance young children's developmental and learning outcomes (Institute of Medicine and National Research Council, 2015; Snyder, Hemmeter, et al., 2011; Winton et al., 2016). What do we mean when we say that professional development is a competency driver? Much like a navigation system, professional development should provide a road map toward desired destinations of quality practice and quality outcomes (Snyder, 2015).

In the theory of change shown in Chapter 1, we illustrated the important relationships among professional development, including PBC, and the desired destinations of fidelity of effective practices implementation and positive child and family outcomes. To reach these

> **Key Point to Remember**
> Professional development should provide a road map toward desired destinations of quality practice and quality outcomes.

desired destinations, quality professional development is critical. By quality professional development, we mean the use of research-informed strategies to support adult learning and to foster learners' competence and confidence to implement effective practices.

For professional development to be an influential competency driver—for its navigation system to function properly—a clear understanding is needed about what will emerge when entering the term *professional development* into the navigation system. A research-informed framework is needed to guide professional development decisions and efforts along the way. Yet, there are many different perspectives about what professional development is and how it is defined (Howes et al., 2012; Winton et al., 2007). Moreover, there are differing perspectives about what types of professional development should be provided for which practitioners and caregivers and for what purposes. An agreed-upon definition for early childhood professional development that can be used consistently across Head Start and Early Head Start, early care and education, pre-Kindergarten (pre-K) programs, early intervention, and early childhood special education is important to promote coherent and aligned professional development systems across programs where practitioners are often interacting with each other for the benefit of children and families (Snyder, 2015).

In 2008, the National Professional Development Center on Inclusion (NPDCI) identified a significant need to develop a shared definition for professional development in early childhood. To advance efforts to reach consensus about a shared definition, they offered a definition of professional development. We have adapted this definition as follows: *professional development* refers to facilitated teaching and learning experiences that are equitable, transactional, and designed to support the acquisition of knowledge, skills, and dispositions as well as their application in practice (NPDCI, p. 3).

Key Point to Remember

Professional development is defined as facilitated teaching and learning experiences that are equitable, transactional, and designed to support the acquisition of knowledge, skills, and dispositions as well as their application in practice.

(NPDCI, 2008, p. 3)

This definition of professional development has several positive features. First, it encompasses many different forms and formats of professional development. It can encompass both preservice and in-service training, which historically has been considered two separate systems (Winton et al., 2016). It emphasizes the importance of learning experiences being equitable and transactional between facilitators and learners. Because the definition is broad, it highlights both the acquisition of knowledge, skills, and dispositions as well as applications for use in

practice. In addition to this definition, a professional development framework was described that includes three key components (NPDCI, 2008). The interrelationships among these components are emphasized, and they are situated within a broader context of policies, resources, organizational structures, access and outreach, and evaluation. The NPDCI framework is useful for informing decisions about how to plan, implement, and evaluate professional development.

The first component of the NPDCI framework is the *who* of professional development. This component includes gathering information about the characteristics and practice contexts of learners and the children and families served in these contexts. The diverse qualifications, experiences, cultures, values, motivations, and priorities of learners and the characteristics of the contexts in which they practice are important to consider.

The second component is the *what* of professional development, meaning the content of the facilitated teaching or learning experiences. Decisions about professional development content are often informed by what learners should know, be able to do, or desired dispositions. For example, is the content of the professional development focused on early literacy practices, science practices, or social-emotional practices? Research suggests that having an explicit curricular or content focus in professional development is an important ingredient of quality professional development (Kraft et al., 2018; Snyder, Denney, et al., 2011). When we explicitly relate content to practice in professional development (e.g., early literacy practices), we mean that professional development is focused on the specific actions or behaviors of practitioners or caregivers that support children's development and learning (e.g., children's early literacy skills).

The third component is the *how* of professional development, including how experiences are organized and facilitated to support learning. This refers to both the structural and process features of professional development (Sheridan et al., 2009; Snyder, Denney, et al., 2011). Structural features include the form of the professional development (e.g., online module, workshop), its duration or dose, and the organization of the learning environment, including materials and people in the learning environment. Process features are the strategies used during professional development to facilitate learning and transactions between the facilitator and learner. This includes evidence-informed strategies such as case stories, video examples, microteaching, creation of job aids, back-home plans, modeling, observation, self-monitoring, reflection, and performance feedback (Brock & Carter, 2017; Snyder & Wolfe, 2008).

Aligning the *Why* and *How* of Professional Development

We have used the NPDCI framework in our professional development work, including in our PBC activities. We have adapted the model to include a fourth component: the *why* of professional development. This component involves addressing why the professional development is being provided by identifying the intended outcomes for learners (e.g., awareness/knowledge, skill demonstration, use in context).

Building on conceptualizations first described by Harris (1980), McCollum and Catlett (1997) used a figure to illustrate the importance of alignment between the *how* and *why* of professional development while simultaneously considering the complexity of required learner synthesis and application. Figure 2.1 shows an adapted version of this figure. As illustrated in Figure 2.1, the *why* of professional development is shown on the *y*-axis. From a practice-focused perspective, we could

> **Four Components of a Professional Development Framework**
>
> **Who:** Gathering information about the characteristics and contexts of learners and children and families in these contexts
>
> **What:** Content focus of the facilitated teaching and learning experiences
>
> **How:** Structural and process features of the facilitated teaching and learning experiences
>
> **Why:** Desired learning outcomes

be providing professional development because learners want to be aware of, know about, or know more about a practice (e.g., knowing the importance of embedding math story problems in everyday activities or knowing more about why it is important to teach children to express emotions). Alternatively, professional development might focus on skill demonstration outcomes. Building on earlier examples, learners might demonstrate they can use embedded instruction practices to teach math story problems or they might demonstrate strategies to teach children emotion words as part of a simulation activity in a workshop. More recently, based on seminal work conducted by Joyce and Showers (2002) about the importance of supporting "executive implementation" in practice contexts, an important *why* of professional development is the use of knowledge, skills, and dispositions in practice contexts—what we refer to as practices within the PBC framework. Building further on the examples, this means learners would be able to use embedded instruction practices with fidelity to teach math story problems in their everyday classroom activities or they would be able to use practices that support caregivers to teach their young children emotion words.

On the *x*-axis of Figure 2.1 is the continuum of learner synthesis and application. Looking at the *x* and *y* axes together, the figure shows examples of *how* strategies that might be used in professional development based on the *why* or the desired outcomes. For example, if the desired

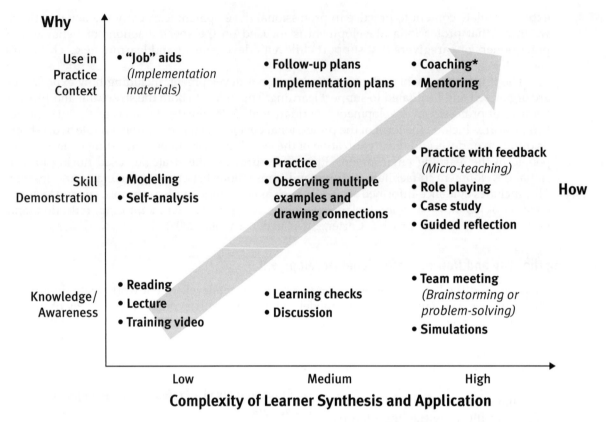

Figure 2.1.   Aligning the *how* and *why* of professional development by the complexity of synthesis and application required. From Snyder, P. (2014), NCQTL Front Parch Series. Available at https://eclkc.ohs.acf.hhs.gov/video/supporting-quality-teaching-learning-conversation-about-professional-development. Adapted from: McCollum, J. & Catlett (Eds.), *Reforming personnel preparation in early intervention: Issues, models, and practical strategies* (105–125); reprinted by permission.

why outcome is that a learner will gain knowledge about embedded math story problem practices, at the lowest level of learner synthesis and application, a brief on-line learning module and handout (two *how* strategies) might achieve that outcome. If the *why* is demonstrating skilled use of an embedded math problem practice, the *how* strategies might include modeling the practice either on video or face to face (lower level of learner synthesis or application). Alternatively, for the same *why* outcome at a higher level of synthesis and application, opportunities for repeated practice with feedback might be provided during a workshop series. If we want learners to use practices in context, our *how* strategies might include job aids at the lower level of synthesis and application. For example, in follow-up to a workshop series on dialogic reading (Whitehurst, n.d.), learners might be given books focused on emotion words and they might insert dialogic reading practices prompt cards in the book for use during storybook reading. At higher levels of synthesis and application, learners might participate in PBC to support their implementation of how to teach emotions using dialogic reading practices and how to implement other effective practices for teaching emotions as reflected in the Pyramid Model (Hemmeter et al., 2020).

In Figure 2.2, we superimpose examples of facilitated teaching or learning experiences. A learner reviewing an online module about effective literacy practices is a low-complexity *how* strategy at the awareness or knowledge level. Home visitors writing back-home plans to support their implementation of early literacy practices is a medium-complexity *how* strategy to support a use in practice outcome. Teachers engaging in PBC to support their fidelity of implementation of responsive interaction practices with children is a high-complexity *how* strategy to support use of the practices in job-embedded contexts. It is important to acknowledge that in quality professional development, more than one of these *how* strategies or other evidence-informed strategies not shown in the figures would be used to support learners to achieve desired outcomes.

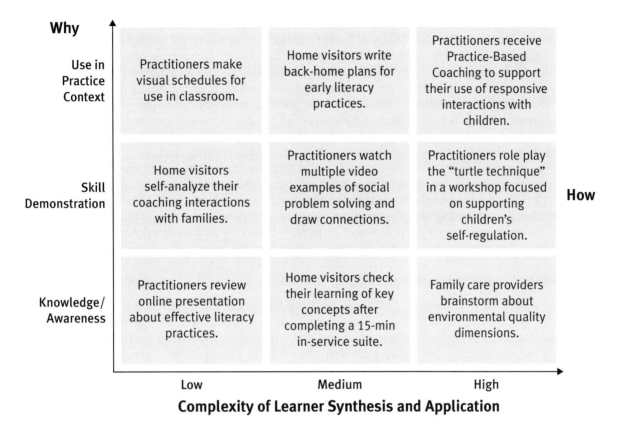

Why

	Low	**Medium**	**High**
Use in Practice Context	Practitioners make visual schedules for use in classroom.	Home visitors write back-home plans for early literacy practices.	Practitioners receive Practice-Based Coaching to support their use of responsive interactions with children.
Skill Demonstration	Home visitors self-analyze their coaching interactions with families.	Practitioners watch multiple video examples of social problem solving and draw connections.	Practitioners role play the "turtle technique" in a workshop focused on supporting children's self-regulation.
Knowledge/ Awareness	Practitioners review online presentation about effective literacy practices.	Home visitors check their learning of key concepts after completing a 15-min in-service suite.	Family care providers brainstorm about environmental quality dimensions.

How

Complexity of Learner Synthesis and Application

Figure 2.2.   Example professional development experiences aligned with desired outcomes and continuum of complexity of synthesis and application. From Snyder, P. (2014). Supporting Quality Teaching and Learning: A Conversation about Professional Development. Retrieved from https://eclkc .ohs.acf.hhs.gov/video/supporting-quality-teaching-learning-conversation-about-professional-development. Adapted from Winton, P. J., McCollum, J.A. & Catlet, C. (1997). *Reforming personnel preparation in early intervention: Issues, models, and practical strategies* (105–125); reprinted by permission.

Professional Development and Practice-Based Coaching

Figures 2.1 and 2.2 are helpful heuristics for planning, implementing, and evaluating professional development, particularly because calls to rethink and reshape professional development have been issued in recent years (Odom, 2009; Snyder et al., 2017; Snyder, Hemmeter et al., 2011). General consensus exists that professional development should not be defined by episodic, one-shot, uncoordinated, poorly planned, primarily didactic teaching and learning experiences. Quality professional development should be guided by desired outcomes (*why*) and the *who, what,* and *how* should be informed by the science of how people learn and the growing body of professional development research (Institute of Medicine and National Research Council; 2015; National Research Council, 2000).

> **Key Point to Remember**
>
> Quality professional development should be guided by desired outcomes (*why*) and the *who, what,* and *how* should be informed by the science of how people learn and the growing body of professional development research.

For example, a cohesive workshop series might be designed to build knowledge and provide opportunities for learners to demonstrate skills implementing Pyramid Model (Hemmeter et al., 2016) or embedded instruction practices (Snyder et al., 2018). If these *why* outcomes are desired, then the *how* strategies (structural and process features of the professional development) should align with them. If use of Pyramid Model or embedded instruction practices in context is a desired professional development outcome, workshops alone are likely not going to be sufficient for most learners.

In implementation science, fidelity of implementation (use) of effective practices in authentic contexts is emphasized (Kelly & Perkins, 2014). As described in Chapter 1, PBC was conceptualized as a form of professional development that would support use of effective practices in context. In all but one study shown in Chapter 1 (Table 1.3), knowledge or skill demonstration forms of professional development (e.g., workshop series, brief trainings, online video exemplars, web-based modules, implementation guides, materials) were provided to learners. In addition, PBC was provided to achieve desired practice-focused outcomes. In these studies, PBC served as a bridge connecting facilitated teaching and learning experiences that occurred outside of practice contexts to those that that occurred in practice contexts. When PBC is implemented with fidelity, there are opportunities for learners to continue to enhance their knowledge, skills, and dispositions through repeated opportunities to implement effective practices, reflect and receive feedback on their implementation, and participate in additional facilitated teaching and learning experiences. Professional development, including PBC, should be viewed as an ongoing journey with different itineraries based on learner strengths and needs rather than a single destination that uses the same road map for every learner.

Practice-Based Coaching Framework

As described in Chapter 1, PBC is an evidence-based coaching approach (Snyder et al., 2015). PBC is a transactional, individualized, and cyclical process used to support coachees' implementation of effective practices that lead to positive developmental and learning outcomes for infants, toddlers, and young children. By effective practices, we mean the observable and measurable actions or behaviors of a coachee that involve manipulating the physical, temporal, interactional, or instructional environment to support child adaptation, development, and learning. These effective practices are at the center of the PBC framework.

> **Key Point to Remember**
>
> *Effective practices* refers to the observable and measurable actions or behaviors of a coachee. Practice can involve manipulating the physical, temporal, interactional, or instructional environment to support child adaptation, development, and learning.

To characterize key components and features of PBC, we have developed a PBC framework. Three key components are part of the PBC framework, as shown in Figure 2.3. The components are 1) shared goal setting and action planning, informed by practice-focused strengths and needs assessment information; 2), focused observation; and 3) reflection and feedback. In Table 2.1, we provide a brief description of each PBC component and related implementation feature and we list examples of theoretical or empirical evidence for each component or feature. In Table 2.2, we describe actions associated with a PBC cycle as part of shared goal setting and action planning, focused observation, and reflection and feedback. In Chapters 3 through 10, we elaborate further on the components and features by providing additional theoretical, empirical, or practice-based rationales for their inclusion in the PBC framework. We provide essential information and resources about how to implement the PBC components and features with fidelity. We use case stories to illustrate how the components and features can be applied in diverse early childhood contexts. A brief overview of each chapter is presented here.

PBC takes place in the context of a collaborative coaching partnership. In PBC, enabling empowering and equitable partnerships are created between coachees and coaches to support fidelity of practice implementation. In Chapter 3, we describe essential features of collaborative partnerships and strategies for building and sustaining these partnerships over time.

As part of our work related to developing, validating, and evaluating PBC, we have identified evidence-informed coaching strategies (Snyder et al., 2015). We have examined the frequency, intensity, and utility of these coaching strategies over time. Based on our research and feedback received from coaches and coachees, we have identified essential and enhancement coaching strategies for use in PBC. These strategies are detailed in Chapter 4. Definitions

Figure 2.3. Practice-Based Coaching framework. From Snyder, P. A., Hemmeter, M. L., & Fox, L. (2015). Supporting implementation of evidence-based practices through practice-based coaching. *Topics in Early Childhood Special Education*, *35*(3), 133–143. https://doi .org/10.1177/0271121415594925; reprinted by permission.

of the strategies are provided and examples of how and when these strategies can be used are described.

Practice-focused strengths and needs assessments refer to processes that involve conducting observations or gathering perspectives about practice implementation relative to a defined set of effective practices (Snyder & Wolfe, 2008). This information is used to prioritize PBC goals and guide action planning, focused observation, and reflection and feedback. Chapter 5 provides information about the essential features of strengths and needs assessments, guidance for how to conduct them, and example forms and formats. Strengths and needs assessment data for the three case stories are shared to illustrate how this process can be conducted.

Goals and action plans are essential road maps that guide continuous cycles of PBC. In Chapter 6, we describe how to write specific, measurable, achievable/action-oriented, relevant/realistic, and time-framed (SMA^{2}R^{2}T) goals and accompanying action plans to guide PBC implementation. We illustrate how goal setting and action planning is informed by strengths and needs assessments. Resources to support writing goals and action plans are provided. We use the case stories to illustrate how goals and action plans were developed collaboratively by coachees and coaches based on strengths and needs assessment data and practice implementation data.

Chapter 7 provides information about focused observations and why they are an important component of PBC. We describe what it means to conduct focused observations and illustrate strategies for how to conduct them. Coaching strategies that might be used during focused observations are described. Resources used to record information from focused observations are shared. Descriptions of how focused observations were conducted in the case stories and example artifacts from the focused observations are shared.

Reflection and feedback about practice implementation is an essential component of PBC. In Chapter 8, we describe theoretical and empirical evidence that supports the importance of

Table 2.1. Description of Practice-Based Coaching components and features and relevant theoretical or empirical support

PBC component or feature	Description of the component or feature	Theoretical or empirical support
Goal setting and action planning	The action plan serves as a road map for coaching. The goal and action plan are differentiated based on the practice-focused strengths and needs of the coachee. Goals and action plans guide PBC implementation, document progress, and provide data for making informed decisions about progress toward fidelity of practice implementation and the need for additional professional development supports, including PBC.	• Cusumano & Preston (2018) • Frates et al. (2011) • Kraft et al. (2018) • Snyder et al. (2015)
Focused observation	During focused observation, fidelity of practice implementation data are gathered. When appropriate, enhancement strategies, such as modeling, verbal or gestural prompts, or environmental arrangements, might be used to support coachees' practice implementation. Focused observation can serve as an event that sets the occasion for a coachee to implement the effective practice in their natural setting, enhancing acquisition, fluency, maintenance, and generalization of practice implementation.	• Cusumano & Preston (2018) • Kraft et al. (2018) • Kretlow & Bartholomew (2010) • Seniuk et al. (2013)
Reflection and feedback	Guided reflection and performance feedback about practice implementation support coachees to monitor and evaluate their fidelity of practice implementation. Reflection helps coachees identify implementation fidelity successes and problem-solve when practice implementation challenges occur. Reflection supports coachees' self-efficacy about practice implementation. Performance feedback about practice implementation, including supportive and constructive feedback, affects future practice implementation and engages the coachee in identifying motivations and strategies for enhancing practice implementation.	• Barton et al. (2011) • Crow & Snyder (1998) • Cusumano & Preston (2018) • Frates et al. (2011) • Hemmeter et al. (2011) • Kraft et al. (2018) • Lorio et al. (2020) • Seniuk et al. (2013) • Shannon, Snyder et al. (2021)
Coaching cycle	A cycle begins when a goal(s) and action plan steps are specified and focused observation and reflection and feedback are implemented in the context of a collaborative partnership. A coaching cycle occurs in each coaching session.	• Snyder et al. (2015)
Coaching manuals and coaching logs	Manuals are used to describe how the components and features of PBC should be implemented during each phase and cycle of PBC.	• Snyder et al. (2015)
Coaching strategies	Refers to actions or behaviors coaches use while implementing PBC with coachees. Strategies have been identified as essential or enhancement. Essential strategies are observation, reflective conversation, supportive feedback, constructive feedback, providing resources or materials; and goal setting, graphic feedback, and video feedback, as appropriate. Enhancement strategies include side-by-side support cues; other help in practice setting; problem solving; role play; video examples; modeling; environmental arrangements; graphing.	• Hemmeter et al. (2016) • Snyder et al. (2015) • Snyder, Hemmeter et al. (2018)
Collaborative partnership	Enabling, empowering, and equitable collaborative partnerships are created between coachees and coaches to support fidelity of practice implementation. In a collaborative partnership information is gathered about the coachees' and coaches' priorities and motivations; their learning history and learning preferences; their knowledge, skills, and dispositions; and their practice setting characteristics. This information is used to individualize PBC as a facilitated learning experience for each coachee and coach.	• Cusumano & Preston (2018) • Shannon, Snyder et al. (2021) • Snyder et al. (2015)
Differentiated delivery format	PBC can be delivered onsite, virtually, or using a blended format. It can be implemented one to one with an expert coach, with a peer, or in small groups.	• Bishop et al. (2015) • Hemmeter et al. (2016) • Kraft et al. (2018) • Shannon et al. (2019) • Snyder, Hemmeter et al. (2018)
Effective practices	*Effective practices* refers to practices for which there is empirical evidence that when implemented with fidelity, they result in positive outcomes for children and families (Snyder et al., 2017). In PBC, these practices are defined as the observable and measurable actions, behaviors, or skills demonstrated by the coachee.	• Crow & Snyder (1998) • Cusumano & Preston (2018) • Seniuk et al. (2013)
Practice-focused strengths and needs assessment	Strengths and needs assessment refers to processes that involve conducting observations or gathering perspectives about practice implementation for a defined set of effective practices and using this information to prioritize PBC goals and guide action planning, focused observation, and reflection and feedback. Strengths and needs assessment also builds and maintains collaborative partnerships.	• Seniuk et al. (2013) • Snyder et al. (2015) • Snyder & Wolfe (2008)

Table 2.2. Summary of actions within a Practice-Based Coaching cycle

Shared goals and action planning	Focused observation	Reflection and feedback
• Identify practice-focused strengths and needs based on strengths and needs assessment or other practice implementation tool. • Set goal(s) for practice implementation. • Create an action plan to support goal achievement, including how achievement will be measured. • Specify timelines for goal achievement and action plan steps. • Identify materials and resources needed to meet the goal.	• Observe practice implementation to assess progress toward meeting goals. • Model, demonstrate, or prompt the practice as needed. • Collect data on practice implementation. • Observe practitioners' or children's responses to practice implementation as appropriate.	• Reflect on the observation and progress toward goal and action steps completion. • Provide supportive and constructive feedback about practice implementation. • Acknowledge successes and problem-solve implementation challenges, as needed. • Using data from strengths and needs assessment or other practice implementation tools, assess whether a goal is achieved, whether the goal should be continued, or whether the goal or action steps should be modified. • Identify additional resources or materials to support practice implementation as needed.

Adapted from von der Embse et al. (2019).

reflection and feedback. Strategies and resources for providing reflection and feedback are provided. Examples of how reflection and feedback were provided in the case stories are included.

Practice-Based Coaching Implementation and Supports for Measuring Implementation Fidelity

PBC has been successfully implemented with practitioners and caregivers in a variety of early childhood settings, including Early Head Start/Head Start, early care and education programs, public and private pre-K programs, inclusive preschool programs serving children with and without disabilities, and early intervention programs. Program- or system-wide implementation of PBC has been described in the literature, particularly to support implementation of Pyramid Model practices (Johnson, 2017; von der Embse et al., 2019). In Chapter 9, we describe structures and processes for implementing PBC and resources that can be used to measure fidelity of PBC implementation.

Phases of PBC Implementation Four major phases generally are associated with the implementation of PBC. Phase I is orientation, where coachees and coaches learn about PBC and how it will be implemented. Practice-focused strengths and needs assessments are initially completed during this phase. The collaborative partnership begins. In Phase II, clarification and verification of practice-focused strengths and needs assessments occurs and initial goals and action plans are developed. The collaborative partnership is expanded. In the third phase, the PBC cycle, including shared goal setting, focused observation, and reflection and feedback is completed a number of times. Goals, action plans, and strengths and needs assessments are updated, as appropriate, based on practice implementation data and ongoing strengths and needs assessments. This information guides coaching actions and decisions in each coaching cycle. The collaborative partnership continues in Phase III, with the coachee assuming more of a leadership role over successive coaching cycles. The fourth and final

> **Four Phases of PBC Implementation**
> **Phase I:** Orientation to PBC
> **Phase II:** Initial strengths and needs assessment, goal setting, and action planning followed by focused observation, reflection and feedback
> **Phase III:** Additional PBC cycles implemented with updated strengths and needs assessment, goal setting, and action planning as appropriate
> **Phase IV:** Assessment and review of goals and accomplishments; plan for sustained practice implementation

phase involves an assessment and review of goals and accomplishments related to fidelity of practice implementation. It also involves development of a plan for sustained implementation of practices that have been the focus of professional development and PBC. This phase includes the identification of future professional development, including PBC, when appropriate. This professional development might be focused on the practices that have been the focus of PBC or on other effective practices. The final phase is designed to emphasize that implementation of practices should be sustained and that future professional development should be ongoing and cohesive rather than episodic and disconnected (Snyder et al., 2015).

Professional Development for Practice-Based Coaching Coaches   Artman-Meeker et al. (2015) reviewed 49 studies focused on coaching practitioners to implement intervention practices in early childhood settings. Less than 50% of the studies reported providing coaches with professional development or follow-up support on coaching, including coaching strategies. Less than one third reported providing professional development on the practices that were the focus of coaching. The importance of this dual emphasis for coach professional development was also supported by Kraft et al. (2018). These authors conducted a meta-analysis of 60 professional development studies that included coaching, 31 of which were conducted in early childhood settings. They concluded that building a cadre of capable coaches whose expertise is matched to the diverse needs of coachees is essential for installing, implementing, and sustaining a robust coaching system.

Within PBC, our professional development support for coaches often uses parallel processes to those the coach is implementing with coachees. This includes strengths and needs assessments related to coaching and the practices that are the focus of coaching, goal setting and action planning, focused observations of coaching, and reflection and feedback about coaching implementation, including feedback about fidelity of PBC implementation. Chapter 9 describes the importance of providing initial and ongoing professional development support for coaches on both PBC *and* the practices that are the focus of PBC.

Key Point to Remember

Coaches should receive professional development support focused on PBC and the effective practices they are supporting coachees to implement.

Coaching Manuals and Fidelity Checklists   To ensure that PBC is implemented with fidelity, coaching manuals and fidelity checklists, including coaching logs, have been developed and validated for acceptability, feasibility, and utility. These materials have been used in a variety of research studies (see Chapter 1), in training and technical assistance activities, and in program- or systemwide implementation activities (e.g., Early Childhood Learning and Knowledge Center, n.d.; von der Embse et al., 2019). Chapter 9 and materials located in the appendices include examples of a coaching manual, a coaching log, PBC fidelity checklists, and PBC fidelity feedback forms.

Practice-Based Coaching Delivery Formats and Modalities

PBC can be used in different coaching partner formats (expert, reciprocal peer, self) and can involve various delivery modalities (e.g., face to face/live/on site, synchronous virtual, asynchronous virtual). PBC can be provided to an individual, a dyad, or a group. As described in Chapter 1, most PBC studies to date have involved delivery on site by an expert coach to individual teachers. Various other options have been studied or proposed for use, including self-coaching (Bishop et al., 2015; Snyder, Hemmeter et al., 2018), reciprocal peer coaching (von der Embse et al., 2019), and group coaching (Fettig & Artman-Meeker, 2016). Figure 2.4 shows an illustration of various PBC delivery options.

Regardless of the delivery option, the same actions shown in Table 2.2 should be used to implement PBC. How these actions are enacted differs depending on the format and modalities

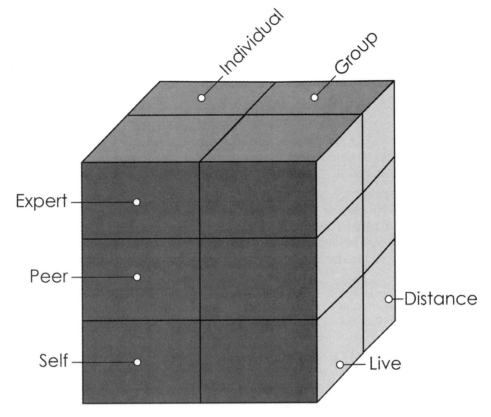

Figure 2.4. Practice-Based Coaching delivery formats and modalities for individuals or groups. From Head Start National Center for Quality Teaching and Learning. (2014). *Leadership academy: Applying practice-based coaching* [PowerPoint slides]; reprinted by permission.

being used and whether coaching is being provided to an individual, dyad, or group. For example, in on-site coaching, the coach might conduct a focused observation in the classroom. In self-coaching, the coachee might arrange for their practice implementation to be video-recorded so they can conduct a focused observation at a later time. Coachees who are involved in on-site coaching might engage in reflection and feedback synchronously with their coach while using a virtual coaching platform. Coachees who are involved in reciprocal peer coaching might use the same virtual coaching platform, but their use is asynchronous, so they engage in reflection and feedback by using commenting and timestamping functions available in the coaching platform. A coachee using self-coaching might use resources available on a coaching platform to engage in reflection and feedback by self-monitoring and self-evaluating their practice implementation. Regardless of modality, it is important to ensure the actions shown in Table 2.2 are implemented with fidelity. Chapter 10 provides additional examples and illustrations of how technology can be used to support PBC implementation. Information is provided about how technology can be used to gather strengths and needs assessment information and facilitate goal setting and action planning, focused observation, and reflection and feedback.

Key Point to Remember

PBC should always involve strengths and needs assessment to inform goal setting and action planning, focused observation, and reflection and feedback. The actions used to implement the PBC components might vary based on the delivery partner or delivery option.

CASE STORIES OF PRACTICE-BASED COACHING IMPLEMENTATION

Case stories are useful for illustrating how the PBC components and features can be implemented in contexts similar to those in which readers want to apply it (Snyder & McWilliam, 2003). We have developed three case stories for illustrating PBC implementation. Each case story differs on relevant dimensions, including the practice contexts in which PBC is implemented, the delivery methods, and the effective practices that are the focus of PBC.

Meet Lynn

Lynn has been working at Helping Hands Childcare Center for 4 years. When Lynn began working at Helping Hands, she was attending college full time to obtain her associate's degree in early childhood education. She started as a volunteer and was hired as a part-time assistant teacher in the infant classroom within her first 3 months volunteering. She was also an assistant teacher in the 4-year-old classroom before finishing her degree. She is now a full-time lead teacher in her current classroom. Lynn has been the lead teacher in the classroom for older toddlers for 2 years. Her classroom currently has 15 children enrolled. All children attend for a full day, from 7:30 a.m. to 5:30 p.m.

Lynn has two teaching assistants. Carl is in the classroom from 7:30 a.m. to 12:00 p.m. Elita comes to the classroom from 12:00 p.m. to 5:30 p.m. Both assistants have worked at the center for less than 4 months. Lynn appreciates having Carl and Elita in the classroom. They usually help her prepare activities and clean the toys when they are in the classroom. They also help with diapering and meal preparation, which gives her more time to spend with the children.

Lynn wants to provide many opportunities for children to explore and learn. She updates the materials in the classroom based on themes every 2 weeks. She joins in children's activities as often as possible. She believes it is important to follow children's interests and to support their learning within engaging activities.

Lynn knows it is important to provide opportunities for toddlers to hear and use language and to interact regularly with adults and peers. In August, Lynn was given an opportunity to attend a local conference focused on early education and learning. Presenters were from a nearby university. Lynn attended two 90-min conference sessions. One session focused on having responsive interactions with children. The other session described strategies for creating a language-rich classroom environment. Since attending the conference, Lynn has been exploring a series of online modules focused on promoting children's language development, which was recommended to her by one of the conference presenters. Each module takes about 10–15 min to complete and includes tips for interacting with young children in ways that support their language development.

Lynn recently learned that her program will be receiving professional development from Sirena, who is a training and technical assistance specialist in a regional child care resource and referral agency. She does not know very much about what Sirena will be doing but is interested in learning more about what professional development opportunities will be available.

Sirena plans to hold monthly lunch-and-learn sessions for teachers to learn about foundational evidence-based interactional and teaching practices that support children's early learning and to talk with their colleagues about how they are implementing these practices. She also plans to provide opportunities for teachers to participate in on-site PBC or self-coaching based on the level of support needed to implement the practices as intended. Sirena was recently trained in PBC and has asked to pilot the on-site PBC that she and her agency leadership team are using with one or two teachers at Helping Hands. The pilot will help her refine the on-site coaching processes as well as develop a resource library and tools to support self-coaching for teachers who would benefit from self-directed professional development.

The center director suggested Lynn might be interested in participating in the pilot of on-site PBC, because she has been engaging independently in professional development opportunities offered outside the center. She knows Lynn has been seeking opportunities to learn more about practices that promote responsive interactions and children's language development.

She suggested Sirena approach Lynn about whether she would be interested in receiving PBC to help Lynn transfer what she has learned from the conference, the online modules, and the lunch-and-learns to her classroom practice.

Lynn is excited about the opportunity to learn more about how she can support responsive interactions and her children's language development. She is nervous about Sirena coming to her classroom because she does not know Sirena and she does not know very much about PBC. When she spoke to Sirena on the phone, Sirena said they would work together to develop a shared goal related to practices that support responsive interactions and children's language development and an action plan to meet the goal. Lynn knows Sirena will need to observe in her classroom each week, and that they will meet after each observation to discuss her progress toward her goal. Sirena said each meeting would include opportunities for shared reflection, supportive and constructive feedback, and opportunities to receive additional resources and materials. Sirena said the information she collects in the classroom will only be used to guide reflection and feedback in their coaching sessions and other parts of PBC, but Lynn still wonders if the information Sirena collects will affect her performance evaluation, which is coming up in 2 months.

Meet Maureen and Maria

Maureen and Maria co-teach in an inclusive Head Start classroom located in a rural area. Maureen is a special education teacher and Maria is the general education teacher. Maureen and Maria also work with an instructional assistant, Adam. There are 17 children in their class and 5 of those children are receiving services associated with an individualized education program (IEP). There are also six dual language learners in the classroom, and Maria is bilingual in Spanish.

Maureen has 4 years of teaching experience in a K–2 special education classroom and this is her first year in preschool and in an inclusive setting. Maria has been a Head Start teacher for 7 years and feels confident with the curriculum. She is excited to have Maureen as her new co-teacher and wants to learn more about strategies for working with young children with disabilities. This year, Maureen and Maria have elected to participate in professional development focused on embedded instruction. As part of a statewide initiative focused on

---

Four Parts of Embedded Instruction (Snyder, Hemmeter et al., 2018)

1. What to Teach—What to teach involves identifying priority skills to teach children. These are skills children are not yet doing, but that are one or two steps ahead of what they can currently do, and that are aligned with early learning foundations and with the children's IEP or individualized family service plan goals. As part of What to Teach, practitioners write priority learning targets. Each target specifies what the target skill is in ways that are observable and measurable, the conditions under which the child is expected to demonstrate the skill, when the child is expected to demonstrate the skill, and information about how the team will know the child has achieved the skill.

2. When/Where/Who to Teach—As part of the When/Where/Who to Teach, practitioners identify everyday activities, routines, and transitions that are natural or logical times to embed opportunities for children to practice the target skills identified in their priority learning targets and who will support embedded instruction.

3. How to Teach—How to Teach involves planning for and implementing embedded learning opportunities that support children to learn target skills within everyday activities, routines, and transitions. As part of How to Teach, practitioners use systematic instructional procedures organized as A-B-Cs (antecedents, behaviors, consequences) to help children learn target skills.

4. How to Evaluate—How to evaluate involves collecting and analyzing data about the implementation of embedded learning opportunities and children's progress toward priority learning targets. These data are used to inform decisions about embedded instruction implementation and outcomes.

supporting preschool inclusion, they will participate in a 12-hr virtual workshop series to learn about embedded instruction practices and will receive practice guides and access to a website to support their use of embedded instruction in the classroom. Four workshops are scheduled in September and January with two 3-hr workshops held on two consecutive days in each of these months. The workshops will provide foundational information about the four parts of embedded instruction, which are described in the box on Page 33.

Maureen and Maria will participate in virtual PBC with their coach, Elley. She will support them to develop shared goals and a classroom-level action plan. Maureen and Maria will video-record each other implementing practices on their action plan and they will share their videos with Elley using a secure video-sharing platform. Every 2 weeks, they will meet with Elley via video conference to review their video and to engage in reflection and feedback about progress on their goals and action plans. Maureen and Maria expect that workshops and coaching will help them build on their current strengths and experiences and enhance their use of embedded instruction practices to individualize instruction for children within ongoing activities, routines, and transitions in their inclusive classroom.

Meet Sam

It's the end of January, and Sam has been working with Kenya, his coach, since August. Sam teaches at Groveland Elementary School. He has 18, 4-year-old children in his classroom, including two children who are dual language learners and three children with IEPs. Sam has been the lead teacher in the 4-year-old class for 3 years, but this is the first year he has participated in PBC. Kenya is a program coach at Groveland. She has been working as a coach for 5 years, including 3 years as a PBC coach. Groveland's approach to professional development is to provide universal, targeted, and individualized implementation supports, including PBC, to teachers who are implementing Pyramid Model practices (Hemmeter et al., 2021). In September, Sam attended a 3-day, 16.5-hr workshop series with the other lead preschool teachers in his school. During the workshops, Sam learned about practices to promote children's social-emotional development and to prevent and address their challenging behavior. He also learned about targeted teaching practices to teach social-emotional skills and how to participate in and support the implementation of an individualized positive behavior support plan. Sam and Kenya have had on-site PBC sessions every other week since September. During their coaching sessions, Sam and Kenya reflect on Sam's progress toward the goals and action plans they developed together to support Sam's use of Pyramid Model practices. Kenya provides supportive and constructive feedback to Sam about his practice implementation. Kenya regularly shares supplemental resources and materials related to Pyramid Model practices implementation that he can use in his classroom.

By January, Sam and Kenya completed four action plans and are getting ready to write their fifth goal and action plan. Sam's previous goals are shown in the box.

To help inform professional development for preschool teachers in their school, Kenya and the professional development team at Groveland perform three observations per

---

Goal 1: I will create and post a visual schedule at eye level for the children and review it with the children before at least four activities throughout the day.

Goal 2: I will create five positively stated classroom rules and teach them at least two times a day during large or small group using role play and games.

Goal 3: I will provide embedded learning opportunities to children during circle time and small-group time on how to appropriately express positive and negative emotions.

Goal 4: I will collect data on the implementation of the behavior support strategies that are part of the individualized positive behavior support plan our team developed for Nora.

year in each preschool classroom using the Teaching Pyramid Observation Tool (TPOT; Hemmeter et al., 2014). In addition, all coaches keep "running TPOTs" that they regularly review with teachers as they engage in PBC sessions and cycles. The running TPOTs serve as ongoing strengths and needs assessments. Kenya conducted the first TPOT in Sam's classroom in September and the second at the beginning of January. Kenya and Sam reviewed these TPOT data and their running TPOT data since August as part of their first coaching session in January. They discussed strengths and priorities for their fifth shared goal and action plan.

SUMMARY

In this chapter, we set the stage for the remaining chapters in the text by describing the PBC framework as it relates to the larger context of early childhood professional development. The key components and features of PBC have been defined. Different formats and modalities for PBC delivery were introduced. Three case stories were introduced by providing summary information about the *who, what, how,* and *why* of PBC implementation. These case stories will be used throughout the remaining chapters to illustrate the application of the PBC in different early childhood contexts.

3

Establishing and Maintaining a Collaborative Partnership

Kathleen Artman-Meeker, Kiersten A. Kinder, and Mary Louise Hemmeter

ESTABLISHING AND MAINTAINING A COLLABORATIVE PARTNERSHIP

"It's all about relationships!" That is something we hear often in the field of early childhood education, and it is true of adult partnerships, as well. When coaching partners report they are understood, valued, and heard, they are more likely to engage in coaching (Johnson et al., 2016) and implement practices with fidelity (Wehby et al., 2012). Partnerships between practitioners and administrators, practitioners and other staff, and families and practitioners are key to the quality of early childhood programs. Partnerships are also the foundation for developing and implementing effective professional development. The partnership that we are focusing on in this book is between the coach and the coachee. Practice-based coaching (PBC) occurs in the context of a collaborative partnership between the coach and the person being coached (the coachee) (Snyder et al., 2015). *Collaborative partnership* refers to the coachee and coach working together to assess the coachee's strengths and needs and to design a plan for supporting the implementation of effective practices (Figure 3.1).

The PBC cycle of strengths and needs assessment, goal setting and action planning, focused observation, and reflection and feedback occur in the context of this partnership. This partnership creates an alliance (e.g., Johnson et al., 2016) and a safe space where coachees can practice new skills, reflect on their practice, problem solve, and receive feedback.

In PBC, coaches have expertise in supporting adult learners and in the practices that are the focus of coaching, and the coachees are experts on their context and setting, their current practice, and the children and families with whom they work. It is the combination of this collective expertise that makes PBC work in terms of supporting coachees to implement effective practices with fidelity.

> **Key Point to Remember**
>
> *Collaborative partnership* refers to the coachee and coach working together to assess the coachee's practice-focused strengths and needs and to design a plan for supporting the coachee's implementation of effective practices.

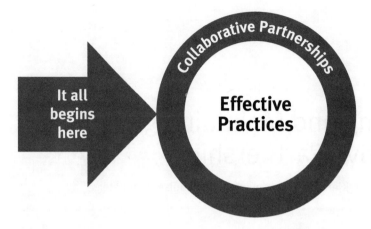

Figure 3.1. Collaborative partnerships in the practice-based coaching framework. Adapted from Snyder, P. A., Hemmeter, M. L., & Fox, L. (2015). Supporting implementation of evidence-based practices through practice-based coaching. *Topics in Early Childhood Special Education, 35*(3), 133–143. https://doi.org/10.1177/0271121415594925; adapted by permission.

All aspects of PBC are collaborative. The coachee and coach work together to identify the practices that will be the focus of coaching, to develop goals and action plan steps to meet those goals, and to plan observations and the coach's role during those observations. These decisions then guide reflection and feedback, which is intended to be a focused and collaborative transaction that involves reciprocal input and reflection from both partners.

In this chapter, we focus on key issues related to establishing and maintaining the collaborative partnership. First, we discuss seven essential characteristics of an effective collaborative partnership. Next, we describe strategies for building rapport with coachees and strategies for enhancing the collaborative partnership. We end the chapter with reflections for coaches and coachees about the role of the collaborative partnership for the success of PBC and build on the case stories from Chapter 2 to illustrate PBC collaborative partnerships in action.

CHARACTERISTICS OF COLLABORATIVE PARTNERSHIP IN PRACTICE-BASED COACHING

Each collaborative partnership reflects the unique values, vision, motivations, and attributes of the people involved in it. The partnership is also influenced by the flexible ways PBC is delivered. Distance, group, or peer coaching partnerships might look very different from one another and from traditional models of coaching. Despite this variability, effective partnerships are common to all of them. This section describes the seven essential characteristics of an effective partnership that apply across PBC delivery formats and modalities.

Shared Vision of Professional Development

The term *partnership* is often considered synonymous with the term *relationship,* but a collaborative coaching partnership is about more than the interpersonal relationship. It is about creating opportunities to nurture adult learning and provide job-embedded professional development. This shared orientation toward learning and real-world application of effective practices gives the partnership purpose and keeps it manageable in scope. In many cases, the first few interactions of a new coaching partnership center around linking content (i.e., from a workshop or course) with the coachee's own practice experiences. Coaches are intentional in the ways they name the practices that support child development and learning; identify the coachee's existing strengths, priorities, and motivations related to practice implementation; and explore ways the coachee would like to enhance or modify their practice implementation.

Shared visions about professional development and practice implementation lead to strong partnerships in which coaches and coachees are comfortable sharing their successes, struggles, and emotions (Shannon, Snyder, et al., 2020). It is important to remember, however, that PBC is a goal-oriented professional partnership. Coaches understand emotions that might arise from learning experiences in professional

> **Seven Essential Characteristics of an Effective PBC Collaborative Partnership**
> 1. Shared vision of professional development
> 2. Shared understanding about the goals of coaching
> 3. Shared focus on specific effective practices
> 4. Choices about effective practices and coaching strategies
> 5. Commitment to the partnership
> 6. Ongoing communication and support
> 7. Celebrations of successful implementation and outcomes

life and are prepared to help make sense of those feelings. They realize that the theory and principles underlying practice are most often simpler than their enactment in real practice contexts. Effective coaches help coachees apply their knowledge and implement effective practices by celebrating successes and persisting through challenges and frustrations.

Shared Understanding About the Goals of Coaching

With the knowledge that coaching is a form of professional development designed to support practice implementation, effective coaches ground coaching experiences within the goals of the organization, team, and individual. This characteristic of a partnership is distinguished from the coaching goals described in Chapter 6, which emphasize the coachee's goals related to specific practices. Here we mean coaching partners link coaching to the goals or vision of the professional development: Why is coaching

> Coaching agreements reflect the unique strengths, needs, priorities, and motivations of coaching partners situated within common elements of an agreement.

happening in the first place? For example, coaching partners may be working together toward implementation of a new curriculum or program. They may be working to achieve a program's school readiness goals for children or to enhance the implementation of individualized plans for children with or at-risk for disabilities.

With shared understanding of the goals of coaching, coaching partners come to an agreement about the types of experiences that will best support the coachee's learning and practice. These agreements unfold through a discussion and ultimately often result in a written coaching agreement that provides details around shared expectations and roles for each coaching partner. Each coaching agreement reflects the unique strengths, needs, priorities, and motivations of the coaching partners, but most coaching agreements have common elements. During the discussion to establish coaching agreements, partners consider details such as the following:

What commitments are necessary for each partner to feel comfortable and supported?

When and how will coaching sessions occur? How frequently?

What is the coach's role during an observation?

How will each coaching partner prepare for goal setting, observations, and reflection and feedback?

What information is considered confidential and what might be shared with others and in what way?

What data will be collected or used as part of coaching and why?

A sample coaching agreement is shown in Figure 3.2 and Appendix VI.Q has examples of elements that might be considered when developing coaching agreements.

It is also important to learn about the context in which coaching takes place and how that context facilitates the larger goals of coaching. Coaches and coachees take time to discuss or reflect on how they come to be a part of this professional development experience. They take time to think separately and together about the previous experiences that have shaped each partner's expectations for this coaching partnership. For coaches who are external to a program or context (i.e., external consultants or representatives of training and technical assistance systems), extra time must be given to learn about how coaching is being conceptualized in the program. For example:

> **Tools for Coaches in the Appendices**
>
> *Appendix VI.Q: Example Elements for Coaching Agreements*
>
> Elements that might be included in coaching agreements for coachees, coaches, and administrators. Elements are organized under the structural and process features of PBC because these relate to building rapport and maintaining and enhancing the collaborative partnership. Elements selected for inclusion on coaching agreements should be written so they are appropriate and individualized for the context in which PBC will be implemented and for the coaches and coachees who will be involved in PBC implementation.

Has PBC been adopted by the entire program or is an individual coachee reaching out for support?

How has coaching been introduced?

Is PBC voluntary or considered mandatory?

What are a coachee's perspectives about coaching relative to goals in the practice context? Is it seen as punitive to correct problems in the program or the individual coachee, or is it seen as an option for job-embedded professional development support and enhanced learning?

Is coaching aligned to a specific curriculum or initiative, and what are the coachee's perspectives about that curriculum or initiative?

Responses to each of these questions impacts the ways partnerships will unfold. When coaches are aware of organizational and leadership factors related to PBC implementation and when these factors align with supports for professional development and effective practice, they can more skillfully and thoughtfully engage with the coaching partners who practice in that context (Metz et al., 2013).

Shared Focus on Specific Effective Practices

As coaching partners come to understand, clarify, and verify their roles and the overarching goals of coaching, they can then focus on a specific set of effective practices expected to support child development and learning. Effective practices are the content of coaching. Skilled coaches help coachees see the alignment between what they learned in a professional development event and what happens with implementation in their practice context (Joyce & Showers, 2002). They facilitate processes in which the coachee identifies a finite set of observable and measurable practices that they are ready to implement and that will be beneficial to child development and learning (Peterson, 2013; Powell & Diamond, 2013). This is essential to making coaching interactions supportive for coachees.

> **Key Point to Remember**
>
> Skilled coaches facilitate processes to help coachees identify a finite set of observable and measurable practices that will be beneficial to child development and learning.

Teacher–Coach Agreement
Implementing the Pyramid Model for
Social-Emotional Competence in Young Children

Coach's Responsibilities:

As I coach you to implement the Pyramid Model with fidelity, I commit to:

- Maintain your confidentiality.
- Observe you during your different daily routines.
- Watch, listen, and learn from you about your educational beliefs and values.
- Focus on your strengths, your emerging skills, and your individual professional goals for implementing the Pyramid Model.
- Use a variety of tools to assess your strengths.
- Offer guidance and support that will address emerging skills identified on the TPOT and the Inventory of Practices.
- Understanding your unique learning style, so that I can adapt my coaching to your individual needs.
- Support you in creating your professional development plans in areas that you prioritize for your growth.
- Follow through to encourage systematic teaching practice changes.
- Be organized and prepared for our monthly teacher–coach meetings to review progress and revise goals.
- Be approachable and trustworthy.

I commit to being respectful, non-judgmental, and supportive in all our coaching interactions in order to contribute to a positive collaborative relationship.

Teacher's Responsibilities:

As I work with you to implement the Pyramid Model with fidelity, I commit to:

- Build positive relationships with my children, families, peers and the coach.
- Design supportive environments that will encourage children's positive behavior.
- Learn to implement the variety of social-emotional strategies embedded into the Pyramid Model.
- Recognize when a child's behavior indicates the need for individualized intensive interventions.
- Collaborate as a team with every adult who is influential in the child's life when creating a functional behavior support plan.
- Provide the coach with a self-assessment on the Inventory of Practices when requested.
- Take charge of prioritizing my own goals identified as emerging skills on the TPOT and the Inventory of Practices.
- Work to successfully implement changes in my teaching practices.
- Be organized and prepared for our monthly teacher–coach meetings.
- Be approachable and trustworthy.

I commit to being open to suggestions, ready to ask for what I need, and willing to change my teaching practices when skills have been identified in order to contribute to a positive collaborative relationship.

_____   _____
Signature of Teacher   Signature of Coach

ChallengingBehavior.org

Rev. 02-2021

Figure 3.2.   Sample coaching agreement. *Note:* Appendix VI.Q contains examples of elements that might appear in coaching agreements. Compare the written statements that appear in this coaching agreement to the elements listed in Appendix VI.Q. Which elements were used in this agreement? National Center for Pyramid Model Innovations (2018). *Coaching*. Challenging Behavior. https://challengingbehavior.cbcs.usf.edu/Implementation/coach.html

A focus on an explicit set of practices is important for several reasons. First, it helps coaches avoid global evaluations of practice quality, which can feel subjective or overwhelming to a coachee. Second, it avoids "gotcha" moments in which a coachee might feel unprepared or defensive about the coach's feedback. Third, a focus on a defined set of practices helps build coachee autonomy in coaching. The practices are transparent and coachees can make their own decisions. This avoids the feeling of "Just tell me what to do!" that can sometimes occur when practices or coaching expectations are unclear. Fourth, a focus on practices helps build a spirit of experimentation and curiosity rather than only performance. Coachees are less likely to feel like they must show everything they can do and have perfect implementation if they have been encouraged to focus on a small number of practices in each coaching cycle.

Choices About Effective Practices and Coaching Strategies

Coaching is an adult learning strategy, and adult learning should be grounded in choice (Knight, 2009). Effective partners share decision-making responsibilities about coaching content (i.e., effective practices that are the focus of coaching), structures (i.e., arrangements for the delivery and receipt of coaching), and processes (i.e., interactions aimed at supporting practice implementation) (Powell & Diamond, 2013). Shared decision-making about coaching structures and processes is especially important when deciding on coaching content. Coaches, particularly those with a great deal of experience or expertise about a curriculum or set of practices, might want to identify independently a good starting point for coaching. It might be faster or more efficient to direct early conversations toward practices the coachee is likely to implement successfully. Coaches might want their coachees to experience a quick win. Although these are important considerations, coaches must also ensure that coachees' priorities and preferences are gathered and honored. To this end, coaches may encourage a coachee to come up with a guiding question about their practice (e.g., "How do children respond to different kinds of questions at group time?" or "How do I support children's transitions?"). These types of questions can help facilitate collaborative, reflective conversations about practice-focused goals and coaching structures and processes as part of the partnership.

In addition to considering the content and structure of PBC, partners work together to make decisions about coaching partnership interactions and the coaching strategies they each prefer. They decide together when and how to observe in the practice setting, whether and when the coach will model or demonstrate practices, and what data will be helpful to the coachee. They also work with program leaders to make decisions about who is involved in the coaching partnership. For example, is only the lead teacher participating, or will the whole team be coached? If only the lead teacher is participating, then the partners work together to develop strategies for sharing information with the team and building action plans that incorporate the team. Figure 3.3 shows a sample Preferred Coaching Strategies Checklist that can be used to inform discussions about coaching processes and enhance the collaborative partnership.

> In addition to the content and structure of PBC, partners work together to make decisions about coaching partnership interactions and the coaching strategies they each prefer.

Commitment to the Partnership

Commitment to the partnership means that each partner is dedicated to agreed-upon practice implementation goals, action plans, and coaching structures and processes. The coaching agreement helps specify shared commitments and expectations for coaching, and those expectations should be upheld. Follow-through is key. Effective coaching partners ensure that meetings start and end on time, observations respect schedules, and changes are communicated in advance using preferred methods (e.g., text, e-mail, message left at front desk).

Preferred Coaching Strategies Checklist

Instructions: Please mark your preferred enhancement coaching strategies using the checklist below. Please feel free to add comments as well!

Coachee: Lynn **Date:** October 15

Enhancement Coaching Strategies	I'd like to try this strategy	Notes
1. **Side-by-side support cues:** The coach supports your practice implementation in the moment, verbally, with gestures, or with visual cues, or through technology (e.g., bug-in-ear).		
2. **Other help in practice setting:** The coach provides support to you or children, which is not directly related to your goal or action plan (e.g., wiping up spilled paint, sitting on the floor beside a child at circle).	X	
3. **Problem solving:** An interaction between you and the coach to solve an identified practice implementation issue. Problem-solving involves four steps: 1) identify the implementation issue, 2) generate potential solutions, 3) decide on a course of action, and 4) evaluate pros and cons of the selected course of action.	X	
4. **Role play:** In a role play, you and the coach take on other roles related to practice implementation (e.g., coach acts as child, coachee acts as adult).	X	
5. **Video examples:** Video examples show how another practitioner uses a practice in a similar implementation setting.	✓	
6. **Modeling:** Modeling is demonstrating or showing you how to implement a practice that is the focus of a goal or action plan.		
7. **Environmental arrangements:** The coach helps you modify or enhance your practice setting or materials in your setting to set the occasion for you to implement a practice.		
8. **Graphing:** You and your coach work together to graph data you or your coach has collected about your practice implementation or child behaviors.		
9. **Other:** *In what other ways would you want your coach to help?* I like to read about things so I can really think about them before we meet or before we share them with the staff and parents.		

Figure 3.3. Preferred Coaching Strategies Checklist: Example for Lynn.

Commitment to the partnership also means honoring confidentiality. Details of coaching conversations are not shared, and both coaching partners are sensitive to one another's strengths and needs. A committed partnership evolves over time but only when partners can rely on one another. Commitment to the partnership sets the occasion for coachees to gain confidence and competence to assume a leadership role and engage in collaborative decision making about practice implementation (Shannon, Snyder, et al., 2020).

> Commitment to the partnership means each partner is dedicated to agreed-upon practice implementation goals, action plans, and coaching structures and processes.

Ongoing Communication and Support

Effective partnerships are built on clear and consistent communication. This is related to commitment to the partnership, but it acknowledges the roles coaches have outside of their scheduled interactions with coachees. Effective partnerships are built on cumulative and reciprocal transactions that build trust and let the partner know that they are important. Respectful communication behaviors include calling ahead if running late, rescheduling a meeting when a practitioner is in the midst of an emergency, cleaning up

> Effective partnerships are built on clear and consistent communication. The cumulative and reciprocal transactions build trust and let the partner know they are important.

spilled paint when observing in the classroom, and sending an e-mail with notes summarizing a coaching conversation. However, ongoing communication and support can go beyond these basic behaviors. Coaches might e-mail asking if they can bring a book from the library for a practitioner's activity next week. They might send a text message after a celebration or difficult day. They might drop a hand-written note in the school mailbox to recognize an accomplishment.

A collaborative partnership is also built on the knowledge that adults have complex lives. Coaching partners are a source of support as each juggles professional and personal responsibilities. New babies, aging parents, health or financial issues, and job stressors affect coaches and coachees. Trust develops when coaches do their best to be sensitive to coachees' needs. They show knowledge of the coachee's situation and adjust accordingly (e.g., "I know your licensing visit is in 2 weeks, so would you like to wait until that's over for my next visit?" or "I can see that these last few weeks have been stressful for your family. Let's take a second to acknowledge all that you've got going on right now . . ."). Coaches also acknowledge their own limitations or complexities (e.g., "We've had some turnover in our administration, and I'm being pulled in lots of different directions. What's the number one way I could support you right now?").

Celebrations of Successful Implementation and Outcomes

A coach is a mirror who helps coachees see their strengths (Jablon et al., 2016). Coaches acknowledge effort and small changes. They acknowledge that practice is hard and much of the work is invisible to others. They recognize the nuanced decision-making and individualization that is required of coachees on a daily basis. Trust is built as coaches focus on small successes: a child who followed a direction, played with a peer, or joined a movement activity because of the coachee's actions. Such celebrations are strong motivators for future practice implementation. Not all adults are comfortable receiving praise, but clear information about the effects of their practice implementation can be transformative. Celebrations of success are especially important when coaching occurs infrequently. Under these circumstances, coaches can set up opportunities for coachees to share and celebrate their successes with a coach. For example, if a coach interacts with a coachee one time per month, they might send an e-mail check-in weekly asking for a "Wow" (practice implementation that went really well) and a "Wonder" (a question the coachee still has about practice implementation). Figure 3.4 offers creative ways to celebrate successes.

Celebrating Success

The environments in which we work can have a significant influence on our well-being and on our level of self-care. Individuals who work in a supportive and caring environment may generally have a better outlook on life and feel better about coming to work every day, even if the work is challenging at times. The following ideas can help you celebrate with coachees, reduce stress, and strengthen the collaborative partnership. Try these ideas and reflect on their effects.

- Send an e-mail to a coachee to let them know you appreciated something they did: "Sam, I really appreciated how hard you worked to create the visual schedule and to review it with children. I saw other members of the classroom team were really motivated by your efforts."
- Congratulate a coachee on an accomplishment by text or e-mail: "Lynn, congratulations on your successful quality assurance visit. You've worked really hard on language support practices in your classroom, and I am sure it will show in the report."
- Treat coachees to a small care package: A small paper sack with a note and a tea bag, hot cocoa mix, or healthy snack can brighten their day.
- Keep a handful of colorful index cards in your coaching kit. Use the cards to jot quick thank-you notes or acknowledgments. Leave a positive note behind after your coaching session.
- Design a coaching recognition board or e-newsletter. With the coachee's permission, share examples of creative, excellent practice implementation. These can be photos or written descriptions. This can become a learning resource for others.
- After observing a coachee's practice implementation, send a note by e-mail or text asking if you can share the example with other coachees.

Figure 3.4. Ways to celebrate successes in collaborative partnerships.

ESTABLISHING RAPPORT

Establishing rapport is the foundation for building and strengthening collaborative coaching partnerships. When coaches and coachees have rapport, coaching becomes a supportive context to ask questions, discuss issues or new ideas, obtain coach's perspectives, reflect, and gather feedback. There is evidence that a strong coach–coachee relationship promotes higher levels and quality of practice implementation in the classroom (e.g., Johnson et al., 2016). Also known as alliance building (Wehby et al., 2012), the process of building rapport with a coachee is individualized, responsive, and transactional. This section describes four key strategies coaches use to build rapport: get to know your coaching partner, get to know the coaching context, establish the coach as a resource, and follow the coachee's lead.

Getting to Know Your Coaching Partner

Effective coaches take time to get to know new coaching partners. This occurs through engaging social interactions, but it also occurs through coaching structures and processes. Coaches begin by getting to know the coachee's coaching and professional development history: What coaching experiences have they had? What professional development experiences have interested or excited them? How do they learn best? What has and has not worked for them in the past? In some cases, coachee's past experiences may have been negative, punitive, or unproductive. This is important to know so that coaches can help coachees understand how PBC might be different than what they have experienced in past coaching experiences.

Rapport is reciprocal, so coaches must also create opportunities for the coach and coachee to get to know one another as people. Coachees should view the coach as competent, approachable, and sincere. Coaches share about themselves and their own professional history: What drew them to coaching? What previous experiences have shaped their approaches? What makes them passionate about the content of coaching? Over time, both coaching partners begin to understand how personal and professional experiences influence coaching and the collaborative partnership.

Four Key Strategies for Building Rapport
1. Get to know your coaching partner.
2. Get to know the coaching context.
3. Establish the coach as a resource.
4. Follow the coachee's lead.

Finally, coaches seek to understand the coachee's motivation for practice implementation or change. What drives the coachee's decisions about practice? What or who are the key influencers in the coachee's professional life? Coachees who have choices in their practice contexts and professional development experiences are more likely to (a) engage in the coaching process and (b) implement practices with fidelity (e.g., Johnson et al., 2014). Understanding the choices available to coachees and what motivates them to make particular choices is a key driver of buy-in. Choice leads to collaboration during the goal setting and throughout the rest of the coaching cycle. For example, a coach who knows that a coachees' practice-focused motivation is primarily around reducing challenging behavior in the classroom will have a different entry point for coaching than for a coachee whose primary motivation is implementing practices associated with a new required math curriculum.

Getting to Know the Coaching Context

Every coaching partnership is shaped by the culture of the individuals, community, and contexts in which the partnership occurs. Part of rapport building is learning about the coachee's practice context. Time spent observing the practice context, and the schedules, activities, and teaming structures and processes, is important. When coaches get to know the practice context, they can better understand and use information about leadership, organizational and competency systems, processes, opportunities, and pressures (Metz et al., 2013). The more the coach knows about a coachee's practice context, the better the coach can be at creating meaningful alliances and tailoring practice-focused learning opportunities with coachees as part of the collaborative partnership.

Coaches look for information on the contexts that sustain and give meaning to teachers' values, beliefs, preferences, and behaviors. They ask questions that reveal the ways coachees' values, beliefs, and preferences influence their behaviors, and they reflect on the influence of their own values, beliefs, preferences, and behaviors (Jablon et al., 2016).

Establishing the Coach as a Resource

Effective coaches are continuous learners and they take steps to neutralize the power dynamics inherent in most coaching interactions. They sit side by side with coachees, they maintain open body language and culturally appropriate interactions, and they make sure coachees have the information they need to be equally prepared and actively participative. Coaches also recognize that some discomfort might occur as the coach and coachee are learning together. They acknowledge their own roles in any discomfort,

Key Point to Remember

Effective coaches are continuous learners and they take steps to neutralize the power dynamics inherent in most coaching interactions. Effective coaches come to be seen as trusted thought and learning partners.

reflect on the discomfort, and work together to make changes that further strengthen the partnership.

Coachees who have trust and confidence in the coach are more likely to have a successful coaching experience (Johnson et al., 2016; Shannon, Snyder, et al., 2020). Effective coaches come to be seen as trusted thought and learning partners. The coach and coachee come together as learners with different and complementary expertise. The coach is able to ask questions that spark the coachee's curiosity, motivation, and connections to previous learning. Coaches have opportunities to see many different practice contexts and coachees. This provides opportunities to share real-world examples and resources developed by coachees in similar roles and types of practice contexts. This cross-pollination of good ideas and resources helps build coachee leadership and a community of practitioners.

Coaches become resources by being flexible and responsive to coachee needs. For rapport building, coaches take actions to be authentic partners in the classroom. For example, coachees might invite coaches to model a new practice while the coachee observes. Coaches may also help out in the practice context when needed. Tying a child's shoe during a busy moment or helping clean up a spill can go a long way toward building trust. Coaches also may help the coachee find resources needed to implement a practice successfully. For example, if the coachee does not have access to a color printer, the coach may be able to help print off-site. If the program's collection of children's books is limited, the coach might help the coachee make connections with the local public library's services for educators. Effective coaches also admit when they do not know the answer, and they commit to learning together with the coachee.

Following the Coachee's Lead

Finally, coaches build rapport by following the coachee's lead. For example, they remember that they are guests in a coachee's classroom, and they honor the decisions the coachee makes. Coaching is not a top-down method of professional development. PBC is aligned with specific practices, but effective coaches help teachers identify the many choices they have about when and how to implement practices. They help coachees build strategies to advocate for themselves and their own learning. They might provide coachees with questions and comments similar to those shown in Figure 3.5 (McLeod et al., 2017). Above all, coaches model openness by learning alongside the teacher and being open to the many ways the partnership will unfold while following the coachee's lead.

CONCRETE STRATEGIES FOR BUILDING COLLABORATIVE PARTNERSHIPS

Beyond the general strategies described as part of building rapport, the National Center for Systemic Improvement (NCSI, 2014) identified three key categories and associated strategies coaches use to build partnerships or alliances: effective communication, building collaboration, and sharing expertise. We summarize these categories and strategies and offer examples adapted from NCSI's work.

First, coaches use effective communication strategies. Drawing on a large body of literature on interpersonal communication, coaches should paraphrase or summarize ("It sounds like you've tried a lot of strategies with Lee, but you haven't seen much change"), they ask open-ended questions ("Can you tell me more about that?"), they affirm ("I can tell you've worked really hard on this"), and they remain nonevaluative. Second, they build a spirit of teamwork and collaboration with a coaching partner. They comment on and build upon the coachee's successes ("The visual schedule was such a success. I think this new adaptation will be help the children know what to do"), they remain goal oriented ("This week you were working on commenting positively during transitions"), and they work with the coachee to identify steps toward a goal ("For next week, it sounds like you will do. . ."). Finally, coaches share their expertise in ways that support learning without driving the partnership. Effective coaches name effective practices throughout the coaching cycle, can be trusted to share their knowledge

Questions and Comments for Coachees

	Ask questions:	Communicate what you want:
Collaborative partnership	• Tell me about your experience in the classroom before you were a coach. • Tell me about your experience as a coach. • What are your goals for our coaching sessions?	• Let me tell you about my day and the children in my class. • My long-term goals for coaching are _____. • When it comes to coaching, I'm nervous about _____. • When it comes to coaching, I'm excited about _____.
Goals and action plans	• What strategies have you seen other teachers use successfully? • What supports do you think would help me implement this action plan? • What data can we collect about this practice?	• I've read about _____ and want to try it out in my classroom. • I feel like I am _____ but want ideas about how do it better or more often. • I need help engaging with [a specific child]. • I have some ideas and need some help planning how to implement them.
Observation	• What supports do you feel comfortable providing to coaches (e.g., modeling, cueing)? • How do you collect data?	• I'd like you to focus on _____. • I'd like you to tell me how many times I _____ in this lesson. • Watch [a specific child] and tell me how she is engaged in the lesson.
Reflection	• How do you think it went when you observed? • What would your next steps be if you were in the classroom? • What do you think would happen if I did _____? • Why do you think it worked well for [specific child] but not for [another specific child]? • Did you notice something I didn't see?	• I think it went well when I _____ because I saw [a specific child] do _____. • It felt good when the children _____ when I did _____. • It did not go well when I _____. I know this because _____.
Feedback	• What went well as I used the practice(s)? • What did you see the children do as a result of the practice(s) I used? • What could I do differently next time?	Choose your feedback fit and tell your coach: • "Cut to the chase." You like to get right to the point and would like the coach to tell you what they observed in your classroom. No need for small talk. • "Show me the data." You like evidence of how you are implementing the practices and how the children are benefiting. You prefer the coach to collect and share specific data on the action plan goals. • "Focus on the positive." You first like to hear about what went well during the observation before receiving suggestions for improving your teaching.

Figure 3.5. Discussion starters for coachees to build a coaching partnership. Republished with permission of National Association for the Education of Young Children, from McLeod, R., Artman-Meeker, K., & Hardy, J. K. (2017). Preparing yourself for coaching: Partnering for success. *Young Children*, *72*(3), 75–81. Permission conveyed through Copyright Clearance Center, Inc.

and experience, and communicate clearly without jargon. Figure 3.6 lists 11 concrete strategies coaches can use to build the collaborative partnership, and Figure 3.7 shows a summary of communication strategies.

COACHING VERSUS SUPERVISION: ISSUES AND POTENTIAL SOLUTIONS

For the purposes of this book and in our work on PBC, we view the coach as someone whose job is to support coachees in a nonevaluative, nonjudgmental way. By this, we mean that a coach should not be evaluating the coachee's job performance or making decisions about raises or other personnel issues with respect to the coachees they are supporting. Our recommendation

---

Concrete Strategies to Build the Collaborative Coaching Partnership

1. Develop a coaching agreement. See Figure 3.1 and Appendix VI.Q for samples.

2. Respect the coachee's time. Begin the session on time and limit your session to the agreed-upon length. Build your schedule around the coachee and prioritize their availability. Signal transitions and make concrete plans (e.g., "It looks like we've got 5 more minutes. What should be our next steps?").

3. Build goals collaboratively. Come to agreement about the focus of coaching. Coachees who took active roles in developing implementation goals and action plans reported more positive relationships with their coaches.

4. Spend time in the coachee's practice context or observe what occurs via video. Coachees who reported more time spent by coaches observing and completing strengths and needs assessments report higher levels of alliance with their coaches.

5. Be a learning partner. Actively seek to learn about the practice culture and the cultures of the coachees, children, and families. Approach each interaction as a learning partner.

6. Build your interpersonal skills (Pierce, 2015). Use active listening strategies such as summarizing ("It sounds like…is that right?"), open-ended questions ("Why is that important to you?"), and affirmations ("Your team has been working really hard, and it shows").

7. Make connections and be goal oriented in collaborations (Pierce, 2015). Make connections with the coachee's previous accomplishments ("Let's look back at what we've accomplished so far…") and keep conversations goal oriented ("This week your goal was…"). Use collaborative language; using words like "we" and "our" signals teamwork.

8. Communicate clearly. Practice implementation is often complex, so effective coaches communicate clearly about small steps. They explain concepts and offer examples. They avoid jargon.

9. Learn together. Attend and actively participate in professional development events with coachees so you hear the same content. Make connections between the professional development events and the coachee's practice context.

10. Celebrate successes. Share celebrations of the coachee's practice implementation and the effects on child learning. Small successes can make a big difference.

11. Continue to grow as a coach. Reflect on your own strengths and needs around coaching practices. Seek feedback from your coaching partners about what is working (or not) and adjust your approaches based on feedback.

Figure 3.6.   Concrete strategies to build the collaborative coaching partnership.

would be that coaches and supervisors are different people. That is, coaches provide ongoing support to coachees around implementing practices and do not have responsibility for evaluating coachees and making recommendations about their job performance, pay, or stability. Coaching is designed to be a safe space—a space where coachees can try new things, perhaps have things not go well, reflect, improve, and try again without worrying that it will affect their job security. It is difficult for coachees to feel supported and safe in a collaborative partnership if they are worried about their job performance.

What happens in a small program or practice context where there is not enough staff to have both a coach and a supervisor? We would suggest that programs consider how they might allocate staff time differently so that these roles can be separated. For example, a program might have an excellent veteran practitioner who could be given some time to support other practitioners. Coaching might occur through video-recorded observations rather than live observations,

Interpersonal Skills: Effective communication. Building trust. Nonevaluative and nonjudgmental language.	• **Summarize:** "What I hear from your comment is…" • **Open-ended questions:** "Can you tell me more about that?" • **Affirm difficulty of change:** "This is really hard!" • **Nonevaluative language:** "Coaching is about supporting your teaching practice, not about evaluating how you teach."
Collaboration: Meeting needs and goals. Conveying that improving teaching is teamwork.	• **Refer to past accomplishments:** "This week you hoped to accomplish…" • **Refer to current goal:** "Your goal for the week is…" • **Help teacher progress toward goal:** "Let's talk about what we'll do to meet that goal. I can…. What do you think you will try to do?"
Expertise: In teaching in the content area.	• **Refer to effective teaching practices:** "Learners who struggle to show mastery benefit from explicit and systematic instruction. Explicit means…." • **Convey deep content-area knowledge:** "We know that effective reading instruction focuses on the five pillars of reading. These include…." • **Explain complex concepts succinctly:** "The Tier 3 learner may show challenging behavior because…."

Figure 3.7. Coaching strategies to build alliances with teachers. From Pierce, J. D. (2015). *Teacher-coach alliance as a critical component of coaching: Effects of feedback and analysis on teacher practice* (Doctoral dissertation, University of Washington). Retrieved from http://hdl.handle.net/1773/33786

making it possible for the veteran practitioner to be a coach without missing time in their own setting. Another possibility might be for two administrators to split the roles—they each coach half the practitioners and supervise the other half.

When it is not possible to have multiple people serving in these roles, there are several steps programs can take to try to ensure that coaching can be a safe space. First, the coach should be clear about when they are observing or meeting with the coachee in their role as a coach versus in their role as a supervisor. Second, the coach and coachee can develop an agreement or a coaching contract (see Figure 3.2) that specifies the roles and expectations of the coach and the coachee. One of the points that can be clarified in the coaching agreement is that coaching data are only used to support the coachee and are not used in evaluating the coachee. Finally, it will be important, at the program level, to establish some guidelines for the coaching partnership with respect to the goal of coaching versus the goal of supervision (Figure 3.8). As with all partnerships, transparency will be key. Relevant issues should be discussed and agreed on before coaching begins.

EVIDENCE ABOUT SUCCESSFUL COLLABORATIVE PARTNERSHIPS: PERSPECTIVES FROM COACHEES AND COACHES

Building rapport and identifying shared goals are important steps to establishing the collaborative partnership. As with any partnership, however, collaborative partnerships develop over time. Often, PBC is viewed by coachees as something new—they report not being used to someone who is there to support them and not evaluate them. It may take time for coachees to trust the coach, for the coach to establish credibility, and for the partnership to be equitable and

---

Tips for Separating Coaching and Supervision

- Keep your responsibilities as a supervisor (evaluation, monitoring, and compliance) separate from coaching in order to create a safe space for the coachee to try new things, get supportive and constructive feedback, and ask for help.
- When you engage with the coachee, make sure the purpose is transparent and the coachee is aware of the role you are playing (supervisor or coach).
- When conducting a practice-based coaching session, make sure the coachee is aware that the visits are coaching related.
- Make it clear to the coachee how the data you collect will be used and shared, either as a part of the coachee's strengths and needs assessment or for compliance with standards.
- Include language in your program handbook or coach training about the distinction between coaching and supervision.

Sample Language for Guidelines That Distinguish Coaching and Supervision

"We expect all children to leave Head Start ready for Kindergarten. Supervisors and coaches help us achieve that goal. The supervisor monitors our classrooms and home visits to make sure we are in compliance with Head Start guidelines and agency policy and procedures. As part of ongoing monitoring, the supervisor will make a number of visits to a teacher's classroom or accompany home visitors on visits with families. These visits will be announced or unannounced, as per agency guidelines. The supervisor will review records, timesheets, and paperwork to ensure compliance. The supervisor and teacher will discuss visits afterward, and the teacher will receive the results of these performance reviews in writing.

Another important job is to support the teacher's work with children through coaching. To do this, the coach and teacher will work together to set goals, monitor progress, and assess outcomes. The coach and teacher meet as needed and the coach will spend time observing the teacher. These coaching experiences will always be scheduled with the teacher in advance. Although results of performance reviews may contribute to coaching (the coach and teacher may look at the written performance review and decide to set a goal to increase communication with families), what a teacher does during coaching visits and meetings will not negatively influence their performance review.

The goal during coaching is to reflect, discuss, and try new things. If something doesn't go well, the teacher and coach will talk about it and brainstorm ways to make it better. If during coaching visits, the coach sees an issue that needs to be addressed right away (health and safety concerns), the coach must meet their professional obligations by filing a report. But the teacher and coach will talk about the problem immediately and the coach will do their best to make sure the response is transparent and clear to the teacher."

Figure 3.8. Tips for separating coaching and supervision. Adapted from Head Start National Center on Early Development, Teaching, and Learning, (2021). *Program Leaders' Guide to Practice-Based Coaching.* https://eclkc.ohs.acf.hhs.gov/document/program-leaders-guide-practice-based-coaching

collaborative. Having repeated success implementing new practices, addressing "problems of practice," or problem-solving difficult issues and situations will build both trust and credibility.

Research has shown that the collaborative coaching partnership is essential to the success of PBC (Shannon et al., 2015; Shannon, Snyder, et al., 2020). Coachees consistently describe the quality of the collaborative partnership as an important part of their experience. Reciprocity, approachability, and open-mindedness have all been associated with coachee empowerment and engagement in coaching. Coachees who have participated in PBC have reported being empowered because of the focus on building strengths instead of needing to be "fixed" (Hemmeter et al., 2016). Coaches and coachees build a sense of *we* and a shared purpose toward enhancing effective practices.

COLLABORATIVE PARTNERSHIPS IN THE CASE STORIES

In the sections that follow, we return to the case stories introduced in Chapter 2 and illustrate how coaches and coachees are engaged in building collaborative partnerships as part of PBC. As you read each case story, consider if and how the seven essential features of collaborative partnerships are reflected in the actions and behaviors of coaches and coachees. Identify which of the four rapport building strategies are being used and how coaches are engaging in effective communication, building collaboration, and sharing expertise. At the end of each case story, guiding questions are provided. Use these questions to guide further reflection about how you can build collaborative partnerships with coachees. Discuss your ideas about collaborative partnerships with other coaches or with coachees.

Lynn

Lynn read the e-mail from her director a few times, trying to make sense of it. "Great news!" it read. "Helping Hands will be receiving professional development from Sirena Sims, a training and technical assistance provider at the Region 4 resource and referral agency. Stay tuned for professional development opportunities coming your way. A few of you will be selected to receive coaching." Professional development was something Lynn was already familiar with because she recently attended workshops on responsive and language-rich interactions with children. She had been viewing online modules on those topics as well. But what did it mean to be selected for coaching? Was it going to be something only people who were doing poorly received? It always seemed that way in the past. If someone came into your classroom, it felt like everything happening was being scrutinized, putting the classroom staff on edge. Lynn had been trying out some new practices she had learned from her online modules, and she did not feel like she was ready for a stranger to come in and to judge these new practices. She hoped she would not be selected.

When Sirena called Lynn to see if she would be interested in being part of the PBC pilot program, Lynn was hesitant. What could she expect? How much extra work would it be? Was she going to have to put a bunch of new things in place? As a relatively new teacher, she did not know everything there was to know about teaching 2-year-olds, but she also felt confident about the way her classroom was running. Was this coach going to come and change it all? And she did not say this at first, but she was worried she was being targeted for extra help. Maybe she should not be so confident after all.

During that first phone call with Lynn, Sirena immediately sensed Lynn's trepidation. Lynn agreed to being part of the PBC pilot, but Sirena knew it was going to be even more important to develop a collaborative partnership with Lynn. Sirena was still thinking about it the next morning and decided to start right away with a quick stop the next day to say hello in person. With her biggest smile, Sirena came into the classroom and gave Lynn a warm greeting. She noticed that Lynn seemed surprised to see her in the classroom, and Sirena wondered if Lynn had missed the e-mail she sent that morning. Sirena made herself at home in the classroom interacting with children, helping a few children wash their hands before snack, and joining in singing "Wheels on the Bus" with the class. She had taught for many years and enjoyed being part of a classroom community. As she left, Sirena reminded Lynn that she would be coming in during planning time that day to have their first coaching session. Lynn mustered a smile and a nod but immediately thought of all the things she had done wrong in the last 20 min that Sirena might point out to her later.

Sirena joined Lynn in the teacher work room later, prepared with a draft agenda to share with Lynn and a coaching agreement to review together. She opened the session by telling Lynn how much she enjoyed being part of her classroom that day and marveled at her use of visuals with the songs. Sirena shared that music was something she loved doing when she taught and went on to explain some of her past positions and why she wanted to become a coach. Sirena made sure the conversation was not one sided—she asked questions about Lynn's previous teaching experiences and education, and what she likes most about her job. They realized they both loved reality television shows and laughed about how a toddler classroom had plenty of reality to go around! Sirena also asked about Lynn's preferred modes of communication and learned that Lynn does not regularly check her e-mail, especially in the mornings before work because she is busy getting her young children ready for school. She preferred to receive texts and did not mind having reminders. Sirena realized that her drop-in visit that morning was a surprise and made a note to be sure to give more notice next time and to use texts rather than e-mails.

Sirena shared the draft agenda with Lynn and pointed to each agenda item as she described it. She said Lynn should ask questions or stop Sirena if she needed time to think further about any of the agenda items or to ask questions. After reviewing the items on the agenda, Sirena asked Lynn if she had anything she wanted to add. Lynn said, "No, not now," but she was impressed that Sirena had asked for her input.

As the meeting went on, Lynn felt more at ease, especially learning that Sirena had been in the trenches before. It was nice to hear that Sirena had noticed the effort she had made creating the song visuals. As the session proceeded, Sirena brought out a visual of the PBC cycle and explained they were about to go on a coaching journey together. She talked through each component briefly, and as she did, Lynn started to better understand what it was going to mean to have a coach. Her initial fears about receiving coaching because she was not good enough were beginning to subside.

Next, Sirena shared a document called a coaching agreement with Lynn. As they talked through each of their roles in the PBC process, it really helped Lynn understand that this experience was going to be different from her previous experiences with coaches. Sirena described PBC as a "safe space" to grow and mentioned the choices Lynn would have in the process, including what practices they could focus on implementing. This was such a relief to Lynn. This sounded like work she would *want* to do, not *have* to do. They chuckled that signing the coaching agreement felt a bit official, but it gave Lynn a sense of commitment to the partnership, and having a copy gave her something to refer to when she was unsure of the process or expectations.

The last document Sirena reviewed with Lynn was called the Preferred Coaching Strategies Checklist (see Figure 3.3 and Appendix VI.S). Sirena explained that it would help guide her coaching by helping her to better understand Lynn's learning preferences. She asked Lynn to review and complete it before their next meeting. The more Lynn learned about PBC, the more she understood that her coach was not there to judge her—she was there to support her. That was a quite a change from the past, and it felt really good. Lynn left the meeting excited about what was to come!

Questions for Further Reflection and Discussion

- What did Sirena do to help ease Lynn's initial hesitation around having a coach observe in her classroom? What are some other ways to ease Lynn's uncertainty?

- What has Sirena already done to build rapport with Lynn?

- Was there anything Sirena could have done differently to understand Lynn or the context of the Helping Hands program's PBC initiative?

- What are some important considerations for Sirena as she continues to build a collaborative coaching partnership with Lynn?

- What do you think about the coaching agreement? How does it help build a collaborative partnership?

- What insights does the Preferred Coaching Strategies document Lynn will complete offer Sirena? How does it support Lynn?

Sam

Sam looked at his e-mail and started to get angry. How was he going to fit it all in? He was still working on getting his portfolio documentation completed for the second checkpoint, but it felt like he was putting out fires in the classroom with challenging behaviors popping up throughout the day. And now he needed to plan an activity for the parent literacy night next week too? His previous assistant Bryanna, had been out all last semester with a knee injury, and although he was glad to have Jamie now, instead of the revolving door of substitute teachers coming in and out of the room, she was new and did not really know much about the classroom. She was new to Groveland, new to the classroom, and new to early childhood settings and the Pyramid Model as well. Things felt out of control. Sam was shaking his head in frustration when his coach, Kenya, arrived.

When Kenya saw Sam, she knew the coaching session she had planned was going to change. She had heard that the teachers were being asked to help with literacy night and it was not being well received, especially given it was nearing the end of the portfolio documentation collection window. These types of requests typically did not ruffle Sam, but the last two times Kenya was in the room, she noted how overwhelmed Sam had seemed. Kenya had been planning to suggest identifying a new implementation goal and action plan but wanted to be sensitive about real-life issues Sam was experiencing.

Sam was both glad to see Kenya and frustrated because he had forgotten all about their coaching session and it felt like one more thing he had to do. He knew Kenya would listen to him. He could talk to Kenya without concern for it being shared with anyone else. Kenya had held up that part of their coaching agreement again and again. It was helpful, especially in times like this, to know he could let off some steam without fear of repercussions.

As Sam talked about all that was going on, Kenya nodded and made supportive statements such as, "These additional demands are really upsetting. How can I best help?" However, Kenya knew that her role as a PBC coach meant it was important to not only be a sounding board and offer help, but also to guide Sam to use his strengths to solve the issues at hand while simultaneously supporting his implementation of effective practices. Kenya shared a similar experience when her assistant quit mid-year, and she had used a roles and responsibilities matrix to help anyone coming into the classroom know what tasks they could complete at each time of the day. Kenya knew Sam really enjoyed engaging in supportive conversations with the children, and this would be a way to ensure that he had time to engage in those conversations. Also, Kenya pointed out that Sam mentioned struggling with frequent challenging behaviors in the classroom, so together they identified a new implementation goal and action plan steps focused on reviewing the rules and expectations more frequently. Sam agreed that this would not only help individual children, but it would also help the other adults in the classroom learn the expectations as well!

As he drove home that day, Sam thought about how Kenya understood what the underlying issues were and was able to support him to engage in problem solving and decision making that led him to a more productive path. He also was glad to be reminded of what he loved about his job—connecting with children—and he appreciated that his coach knew what motivated him to come to work every day. Sam knew his plate was still full, but Kenya was able to help him identify an implementation goal and related action steps to gain some forward momentum and continue to prioritize what was important for him, his team, and the children.

Questions for Further Reflection and Discussion

- What are some strategies Kenya likely has used previously to build the rapport she has with Sam?

- What words do you think Sam might use to describe his collaborative partnership with Kenya? How do these words reflect a collaborative partnership?

- What were some of Kenya's key actions or behaviors during her coaching session with Sam when he was frustrated by other issues occurring in his practice context?

- What strategies did Kenya use to help Sam refocus on his implementation of effective practices?

- How engaged was Sam in identifying his new implementation goal and action plan? What might Kenya have done differently to further engage Sam?

Maureen and Maria

It was a year of firsts for Maureen. It was her first time teaching preschool children, first time co-teaching, first time teaching in an inclusive setting, and first time participating in coaching. She was taking it all in and was grateful for the professional development she was being offered.

After attending the first round of embedded instruction virtual workshops, she felt really good about what she and her co-teacher Maria had started implementing in the classroom. Their coach Elley had been helpful too—pointing out embedded instruction learning opportunities on the video they had uploaded for her to watch. This was the one part of her PBC experience that Maureen still struggled with—being recorded on video. There was something that still did not feel comfortable. She went along with it because it did not seem to bother Maria at all and she knew it was something that had to be done. How else would Elley know what was happening in the classroom?

After watching Maureen and Maria's video, Elley sat back in her chair and thought, "Why can't all teams look like this?" She was already beginning to see changes in their embedded instruction practices after the workshop. They worked well together and their strengths complemented each other. There was something Elley could not quite understand, however. Maureen seemed stiff and uncomfortable throughout the video. When she used the practices, she seemed a bit robotic. Elley had just started working with this team and had only had a handful of PBC sessions with them, so she was still learning their interaction styles—but something was amiss. Elley reflected on what could be causing this reaction. She wrote down some open-ended questions to bring up in the next coaching session to learn more about how Maureen was feeling.

At their session, after providing both supportive and constructive feedback on their use of embedded instruction learning opportunities, Elley took a deep breath and said, "Talk to me a bit about the process of recording video. Is anything surprising to you?" Maria quickly answered and said that the uploading process was a lot easier than she had expected and the kids really did not seem to notice what was going on after their initial interest in the camera. Maureen was quiet. Elley asked her if there was something she wanted to share, and Maureen shrugged. Elley did not want to assume she knew what Maureen was thinking or feeling, so she looked back on the notes she had prepared for the meeting. Elley said, "I'm not sure I ever told you about my experience being recorded on video for a class I was taking, have I?" She then described her experience with self-recording and how she could not stop thinking about what she looked like and the "mistakes" she had made. She offered to share a blog article that helped her reframe her experiences with recording video. One suggestion the article described was focusing on the child in the video and watching their reaction. Elley said that after she did that a few times, her whole approach and reaction to recording video changed. She suggested that Maureen and Maria watch their video again but focus on the child's reaction, because they were skilled educators and it showed. Elley focused on what Maureen was doing with the child rather than only what she was saying. It seemed like Maureen's body language relaxed a bit—she sat up a little straighter and a gentle smile appeared. Maria offered to talk about the resource at their next classroom team meeting—and she thought the whole team could benefit from it.

After they disconnected the video chat, Elley took a few minutes to reflect on the session and complete her coaching log. She noted that she should remember to use this resource and recommendation in future sessions and point out child reactions to teachers' practice implementation on the next video they uploaded. She knew she had not magically changed Maureen's comfort level, but her role as a PBC coach was not to fix issues. Instead, by guiding them to a resource Maureen and Maria could look at together, they had some ownership of their

---

Questions for Further Reflection and Discussion

- What collaborative partnership strategies did Elley use when approaching the topic of recording video with Maureen?

- What could Elley have done differently to address the topic of recording video?

- Why do you think the topic of recording video was important to address?

- What collaborative partnership strategies have you used when coaching multiple coachees at the same time?

- How is building a collaborative partnership different when there is more than one coachee?

- What might be challenging about coaching multiple coachees at the same time?

own professional development. As she hit "send" on an e-mail to Maria and Maureen with the blog link and a reminder for their next steps and meeting time, Elley felt confident that this team was going to make some amazing growth!

SUMMARY

PBC begins with establishing rapport and building collaborative partnerships over time. Strategies to establish rapport and build and enhance collaborative partnerships have been shared in this chapter along with illustrations about how these strategies were used in the case stories. As illustrated in the PBC model, collaborative partnerships wrap around the three components of PBC: 1) shared goals and action planning, 2) focused observation, and 3) reflection and feedback. Strategies used to build rapport and maintain and enhance collaborative partnerships, along with the coaching strategies described in Chapter 4, are essential coaching processes. These processes help support the successful implementation of strengths and needs assessments described in Chapter 5 and the PBC components (i.e., shared goals and action planning, focused observation, and reflection and feedback) described in Chapters 6, 7, and 8.

4

Coaching Strategies and Definitions

Darbianne Shannon, Crystal Bishop, Patricia Snyder, and Tara McLaughlin

COACHING STRATEGIES AND DEFINITIONS

Practice-Based Coaching (PBC) is a transactional process. It includes coachee and coach engagement in a collaborative partnership and cyclical processes of goal setting and action planning, informed by strengths and needs assessment; focused observation; and reflection and feedback. Coaching strategies are the actions or behaviors used by coaches throughout PBC cycles. These strategies are *how* coaches support coachees to engage in each component of the PBC cycle. Coaching strategies facilitate and enhance the collaborative partnership and guide implementation of the PBC components. Although various coaching strategies have been described in the literature, to date few studies have documented the types and dose of strategies used to optimize coaching implementation (Artman-Meeker et al., 2015; Johnson et al., 2018). In this chapter, we present the coaching strategies that have been defined and used in PBC research and practice (Snyder et al., 2015). When these coaching strategies are implemented with fidelity as part of PBC, evidence has shown

associated changes in coachees' practice implementation, their self-efficacy about practice implementation, and the value they place on their collaborative coaching partnership (Hemmeter et al., 2016; Shannon, Snyder et al., 2021; Snyder et al., 2018).

> **Key Point to Remember**
> Coaching strategies are the actions or behaviors used by coaches throughout PBC cycles.
>

PRACTICE-BASED COACHING STRATEGIES

Two categories of coaching strategies are used in PBC: 1) essential and 2) enhancement. Essential strategies are fundamental for implementing PBC with fidelity. Enhancement strategies are those the coachee and

> **Key Point to Remember**
> Two categories of coaching strategies are used in PBC: essential and enhancement.
>

coach agree will further support the coachee's fidelity of practice implementation and that the coachee prefers to be used.

Essential Coaching Strategies

A coaching session occurs each time the cyclical components of PBC are implemented. These components can be implemented on-site or virtually, and each component can occur synchronously or asynchronously (see Chapter 2). Regardless of the delivery format, five essential coach-

> **Tools for Coaches in the Appendices**
>
> *Appendix VI.R: Coaching Strategies Quick Reference Guide*
>
> This is a resource summarizing the essential and enhancement coaching strategies used in PBC.

ing strategies are used in every coaching session: 1) observation, 2) reflective conversation, 3) supportive feedback, 4) constructive feedback, and 5) identifying or providing resources or materials. Three essential coaching strategies are used periodically across coaching sessions: 1) goal setting, 2) graphic feedback, and 3) video feedback. Each of the essential coaching strategies (see the Box to the right) is defined and described in this chapter, including information about why the strategy is essential and how it might be used.

When all PBC components are delivered on-site, a coaching session involves a focused observation conducted by the coach in the coachee's practice context followed by a reflection and feedback meeting. When PBC is delivered virtually, focused observation might be conducted synchronously via live streaming from the coachee's practice context, or the coach might conduct a focused observation asynchronously by reviewing a video of practice implementation. The reflection and feedback that follow the focused observation might be facilitated virtually using video-conferencing technology, or the

> **Essential Coaching Strategies**
>
> *Used in every coaching session:*
> - Observation
> - Reflective conversation
> - Supportive feedback
> - Constructive feedback
> - Identifying or providing resources or materials
>
> *Used periodically in coaching sessions:*
> - Goal setting
> - Graphic feedback
> - Video feedback

coach and coachee might use a virtual coaching platform to engage in asynchronous reflection and feedback about practice implementation using video annotations. For a self-coaching session, the coachee would likely conduct a focused observation of their practice implementation, often by reviewing a video, and would engage in self-reflection and self-feedback about their practice implementation. In each of these formats, the essential strategies are implemented and are adjusted, as needed, based on the format.

Observation   Observation is watching, listening, and taking objective notes about the coachee's actions or behaviors related to practice implementation. Observation also might involve watching, listening, and taking objective notes about the practice setting or how children respond when a coachee implements a practice, when appropriate. The observed practice is aligned with the goal specified on the action plan that is guiding the current coaching cycle. The observation strategy is used during focused observation, which can occur on-site, virtually via live streaming, or asynchronously by video review. Observation notes often include information about how often, how well, or how long a practice is implemented. Observation is an essential strategy because information gathered as part of the observation is used to facilitate reflection and to provide performance-based supportive and constructive feedback (Kretlow & Bartholomew, 2010). Chapter 7 provides additional information about conducting a focused observation.

Reflective Conversation Reflective conversation is an interaction between the coachee and coach that prompts the coachee to consider their actions related to practice implementation and how practice implementation affects children or others. It involves the coachee's or coach's description of select coachee actions from the focused observation followed by questions that invite the coachee to reflect on those actions (e.g., "I noticed you implemented embedded instruction learning trials in large group today. How did implementing trials in large-group compare to small-group?"). When facilitating reflective conversation, use of open-ended questions (e.g., "How did you use the activity matrix today?") and clarifying questions (e.g., "Did you try a verbal or gestural prompt when you implemented the embedded learning opportunity with Jamal?") is recommended.

Reflective conversation is an essential coaching strategy because it supports the collaborative partnership by facilitating interactions between the coachee and coach. It can occur throughout the coaching cycle in shared goal setting and action planning, focused observation, or reflection and feedback. Reflective conversation provides ongoing strengths and needs assessment information about the coachee's confidence and competence about practice implementation (Frates et al., 2011). Providing opportunities for the coachee to reflect on the use of targeted practices can also help to ensure that implementation supports and challenges are identified and to support sustained practice implementation after coaching ends (Sanetti et al., 2015). When preparing for reflective conversations, coaches might find it helpful to note the open-ended questions they plan to ask. When using reflective conversation, it is important to plan for and provide opportunities for the coachee to process the reflective questions and to share their perspectives. When reflective conversation occurs during an on-site or virtual meeting, this might include providing ample wait time for the coachee to respond. When reflective questions are posed asynchronously using a virtual coaching platform, it is important to ensure that the coachee has an opportunity to view, reflect on, and respond to questions. Examples of reflection starters are shown in Table 4.1. Chapter 8 provides additional information about the reflection and feedback component of PBC.

Performance-Based Feedback Performance-based feedback is an evidence-based practice for supporting individuals to learn new behaviors, skills, or practices (Fallon et al., 2015). Within PBC, it involves specific feedback about a coachee's practice implementation. Practitioners have reported they find performance feedback, when provided as part of PBC, to be useful, acceptable, and appreciated (Shannon et al., 2015). The essential performance-based feedback strategies used in PBC are supportive feedback and constructive feedback. Graphic and video feedback can also be used as forms to enhance the use of performance feedback.

Key Point to Remember

Performance-based feedback is an evidence-based practice that supports individuals to learn new behaviors, skills, or practices.

Supportive Feedback Supportive feedback is the provision of positive descriptive information, verbal or written, about the coachee's actions related to practice implementation as specified in the goal and action plan. Supportive feedback might be provided about forms or materials used to implement a practice (e.g., use of the activity matrix in embedded instruction or use of visual schedule in Pyramid Model), practice implementation, or use of data related to practice implementation, child progress, or child outcomes. Supportive feedback should *always* describe what the coachee did that supported implementation of targeted practices or outcomes of practice implementation. A clear description of what was observed helps the coachee to know what it looks like or sounds like to use a practice as intended. In addition, connecting the coachee's use of practices to positive child development or learning can be reinforcing and encourage sustained use of the practice (Shannon et al., 2015). Supportive feedback is provided during every coaching cycle as part of reflection and feedback.

Table 4.1.   Example questions for facilitating reflective conversation by type of information gained

Reflection starter questions	Information gained
Objective questions	
What happened when _____?	• How the coachee recalls or interprets an observation of practice implementation • If the coachee is attending to implementation of practices, child(ren)'s or others' responses, or materials and settings
What have you tried with _____?	• Coachee's previous knowledge or experiences • Practices coachee has tried in the past
Interpretive questions	
How is it going with _____?	• Coachee's perspective about how practice implementation is going for the coachee, for a child(ren), or for others • Coachee's perspective about how materials or other environmental supports are helping with implementation • Information about barriers the coachee has experienced
Why do you think _____?	• Coachee's perspectives about relationships between the setting, materials, or practices used and an implementation outcome for the coachee, for children, or for others
What do you think would happen if _____?	• Coachee's perspectives about outcomes associated with practice implementation or use of materials
Comparative questions	
Knowing _____, what might you try next time?	• How coachee might modify their practice-focused actions or behaviors based on an experience in the implementation setting or feedback received from the coach
How did that compare to _____?	• Extent to which the coachee found their practice-focused actions or behaviors or materials used similar to or different from previous practice-focused actions or behaviors or materials used
Clarifying/Closed-Ended questions	
Is the _____ working for you?	• If the coachee is satisfied with an implementation setting, material, or practice, given strengths and needs they identified or goals and action steps they specified
Did you try _____ or _____?	• Clarifying the materials, practices, or actions the coachee tried in a given situation or implementation setting
Do you want to try _____?	• If the coachee would like to try to use a different approach to practice implementation or different materials
Do you want _____ or _____?	• Coachee's preference, given a choice

---

Tools for Coaches in the Appendices

Appendix V.M: Tips for Providing Supportive Feedback Within the Practice-Based Coaching Framework

This is a quick reference guide for providing supportive feedback.

It might also be provided briefly during a focused observation or during goal setting and action planning. Coaches should prepare for providing supportive feedback by identifying several strengths of the coachee's implementation of the practices, including how their actions supported children (see Table 4.2). Coaches should also build on reflective conversations by linking experiences shared by the coachee to practice implementation and child outcomes.

Constructive Feedback   Constructive feedback is the provision of data-informed or performance-based suggestions or supports for enhancing the fidelity of practice implementation as specified in the goal and action plan (Barton et al., 2011). This feedback can be provided verbally or in written format depending on the delivery format for coaching. Constructive feedback should support the coachee to implement the practice more often, more fluently, across contexts or children, or to maintain or adapt practice implementation. Like supportive feedback, constructive feedback might be provided about forms or materials used to implement a prac-

Table 4.2. Supportive feedback nonexamples and examples of observed practice implementation and importance for children for each case story

Case story	Non-examples	Examples of observed practice implementation and connecting to importance for children
Lynn	You did a great job with expansions!	**Observed:** When Herb reached for the truck and said "uck," you repeated and expanded by saying, "A big yellow truck!" **Importance for children:** Repeating what Herb said acknowledged his communication and adding descriptive words gave him a language model.
Maureen and Maria	I love the activity matrices!	**Observed:** I noticed you posted your activity matrix. You both referred to it at least two times and you embedded learning opportunities in the planned activities. **Importance for children:** Using your activity matrix as a visual cue to remind you to embed learning opportunities helps to ensure that children receive sufficient opportunities to practice their priority learning target skills.
Sam	You did a great job with expectations!	**Observed:** At the beginning of centers, you went to dramatic play and reminded Nora to ask her friend for a turn if she wanted a toy, and you pointed to the posted visual for taking turns. **Importance for children:** Reminding Nora to ask for a turn before she takes a toy from a peer helps her remember expectations for playing respectfully in dramatic play.

tice, practice implementation, or the use of data related to practice implementation, child progress, or child outcomes. Constructive feedback is *not* telling the coachee they did something wrong (e.g., that was not the right way to teach children expectations or that was an incor-

>
>
> **Key Point to Remember**
>
> Constructive feedback is the provision of data-informed or performance-based suggestions or supports for enhancing the fidelity of practice implementation.

rect embedded instruction learning trial). Rather, constructive feedback provides an objective description of observed practice implementation and actionable suggestions or supports for enhancing fidelity of practice implementation.

Many coaches report that they have difficulty providing constructive feedback, particularly when they do not understand what is and is not constructive feedback (Snyder et al., 2015). To assist coaches, we have specified four features that typically are included when constructive feedback is provided as intended. Each feature and an accompanying example are shown in Table 4.3. The features of constructive feedback support a coachee to reflect on and self-evaluate

Table 4.3. Four features of constructive feedback with examples

Feature	Why is this feature essential?	Example
Provide an objective description of what the coach observed related to the practice implementation goal specified in the action plan.	Helps the coachee to identify when, how, and with whom they are currently implementing the practice.	There were four times when children called out during the story and you said, "Remember, listening ears." This was a positive verbal reminder for one of your carpet-time rules.
Provide information about the practice and how it can benefit the coachee, children, others, or the practice context.	Supports the coachee to understand why the practice is important and to consider the fit between the suggestions for practice enhancement and their implementation setting.	Many children benefit from reminders they can see and hear. Posting the carpet rules with visuals would really support children like Lucas and Mikayla to remember what is expected and appropriate behavior.
Identify with the coachee one to three suggestions or strategies for enhancing the coachee's implementation of the practice.	Provides the coachee with options for how the practice could be implemented. Choice facilitates the collaborative partnership and increases the likelihood the coachee will use or continue to use the practice.	We could post the rules on the chart stand or below the white board. Once the rules are posted, you could use a song, your teacher's helper, or role play to review the rules when you begin whole-group.
Provide a reflective prompt so the coachee has an opportunity to decide what they will do differently, more often, or with enhanced fidelity in the future.	Provides an opportunity for the coachee and coach to confirm their shared understanding of the actions that will be taken by the coachee to enhance their use of the practice.	Do you think either of those ideas will work, or do you have other ideas that are a better fit for you or your classroom?

their practice implementation. Constructive feedback is an essential coaching strategy for each coaching cycle. Constructive feedback is always provided during the reflection and feedback component of PBC, and it can be provided during other parts of a coaching cycle if it is brief and requested by the coachee. In the absence of constructive feedback, the coachee is unlikely to know whether or not the practice is being implemented with fidelity and how to enhance their use of the practice when it does not work well, and this can lead to abandoning use of the practice (Kretlow & Bartholomew, 2010).

When providing constructive feedback, the coach should emphasize the constructive intent of the feedback (i.e., how it will benefit the coachee, children, or others with whom the coachee interacts) and, when possible, identify strengths the coachee already possesses that would support enhanced fidelity in the future. Coaches should limit constructive feedback to practices that are the focus of the current action plan or have been the focus of previous action plans. Providing constructive feedback about other actions or behaviors that are not or have not been part of an action plan might compromise the collaborative partnership. In addition, providing constructive feedback about topics that are not aligned with the targeted PBC practices may overwhelm or frustrate the coachee. Coaches should consider and note the constructive feedback they intend to provide, talk with other coaches about how they provide constructive feedback, and use tools that provide tips for engaging in constructive feedback.

Tools for Coaches in the Appendices

Appendix V.N: Tips for Providing Constructive Feedback Within the Practice-Based Coaching Framework

This is a quick reference guide for providing supportive feedback.

Identifying or Providing Resources or Materials   In every PBC cycle, the coach should help the coachee identify or provide resources or materials to support their knowledge about or use of a practice that is the focus of the current goal and action plan. Resources might include practitioner-friendly websites, practice briefs, or demonstration videos that help the coachee learn more about a practice. They might also include planning forms or materials to support practice implementation, including learning how to use existing materials in the practice setting in new ways.

Materials and resources should come from a trusted source and should be reviewed for alignment with the effective practices that are the focus of coaching. Matching materials and resources to the strengths and needs of the coachee and the children they support is important. Coaches should be knowledgeable about available resources and materials and, when possible, have an organized repository of vetted materials and resources. Knowing the focus of the current goal and action plan helps coachees and coaches to identify categories of materials or resources that might be helpful during the coaching cycle. Coaches often benefit from collaborating with other coaches to identify and build a library of relevant materials and resources that are available to support coachee knowledge and implementation of the practices that are the focus of PBC.

Goal Setting   Goal setting is a collaborative process between the coachee and coach that includes discussion about the coachee's practice-focused strengths and needs and the identification of a coaching priority for the current coaching cycle. In PBC, the goal is recorded on the action plan as an implementation goal and includes three parts: 1) an observable and measurable practice, 2) how much or how often the practice will be seen or heard, and 3) when or with whom the practice will be implemented. Writing the goal down provides shared vocabulary and transparency about what the coach will be supporting the coachee to do. Initial goal setting occurs at the beginning of the collaborative coaching partnership. After the initial goal is identified, the goal and action plan are reviewed at the end of every coaching cycle to consider progress and next steps. How long the same goal and action plan are used across successive coaching cycles varies depending on the strengths and needs of the coachee and the complexity of the practice. Typically, an action plan should be met and the goal completed in 2–4 weeks.

Goal setting is an essential coaching strategy, but it only occurs as part of a PBC cycle when a goal has been met, a new goal is needed, or the current goal needs to be revised. Goal and action plan review occurs in every coaching cycle. Chapters 5 and 6 provide additional information about the processes for conducting practice-focused strengths and needs assessments and developing goals and action plans.

Graphic Feedback Graphic feedback is a form of performance-based feedback and is used to supplement verbal or written supportive or constructive feedback. It is a visual display of coachee data or child data and includes verbal or written information that is used to provide performance feedback and to analyze and communicate about coachee's practice(s) implementation. To provide graphic feedback, coaches or coachees should (a) collect data about the coachee's implementation of the targeted practice or a child's behavior related to the practice, (b) summarize the data collected in a visual display, and (c) support the coachee to analyze and reflect on the data displayed.

Graphic feedback is an essential strategy because visual data displays help coaches and coachees to identify patterns or trends in practice implementation over time (e.g., Barton et al., 2020; Hojnoski, Gischlar, et al., 2009). Graphic displays of data help inform celebrations about progress and goal attainment as well as opportunities for future coaching priorities or goals and action plans. When graphic feedback is used, it facilitates the use of other essential coaching strategies, including reflective conversation, supportive feedback, and constructive feedback (Barton et al., 2011; Fallon et al., 2015). It can also facilitate use of problem-solving and other enhancement coaching strategies.

When reviewing graphs, build on the coachee's data literacy skills by providing an orientation to the graph with an explanation of key variables represented or the colors and symbols included. Pose comments or questions to guide the coachee in the process of analyzing and reflecting on the data and to link the graphic display with verbal or written supportive and constructive feedback. Ensure that the content of graphs is aligned with the goal and action plan, the complexity of graphs is aligned with the coachee's data literacy skills, and a balance of supportive and constructive feedback is provided. Coaches should never use graphs solely to provide constructive feedback.

> **Tips for Using Graphic Feedback**
> - Align the graph with the goal and action plan.
> - Provide an orientation to the graph.
> - Pose questions to analyze and reflect on the graph.
> - Balance supportive and constructive feedback.

Graphs can be developed by hand or by using computer-based software (e.g., Numbers, Excel), templates (e.g., https://brookespublishing.com/download-your-materials/tpot-scoring-spreadsheet/). Graphic feedback is required periodically but can be used more often if it is a preferred coaching strategy identified by the coachee. Those using PBC often use graphic feedback at least once per action plan or in specified weeks of coaching when a predetermined coaching calendar is being implemented (e.g., weeks 3, 6, 9, 12, and 15 of a 16-week coaching period). Providing graphic feedback is recommended at the end of coaching to summarize the coachee's overall practice implementation achievements and to identify goals for sustaining or enhancing practice.

Video Feedback Video feedback is a form of performance-based feedback and can be used to supplement the provision of verbal or written supportive or constructive feedback. It includes (a) collecting video of the coachee implementing the targeted practice, (b) reviewing brief video clips of practice implementation (e.g., 30 s to 2 min) with the coachee during reflection and feedback, and (c) supporting the coachee to analyze and reflect on practice implementation. Video clips can be collected by the coachee or the coach. The coach can provide verbal or written comments or questions to guide the coachee in the process of observing, analyzing, and reflecting on their actions and behaviors and those of children in response to their practice implementation. Video feedback is an essential strategy because it can take the coachee back to a specific experience in the implementation context (Trivette et al., 2009). In addition, video can be reviewed multiple times to receive feedback about different aspects of implementation, including fluency of practice implementation or how practice implementation supports child engagement and learning. Video feedback facilitates other essential coaching strategies including reflective conversation, supportive feedback, and constructive feedback (Nagro et al., 2017). It can also facilitate use of problem-solving and other enhancement coaching strategies.

Tips for using video feedback include the following: 1) Ensure that video clips are brief and aligned with the action plan goal, 2) provide both supportive and constructive feedback, and 3) connect video feedback to reflective conversations about practice implementation. Video should *never* be used to provide only constructive feedback. Before using video, confirm the video policy for the practice context to ensure compliance with requirements for approved video-recording devices, storage, and file-sharing policies. Video feedback is a periodic essential strategy when face-to-face coaching occurs, but it is used in every coaching session if coaching is occurring asynchronously using video, such as through a virtual coaching platform.

Tips for Using Video Feedback

- Ensure that video clips are brief and aligned with the goal and action plan.
- Provide both supportive and constructive feedback.
- Connect video feedback to reflective conversations about practice implementation.

Enhancement Coaching Strategies

Enhancement coaching strategies are used when they are judged by the coachee and coach as strategies that would further support fidelity of practice implementation (see the following Box). These strategies should be appropriate for the current goal and action plan and preferred by the coachee. There are two enhancement coaching strategies that can only be used during either on-site or live-streamed focused observations (i.e., side-by-side support cues; other help in practice setting). The remaining enhancement strategies can be used in various coaching delivery formats but may need to be adjusted based on the format. Before using enhancement strategies, check with the coachee to ensure that the coaching strategy is (a) acceptable and useful given the current practice context, (b) appropriate given the delivery format for PBC, and (c) judged by the coachee and coach to be a strategy that will support practice implementation.

Enhancement Coaching Strategies

- Side-by-side support cues
- Other help in practice setting
- Problem-solving
- Role play
- Video examples
- Modeling
- Environmental arrangements
- Graphing

Side-By-Side Support Cues   Side-by-side support is provided during focused observation when it occurs on-site or via live streaming and is used to guide the coachee's implementation of practices in the moment. When providing support cues, the coach either stands or sits in proximity to the coachee and provides verbal, gestural, or visual cues or uses wireless technology to cue (e.g., bug-in-ear) while the coachee is implementing a practice. The coach might use verbal support to engage in a brief exchange with a coachee (e.g., "Do you think a choice would work?") or to prompt (e.g., "Try hand over hand"). Gestural or visual supports (e.g., pointing or directing attention to an activity matrix to remind the coachee of the child's learning target) often require the coach and coachee to agree to use conventional gestures (e.g., thumbs up) and symbols or to plan ahead for which cues will be used and for what purpose. Side-by-side support provides just-in-time assistance to the coachee. It can also build the coachee's awareness of opportunities to use the practice or confidence that the practice is being implemented as intended. Coaches should plan to fade cues over time to ensure that the coachee can independently implement and sustain the practice.

Other Help in Practice Setting   Other help in the practice setting is a strategy for providing support to the coachee during focused observation that is not directly related to the goal or action plan (e.g., wiping up spilled paint, sitting beside a child at circle who benefits from adult proximity). Other help should be used to facilitate the collaborative partnership or to reduce distractions that might prevent the coachee from implementing practices that are the focus of coaching. The coach can participate in the activities and routines of the classroom if the coachee has expressed that this is a preferred coaching strategy. Nevertheless, providing other help should not prevent the coach from observing, collecting data on the coachee's implementation of practices, or providing implementation support through other requested and appropriate enhancement strategies.

> **Key Point to Remember**
> Providing other help in the practice setting can facilitate the collaborative partnership and practice implementation. Nevertheless, it should not prevent the coach from observing and collecting data on the coachee's implementation of practices.

Problem Solving   Problem solving is an intentional interaction between the coachee and coach about solving a practice implementation issue. It is designed to support the coachee through a systematic process involving four steps: 1) identify the practice implementation issue, 2) generate options or potential solutions, 3) decide on a course of action, and 4) evaluate potential pros or cons of the selected course of action (Snyder & McWilliam, 2003). Problem solving is an enhancement strategy often initiated by the coachee to access support for an identified issue or need in the practice setting (Shannon et al., 2021). Problem solving of a personal nature or related to larger programwide or personal concerns typically are not a focus in PBC unless these issues are preventing the coachee from participating in the coaching process. Problem solving is sometimes confused with constructive feedback. Although they both address implementation, they differ in important ways. Table 4.4 shows the similarities and differences between them.

Table 4.4. Similarities and differences between constructive feedback and problem solving

Similarities	Differences	
Both	Constructive feedback	Problem solving
Coaching strategies used within practice-based coaching	Essential strategy that must occur in every session	Enhancement strategy used when preferred or appropriate for supporting the coachee
Support practice implementation	Guided by the focused observation and is designed to enhance the coachee's use of a practice (e.g., use practices more often, more fluently, across contexts or children, or to maintain or adapt practice implementation)	Guided by a practice implementation issue or challenge that is identified by the coachee or the coach
	Does not require the identification of an implementation issue or challenge	Issue or challenge is preventing the coachee from engaging in coaching or implementing the practice
Support coachee to generate strategies or options	Coach ensures that the coachee has one to three strategies for how to enhance their implementation	Both the coachee and coach generate options or potential solutions to address an implementation issue or challenge
	Strategies might be identified by the coachee	Explicit evaluation of the pros and cons of the options or potential solutions
	Coachee states the strategy they intend to try out	Coachee states the option or potential solution they intend to try out

Role Play   Role play is a simulated situation designed to help the coachee learn to implement a practice. The coachee might take on the role of child(ren) while the coach demonstrates a practice, or the coach might take on the role of child(ren) while the coachee demonstrates a practice. Role play gives the coachee or coach an opportunity to demonstrate practices and is most effective when paired with real-life applications (Trivette et al., 2009). Role play can be formally or informally implemented. Formally, the coachee might want to use role play to develop or practice a systematic written plan for implementing a practice. During a formal role play, the coachee typically has a plan for what they are going to say or do, or the steps to take. Role play can also be used informally as the coachee and coach engage in constructive feedback or problem-solving discussion (e.g., "If I were Isabell and I was running between centers in the classroom, what could you say to me?"). Role play might also be used when modeling (e.g., "If you were Kyree writing, I might use a physical prompt by cupping my hand behind yours like this. Show me how you think Kyree might respond to that type of support").

Video Examples   Video examples are used to demonstrate how another practitioner or caregiver in a similar setting implements a practice or practices that are the focus of coaching. Video examples should be brief (e.g., from 30 s to 2 min) and should be well aligned to the goal and action plan. Prepare the coachee for engaging with the video by stating what the coachee should focus on when watching the video and why the video was selected. For example, the coach might share a video that demonstrates how to expand children's language by saying, "This video has some great examples of ways to expand children's verbal and nonverbal communication. As we watch, let's write down some of the examples we see." Alternatively, the coach might also provide a longer video example (e.g., 5–10 min) as a resource for the coachee to watch between sessions to learn more about a particular practice. Video examples are similar to video feedback but differ in one important way. Video examples are prerecorded and include another practitioner or caregiver in a similar practice context, whereas video feedback is specific to the coachee's implementation of a practice.

> The coach should prepare the coachee for engaging with video examples by stating what to focus on when watching the video and why the video was selected.

Modeling   Modeling is demonstrating or showing the coachee how to implement a practice that is the focus of a goal or action plan. Modeling can occur synchronously during focused observation or reflection and feedback. It can also occur asynchronously using a video model of practice implementation. As part of focused observation, the coach would implement a practice while the coachee watches. Immediately following the model, the coach would give the coachee an opportunity to implement the modeled practice. As part of reflection and feedback, the coach might demonstrate how to implement a practice while the coachee watches. For example, in an on-site meeting, the coach and coachee might walk to the circle time area where the coach models what the coachee might say or do in the future. Sitting in the coachee's circle time spot the coach says, "Here are ways you might give Yerelyn a positive reminder about circle time rules using your visual cues: acknowledge other children's positive behavior and give descriptive praise to Yerelyn." The coach models how to point to the behavior expectations and says, "Feet on floor, Yerelyn. Luke has his feet on floor! Yerelyn, now you have your feet on the floor!" in a positive tone.

Modeling and video examples are useful enhancement strategies because they illustrate how a practice could be implemented in the coachee's context. Coaches should use modeling and video examples when the coachee and they identify the coachee is motivated and ready to use the practice. Coachees might be less motivated to implement a practice if they are unable to implement the practice as demonstrated by the coach or video example or if children respond differently when the coach implements the practice compared to when the coachee implements the practice. Models are most useful when they demonstrate a practice the coachee can successfully implement with minimal support following the coach or video model.

Environmental Arrangements Environmental arrangements are when the coach helps the coachee to modify or enhance the physical, temporal, or social aspects of the practice setting or materials in the setting that set the occasion for the coachee to implement a practice. Environmental arrangements can occur during focused observation or over a more extended time period if it is a preferred coaching strategy or appropriate for specific practices. For example, during a focused observation the coach might quickly add materials to a center to help set the occasion for the coachee to join in children's play and engage in supportive conversations. Alternatively, the coachee and the coach might work together to identify the preferred place to post a visual schedule in the classroom. Coaches should follow the coachee's lead when using environmental arrangements to ensure suggested arrangements are feasible and acceptable and will support practice implementation from the coachee's perspective.

Graphing Graphing is an enhancement strategy when the coach and coachee work together to graph data that have been collected for coachee practice implementation or for child behaviors. Coachees often benefit from support to learn how to graph data and enhance their data literacy skills (Fox et al., 2014; Hojnoski, Caskie, et al., 2009). Graphing differs from graphic feedback because data that are graphed are not directly connected to the provision of feedback.

INTRODUCING COACHING STRATEGIES TO COACHEES

Early in the coaching partnership, coaches should review the Preferred Coaching Strategies Checklist (see Appendix VI.S) with the coachee. This can be done during an on-site or virtual meeting or through asynchronous correspondence. This checklist provides transparency about the coaching process by defining and describing which strategies are essential for PBC and will be used in each PBC cycle. It also includes a menu of the enhancement strategies with a brief description and a check box for whether the strategy is preferred by the coachee for use. The menu of enhancement strategies is used to facilitate discussion about how the coachee would like to be further supported by the coach (Shannon et al., 2019). Over time, as the coach and coachee develop their collaborative partnership and address different practices across coaching cycles, the coachee's strategy preferences might change. Structured opportunities to update or reference the coachee's preferred strategies might occur each time a new goal and action plan is developed or as part of reflection and feedback, which includes planning for the next coaching cycle.

> **Tools for Coaches in the Appendices**
>
> *Appendix VI.S: Preferred Coaching Strategies Checklist*
>
> This is a resource that defines and describes essential coaching strategies and is used to gather information about a coachee's preferred enhancement strategies.

FIDELITY OF IMPLEMENTATION OF COACHING STRATEGIES

As described in Chapter 1, fidelity of implementation is doing an action or behavior as intended or as it should be done. Across studies where PBC has been used, coaches' adherence to and the quality with which they implemented the essential PBC strategies resulted in coachees' practice fidelity, and, in turn, positive developmental and learning outcomes for children (Snyder et al., 2015). To implement PBC strategies with fidelity, coaches need advanced knowledge about PBC processes, including the coaching strategies, and how to apply those strategies in relation to the practices that are the focus of coaching (National Research Council, 2015; Shannon, Snyder, et al., 2021).

Coaches need ongoing support and performance-based feedback about their implementation of PBC, including their use of the essential and enhancement coaching strategies. Initial PBC coach training should define and describe PBC processes and the essential coaching strategies. Multiple written and video examples, reflection, discussion, and role play with feedback supports coaches to acquire foundational confidence and competence to implement PBC, including the coaching strategies (Durlak & DuPre, 2008, Trivette et al., 2009).

Coaches also benefit from the provision of job aides, including a coach manual, coaching log, and quick reference guides. A coach manual should (a) summarize the key components of PBC; (b) define the coaching strategies with examples appropriate for the coach's practice context, delivery format, and practice focus; and (c) contain guidelines for implementation of PBC (e.g., reflection and feedback protocols or logs, lists of practices to be implemented, dose of coaching, timelines for coaching, decision criteria for providing coaching). A coaching log can be used to record the number of the coaching session, duration of the coaching session, delivery format, who participated, the implementation settings observed, and any unexpected or unusual events that occurred). The coaching log also specifies a logical sequence and place to record coach actions or behaviors, including the use of coaching strategies. A coaching log can serve as a visual prompt to remind the coach to implement and record their use of the essential and enhancement coaching strategies during the coaching session (Durlak & DuPre, 2008).

Tools for Coaches in Appendices

Appendix VI.T: Practice-Based Coaching Log

This is used to guide and document information about fidelity of PBC implementation, including coaching strategies.

Coach fidelity of implementation of PBC, including the coaching strategies, should be measured in each session by the coach's self-reported implementation on the coaching log. In select coaching sessions, audio or video observation or a record of coach and coachee communication within a virtual coaching platform should be collected and rated by a trained observer or lead coach within a program for fidelity-of-implementation checks. This information can be used to provide the coach with performance-based feedback about coaching dose (i.e., planned versus implemented coaching sessions; frequency, intensity, and duration of sessions), delivery formats for coaching sessions and coaching components (e.g., virtual observation from video, asynchronous reflection and feedback), adherence (i.e., Did the PBC process and coaching strategies occur as intended, yes or no?), and quality (e.g., How well did the coach use the strategies to facilitate the collaborative partnership and the PBC components?). Coaches need performance-based feedback about their fidelity, as well as ongoing supports to maintain and enhance their implementation of PBC, including coaching strategies (Fallon et al., 2015; Snyder et al., 2015). Individual or small-group meetings with experienced PBC coaches or participation in a coaching network can provide coaches with ongoing professional development and support. Coach networks or professional learning communities support coaches' ongoing fidelity of implementation of PBC, including coaching strategies. These networks can provide access to (a) peer exemplars and resources drawn from the real-world use of the coaching strategies within the network and (b) expert exemplars and resources from trusted external sources provided by coach network facilitators. Chapter 9 describes further how fidelity-of-implementation feedback, job aids, and coach networks can be used to support coaches to implement PBC processes and coaching strategies with fidelity.

REVISITING THE CASE STORIES

In the sections that follow, we return to the case stories introduced in Chapter 2 and illustrate how Sirena, Elley, and Kenya are implementing essential and enhancement coaching strategies as part of the PBC cycle. As you read each case story, consider if and how the essential coaching strategies are used in the case story. Determine which enhancement coaching strategies are used and if there are other enhancement strategies you might consider using. At the end of each case story, guiding questions are provided. Use these questions to guide further reflection about how you can implement essential and enhancement coaching strategies with coachees using different delivery formats. Discuss your ideas with other coaches.

Lynn and Coach Sirena

As Sirena prepared for her coaching session with Lynn, she reviewed the Preferred Coaching Strategies Checklist and the action plan they completed together. Sirena printed a practice brief about expanding children's language to share with Lynn given that she indicated she prefers to have resources she can read and share with her team or families. When Sirena reviewed the current action plan, she remembered that they planned for her to record video of Lynn's interactions with children during free choice and mealtimes. They planned to use the video to reflect on Lynn's current practice implementation and to facilitate a role play around strategies for using expansions when they met after the focused observation. Sirena made sure to take her video camera and computer so they would be able to watch the video together.

When Sirena arrived for the focused observation, she greeted Lynn. Before beginning her observation, she said, "We had originally planned to take some short videos during free choice and lunch so we could watch them together when we meet later. Do you still want to do that? We can easily adjust our action plan if today isn't a good day and I can just take notes while I observe." Lynn said she had been preparing for Sirena to video and thought watching her videos would be really helpful, even if she was a little reluctant to see herself on film. Sirena said, "Great! First, I'll get settled and take some notes, and then I will try and get about 10 minutes of you interacting with different children during free choice and lunch. We won't watch everything together, but that will help make sure we have plenty of video to choose from when it's time to meet."

Sirena found a place in the classroom where she could observe Lynn's interactions without disrupting the classroom activities. As she observed, she collected data about the number of times Lynn repeated what children said or expanded their language by describing children's experiences or adding new words to what they said. She also wrote notes about specific phrases Lynn said. Then she collected video of Lynn interacting with different children during free choice and lunch. When the focused observation was over, she arranged to use the teacher resource room at Helping Hands to review her video and her notes so she could prepare for meeting with Lynn at nap time.

Sirena started the meeting with reflective conversation about Lynn's progress toward her goal. Then, she said, "When we wrote our action plan, the first step was to watch a video online and to practice writing expansions. Have you had a chance to do that?" Lynn replied that she had watched the video and had started trying out expansions by adding descriptive words to what children said.

Sirena asked, "What have you noticed about how children respond when you add descriptive words?" Lynn said, "I haven't really noticed much change yet, but I think over time it will help them use additional or new words to talk about what they do or what happens in the classroom." Sirena mentioned that it can be difficult to notice everything in a classroom, and that some practices would take more time to implement and to lead to child gains. She reminded Lynn that her idea to watch video of herself interacting with the children was a really good way to identify when and how she was expanding children's communication, and how her use of expansions helps to build children's language. As they watched a short video clip, Lynn noted that when she added

Questions for Further Reflection and Discussion

- How did Sirena use the Preferred Coaching Strategies Checklist and action plan to prepare for implementing essential and enhancement coaching strategies?

- What essential and enhancement coaching strategies did Sirena implement during focused observation?

- What essential and enhancement coaching strategies did Sirena implement during reflection and feedback?

- How did Sirena's use of the essential and enhancement coaching strategies facilitate continued development of the collaborative partnership?

- How did Sirena's use of essential and enhancement coaching strategies support Lynn's implementation of practices that were the focus of her action plan?

- What other enhancement strategies might you have considered using? Why?

new words to what Aiden said in the art area during free choice, Aiden repeated the new words Lynn added. Sirena provided supportive feedback that confirmed Lynn's observation, "That's right. I wanted to show you this example because when Aiden said, 'I draw,' you responded to what he said and added information about what he was drawing by saying, 'You're drawing a pink cloud.' This is a really nice example of how your expansion helped him build language, because he repeated, 'Pink cloud'!" As they watched the video further, both Lynn and Sirena noted that Lynn repeated children's phrases more often than she expanded on them. Sirena gave constructive feedback by first describing the number of times Lynn repeated what children said and by explaining that this practice was a great starting point for expansions. They then discussed a few ways Lynn might enhance her use of expansions and decided to review more video clips and to write down some words Lynn might use in each activity. They also used the video to brainstorm and role play some of the ways Lynn might have expanded children's language during free choice and lunch. Lynn asked if she could keep one of the video clips and practice writing some more expansions on her own. Sirena shared two video clips with Lynn and gave her the practice brief she printed as a resource to provide additional ideas for expansions.

Maureen, Maria, and Coach Elley

Maureen and Maria sent an e-mail to Elley 3 days before their scheduled meeting to let her know that they had uploaded their focused observation video to the virtual coaching platform. Maureen uploaded 15 min of video from snack and free choice. Maria uploaded 15 min of video from free choice and small groups. In the e-mail they wrote, "Embedding learning opportunities is becoming more natural for us, and we are already noticing child progress! We might even need to write a new priority learning target for Aaron. One thing we are still struggling with is embedding learning opportunities across different activities. When we meet on Friday, can we revisit the idea of learning target-activity fit we discussed during the workshops and discuss some strategies for spreading the opportunities throughout the day?" Elley responded to their message thanking them for uploading their video and for sharing what they would like specific feedback about. She said they could brainstorm strategies together during their meeting, and she also shared a link to a page on the embedded instruction website that included considerations for planning when to embed learning opportunities and more information about fit. She knew an upcoming action step on their action plan was to make an activity matrix and suggested this might help them think about how they could distribute embedded learning opportunities throughout the day.

As Elley watched each video, she collected data about the number of embedded learning opportunities she observed in each activity for three children's priority learning targets. After reviewing her notes and the data she collected, Elley decided to make a graph showing the number of activities where learning opportunities were embedded for each priority learning target. Elley used the virtual coaching platform to annotate the videos and provide written supportive feedback about Maureen's and Maria's implementation of embedded learning opportunities. In her observation notes, she wrote down constructive feedback she could give that would support Maureen and Maria to provide embedded learning opportunities throughout the day in activities that would be natural or logical fits for the priority learning targets.

Elley, Maureen, and Maria met by video conference during Maureen and Maria's planning time. Elley began by reviewing the action plan goal and action steps with Maureen and Maria. She said, "You mentioned in your e-mail that embedding learning opportunities is becoming more natural for you. What do you think has changed?" Maureen and Maria said they had been using their planning time to review together sections of the practice guide they had received at the workshop and that when they developed lesson plans, they discussed how they could embed learning opportunities. After hearing their reflections, Elley provided supportive feedback about their collaborative approach to embedded instruction. She used a screen-sharing feature to share the graph she made. First, she explained the parts of the graph and then she emphasized the total number of embedded learning opportunities they provided to each child in each activity from the focused observation. She said, "When you both embed learning opportunities in different activities, you provide more opportunities for children to practice new skills, which helps the children learn and generalize skills."

As they looked at the graph together, Maureen said, "I know you only saw a snapshot and I agree we are embedding more learning opportunities, but I still think we could use some help spreading learning opportunities throughout the day and thinking about fit." Elley asked if there were times of day that were more difficult to embed learning opportunities and why. After some more discussion, Maureen and Maria identified that embedding instruction during planned activities was easier than in routines like meal and snack or in transitions. Elley said, "I noticed that before free choice and small groups you took a minute to remind each other about the children's priority learning targets, and you mentioned that you have started discussing how to embed learning opportunities when you do your lesson planning. Remember, at the workshops we discussed that a classroom activity matrix is a really helpful tool for looking at your daily activities, routines, and transitions and planning when and how many learning opportunities are natural or logical to embed for multiple children. It also serves as a visual reminder that you can refer to throughout the day. You could make an activity matrix that shows your daily schedule and post it in a prominent place in the classroom, or you could make multiple matrices for different areas of the classroom. I have some examples we can look at together." Elley shared her computer screen again and showed pictures of different types of activity matrices. As they looked at the pictures, Maureen and Maria discussed which type of matrix would help them plan for and remember to embed learning opportunities throughout the day. When they decided on a matrix, Elley asked, "Once you have made your matrix, how will you use it to remind yourself when to embed learning opportunities?" As Maureen and Maria reflected, Elley wrote their ideas on the action plan. She showed them the updated action plan and asked them if they had any additional updates they would like to make.

> **Questions for Further Reflection and Discussion**
> - What essential or enhancement coaching strategies did Elley implement during focused observation?
> - What essential and enhancement coaching strategies did Elley implement during reflection and feedback?
> - How was Elley's implementation of essential and enhancement strategies adapted for use in a virtual coaching format?
> - What other enhancement strategies might you have considered using? How might you need to adapt these for use in a virtual delivery format?

Sam and Coach Kenya

"Wow! I can't believe we're on our fifth action plan!" beamed Sam. Kenya said, "Now that we're about halfway through the year, I just want to be sure I'm providing the supports you find most helpful." Kenya gestured to the Preferred Coaching Strategies Checklist document on the table. "When we filled this out in September, you indicated that all of the enhancement strategies would be helpful but said you would prefer they be used during reflection and feedback rather than during the focused observation. In October, we added 'Other Help in Setting.'" Sam looked over the form and said, "I really think with my class that they'll get distracted if you model during the focused observation." Kenya said, "Okay, no problem. This is just an opportunity to check in and see if there are any new strategies you think would be helpful." Sam reread the form and said, "Do you think there is something I should try?" Kenya said, "It's really about your preferences and what you think will be most helpful. With your current action plan, the only one I can think of that might be helpful is side-by-side support cues. An example of how I might use gestural support is when I am observing if you're collecting data as planned. If you forget to move your rubber band to help you keep a count, I could just tap my wrist to cue you. A way I might use side-by-side verbal support could be to draw your attention to a child or group of children that might benefit from a positive reminder about the posted rules." Sam nodded and said, "I'm so busy in the classroom. I may not even see you gesture, but the verbal cue could be helpful. Let's given them both a try and see how it goes!" Kenya smiled reassuringly and said, "If you change your mind at any point, just let me know. We don't need to use those enhancement strategies unless they're going to support you!"

During the next focused observation, as children were transitioning from small groups to circle, Kenya said to Sam, "Toward the end of small groups, I noticed Maddy was starting to poke Sanji in the side. He told her to stop and she did, but you may want to give a quick reminder about keeping hands in lap during circle." When Maddy got to circle, Sam said, "Hey Maddy, thanks for coming to the carpet! Remember to sit down on your spot with your hands in your lap so we can stay safe." When she sat with her hands in her lap, Sam gave her a smile and pat on the back and said, "That is exactly how we sit at circle. Thanks for showing your friends how they can sit too!" As he moved a blue rubber band from one wrist to the other, Kenya gave him a thumbs up. He nodded and smiled, and then he sat down and began reviewing the circle-time rules.

When they met following the focused observation, Kenya said, "We tried out some new coaching strategies today! I know you weren't sure how it would go, so I wanted to check in to see how helpful you thought using side-by-side support was today." Sam said he really appreciated the verbal cue to give Maddy a reminder when she got to the carpet for circle. "As soon as you said it, I realized that would help to prevent her from touching the other children. I might have missed it if you hadn't given the cue, but it made such a difference. I think she really liked being the model for her classmates, too. I was worried it might be distracting, but it wasn't at all!" Kenya said, "I'm glad you found it helpful. We also tried out a gestural cue today. I didn't really have to remind you to move your rubber bands because you did it every time! Because you didn't need the reminder, I just tried a thumbs up. How was that?" Sam replied, "The thumbs up was a real confidence boost for me. I'm still not sure I'll notice the gestures every time, but I would like to continue using both types of side-by-side support when you observe in the classroom. I didn't realize something so simple could be so helpful."

Questions for Further Reflection and Discussion

- How did Kenya use the Preferred Coaching Strategies Checklist to introduce additional enhancement strategies?

- How did Kenya's use of the Preferred Coaching Strategies Checklist facilitate her ongoing collaborative partnership with Sam?

- How did Kenya's use of side-by-side verbal and gestural cues support Sam's confidence and competence to implement practices that were the focus of his goal and action plan?

- In what other ways might you propose the use of enhancement strategies to coachees as the collaborative partnership evolves over successive coaching sessions?

SUMMARY

Coaches should always use the essential coaching strategies to ensure that they are implementing PBC with fidelity (as intended) and should select enhancement strategies when they are preferred by the coachee or appropriate for enhancing the knowledge and skills of the coachee. Coachees and coaches often identify several things coachees are doing well in addition to opportunities for growth. To avoid overwhelming the coachee and to make the most of each coaching session, coachees and coaches should agree on focused and cohesive strategies that align with the implementation goal and action plan for each coaching cycle. The essential and selected enhancement strategies should be implemented to support the coachee to use effective practices with fidelity.

5

Effective Practices and Strengths and Needs Assessments

Darbianne Shannon, Tara McLaughlin, and Patricia Snyder

EFFECTIVE PRACTICES AND STRENGTHS AND NEEDS ASSESSMENTS

Strengths and needs assessments are used within Practice-Based Coaching (PBC) to help clarify and verify practice-focused strengths and needs from coachees' and coaches' perspectives. Strengths and needs assessments are important for several reasons. First, they offer the coachee and coach a sense of ownership in coaching and coaching processes. Coachees and coaches are more likely to commit to and build a collaborative partnership when the practice-focused goals identified through strengths and needs assessments are realistic, important, and motivating (Snyder & Wolfe, 2008). Second, by engaging in strengths and needs assessments, coaches support coachees to develop shared understandings about the meanings of terms relevant to the specific practices that are the content focus of PBC (Gallegos, 1979). Shared understandings of practice-relevant terms (e.g., embedded instruction, behavior expectations, visual schedules) help coachees and coaches engage in clarifying and verifying strengths and needs. Third, initial strengths and needs assessments provide baseline information that can be used as part of subsequent assessments to show how strengths and needs shift over time as fidelity of practice implementation changes. Finally, strengths and needs assessments provide a shared and transparent focus for PBC as they specify explicitly the effective practices that are the focus of coaching (Snyder et al., 2015).

> **Key Point to Remember**
>
> Strengths and needs assessments are used in PBC to help clarify and verify practice-focused strengths and needs from coachees' and coaches' perspectives. They help inform shared goal setting and action planning.

An assessment of strengths helps the coachee and coach identify perspectives about implementation strengths relative to a defined set of practices. Assessments of needs help identify the gap between what is and what should be in terms of fidelity of practice implementation (Snyder & Wolfe, 2008). In PBC, assessment of both strengths and needs is important, given the goal of coaching is to build on existing strengths and address identified needs. Clarifying and verifying both strengths and needs helps individualize goal setting and action planning by prioritizing goals that build on a coachee's strengths and address their identified needs.

> Clarifying and verifying both strengths and needs helps individualize goal setting and action planning by prioritizing goals that build on a coachee's strengths and address their identified needs.

Strengths and needs assessment information can be obtained in various ways: using instruments, analyzing documents, observing practice implementation, conducting interviews, or using consensus techniques such as a priority matrix or Delphi technique (Snyder & Wolfe, 2008). Assessments can be formal (e.g., use of an instrument) or informal (e.g., on-the-spot discussions during a coaching session). In PBC, both formal and informal methods are used to gather strengths and needs assessment information. Formal strengths and needs assessment instruments are used initially and periodically in successive coaching cycles as part of shared goal setting and action planning. Informal, on-the-spot discussions about strengths and needs occur during every coaching session, even when a formal assessment is not completed. One advantage of formal instruments is that the set of observable and measurable practices that are the content focus of PBC are the items on the instrument. The use of informal assessments helps further clarify and verify individualized strengths and needs while retaining an emphasis on the practices that appear on the instrument. Coaches have an important role in supporting both formal and informal assessments and in supporting the clarification and verification of coachees' strengths and needs.

This chapter is organized around three steps for developing and using formal practice-focused strengths and needs assessments within PBC. The steps are 1) specify the practices to be the content focus of coaching so they are observable and measurable, 2) design or select the strengths and needs assessment instrument, and 3) use strengths and needs assessment information as part of PBC implementation.

Key Point to Remember

In PBC, both formal and informal methods are used to gather strengths and needs assessment information. Strengths and needs assessment instruments are often used initially and periodically in successive coaching cycles as part of shared goal setting and action planning. Informal on-the-spot discussions about strengths and needs occur during every coaching cycle, even when an instrument is not completed.

Steps for Developing and Using Formal Practice-Focused Strengths and Needs Assessments

1. Specify the practices to be the content focus of coaching so they are observable and measurable.

2. Design or select the strengths and needs assessment instrument.

3. Use strengths and needs assessment information as part of PBC implementation.

PRACTICE SPECIFICATION

PBC has an explicit focus on supporting coachees to implement effective practices with fidelity to promote development and learning outcomes for infants, toddlers, and young children (Snyder et al., 2015). As described in previous chapters, practices are statements of observable and measurable actions or behaviors of the coachee. Observable means the practices can be seen or heard in the practice context. Measurable means the practices are written in a way that two people could agree the practice is being implemented. Explicit statements of practices give the coach and coachee a shared understanding and vocabulary. *Effective practices*

Tools for Coaches in the Appendices

Appendix VII.AC: Effective Practices in the Practice-Based Coaching Framework

This is a resource highlighting key characteristics of effective practices used in the context of PBC.

are defined as those informed by the best-available research evidence, collective wisdom, and values of the field to support child development and learning (Snyder, 2006; Snyder & Ayankoya, 2015). Shared knowledge of the practices that are the focus of PBC facilitates job-embedded collaboration between the coachee and coach around the identification of coaching priorities, goal setting and action planning, fidelity of practice implementation, reflection, and performance feedback (Crow & Snyder, 1998).

Competencies Versus Practices

When selecting practices, it is important to distinguish between competencies and practices. Competencies are defined as statements of what individuals need to know, are able to do, or dispositions they should possess. Competencies or standards are often developed by national organizations (e.g., Professional Standards and Competencies for Early Childhood Educators developed by the National Association for the Education of Young Children [NAEYC], 2020; Council for Exceptional Children, Division for Early Childhood [CEC-DEC], 2017) or states (e.g., California Early Childhood Educator Competencies developed by California Department of Education [CDE] and First 5 California, 2011) and often inform program or practitioner-level accreditation, licensing, or certification. In contrast, in PBC, we define *practices* as statements of observable and measurable actions or behaviors that are indicators of competence. Competencies typically align to several explicit observable and measurable practices, as shown in Table 5.1. PBC builds coachees' practice implementation and self-efficacy about a defined set of practices. When coachees' perspectives about practice confidence and competence align with observed implementation, competence is demonstrated.

> **Key Point to Remember**
>
> Competencies are statements of what individuals need to know or are able to do, or dispositions they should possess. Practices are statements of observable and measurable actions or behaviors and can be indicators of competence.

PBC has been identified as a content-ready coaching framework. This means it can be used with various early childhood professional competencies or curricular or content domains. Practice content must be stated, however, in ways that the practice can be directly observed and measured. Practices are often organized in sets under curricular or content area domains, pedagogical or interaction competencies, or logical categories (e.g., environmental arrangement practices, interactional practices, instructional practices, literacy practices, science and math practices, language practices, technology practices, family capacity building practices, social-emotional

Table 5.1.　Examples of aligning competencies and effective practices

Domain	Competency	Example practices
Family–teacher partnerships and community connections	2a: Know about, understand, and value the diversity of families (NAEYC, 2020, p. 9).	• Coachee differentiates communication strategies to meet the needs of each family • Coachee creates frequent opportunities for families to participate in classroom activities
Child observation, documentation and assessment	3a: Understand that assessments (formal and informal, formative and summative) are conducted to make informed choices about instruction and for planning in early learning settings (NAEYC, 2020, p. 9).	• Coachee collects observation data about children's behaviors or skills during daily activities and routines • Coachee summarizes data to inform assessment ratings and children's instructional goals
Developmentally, culturally, and linguistically appropriate teaching practices	4a. Understand and demonstrate positive, caring, supportive relationships and interactions as the foundation of early childhood educators' work with young children (NAEYC, 2020, p. 10).	• Coachee verbally responds to children's communication • Teacher asks children open-ended questions about classroom activities or materials • Coachee labels emotions for self and others

Note: Domains and competencies listed were drawn from NAEYC (2020).

practices, embedded instruction practices, positive behavior support practices, assessment practices). Programs and
coaches will often address several sets of practices over
time and might "bin" or "tier" practices to address them in
a logical or hierarchical sequence. For example, a decision
might be made to focus on foundational practices that enhance environmental quality and later
shift focus to differentiated instructional practices.

> PBC is a content-ready coaching framework that accommodates various effective practices.

Other Sources to Help Inform Practice Specification

Beyond using competencies to inform the specification of practices used in PBC, practitioner
and child data can be used. These data can be used to help inform decisions about practice
specification. Moving from desired distal outcomes (i.e., child development and learning) to
the identification of effective practices that support these outcomes as a focus for professional development, including PBC, is known as *backward mapping* (Guskey, 2014). This means mapping backward from desired child outcomes to effective practices likely to affect child outcomes and to professional development, including PBC, that will support fidelity of implementation of effective practices. An example backward mapping process is illustrated in Figure 5.1.

Key Point to Remember

Backward mapping means mapping backward from desired child outcomes to effective practices likely to affect child outcomes and to professional development, including PBC, that will support fidelity of implementation of effective practices.

When backward mapping is used to help inform practice specification, the first source of
information examined is child-level outcome data. Examining these data helps identify child-
level strengths and needs and whether desired outcomes are being achieved by all children,
subgroups of children (e.g., children with disabilities, children who are dual language learners),

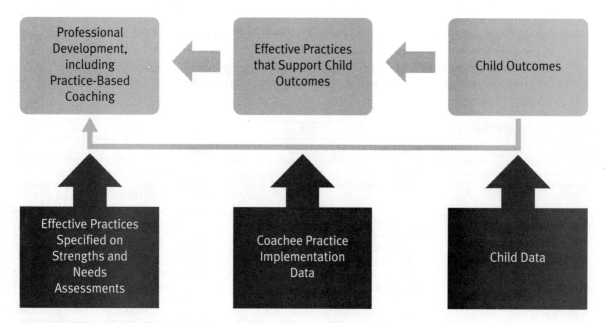

Figure 5.1. Mapping backward from child outcomes to effective practices that are the focus of professional development, including practice-based coaching.

or individual children. Child-level data show patterns of strengths or needs about what children know or are able to do. Mapping backward from child-level data involves making decisions about what coachees need to know or be able to do to support child-level outcomes, that is: What are the effective practices that when implemented as intended would be expected to affect child-level outcomes?

Gathering data about coachees' implementation of these effective practices through both strengths and needs assessments and through direct observations of practice implementation helps inform decisions about the specification of practices for professional development, including PBC (Gentile, 2006). When backward mapping is used, professional development providers, training and technical assistance teams, or program leadership teams can specify content and construct practice lists for strengths and needs assessments. They do this by summarizing and analyzing child-, practitioner-, and program-level data to identify the practices likely to enhance child outcomes (Fox et al., 2014).

Observation Instruments To facilitate the specification of practices for formal strengths and needs assessments, existing judgment-based rating scales or direct observation instruments can be used. Measures of practice implementation fidelity, such as the Teaching Pyramid Observation Tool (Hemmeter et al., 2014) or the Teaching Pyramid Infant–Toddler Observation Scale (Bigelow et al., 2019), can be used. Performance checklists, available through the Early Childhood Technical Assistance Center, which are based on the *Division for Early Childhood Recommended Practices* (DEC, 2014), also contain practices that might be used to construct strengths and needs assessments. Another resource is the Head Start Early Learning Outcomes Effective Practice Guides. These guides provide sets of practices aligned with the five central child outcome domains of the Head Start Early Learning Outcomes Framework (ELOF; Office of Head Start, 2015). The domains are approaches to learning; social-emotional development; language and literacy; cognition; and perceptual, motor, and physical development.

> To help specify practices for formal strengths and needs assessments, existing judgment-based rating scales or direct observation instruments can be used.

> **Tools for Coaches**
>
> Existing practice checklists from the Early Childhood Technical Assistance Center, which are based on the Division for Early Childhood Recommended Practices (http://ectacenter.org/decrp/type-checklists.asp) and the Office of Head Start (https://eclkc.ohs.acf.hhs.gov/school-readiness/effective-practice-guides/introduction), can be used to inform strengths and needs assessments.

The use of existing instruments can be ready-made tools that coaches use to collect data on fidelity of implementation or changes in practice implementation over time. The design of an observation instrument will affect whether it is practice-list ready or requires additional effort to specify observable and measurable practices. For example, some instruments might be designed to provide global or average ratings rather than ratings for explicit observable and measurable practices. If these types of instruments are used to help inform decisions about specifying practices for inclusion on strengths and needs assessments, program leadership or coaches will need to ensure that the practices included on strengths and needs assessments are observable and measurable.

Evaluating Effective Practices for Inclusion on Strengths and Needs Assessments

From each of the sources described above, program leadership or coaches could potentially identify hundreds of practices. Focusing on high-leverage practices, those that have been shown through rigorous research to promote positive learning and development outcomes for children, is key (Ball & Forzani, 2011). Program leadership and coaches should consider these practices along with their professional wisdom and experience and their characteristics, values, and preferences when evaluating practices for inclusion on strengths and needs assessment (National Professional Development Center on Inclusion [NPDCI], 2008; Snyder, 2006). In the absence of this wholistic approach to the specification of high-leverage effective practices, barriers associated with contextual fit might be encountered (Horner et al., 2014; McLaughlin et al., 2012). As Montrose Wolf (1978) noted more than 40 years ago, ". . . if the participants [coachees] don't like the treatment [practices] then they may avoid it [them], or run away, or complain loudly. And thus, society will be less likely to use our technology [effective practices], no matter how potentially effective and efficient it [they] might be" (p. 206). Select and promote practices that can be feasibly implemented in the practice context and ensure that coachees know how their use of the practices will support child development and learning.

A specified set of practices organized in a coherent way is needed to implement PBC with fidelity. Each practice should be evaluated for quality and utility. The Checklist for Evaluating Effective Practices for Practice-Based Coaching shown in Figure 5.2 and in Appendix VII.AD can be used to help guide decisions about practices. Use of the checklist guides consideration of each practice to determine whether or not it is observable (i.e., can be seen or heard), measurable (i.e., written in a way two people could agree when it occurs), feasible (i.e., it is possible for the coachee to implement in practice context), and aligned with desired child outcomes. Program leadership teams, coaches, coachees, and other stakeholders might use the checklist as they are planning for professional development, including PBC. Effective practices are foundational for PBC. Time spent on the specification of effective practices to ensure their quality and utility is a good investment and will help support fidelity of PBC implementation.

Tools for Coaches in the Appendices

Appendix VII.AD: Checklist for Evaluating Effective Practices for Practice-Based Coaching

This is a resource for considering the extent to which practices selected to be the focus of professional development, including PBC, are observable, measurable, feasible, and aligned with desired child outcomes.

Why Do Effective Practices Matter?

> The specification of practices helps focus coaching on an explicit set of actions or behaviors rather than on the universe of things that could be addressed.

Clarity and specificity of an identified set of practices supports coachees and coaches to be confident and competent about PBC and provides a shared language for the coachee and coach to establish a collaborative partnership and coaching priorities. The specification of practices also helps focus coaching on an explicit set of actions or behaviors rather than on the universe of things that could be addressed. A focused set of practices provides transparency for the coachee and coach and establishes mutual expectations about the focus of PBC. As described in Chapter 3, transparency is important for the collaborative partnership.

DESIGNING A STRENGTHS AND NEEDS ASSESSMENT

Once effective practices are specified, they can be populated into a strengths and needs assessment instrument. As noted previously, various strengths and needs assessment methods have been described in the literature (e.g., rating scales, interviews, priority matrix, critical incidents). Consideration should be given to the advantages and disadvantages of these different methods. Snyder and Wolfe (2008) provided detailed descriptions and examples of several strengths and needs assessment methods (e.g., instruments, document analysis, observations, interviews, focus groups, priority matrix, critical incidents, consensus methods), which can be matched to various target respondents and purposes.

Program: Helping Hands			**Date:** August 14				
Focus for PBC: Oral Language Facilitation			**Age of Children:** Toddler and Preschool				

Practice	Observable		Measurable		Feasible		Child outcomes	
	Yes	No	Yes	No	Yes	No	Yes	No
1. I talk to children throughout the day during activities and routines.								
2. I respond immediately and positively to children's attempts to communicate.								
3. I have back-and-forth conversations or exchanges with children, appropriate for their developmental level.								
4. I talk about many different things children are feeling, doing, or experiencing throughout the day.								
5. I use a wide range of words to describe objects, actions, and experiences throughout the day.								
6. I describe my actions as I am doing them.								
7. I describe children's actions as they do them (i.e., self-talk).								
8. I add more words or ideas to what children say.								
9. I ask open-ended questions to facilitate children's use of language.								

Key: Observable, can be seen or heard; measurable, written in a way that two people could agree when it occurs; feasible, feasible for coachee to implement in practice context; outcomes, likely to lead to desired positive child developmental and learning outcomes when implemented with fidelity.

Figure 5.2. Example checklist for evaluating effective practices for practice-based coaching (PBC).

Formats for Practice-Based Coaching Strengths and Needs Assessments

Most strengths and needs assessments used to date in PBC have been either observational measures of fidelity of practice implementation (e.g., Teaching Pyramid Observation Tool [TPOT™]; Hemmeter et al., 2014; Teaching Pyramid Infant–Toddler Observation Scale [TPITOS™]; Bigelow et al., 2019) or judgment-based rating scales developed to align with a set of effective practices, such as embedded instruction (Snyder, Hemmeter, et al., 2018; see Figure 5.3). When rating scales are used, various scale response options and anchors might be used. Selection should be determined by the type of strengths and needs information being sought (see Table 5.2). Response options and anchors can be written so that information is gathered about the coachee's use of or knowledge about the practice, practice self-efficacy, practice fit in context, and the extent to which the coachee believes the practice is beneficial for supporting child development and learning. Response options can also be written to gather information about current and future practice implementation. Use of current and future-oriented response options and anchors provides information about coachees' motivations and preferences for change (Grant, 2011). By using different response options and anchors on a strengths and needs assessment instrument, more than one type of information can be gathered. For example, as shown in Figure 5.3, information is gathered about the coachee's current knowledge, use, and need for support to use a practice.

It is also important to ensure that response options and anchors are nonjudgmental and strengths based. When data are being gathered in a job-embedded context, coachee and coach roles and the extent to which a collaborative partnership has been established can affect the coachee's self-report. Strengths-based response options help to gather valid information from the coachee. For example, a response option that reads "I need support to use this practice" and "I would like support to use this practice" are similar. When answering "I need support to use this practice," the coachee would need to be confident that requesting support would not result in negative judgments. In contrast, "I would like support to use this practice," indicates that the coachee is inviting support to gain competence in using the practice as intended. Similarly, when asking the coachee to rate whether they use a practice, changing the low end of the scale from "Never" to "Not yet" communicates a strengths-based and promotive approach to self-assessment.

> It is important to ensure that response options are nonjudgmental and strengths based. Strengths-based response options help to gather valid information from the coachee.

Tools for Coaches in the Appendices

Appendix II.D: Designing Your Strengths and Needs Assessment: Being Intentional About Response Options and Anchors

This is a resource for considering different response options and anchors that might be used on a formal strengths and needs assessment instrument.

Coachee and Coach Strengths and Needs Assessments

Within PBC, both coachees and coaches complete strengths and needs assessments. These strengths and needs assessments each have the same practices. How the practices are written might be identical or they might vary in length or format based on the respondent. For example, during an initial coaching cycle, the coach might gather strengths and needs assessment information for an entire set of practices using an observation rating scale or fidelity measure (e.g., complete all indicators on the TPOT; Hemmeter et al., 2014). The coachee might complete a strengths and needs assessment for a targeted set of practices from a larger set (e.g., Schedule and Routines indicators on the TPOT). The documents might also provide space for open-ended responses or notes from the coachee or coach that summarize strengths and needs across the set of practices or acknowledge other learning experiences that might contribute to the identified priorities for PBC (see Figure 5.4).

Embedded Instruction Teaching Practices	How much do you know about this practice?		How often do you use this practice?		I would like support to use this practice.	
	Just learning	I could teach others	Not often	Every day	Not right now	Very much
1. Identify and align **target skills** for children.	1 2 3 4 5		1 2			
2. Write high-quality **priority learning targets**.			2 3 4 5		1 2 3 4 5	
3. Use high-quality activities to provide multiple and meaningful **embedded learning opportunities**.			3 4 5		1 2 3 4 5	
4. Develop an **activity matrix** to plan when and how many learning opportunities to embed within and across activities.	1 2 3 4 5		1 2 3 4 5		1 2 3 4 5	
5. Plan and implement embedded learning opportunities as **complete learning trials**.	1 2 3 4 5		1 2 3 4 5		1 2 3 4 5	
6. Collect and analyze **data on embedded instruction implementation** and child progress to inform instructional decisions.	1 2 3 4 5		1 2 3 4 5		1 2 3 4 5	

Callout boxes:
- Used to gather information about practice knowledge
- Used to gather information about use of practice and need for support in job-embedded context
- Underlined terms important for respondents to have shared understanding of meaning.
- **Specific statements** of embedded instruction actions and behaviors. (i.e., practices)

Figure 5.3. Example formal strengths and needs assessment for six embedded instruction practices. From Bishop, C. D., Shannon, D. & Snyder, P., (2018). *Constructing a coaching roadmap: Tips for collaborative goal setting and action planning* [Pre-conference workshop]. International Division for Early Childhood Conference. Orlando, FL; reprinted by permission.

Table 5.2.   Considerations when selecting formal strengths and needs assessment rating scale response options and anchors

Response options	Rating scale anchors		Current or future use	Considerations
	Low end	High end		
	Practice use			
I <u>use</u> this practice.	Not yet	Always	Current	• Gathering *use* perspectives on a strengths and needs assessment in conjunction with direct observations of practice implementation provides important "say–do" correspondence information. Say–do is the correspondence between what a person says they do and what they do.
I would like to <u>use</u> this practice.	Not yet	Very much	Future	
I would <u>like support</u> to use this practice	Not yet	Very much	Current	• Responses at the high end of the rating scale for "I would like to use this practice" or "I would like support to use this practice" can help the coach and coachee prioritize a practice to enhance motivation and buy-in and build rapport to establish a strong foundation for the collaborative partnership.
	Frequency and fluency of use			
How often do you <u>use</u> this practice?	Seldom	Daily	Current	• Gathering perspectives about frequency and fluency of use on a strengths and needs assessment in conjunction with direct observations of practice implementation provides important say–do correspondence information.
I can implement this practice <u>accurately and quickly</u> when appropriate.	Not yet	Always	Current	• If a coachee reports their use of a practice is at the low end of the rating scale, this might be an important priority for coaching support if the coachee expressed a desire to learn about or use the practice. • If a coachee reports they are using a practice daily, this might be an important priority for coaching support if the practice is not being implemented with fidelity. • If a coachee reports they can implement the practice accurately and quickly, this might be an important priority for coaching support if the practice is not being implemented with fidelity.
	Practice knowledge			
I <u>know about</u> this practice.	Just learning	I could teach others	Current	• If coaching is not provided in conjunction with other facilitated learning experiences (e.g., workshops, online modules), coaches might ask coachees whether there are any terms on the strengths and needs assessment that are unfamiliar or whether the coachee has questions about any of the practices before they complete the strengths and needs assessment (e.g., "We have not worked on these practices together yet. Are there any practices that you want to talk about briefly before you complete the strengths and needs assessment?").
I want to <u>learn more</u> about this practice.	Not yet	Very much	Future	• Let the coachee know that an important step that often appears on action plans is to learn more about a practice and that the coach will work with the coachee to identify relevant materials and resources.
	Practice confidence			
I am <u>confident</u> using this practice.	Not yet	Very	Current	• Confidence is part of self-efficacy. If a coachee indicates they are not yet confident about using the practice, the coachee might want to learn more about the practice or might benefit from feedback about their implementation of the practice to build their confidence.
	Practice fit in context			
This practice is a <u>good fit</u> for my context.	Strongly disagree	Strongly agree	Current	• Perspectives about fit provide information about alignment or acceptability of practice. If the coachee does not believe the practice is a good fit for their context, the coachee and coach should discuss the reasons why.
This practice is <u>aligned with the values</u> of the program in which I work.	Less aligned	More aligned	Current	• If a coachee indicates a practice is not a good fit, consider other practices that are rated as having better fit to enhance motivation and build the collaborative partnership.
I could <u>integrate</u> this practice into my activities and routines.	Strongly disagree	Strongly agree	Future	• Once the coachee and coach have an established collaborative partnership, the coach might engage the coachee in a reflective or problem-solving conversation to identify practice implementation challenges and potential solutions to enhance fit.

Table 5.2. Continued

Response options	Rating scale anchors		Current or future use	Considerations
	Low end	High end		
Practice effects on child outcomes				
I believe this practice is <u>important for supporting children's development and learning.</u>	Strongly disagree	Strongly agree	Current	• If the coachee does not rate the practice as important for children's development and learning, it is unlikely to be a good place to begin coaching and might indicate a need to clarify misunderstandings or to support the coachee to learn more about relationships between practice implementation and child outcomes.
Using this practice will <u>help children learn.</u>	Strongly disagree	Strongly agree	Future	

Note: Rating scale anchors can be binary (Yes/No) or Likert type (e.g., from 1 to 5).

Embedded Instruction for Early Learning

Strengths: List three things about your current instructional practices that you are confident about and that you believe are strengths that support your implementation of embedded instruction (e.g., We know our students' individual interests and what they like, We offer a variety of toys in each center).

Three things we are confident about and are strengths:

1. We have been working with children with disabilities for several years.

2. We know our children well and can identify their preferences or materials they find motivating.

3. Even though we just started working together, we work well together, and our combined experiences and knowledge will help us use embedded instruction in our classroom.

Priorities: List your top three priorities for embedded instruction coaching support to inform your first action plan goal.

Three priorities for coaching are:

1. We want to learn more about how to write priority learning targets that are observable and measurable.

2. We need some help planning how to embed learning opportunities in multiple activities throughout the day, especially during free play and meals.

3. We need to monitor children's progress on their priority learning targets so we know when to provide more support or work on something new.

Figure 5.4. An example of open-ended strengths and needs assessment data for Maureen and Maria. From Bishop, C. D., Shannon, D. & Snyder, P., (2018). *Constructing a coaching roadmap: Tips for collaborative goal setting and action planning* [Pre-conference workshop]. International Division for Early Childhood Conference. Orlando, FL; reprinted by permission.

Complexity and Utility

Final considerations when designing strengths and needs assessments are complexity and utility. If the strengths and needs assessment document is too complex or burdensome, it might detract from the intended purposes for the strengths and needs assessment. We are frequently asked how many practices and response options should be included in a strengths and needs assessment. Our experiences with PBC suggest that practices included on a coachee strengths and needs assessment should range from 5 to 15 practices and there should be three or fewer response options for each practice on a given strengths and needs assessment. If a larger set of practices (e.g., Pyramid Model; Hemmeter et al., 2016) is the focus of PBC, strengths and needs assessments that contain select practices from the larger set can be used over time. Similar competency areas, practice domains, logical practice implementation sequences, or hierarchies of practices that increase in complexity are possible structures for grouping practices across linked strengths and needs assessments.

> **Tools for Coaches in the Appendices**
>
> *Appendix II.E: Key Considerations for Strengths and Needs Assessments*
>
> This checklist can be used to examine the quality and utility of formal strengths and needs assessments.

USING THE STRENGTHS AND NEEDS ASSESSMENT WITHIN PRACTICE-BASED COACHING

Strengths and needs assessment is not explicitly depicted in the PBC visual model, but it is fundamental for implementing PBC with fidelity. Once a set of practices has been specified and a strengths and needs assessment developed, guidance should be provided to both coachees and coaches about when and how to use the assessments. This section addresses three questions coachees and coaches often have about the strengths and needs assessment: 1) Why do coachees and coaches complete the strengths and needs assessment? 2) When is the strengths and needs assessment used? and 3) How is the strengths and needs assessment used? Coaching manuals should include more detailed information and timelines to support coachees and coaches to use strengths and needs assessments.

Why Do Coachees and Coaches Complete the Strengths and Needs Assessment?

Coachees' strengths and needs assessments are used to gather coachee perspectives about the practices. Coach assessments gather the coach's perspectives about the coachee's knowledge about and implementation of the practices. It is important for both coachees and coaches to complete a strengths and needs assessment to clarify and verify strengths and needs from each person involved in the collaborative partnership (Snyder & Wolfe, 2008).

Perspectives of coachees are based on their current understanding of practices and with support and implementation experiences, their perspectives will change over time. PBC is often provided in conjunction with workshops or other facilitated learning experiences that provide coachees with knowledge and skills (Artman-Meeker et al., 2015; Snyder et al., 2012). These learning experiences should provide opportunities for coachees to learn about the effective practices, observe the practices being implemented using in situ or video models, and try out the practices with feedback (Snyder et al., 2012; Trivette et al., 2009). Conducting PBC strengths and needs assessments after coachees have gained foundational knowledge and skills will enhance the validity of their responses.

> It is important for both coachees and coaches to complete a strengths and needs assessment to clarify and verify strengths and needs from each person involved in the collaborative partnership.

Perspectives of coaches about coachee strengths and needs are based on their interactions with coachees during workshops or other facilitated learning experiences and on their observations of coachees' practice implementation. Coaches might also review child-level data or documents from the coachees' practice context that are aligned with the PBC practice focus (e.g., daily schedule, data collection forms, classroom rules) to inform their assessments. Perspectives of coaches might not always be congruent with coachees' perspectives. An important part of the collaborative partnership is to share perspectives about strengths and needs and use this information to identify a coachee's practice implementation goals.

When Is the Strengths and Needs Assessment Used?

As described previously, assessments can be formal (e.g., use of an instrument) or informal (e.g., on-the-spot discussions during a coaching session). The formal strengths and needs assessment is completed by the coachee and coach early in the coaching process. Following the initial assessment, formal assessments occur periodically throughout coaching cycles to inform goal setting and action planning. Informal strengths and needs assessments are done in every coaching cycle. In situations where a predetermined coaching sequence is in place, one might prespecify when formal assessments are done (e.g., Sessions 1, 8, and 16 of a 16-week coaching sequence). Formal assessments should always be completed at the beginning and end of a coaching sequence to demonstrate coachee growth, measure the impact of PBC on coachee's implementation of practices, and identify priorities for additional professional development experiences.

How Is the Strengths and Needs Assessment Used?

The strengths and needs assessment is used in two primary ways. The first is to inform coachee and coach shared goal setting and action planning through the identification and development of action plan goals. The second is to provide information for data-informed decision making. Data-informed decision making can occur at an individual, program, or system level.

Develop Shared Goals and Action Plans Verbal or written discussions about data from strengths and needs assessments guides the development of the action plan goal. Table 5.3 provides a recommended sequence for coachees and coaches to review and discuss the assessments, including example prompts and tips for coaches who are facilitating the process. The sequence represents a logical flow that applies to most strengths and needs assessment processes. Nevertheless, the coach should be responsive to the coachee and modify the sequence, as appropriate, to meet individual needs. The coachee and coach should *always* identify strengths before considering needs and coaching priorities. All coachees have practice-related strengths. It is the coach's role to support the coachee to recognize and build on those strengths. Coaches are strongly encouraged to role-play facilitating the strengths and needs assessment process and to receive feedback from other coaches before engaging in their first strengths and needs assessment interactions with coachees.

Key Points to Remember

The coachee and coach should always identify strengths before considering needs and coaching priorities.
All coachees have practice-related strengths. It is the coach's role to support the coachee to recognize and build on those strengths.

Inform Decision Making Strengths and needs assessment data can be summarized, analyzed, and used for several purposes. It can be used to make data-informed decisions about the content focus and dose (i.e., frequency, duration, and delivery format) of professional development and PBC for an individual, program, or system. Formal and informal strengths and needs assessment data can be used to review and celebrate progress as part of each coaching cycle and over time. It can be used to inform decisions about goals and action plan steps. Data gathered using strengths and needs assessments are the most proximal measure of the

Table 5.3.   Discussing the strengths and needs assessment: sequence, example prompts, and tips

Sequence	Example prompt(s)	Tips
Make the coachee and coach strengths and needs assessments documents visible for reference.	"Were you able to complete the strengths and needs assessment?" "What are your initial thoughts about your responses to the strengths and needs assessment?"	• Send a reminder for the coachee to have the completed strengths and needs assessment available when it will be discussed. • Ensure that you have access to a blank copy that can be completed together if the coachee has not completed it. • Ensure that ratings or other information on your strengths and needs assessment will not compromise the collaborative partnership. If needed, prepare a separate summary or list that identifies practice strengths, even if they are not directly related to the practices that are the focus of practice-based coaching (PBC).
Provide the coachee with a **brief** orientation to the strengths and needs assessment	"Today, we're going to share practices strengths and priorities. Then, we'll develop an initial practice implementation goal and action plan!"	• Always discuss strengths first. • Frame needs as opportunities to close gaps between what is and what is desired, and for collaboration and support around a priority the coachee selects. • Do not provide constructive feedback during the coachee's reflection on their strengths and priorities for coaching.
Invite the coachee to share their strengths by using open-ended reflective questions.	"Which practices are strengths for you?" "Which practices are important for you?"	• As the coachee shares, take notes and seek opportunities to acknowledge and affirm the coachee's self-identified strengths. • Clarify and verify practices as needed. • Provide evidence from an observation confirming the coachee's strengths related to select practices. • Highlight alignment between the coachee's and the coach's strengths and needs assessments.
Invite the coachee to share their priorities for coaching using open-ended reflective questions.	"Which practices would you like to prioritize?" "Why are these practices important to you?"	• As the coachee shares, take notes and seek opportunities to acknowledge the coachee's self-identified priorities. • Clarify and verify practices as needed. • To the extent possible, if the practices have a logical implementation sequence, be prepared to help the coachee understand how they will benefit from starting with a particular practice and when it is logical to support their top priorities if they are out of sequence. • When the coach identifies a priority that the coachee did not identify, the coach might present the potential priority by focusing on the benefit of implementing the practice for the coachee or for children.
Summarize and confirm the coachee's strengths and priorities using a **brief** list.	"To summarize everything, strengths we're going to build on are _____ and top priorities for PBC are _____. Did we miss anything?"	• Be sure that notes reflect the collaborative discussion and coachee priorities. • When appropriate, frame the priorities in a logical sequence when summarizing. • When appropriate, consider opportunities to blend priorities to incorporate several high-leverage practices in implementation goals. • Follow the coachee's lead in selecting the first priority. • In subsequent strengths and needs assessment discussions, the coachee and coach will have additional information to make decisions about potential next steps that are a good fit for the coachee and the practice setting.

effect PBC is having on the coachee's perspectives about practice implementation. Thus, these data can inform decisions about whether PBC is achieving intended outcomes related to strengthening coachee practice confidence and competence. Strengths and needs assessment data provide value-added information when used in conjunction with measures of global environmental and practice quality. For this reason, strengths and needs assessment data should be used not only to inform coaching-related decisions but also as part of program- or systemwide data-informed decision making (Fox et al., 2014).

> Data gathered using strengths and needs assessments are a proximal measure of PBC effects on the coachee's perspectives about practice implementation.

REVISITING THE CASE STORIES

We return to the three case stories to illustrate the major topics discussed in this chapter. For Maureen and Maria, we specify the practices that are the content focus of coaching and illustrate how these practices are observable and measurable. For Lynn, we describe how the strengths and needs assessment instrument was designed by Sirena and the leadership team at Helping Hands. For Sam and Kenya, we illustrate how strengths and needs assessment information is being used as part of PBC implementation. As you read each case story, consider what you or others with whom you work might do to support the development and use of strengths and needs assessments. At the end of each case story, questions for reflection and discussion are provided. Use these questions to guide further reflection and discussion about using strengths and needs assessment with other coaches or others with whom you work.

Maureen and Maria Demonstrate Competence

In Maureen's and Maria's program, each teacher has an annual individualized professional development plan (IPDP) aligned with their program's annual performance assessment. Their program provided a list of early childhood educator competency statements and each teacher was encouraged to select one of three competencies for their IPDP focal area. Maureen and Maria reviewed the list carefully and selected the following competency statement: "Knows typical and atypical development. Plans developmentally appropriate environments, interactions, and experiences for the home and learning environment" (CDE and First 5 California, 2011, p. 153). To support Maureen and Maria with this competency, their program administrator suggested two resources: the Desired Results Development Profile (CDE, 2015) for information about developmental and learning continua for young children from birth to Kindergarten entry and the California Preschool Curricular Frameworks (CDE, 2010) for developmentally appropriate activities and interactional practices. Although Maureen and Maria gained knowledge from these sources, they were still uncertain about what practices they and their assistant Adam could use to support the children in their inclusive preschool classroom. When they e-mailed their administrator to inquire about additional learning experiences aligned with this competency, she suggested the embedded instruction for early learning virtual workshop series being offered by the state training and technical assistance network.

Following the embedded instruction virtual workshop series, Maureen and Maria were thankful to have learned about the observable and measurable embedded instruction practices on their strengths and needs assessment (see Figure 5.3). The practices helped them to think about specific actions they could take to enact the professional competency on their IPDP and to support the children in their inclusive classroom. They e-mailed their strengths and needs assessment to their embedded instruction coach, Elley, whom they had enjoyed meeting and interacting with during the virtual workshop series. They also uploaded a video clip of their classroom instruction to the coaching platform. Elley reviewed the video and strengths and needs

Questions for Further Reflection and Discussion

- Why might competencies, as they are typically written, be challenging for teachers like Maureen and Maria to connect to practices they implement or would like to implement in their classroom?

- What organization-, state-, or program-level competencies might inform or be aligned with practices that are the focus of professional development, including PBC, in the practice contexts in which you work?

- What did Elley do to help Maureen and Maria further connect their IPDP to their strengths and needs assessment focused on embedded instruction practices?

- Why would attending the embedded instruction workshops together before completing the strengths and needs assessment be beneficial for Maureen and Maria? For Elley?

assessment Maureen and Maria had uploaded to the coaching platform along with the priority learning targets they had written during the workshop series. Then, she completed her coach strengths and needs assessment in advance of their first coaching meeting.

Later that week, Maureen, Maria, and Elley met by videoconference. Elley screen-shared Maureen and Maria' strengths and needs assessment and asked them to reflect on aspects of their classroom that would be strengths when implementing embedded instruction and to identify their top priorities for coaching. They talked further about their IPDP, the state competencies, and why they joined embedded instruction. Together, they decided to focus their first shared goal and action plan on the following practice: "Develop an activity matrix to plan when and how many learning opportunities to embed within and across activities and try it out in the classroom before our next coaching session." As Elley wrapped up their discussion of the strengths and needs assessment she said, "Using an activity matrix is a practice aligned with the state competency. I think it will be a useful tool for you to develop and implement activities to support children's individual learning needs and plan specifically for children who may require more support." Maureen and Maria were excited to write their first action plan goal!

Lynn's Program, Helping Hands, Identifies Effective Practices

As part of their participation in their state's quality improvement system, the leadership team at Helping Hands is working closely with Sirena, a training and technical assistance specialist in a regional child care resource and referral agency who will also be coaching teachers in their program. With Sirena's support, the leadership team reviewed their child outcome data over the last 2 years. They identified that children's oral language skills are not meeting expectations as outlined in their programwide improvement plan. After discussing their child-level data, Sirena suggested that the leadership team might want to review the Classroom Assessment Scoring System (CLASS™) Toddler (La Paro et al., 2011) program-level data provided by their state quality rating and improvement system to identify strengths and needs regarding practices teachers were using to promote children's oral language. The team reviewed their data and noted several dimensions of their Emotional and Behavioral Support were above average! They also noted a need for support in the Quality Feedback and Language Modeling dimension of the Engaged Support for Learning domain. The team decided to focus their professional development over the coming months, including PBC, on identifying practices to support children's oral language.

> **Questions for Further Reflection and Discussion**
> - What sources of data did the Helping Hands leadership team use to identify the content focus of their practices?
> - Why might Sirena have encouraged the leadership team to use published judgment-based observation measures to help them identify and specify the oral language practices for the formal strengths and needs assessment?
> - How did the team select teachers to participate in PBC? What might be the benefits of this approach? What might be another strategy for selecting coachees for PBC support? What strategies have you used to make decisions about PBC participation?
> - How might the leadership team use summarized strengths and needs assessment and practice implementation data at their next leadership team meeting? How can they ensure that the data will not be used as part of performance evaluations in the program?
> - Why is it important to consider the age of the children when identifying and specifying practices?

The leadership team worked together with Sirena to identify a set of nine practices. The practices the team identified were informed by several sources, including the language modeling section of the CLASS Toddler (La Paro et al., 2011) and from the TPITOS (Bigelow et al., 2019). With support from Sirena, the team used the checklist shown in Figure 5.2 to determine if the identified practices were (a) observable, (b) measurable, (c) feasible for practitioners to implement, and (d) likely to support children's oral language skills when implemented with fidelity.

The team knew that teachers would need support to learn about and use the identified practices. They decided to organize and deliver a monthly lunch-and-learn session, with Sirena's support, focused on oral language facilitation strategies using materials available from the resource and referral agency. They also identified teachers to participate in on-site coaching with Sirena. The team focused initially on teachers whom they believed would be motivated to participate in PBC and who might serve as model demonstration classrooms for other teachers to visit as they learned about the oral language facilitation practices at the lunch-and-learn sessions. The team selected Lynn from the toddler room and Yalonda from the preschool classroom to participate in PBC initially. At the next quarterly leadership team meeting, they agreed to examine teacher strengths and needs assessment data for toddler and preschool teachers collected at the first lunch and learn and practice implementation data from Sirena's coaching sessions. They also planned to identify practices that were aligned with their focus on oral language development for the infant classrooms.

Sam and Kenya Use Teaching Pyramid Observation Tool Strengths and Needs Assessment Data to Identify a New Goal

In preparation for writing their fifth goal and action plan, Kenya made a graph showing the percentage of Pyramid Model practices implemented in Sam's class, as measured by the TPOT (Hemmeter et al., 2014) in August and January. Although she completed the full TPOT measure as part of her formal strengths and needs assessment observation in January, Kenya chose to graph the items that aligned with Sam's Practice Implementation Checklist to keep the conversation focused (see Figure 5.5). She also jotted down some reflective questions she planned to use when she and Sam engaged in discussions related to identifying strengths and possible needs or priorities for their next action plan. She sent Sam a quick e-mail reminding him of their meeting and attached the Practice Implementation Checklist (see Appendix I.C), asking Sam to jot down his current perspectives related to each practice and to bring the checklist to the meeting.

As their meeting got started, Kenya reminded Sam of the TPOT data she had collected in August and that she had gathered data using this measure again when she visited in January. She said, "Each of our action plans have zoomed in to focus on a key practice from the TPOT. It's also important for us to zoom out to celebrate everything you've accomplished and to verify what we hope to accomplish next. The data I've collected are one source we'll use to identify next steps, but it is equally important to consider your perspectives about the practices. Looking over the Practice

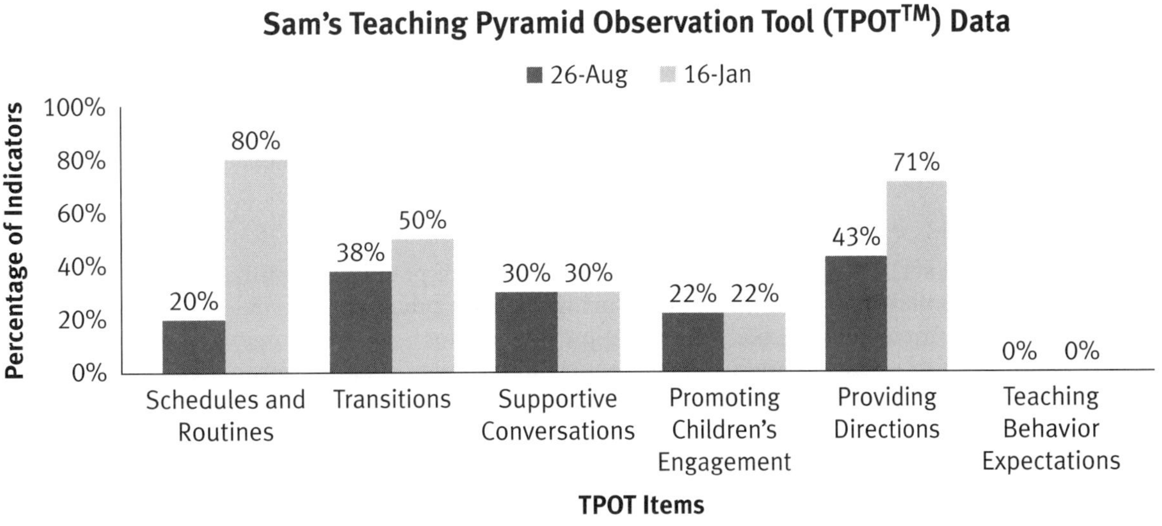

Sam's Teaching Pyramid Observation Tool (TPOT™) Data

■ 26-Aug   ▨ 16-Jan

Figure 5.5. Sam's Teaching Pyramid Observation Tool (TPOT™) fidelity data for select items in August and January.

Implementation Checklist you completed, what are some areas of your TPOT implementation that are strengths?" Sam shared that he had made progress using the visual schedule to teach children the daily routines. He also said, "We haven't really focused on transitions, but I think I've naturally started to use some of those practices as well." Kenya followed Sam's lead and used data from her graph and supportive feedback to affirm his reflections. She said, "I've seen you using a timer and a clean-up song to signal an advanced transition cue before clean-up transitions begin at centers and meals. These are great strategies because they let children know that they have a few minutes to finish what they're working on and to prepare for the next activity. You've also consistently referred to the visual schedule. Our graph shows you've made gains in Schedules and Routines and Transitions!" Sam smiled, "That is really nice to see!"

Sam and Kenya then shifted their conversation to priorities. Kenya said, "Looking over your checklist and the data on our graph, what are some new priorities you have?" Sam paused thoughtfully and then shared that the class had experienced several changes following the winter break, including his new assistant, Jamie, and two new children. He said, "I know making choices and center time is really important for helping children to stay engaged, but centers always feel a bit chaotic. I'm not able to spend time with kids because I'm always redirecting, 'No running—use walking feet' and 'Don't touch that—it's not safe.' Plus, supporting children's engagement looks a little low on the graph. Maybe we need to work on that." Kenya had also noticed and recorded notes about times Sam was more and less successful with reviewing the expectations and rules and where engagement was low at circle and centers. She wanted to keep the conversation goal focused, so she nodded and said, "Centers can be tricky, but as you mentioned, they are also an important part of the day. It seems like we could focus our next action plan on teaching behavior expectations or possibly supporting children's engagement. When children know what's expected, you will be able to focus less on redirection and more on supporting children's engagement through nurturing and responsive interactions with children in centers." Sam was nodding, "Yeah, that makes sense. I do have rules, but maybe rewriting those would be a good place to start." Kenya smiled, "Before we jump into revising your expectations and rules, let's get the action plan goal jotted down. As we discussed, it will help us to stay focused on how and where you can help children to learn the classroom expectations and rules."

Questions for Further Reflection and Discussion

- Which components of the logical sequence for sharing strengths and needs assessments shown in Table 5.3 were implemented in the case story?
- What strategies did Kenya use to support Sam to identify priorities for the new goal?
- What might you have done differently in this interaction with Sam if you were Kenya?
- This is Sam's fifth action plan. How might the conversation be similar or different from coachees and coaches who are meeting to discuss the strengths and needs assessment for the first time?
- Kenya chose to use a graph. How could she have facilitated the conversation using only the Practice Implementation Checklist?

SUMMARY

A specified set of observable, measurable, and effective practices organized in a coherent way are an essential ingredient of PBC. Ensuring that the practices that are the focus of PBC are feasible to implement, a good fit for the practice context, and have been identified based on data-informed strengths and needs is important. Backward mapping from desired child developmental and learning outcomes to practices that support those outcomes to the professional development most likely to support effective practice implementation, including PBC, is recommended. Formal and informal practice-focused strengths and needs assessments are inextricably linked to each PBC component, especially shared goals and action planning, which is the focus of Chapter 6.

6

Shared Goal Setting and Action Planning

Patricia Snyder, Mary Louise Hemmeter, Lise Fox, and Crystal Bishop

GOAL SETTING AND ACTION PLANNING

Shared goal setting and action planning is an essential component of Practice-Based Coaching (PBC) (Snyder et al., 2015). In this chapter, the rationale for the shared goal setting and action planning component within the PBC framework is described. Processes related to initial and ongoing goal setting and action planning are discussed. Information about how to use information from practice-focused coachee and coach strengths and needs assessments to inform goal setting and action planning are described and illustrated with examples. The important characteristics of goals and action plans are shared and examples of goals and action plans are provided. Application activities are guided through use of case stories. The chapter concludes with a section that describes relationships among shared goal setting and action planning, focused observation, and reflection and feedback within the collaborative coaching partnership throughout each PBC cycle.

Rationale for Shared Goal Setting and Action Planning

Goal setting is done to frame and facilitate the development, implementation, and evaluation of an action plan. A *goal* includes an explicit practice statement that describes observable and measurable actions or behaviors of coachees. In PBC, the actions or behaviors specified in a goal align with one or more of the set of practices that are the focus of coaching. Descriptions of how to identify and specify practices by using information from strengths and needs assessments are provided in Chapter 5. Goals make explicit the transition from the current to the desired state of practice implementation.

> **Key Point to Remember**
>
> A goal includes an explicit practice statement that describes observable and measurable actions or behaviors of coachees.

Different categories and types of goals have been described in the literature. Goals might focus on cognitive, behavior, or affective domains. They can be of different types, including outcome goals, distal or proximal goals, approach or avoidance goals, performance or learning goals, developmental goals, and higher- and lower-order goals (David et al., 2016; Grant, 2011; Gregory et al., 2011). In PBC, goals are developmental and outcome focused. They are based on the

> A shared goal is a goal developed collaboratively between a coachee and a coach.

coachee's phase of practice learning (i.e., acquisition, fluency, generalization, maintenance, adaptation) (Haring et al., 1978; Kubina et al., 2009). Initially, goals typically specify practice behaviors or actions proximal to current performance so the goal is viewed as attainable. Goals are also learning or performance based given the emphasis in PBC on fidelity of practice implementation (Snyder et al., 2015). A *shared goal* refers to a goal developed collaboratively by a coachee and a coach. Strategies for developing specific, measurable, achievable/action-oriented, relevant/realistic, and time-framed (SMA^{2}R^{2}T) goals and action plans are described later in this chapter.

Action plans serve as road maps for how goals will be accomplished. They guide initial and ongoing PBC interactions between the coach and coachee. Action steps are subordinate to a PBC goal. A well-constructed plan motivates the coachee to act. It should specify how actions toward goal attainment will be monitored and evaluated (Grant, 2006) by both the coachee and the coach. Actions that appear on the plan should be informed by coachee's priorities, preferences, and motivations. Actions should be those that will allow for the provision of performance-based feedback. Performance-based feedback is essential for providing information about when, how, or if goals and associated actions should be modified (Grant, 2011; Gregory et al., 2011).

> Action plans serve as road maps for how goals will be accomplished.

Shared goal setting and action planning is a goal-directed activity. Along with focused observation as well as reflection and feedback, it guides observable and measurable enhancements, refinements, or changes in coachees' implementation of effective practices. Initial goal

Figure 6.1. Shared goals and action planning in the Practice-Based Coaching framework. Adapted from Snyder, P. A., Hemmeter, M. L., & Fox, L. (2015). Supporting implementation of evidence-based practices through practice-based coaching. *Topics in Early Childhood Special Education, 35*(3), 133-143. https://doi.org/10.1177/0271121415594925; adapted by permission.

setting and action planning sets the PBC cycle in motion. Ongoing goal setting and action planning facilitates the interactive processes among cycles of goal setting and action planning, focused observation, and reflection and feedback, which occur in the context of a collaborative coaching partnership. Ongoing cycles of coaching lead to a series of actions and learning by the coachee, which combine to create practice change (Griffiths, 2005).

To identify goals and plan-associated actions, coachees often benefit from coaches' support to engage in self-assessment of practice implementation and discrepancy analyses. In PBC, discrepancies refer to differences between current and desired practice implementation. One way to engage in discrepancy analyses to inform goal setting is to use strengths and needs assessments.

Using Practice-Focused Strengths and Needs Assessments to Inform Shared Goal Setting

As described in Chapter 5, practice-focused strengths and needs assessments are used to help gather information about a coachee's current implementation of practices, to identify discrepancies between current and desired practice, and to determine priorities for enhancement, refinement, or replacement. The content for a strengths and needs assessment is the set of effective practices identified as the focus of coaching (e.g., embedded instruction practices, social-emotional practices, literacy practices). The practices included on the strengths and needs assessment should be observable and measurable. Except for self-coaching, in all other PBC formats, both coachees and coaches engage in strengths and needs assessments to guide selection of a shared goal for practice implementation.

We recommend formal strengths and needs assessments be completed after a coachee has had other facilitated teaching and learning experiences related to the practices. These experiences should provide opportunities for the coachee to learn about the practice(s), observe the practice(s) being implemented using in situ or video models, and try out the practice(s). It also is important for coachees to learn the meaning of terms or vocabulary words used in the practice statements. For example, as shown in the strengths and needs assessment for embedded instruction shown in Figure 6.2, it would be important to learn the meaning of target skills, priority learning targets, embedded learning opportunities, activity matrix, complete learning trials, embedded instruction implementation, child progress, and instructional decisions.

When an expert or peer PBC format is used, the coachee and coach should complete the same strengths and needs assessment. The coachee self-assesses their strengths and needs. The coach assesses the coachee's strengths and needs. The coach's assessment is based on information gathered during the facilitated teaching and learning experiences that precede coaching or observations that precede initial shared goal setting and action planning. This process provides useful information from both coachee's and coach's perspectives to facilitate shared goal setting and action planning.

> **Key Point to Remember**
>
> Strengths and needs assessments provide useful information from both coachee's and coach's perspectives to facilitate shared goal setting and action planning.

Gathering the coachee's perspectives about their strengths and needs helps identify priorities, preferences, and motivations related to the targeted set of practices, which, in turn, guides goal setting. Self-concordance, which refers to the extent to which a goal is aligned with an individual's preferences, motivations, or values, has been shown to engage and elicit greater effort from coachees (Grant, 2011). As part of shared goal setting and action planning, coaches support coachees to use information from the strength and needs assessment to identify goals and make them personal and concordant. If a coachee is self-coaching,

> Self-concordance, which refers to the extent to which a goal is aligned with an individual's preferences, motivations, or values, has been shown to engage and elicit greater effort from coachees.

Strengths and Needs Assessment

Instructions: Each of the statements listed are skills needed to implement embedded instruction. Read each statement and identify how much you know about the practice, how often you use the practice, and if you would like support to use the practice. Circle one number in each column for each practice.

Used to gather information about knowledge of practice

Used to gather information about use of practice

Used to gather information about support for practice use

Team: _Mauree_____ r 2

Embedded instruction teaching practices	How much do you know about this practice?		How often do you use this practice?		Would you like support to use this practice?	
	Just learning	Could teach others	Not often	Every day	Not right now	Very much
1. Identify and align <u>target skills</u> for children.	1 2 ③ 4 5		1 2 ③ 4 5		1 2 ③ 4 5	
2. Write high-quality <u>priority learning targets</u>.	① 2 3 4 5		① 2 3 4 5		1 2 3 ④ 5	
3. Use high-quality activities to provide multiple and meaningful <u>embedded learning opportunities</u>.	1 2 3 4 ⑤		1 2 3 ④ 5		1 ② 3 4 5	
4. Develop an <u>activity matrix</u> to plan when and how many learning opportunities to embed within and across activities.	③ 4 5		1 2 3 ④ 5			
5. Plan and implement embedded learning opportunities as <u>complete learning trials</u>.	1 2 ③ 4 5		1 2 ③ 4 5		1 2 3 ④ 5	
6. Collect and analyze data on <u>embedded instruction implementation</u> and <u>child progress</u> to inform <u>instructional decisions</u>.	1 2 ③ 4 5		1 2 3 ④ 5		1 2 ③ 4 5	

Vocabulary (terms) important to define for respondent

Specific statements of embedded instruction actions and behaviors. (i.e., evidence-based practice)

Figure 6.2. Practice-focused strengths and needs assessment for six embedded instruction practices.

using a focused assessment helps them to verify and clarify strengths and needs and to identify priority practices to inform goal setting and action planning.

GOAL SETTING

Setting goals logically follows the assessment of strengths and needs. Once priorities for practice are identified through an assessment of strengths and needs, a goal can be written. Goals based on strengths, needs, preferences, priorities, and motivations are important when coaching for behavior change (Frates et al., 2011). Goals are critical in PBC because they identify the practice(s) that will be the focus of coaching. They specify the expectations and aspirations for what the coachee wants to achieve in relation to the specified set of practices. Goals guide the development, implementation, and evaluation of the action plan (Snyder et al., 2015). In turn, the goals and the action plans inform the focused observation as well as the reflection and feedback components of PBC.

When expert or peer PBC is used, the role of the coach is to work collaboratively with the coachee to help them identify and specify goals. We refer to this process as *shared goal setting*. Although the coachee and coach set a shared goal, the goal is the coachee's not the coach's. It is important that the coachee understands the goal is their goal and identifies the goal as feasible and attainable. When self-coaching, coachees also benefit from facilitated teaching and learning experiences that precede goal setting and accompanying resources to help them identify and specify goals (Embedded Instruction for Early Learning, 2016).

Key Point to Remember

Although a coachee and coach work together to develop a shared goal, it is important to remember that the goal is the coachee's goal, not the coach's.

Goals in PBC should be developmental in nature, and outcome focused and performance based. A developmental goal refers to a goal that is focused on refining or improving practice implementation (Gregory et al., 2011). When considering the developmental nature of a goal, it is important to consider a learning or instructional hierarchy that has been described in the literature (Intervention Central, n.d.; Kubina et al., 2009). The goal will be written differently if the coachee is just beginning to learn about and implement the practice (acquisition), wants to implement the practice more accurately and efficiently (fluency), is using the practice fluently in some circumstances or with some children but wants to generalize its use (generalization), or wants to maintain or adapt the use of the practice (maintenance, adaptation). Table 6.1 shows example goals that align with each of these learning phases for Lynn, Maureen and Maria, and Sam. Outcome focused means that the desired practice outcome is explicitly stated in the goal. Performance based means that the goal emphasizes practice(s) implementation rather than knowledge acquisition or desired dispositions. When initial goals are written, we recommend they be proximal to the coachee's current practice implementation so the discrepancy between the current and desired outcome is not too large. Coachees should view goals as realistic and attainable. Goals should be time limited. Typically, they should be achievable within 2–4 weeks and then new goals are written. If a goal is not achieved within 2–4 weeks, it should be reevaluated. The goal might need to be rewritten, associated action plan steps might need to be adjusted, or additional facilitated teaching and learning experiences might need to be provided.

Gregory et al. (2011) recommended a ramped approach to goal setting. This approach involves setting more attainable goals initially and then more difficult goals once initial goals have been achieved. The ramped approach to goal setting is illustrated using the learning hierarchy for Lynn, Maureen and Maria, and Sam in Table 6.1. The ramped approach to goal setting has been demonstrated to result in higher self-efficacy (Gregory et al., 2011). Self-efficacy has been identified to be positively related to the allocation of effort toward goal pursuit and has a role in both goal setting and goal striving (Bandura & Locke, 2003).

Coachees should view goals as realistic and attainable within 2–4 weeks.

Table 6.1. Example goal alignment with learning phases

Learning phase	Lynn	Maureen and Maria	Sam
Acquisition (Just learning)	I will expand what children say by adding at least one descriptive word to objects they name during free choice (e.g., "The car is <u>fast</u>"). I will use at least one expansion with one child during each play time for the next 2 days.	We will practice implementing embedded learning opportunities for one child's priority learning target. We will provide at least one embedded learning opportunity during snack every day for a week.	I will post three positively stated expectations and related classroom rules and review them at least two times a day during large group using role play and games for 3 days this week.
Fluency (Accuracy and efficiency)	I will expand what children say by adding at least one descriptive word to objects they name during play immediately after they say it (e.g., "The car is <u>fast</u>"; "The tower is <u>tall</u>"). I will use an expansion at least one time in each of the five play areas during free-choice time.	We will practice implementing embedded learning opportunities for one child's priority learning target during snack time. We will provide at least five embedded learning opportunities during snack time every day for 1 week.	I will provide at least three positive reminders about the posted expectations and related rules to either an individual child or to a group of children during each large-group time every day for 1 week.
Generalization (Across children or settings)	I will expand what children say by adding at least one descriptive word to objects they name during free choice or mealtimes (e.g., "The car is <u>fast</u>"; "The cracker is <u>crunchy</u>"). I will use an expansion one time with at least three children during each free choice and mealtime for a week.	We will practice implementing embedded learning opportunities for one priority learning target for three children in two classroom activities each day for 1 week.	I will provide at least three positive reminders about the posted expectations and rules to either an individual child or to a group of children during center time and circle time every day for 3 consecutive weeks.
Maintenance or adaptation (Use over time or with modifications)	I will expand what children say and do by describing their experiences (e.g., "You are rocking your baby gently. It looks like you really like playing with babies") or by adding at least one descriptive word to objects they name during free choice or mealtimes (e.g., "The block is <u>heavy</u>"; "The cracker is <u>crunchy</u>"). I will use an expansion one time for at least three children during each free choice and mealtime every day for 2 weeks.	We will implement embedded learning opportunities for all priority learning targets for each of three children. We will provide embedded learning opportunities for each child in all classroom activities as listed on our activity matrix each day for 2 weeks.	I will provide positive reminders about the posted expectations and rules during center time and circle time every day and provide positive descriptive feedback when children follow posted expectations and rules. I will provide positive reminders or positive descriptive feedback to each child at least once during centers and circle time each day for 3 weeks.

Note: Goals in boxes are the current goals for Lynn, Maureen and Maria, and Sam. Underlined words for Lynn's goals are those she will use with children.

Writing Goal Statements

Three essential features should be included when writing PBC goal statements: 1) **the observable action or behavior (practice)** the coachee will do, 2) *how much or how often the practice will be seen or heard,* and 3) <u>when, where and with whom the practice will be implemented</u>. The observable action or behavior (practice) can be considered the WHAT of the goal. How much or how often the practice will be seen or heard refers to QUANTITY. When, where, and with whom refers to the SETTING AND PEOPLE. We use **bold**, *italics*, and <u>underline</u> to highlight these features for coachees and coaches:

Practice = **Bold**

How much/how often = *Italics*

When/where/with whom = <u>Underline</u>

When writing goal statements, this formatting will help ensure there are three essential features that can be easily identified. An example of a practice goal focused on acquisition for Maureen and Maria is as follows: "We will **practice implementing embedded learning opportunities** for <u>one child's</u> *priority learning target*. We will provide *at least one embedded learning opportunity* <u>during snacktime</u> *every day for 1 week*." Broken out into parts, the goal looks like this:

Practice: **practice implementing embedded learning opportunities**

How much/how often: *one child's priority learning target; one embedded learning opportunity; every day for a week*

When/where/with whom: <u>during snacktime; one child</u>

Another example goal associated with a Pyramid Model (Hemmeter et al., 2013) practice and the fluency stage of learning is as follows: "I will **provide** *at least three* **positive reminders about posted expectations/rules** to either an <u>individual child or to a group of children during each large group time</u> *every day for 1 week*." Broken out into parts, the goal looks like this:

Practice: **provide positive reminders about posted expectations/rules**

How much/how often: *at least three [reminders]; every day for 1 week*

When/where/with whom: <u>during each large group time; individual child or group of children</u>

Table 6.2 shows additional examples of goals that have the three essential features and compares them to goals that do not. Figure 6.3 shows common issues that might arise when writing goals and provides tips for addressing these issues.

Essential Features of PBC Goals

1. **Observable action or behavior (practice) the coachee will do**

2. *How much or how often the practice will be seen or heard*

3. <u>When, where, and with whom the practice will be implemented</u>

Table 6.2. Comparison of practice-based coaching goals with and without three essential features

Practice focus	Goal with three essential features	Goals without three essential features
Embedded instruction	I will **provide** *four* **embedded instruction learning trials that include planned or logical consequences** for <u>a child's</u> *priority learning target* <u>during morning circle and snack</u> *each day for 2 weeks*.	I will provide consequences to make my embedded instruction learning trials complete.
	I will **develop and use an activity matrix** that has *three priority learning targets* each for <u>three children</u>. Each learning target for each child will be distributed across at least <u>one teacher-directed and one child-initiated activity</u> *each day for 1 week*.	I will make an activity matrix.
Pyramid Model	<u>Right before children transition from circle to centers</u> *each day for 2 weeks*, I will **use the posted visual behavior expectations as a prompt as I verbally review the center-time expectations**.	I will teach behavior expectations.
	I will **watch** <u>**Brenden and Kyla**</u> <u>during centers and outdoor play and when appropriate to the situation</u>, I will **label their emotions**. I will **ask them to repeat my model**. I will do this *each day for 2 weeks*.	I will teach children to express emotions.
Literacy practices	<u>When reading a book with children</u>, I will **use the PEER (prompt, evaluate, expand, repeat) sequence and focus on completion prompts** (e.g., Humpty Dumpty sat on a _____). I will do this *each day for 3 days*.	I will use dialogic reading with my children.
	During <u>small-group instruction</u>, I will use a set of 10 picture cards, some of which are rhyming words. I will **select two cards from the set, name the picture on each card, and then ask the** <u>**children**</u>, "[_____] and [_____]. **Do these two words sound the same?**" I will *repeat this 5 times* and will do this *once each day for 5 days*.	I will teach rhyming words.

Note: Three essential features should be included when writing PBC goal statements: 1) the observable action or behavior (practice) the coachee will do, 2) how much or how often the practice will be seen or heard, and 3) when, where and with whom the practice will be implemented. The observable action or behavior (practice) can be considered the WHAT of the goal. How much or how often the practice will be seen or heard refers to QUANTITY. When, where, and with whom refers to the SETTING AND PEOPLE. We use bold, italics, and underline to highlight these features for coachees and coaches: **Bold**, observable behavior or action (practice) to be implemented; *italics*, how much or how often the practice will be seen or heard; <u>underline</u>, when/where/with whom the practice will be implemented.

Issue	Why is it an issue?	Tip
Focusing <u>only</u> on making materials (e.g., visual schedule, rules/expectation)	• No observable action the coachee(s) will do in the classroom • Likely to be achieved in <2 weeks	• Focus on how the coachee will use the material to implement a practice. • Make developing/making the material an action step to achieve the goal.
Taking the practice straight from the strengths and needs assessment, practice inventory, or observational tool	• Often too broad • Not individualized to meet the needs of the coachee	• Consider available data about the extent to which the coachee currently uses the practice. • Consider coachee's phase and pace of learning (e.g., acquisition goal if just learning a practice, fluency goal if coachee wants to implement the practice accurately and efficiently). • Focus on how and when the coachee will use the practice and reflect on the goal.
Focusing on too many practices	• The goal is too big to be accomplished in 2–4 weeks • Overwhelming for the coachee	• Break practices down into a logical sequence for multiple action plans. • Consider which practice(s) are high leverage and will have the greatest impact on quality practice.

Figure 6.3.   Common goal-setting issues and tips for addressing them. (Source: Bishop, et. al. 2019).

ACTION PLANNING AND ACTION PLANS

Once a goal is specified, action planning occurs and an action plan is written. Action planning is the process of identifying a set of related short-term activities or steps which, when accomplished, will support goal attainment. Stober and Grant (2006a) noted action planning involves facilitating a coachee's transition from a deliberative frame of reference to an implementation frame of reference. A deliberative frame of reference occurs during action planning when the coachee, with assistance from the coach in expert or peer PBC, carefully identifies and considers the pros and cons of each goal and associated action steps as well as competing goals or action steps. Once the action plan activities or steps are determined and the plan is written, a focus on practice implementation is engaged because concrete and specific actions aligned with the goal have been identified.

PBC Action Plans: Five Parts

1. Goal statement

2. Criterion or goal achievement statement

3. Action steps

4. Resources

5. Timelines for completing each action step

PBC action plans have five parts: 1) goal statement, 2) criterion or goal achievement statement, 3) action steps, 4) resources, and 5) timelines for completing each action step. Figure 6.4 shows an example PBC action plan for Maureen and Maria with these five parts.

Goal Statement

The goal statement on the action plan describes the actions or behaviors (practice) that Maureen and Maria have identified as a priority. In Figure 6.4, the goal has the three key features and is stated as follows, "We will **practice implementing embedded learning opportunities** for *one priority learning target for <u>three children</u>* in <u>*two classroom activities each day*</u>." This goal is focused on generalization of embedded instruction practices because they are prioritizing embedding learning opportunities with multiple children and in multiple activities.

Criterion Statement

The criterion statement describes when or how the coachee and coach will know the goal has been achieved. This is sometimes referred to as a goal achievement statement. The statement

Action Plan

Coachee(s): _Maureen and Maria_ **Coach:** _Elley_ **Date:** _October 5_ **Action Plan:** _1_

Implementation Goal
We will practice implementing embedded learning opportunities for one priority learning target for three children in two classroom activities each day.

Criterion or Goal Achievement Statement
We will know we have achieved this goal when we have collected data (i.e., tally marks on an activity matrix) showing we have implemented at least one embedded learning opportunity for each child's priority learning target in at least two classroom activities each day for 1 week.

	Steps to achieve this goal	Resources needed	Timeline
1	We will revise the priority learning targets we wrote during the embedded instruction workshops. Maureen will email the revised learning targets to Elley for feedback and include Maria on the email. **(Learn more)**	Learning targets Time to revise learning targets Models from the Practice Guide (p. 23) Elley's feedback	10/7 (next coaching session)
2	We will look at examples of activity matrices in the practice guide. Maria will make an activity matrix showing the planned number of opportunities for each priority learning target and activity that we can hang on the wall. Maureen will make a printable version of the activity matrix with space for tally marks. **(Learn more and Make)**	Practice Guide p. 50, 51, 98 Time to make the matrices Printer Materials for wall matrix	10/12
3	We will practice implementing embedded learning opportunities and collecting data during classroom activities. We will take turns collecting data for each other during whole group activities when opportunities are planned. **(Practice and Collect data)**	Paper activity matrix	10/12 and then ongoing
4	We will share and discuss our data each day at naptime and talk together about additional resources or reminders we might need to help us implement embedded learning opportunities for each priority learning target in at least two classroom activities every day. **(Talk to)**	Daily naptime meeting	10/20 (after fall break) and then ongoing
5	We will review our data with Elley at each coaching session to see if we are making progress or have met our goal. **(Summarize and Analyze data)**	Time with our coach to review data Paper activity matrices with data	10/23 and then ongoing

Review		
Review Date 1: _____ ( ) Goal achieved! ( ) Making progress, but not there yet. ( ) Modified or changed my goal.	Review Date 2: _____ ( ) Goal achieved! ( ) Making progress, but not there yet. ( ) Modified or changed my goal.	Review Date 3: _____ ( ) Goal achieved! ( ) Making progress, but not there yet. ( ) Modified or changed my goal.

Figure 6.4. Example Action Plan. From Embedded Instruction for Early Learning. (2018). _Example Action Plan. Embedded Instruction._ Retrieved from https://embeddedinstruction.net/; reprinted by permission from the Anita Zucker Center for Excellence in Early Childhood Studies, University of Florida.

should be observable and measurable. It should be directly linked to the goal statement. In expert and peer PBC formats, criterion statements are generated collaboratively by the coachee and coach. In the self-coaching PBC format, the coachee determines their own goal and criterion statement. Criterion statements are informed by the goal statement, the strengths and needs assessment information, and planned action steps. Criterion statements are used to decide when a goal is met and a new goal and accompanying action plan is needed. They should include information about who will collect data to inform the decision about whether the goal is met and what data will be collected. For the example goal in Figure 6.4, the criterion statement is as follows: "We will know we have achieved this goal when we have collected data (i.e., tally marks on an activity matrix) showing we have implemented at least one embedded learning opportunity for each child's priority learning target in at least two classroom activities each day for 1 week." This criterion statement specifies that the coachees (Maureen and Maria) will be responsible for collecting the data and gives specific information about the criterion (i.e., at least one embedded learning opportunity for each child's priority learning target in at least two classroom activities each day for 1 week) that will be used to measure whether the goal is met.

Action Steps

Action steps are the activities or steps to be completed by the coachee that will help them achieve the goal. Action steps should be clearly linked to and aligned with the goal statement. They should describe who or what will be involved and which specific actions will be taken.

Action steps generally should be logically sequenced based on the coachee's current strengths and needs and with respect to the practice that is the focus of the goal and action plan. Figure 6.5 provides tips for writing action steps that are logically sequenced. The action steps in Figure 6.4 are clearly linked to Maureen and Maria's goal and are written following the tips listed in Figure 6.5. First, Maureen and Maria have planned to *learn more* about the practice by looking at models and reviewing sections of the practice guides they received during the virtual workshop. Next, they needed to *learn more* about and *make* an activity matrix. Then, they specified how they will practice. As they practice, they plan to take turns *collecting* data so they will be able to determine with Elley (their coach) when they have met their goal. This is particularly important for Maureen and Maria to do because they are participating in virtual coaching that involves asynchronous focused observation. Finally, Maureen and Maria have stated how they will *talk to* each other and Elley to *summarize and analyze* data about how many times they embed learning opportunities for each child and in how many activities each day. Each action plan step aligns with Maureen and Maria's goal statement and will help them achieve their goal of generalizing their use of embedded instruction practices across children and activities. In addition, the action steps related to data collection are aligned with the criterion statement and will help Maureen, Maria, and Elley know when the goal has been met.

> Action steps are the activities or steps to be completed by the coachee that will help them achieve the goal. Action steps should be clearly linked to and aligned with the goal statement.

Resources

The resources, material or human, needed to accomplish each action step are also specified on the action plan. Resources might include people (e.g., coach, teaching assistant); materials (e.g., visual cues, toys, books); and handouts, websites, or articles that provide information or illustrations relevant for the action step. Examples of resources linked to each action step are shown in Figure 6.4.

Tip 1	**Identify strategies to learn more about the practice (Learn more)**

Tip 1   **Identify strategies to learn more about the practice (Learn more)**

- *What does the coachee need to learn, watch, read, or analyze to get started?*

Example—Step 1 on action plan: I will watch video examples of teachers providing positive reminders about classroom expectations and rules with Jamie during naptime.

Tip 2   **Specify the actions to be taken (Make, Talk to, Practice)**

- *What does the coachee (or coach) need to make?*

Example—Step 2 on action plan: I will make a list of positive reminder starter phrases and post them in centers or at the circle time carpet where children typically need the most reminders about them (e.g., blocks, dramatic play, story time, music and movement).

- *Who does the coachee need to talk to about the action plan goal and steps?*

Example—Step 3 on action plan: I will share the positive reminders with Jamie and talk with her about them.

- *What will the coachee be seen or heard doing in the classroom?*

Example—Step 4 on action plan: I will continue to review the center and circle expectations and rules with the children. I will give positive reminders to children about the expectations and rules when they are in centers and at circle.

Tip 3   **Specify actions for collecting, summarizing, and analyzing data (Collect, Summarize, and Analyze data)**

- *How will data be collected and summarized?*

Example—Step 5 on the action plan: I will use a rubber-band system to count how many positive reminders I provide to an individual child (blue rubber band) or to a group of children (red rubber band) during centers and circle. I will summarize my rubber-band data each day on a sheet of paper. I will analyze the data with Kenya (coach) during our next coaching session.

- *Be sure actions for summarizing and analyzing data are aligned with the criterion or goal achievement statement.*

Example—In this example, Sam's (coachee's) goal achievement statement is providing at least three positive reminders during center time and circle time (six total) to either individual children or a group of children every day for 3 weeks. The actions for summarizing and analyzing data are aligned with his goal.

Figure 6.5. Tips for writing logically sequenced action steps for action plans with examples for Sam. Adapted from Anita Zucker Center for Excellence in Early Childhood Studies (2019) *Practice-Based Coaching Coach Training*. Adapted by permission from the Anita Zucker Center for Excellence in Early Childhood Studies, University of Florida.

Timelines

Timelines for action steps should be considered in relation to the general timeframe for goal attainment, which is 2–4 weeks. Timelines should take into consideration anticipated breaks or holidays. As shown in the example in Figure 6.4, extra time has been planned between Steps 3 and 4 to account for fall break. Timelines should allow for the coachee to complete action steps between coaching sessions. They do not always need to be anchored to the date of a coaching session. The timelines shown in Figure 6.4 show that some action steps (i.e., Step 1) will be completed by the date of a coaching session because the coach will do them; however, other steps are determined based on when it is feasible for the coachees to complete them and are not anchored to a coaching date. Some action steps (i.e., Steps 3–5) show a beginning date and state that they will be ongoing, because these are actions the coachees will continue to do until the goal is met.

SMA²R²T Goals and Action Plans

A popular framework for goal setting is known by the acronym SMART (David et al., 2016). This acronym has also been used to guide the development of quality goals and objectives in special education (e.g., Jung, 2007). Although the acronym is widely used, different terms have been associated with several of the SMART acronym letters. For example, *A* has been associated with *attainable* but also with *agreed*. *R* has been associated with *realistic* but also with *routines based* (David et al., 2016; Jung, 2007). Although some have called into question the sole use of SMART goals in coaching and mentoring (David et al., 2016), in PBC we assert that it is important for goals and action plans to be SMA²R²T. Our adapted SMART acronym stands for *specific, measurable, achievable/action oriented, relevant/realistic,* and *time framed*. We have described and illustrated previously how to write goals and associated action plans that are SMA²R²T.

> **SMA²R²T PBC Shared Goals and Action Plans**
> - Specific
> - Measurable
> - Achievable/action oriented
> - Relevant/realistic
> - Time framed

PUTTING IT ALL TOGETHER

In this chapter, we have described and illustrated four actions for the PBC component of shared goal setting and action planning: 1) assess practice-focused strengths and needs, 2) review and discuss strengths and needs assessment information, 3) identify and write an observable and measurable goal, and 4) write action plans that align with the goal.

It is important to remember that the action plan provides a road map for coaching. Action plans provide transparency and accountability for the coachee and the coach. In expert and peer PBC, they guide coachee–coach interactions for what will be observed, when coaches or coachees will observe, what data coachees and coaches will collect during focused observations or at other times, what actions or behaviors will be the focus for reflection and feedback, and how fidelity of practice implementation will be measured. In self-coaching, the action plan is an accountability plan, guiding the coachee on what to observe about her or his actions or behaviors and how to self-monitor and self-evaluate practice implementation.

> **Shared Goal Setting and Action Planning**
> 1. Assess practice-focused strengths and needs
> 2. Review and discuss strengths and needs assessment information
> 3. Identify and write an observable and measurable goal
> 4. Write action plans that align with the goal

REVISITING THE CASE STORIES

In this chapter, we illustrated the three essential features of PBC goal statements and the parts of action plans that make up the SMA²R²T framework for PBC shared goals and action plans using the Maureen, Maria, and Elley case story. In the sections that follow, we return to the case stories for Sam and Lynn that were introduced in Chapter 2. First, we will follow Sam and Kenya as they (a) assess practice-focused strengths and needs, related to Pyramid Model practices from the Teaching Pyramid Observation Tool (TPOT; Hemmeter et al., 2014); (b) review and discuss strengths and needs assessment information; (c) identify and write an observable and measurable goal; and (d) write an action plan that aligns with their goal. At the end of the case story, guiding questions are provided. Use these questions to guide further reflection about whether Kenya and Sam applied the SMA²R²T framework and how the framework might be applied using different PBC delivery formats.

In the second case story, we revisit the four actions that were described and illustrated in this chapter related to shared goal setting and action planning. Activities illustrating how these actions were implemented using the Lynn case story are presented. Review the case story information with a colleague and apply the content from the present chapter to write an observable and measurable goal and an aligned action plan for Lynn. Use the action plan template in Appendix III.G. When the goal and action plan are written, use the Action Plan Fidelity Checklist in Appendix III.H to self-check if key parts of action plans and the SMA^{2}R^{2}T framework are included. Reflect on the process with your colleague.

> **Tools for Coaches in the Appendices**
>
> *Appendix III.G: Action Plan Template and Appendix III.H: Action Plan Fidelity Checklist*
>
> These appendices contain a blank action plan and a blank Action Plan Fidelity Checklist that are useful for shared goal setting and action planning.

Sam and Kenya

1. Assess Practice-Focused Strengths and Needs

As Sam and Kenya prepared to write a fifth goal and action plan, they decided that they each would complete a formal strengths and needs assessment to inform their discussion. Sam completed the Pyramid Model Practice Implementation Checklist for practices associated with high-quality environments (Teaching Pyramid Research Project, 2012). The checklist included practices related to schedules and routines, classroom design, promoting children's engagement, transitions, and expectations and rules. Kenya observed in Sam's classroom and completed the TPOT (Hemmeter et al., 2014). Given that Sam had previous goals and action plans focused on practices associated with high-quality environments, Kenya made a graph showing changes in his implementation of practices in these areas from August to January.

2. Review and Discuss Strengths and Needs Assessment Information

When Sam and Kenya met to discuss their strengths and needs assessment information and review previous goals and action plans, Kenya asked Sam to reflect on his use of Pyramid Model practices by discussing areas of strength or growth in practice use. Sam shared that he was regularly reviewing his posted visual schedule to teach the schedule and to prepare children for changes in the schedule. Although he hadn't specifically focused on transitions, Sam reflected that referring to his visual schedule more often has helped his transitions become smoother as well. When Kenya asked what practice Sam might want to prioritize for his next goal and action plan, he mentioned that he was still having difficulty promoting children's engagement in circle and at centers. He reflected that during those times, he frequently had to redirect children. He asked Kenya what she thought about a goal focused on engagement. Kenya said, "Let's look at the TPOT I completed to see which practices you are implementing related to promoting children's engagement. Your large-group activities were structured so that children had opportunities to be actively engaged, and you helped children who needed it to become more actively engaged during centers. One thing I observed and wrote down in my notes was that when children were engaged, you occasionally commented positively on what children were doing or when they were following the rules and expectations." Sam smiled and said, "I didn't even think I did that at all, so I'm glad you saw it a few times! I remember from the workshops learning why it is important to provide positive and descriptive feedback to children when they are engaged or following classroom expectations and rules. I remember seeing a few examples of other teachers doing it. I just get so preoccupied with helping children engage and stay engaged or follow the expectations and rules, that I forget to let them know that they are doing it! I know it when I see it, but I don't tell them."

3. Identify and Write a Goal

Kenya said, "Those are such good observations and reflections about your practice implementation, Sam. Providing more positive descriptive feedback to children when they are engaged in activities or follow the expectations or rules helps them know that they are doing and what is expected during the activity. You also noted, and I saw in my TPOT observation, that your redirections are primarily related to classroom expectations and rules. Another option for a goal could be to focus on teaching expectations and rules more explicitly, the way you have started to do with the schedule. We could work on reviewing the expectations and rules, giving positive reminders about them or giving positive descriptive feedback to children when they are following them. Which focus do you think sounds like the best fit right now?" After thinking it over, Sam decided that he really wanted to focus on providing more reminders about the expectations and rules. He had classroom expectations and related rules he reviewed regularly with the children, but he realized he needed to provide reminders about them, particularly during center and circle time—not just during transitions. And, he thought that providing reminders to children would also help him remember to provide feedback to them about following the expectations and rules during these activities. Together, Sam and Kenya wrote the following goal: I will provide at least three positive reminders about the posted expectations and rules to either an individual child or to a group of children during center time and circle time every day. They agreed the criterion statement should include providing the reminders every day for 3 consecutive weeks.

Questions for Discussion and Further Reflection

- How did Sam and Kenya use their strengths and needs assessment information to inform goal setting?

- Use Figure 6.5 to determine whether the action steps on the plan are logically sequenced. What, if any, action steps might be added, removed, or modified based on what you know about Sam's goal and his phase of learning?

- Use the SMA^{2}R^{2}T framework to determine whether the goal and action plan are specific, measurable, achievable/action oriented, relevant/realistic, and time framed. Where do you see these characteristics reflected in the action plan?

---

4. Write an Action Plan That Aligns With the Goal

After they wrote the goal, Sam and Kenya worked together to write an action plan with a criterion statement, action steps, resources, and timelines. The action plan they wrote is shown in Figure 6.6.

Lynn and Sirena

1. Assess Practice-Focused Strengths and Needs

Lynn has completed the strengths and needs assessment, which includes nine effective practices for supporting children's language development (see Figure 6.7). Carefully examine her strengths and needs assessment responses. Sirena has conducted an initial observation in the classroom focused on the nine practices included on the strengths and needs assessment. She also has completed a strengths and needs assessment about Lynn's practice implementation based on her classroom observations (see Figure 6.8).

2. Review and Discuss Strengths and Needs Assessment Information

Using Lynn's strengths and needs assessment, participate with a colleague in a role play where you take on the role of a coach and your colleague assumes the role of Lynn. Discuss the strengths and needs assessments remembering the information you know about Lynn and Sirena. Ask for clarification and verification of the strengths and needs assessment information (Snyder & Wolfe, 2008). Discuss the rationale for Lynn's top coaching priority and confirm that it remains a priority.

Action Plan

Coachee(s): Sam   **Coach:** Kenya   **Date:** January 30   **Action Plan:** 5

Implementation Goal
Goal I want to achieve:
I will provide at least three positive reminders about the posted expectations and rules to either an individual child or to a group of children during center time and circle time every day.

Criterion or Goal Achievement Statement
My data show I provide at least three positive reminders about the expectations and rules to either an individual child or a group of children in centers and during circle time (6 total) every day for 3 consecutive weeks.

Steps to achieve this goal		Resources needed	Timeline
1	I will watch video examples of teachers providing positive reminders about classroom expectations and rules with Jamie during naptime. **(Learn more)**	Video examples from coach Time to watch videos with Jamie	Fri. 2/1
2	I will make a list of positive reminder starter phrases and post them in centers or near the circle time carpet where children typically need the most reminders (e.g., blocks, dramatic play, story time, music and movement) and share it with Jamie. **(Make)**	Construction paper Computer/printer Planning time	Wed. 2/6
3	I will share the positive reminders with Jamie and talk with her about them. **(Talk to)**	Planning time	Wed. 2/6
4	I will continue to review the center and circle expectations and rules with the children. I will give positive reminders to individual or groups of children about the expectations and rules when they are in centers and at circle. **(Practice)**	Positive reminder starter phrases	Wed. 2/20
5	I will use a rubber-band system to count how many positive reminders I provide to an individual child (blue rubber band) or to a group of children (red rubber band) during center and circle. I will summarize my rubber-band data each day on a sheet of paper. I will analyze the data with Kenya during our next coaching session. **(Collect, Summarize, Analyze data)**	Blue and red rubber bands Paper Time with coach	Wed. 3/6

Review		
Review Date 1: _____ ( ) Goal achieved! ( ) Making progress, but not there yet. ( ) Modified or changed my goal.	Review Date 2: _____ ( ) Goal achieved! ( ) Making progress, but not there yet. ( ) Modified or changed my goal.	Review Date 3: _____ ( ) Goal achieved! ( ) Making progress, but not there yet. ( ) Modified or changed my goal.

Figure 6.6. Goal and Action Plan completed by Sam and Kenya. From National Center for Pyramid Model Innovations (2018). *Coaching*. Challenging Behavior. Retrieved from https://challengingbehavior.cbcs.usf.edu/Implementation/coach.html

Coachee: __Lynn__   Coach: __Sirena__   Date: __October 15__

Coachee Strengths and Needs Assessment

Practice	How often?				Change needed?	Priority (Top 5)	Notes
	Never/ Seldom	Sometimes	Most of the time	Always			
1. I talk to children throughout the day during activities and routines.	1	2	3	(4)	No		
2. I respond immediately and positively to children's attempts to communicate.	1	2	(3)	4	No		
3. I have back-and-forth conversations or exchanges with children, appropriate for their developmental level.	1	(2)	3	4	**Yes**	5	Need to focus on modeling language for children first so they can engage in back-and-forth exchanges
4. I talk about many different things children are feeling, doing, or experiencing throughout the day.	1	(2)	3	4	**Yes**	3	
5. I use a wide range of words to describe objects, actions, and experiences throughout the day.	1	2	(3)	4	No		
6. I describe my actions as I am doing them (i.e., self-talk).	1	2	(3)	4	No		
7. I describe children's actions as they do them (i.e., parallel talk).	(1)	2	3	4	**Yes**	2	
8. I add more words or ideas to what children say.	(1)	2	3	4	**Yes**	1	
9. I ask open-ended questions to facilitate children's use of language.	1	(2)	4	4	**Yes**	4	

Key Strengths

Three strengths I have that I think support implementation of practices:

1. *I try to spend time playing with children in every center. When I visit centers, I talk about the toys children are using.*

2. *I do my best to respond to children as soon as possible. I know it is important to acknowledge when children communicate with me, even if my response is brief.*

3. *I describe what I am doing so children have opportunities to hear more language.*

Coaching Priorities

Three practices I want to prioritize for coaching:

1. *I would like to model more language by describing what children do and say in the classroom. I only do this a little bit right now.*

2. *I need ideas for how to expand children's language. I am not sure what language is most appropriate to use to expand language for children of this age.*

3. *I would like some help to make sure I use a variety of words to describe children's experiences and feelings. I already describe objects they play with but don't really describe their feelings or experiences. I think this is important for children this age.*

Figure 6.7.   Coachee Strengths and Needs Assessment completed by Lynn.

Coachee: _Sirena_   Coach: _Lynn_   Date: _October 15_

Coach Strengths and Needs Assessment

The coachee is doing this now	Coaching priority
1—Not at all/Seldom 2—Some of the time 3—Most of the time 4—Always (or almost always)	1—Not a priority or already fluent 2—Low priority 3—Moderate priority 4—Immediate priority

Practice	The coachee is doing this now . . .				Coaching priority level			
1. Talks to children throughout the day during routines and in play	1	2	③	4	1	②	3	4
2. Responds positively and immediately to children's attempts to communicate	1	2	3	④	①	2	3	4
3. Has back-and-forth conversations or exchanges with children, appropriate for their developmental level	1	②	3	4	1	2	③	4
4. Talks about many different things children are feeling, doing, or experiencing throughout the day	1	②	3	4	1	2	③	4
5. Uses a wide range of words to describe objects, actions, and experiences throughout the day	1	②	3	4	1	2	3	④
6. Describes own actions as they do them (i.e., self-talk)	1	②	3	4	1	2	3	④
7. Describes children's actions as they do them (i.e., parallel talk)	①	2	3	4	1	2	3	④
8. Adds more words or ideas to what children say	1	②	3	4	1	2	3	④
9. Asks open-ended questions to facilitate children's use of language	①	2	3	4	1	2	③	4

Additional Notes/Comments:

Three children became upset during observation; teacher responded immediately and was able to calm or redirect each child successfully.
Teacher repeated child phrase: 10 times; Teacher expanded child phrase: 3 times
Back and forth exchanges: 3 observed
Questions: You want that? What do you have? What shape? Can I have a turn?

Figure 6.8.   Coach Strengths and Needs Assessment completed by Sirena.

3.   Identify and Write a Goal

Based on your discussion with Lynn, identify and write a goal. Be sure the goal has the three essential features: 1) **the observable action or behavior (practice) to be implemented,** *2) how much or how often the practice will be seen or heard, and 3)* when, where, and with whom the practice will be implemented.

4.   Write an Action Plan That Aligns With the Goal

Use the template (Appendix III.G) to write an action plan that aligns with the goal you wrote for Lynn. Use the Action Plan Fidelity Checklist shown in Table 6.3 (Appendix III.H) to ensure that your action plan has appropriate goal and criterion statements; action steps that are specific, aligned with the goal, and in a logical sequence; and resources and timelines that

Table 6.3. Action Plan Fidelity Checklist

Action Plan Indicators	Yes	No
Implementation goal		
1. **Practice oriented:** The goal supports the coachee to <u>implement</u> effective practices with fidelity in context (i.e., action the coachee will do vs. making materials).		
2. **Effective practices:** The goal is directly aligned with one or more of the targeted effective practices.		
3. **Observable:** The goal describes actions or behaviors of the coachee that can be observed (i.e., such that two people could agree when the practice occurred).		
4. **Achievable:** Given the coachee's knowledge, skills, and preferences, the goal is achievable in 2–4 weeks.		
Criterion or goal achievement statement		
5. **Observable:** The criterion statement includes actions or behaviors of the coachee that can be observed (i.e., two people could agree when the practice occurred).		
6. **Measurable:** The criterion statement includes a performance statement including how often *or* how much (i.e., how many times) a practice will be implemented and for how long (i.e., number of days).		
7. **Goal focused:** The criterion or goal achievement statement is aligned with the implementation goal (i.e., includes the same practice and observable actions or behaviors stated in the implementation goal).		
Action steps		
8. **Specific:** The action steps describe observable actions or behaviors the coachee will do (e.g., Read, Watch, Make, Implement, Talk to, Analyze).		
9. **Aligned:** The action steps include key words associated with the practice and observable behaviors specified in the goal.		
10. **Logical sequence:** The action steps occur in a chronological or progressive order, which move the coachee toward accomplishing the goal by meeting the criterion or goal achievement statement specified.		
11. **Resources:** When appropriate, the specific human (i.e., who and for how long) and material resources (i.e., what and where to locate) needed to achieve each action step are specified.		
12. **Timelines:** The timelines for action steps occur within 2–4 weeks and are feasible for the coachee.		
Collaboration		
13. **Utility:** The action plan is written clearly in language the coachee can understand.		

From Embedded Instruction for Early Learning (2016). *Action plan fidelity checklist.* Used with permission from the Anita Zucker Center for Excellence in Early Childhood Studies, University of Florida.

are specified for each action step. As specified in the fidelity checklist, the language used in the action plan should be clear and understood by the coachee—in this case Lynn. If terms or vocabulary words are new for the coachee, be sure to include a definition for the term in a footnote and discuss it with the coachee. The action plan is kept by Lynn. As her coach, you will want to have a copy of the plan. It is important to remember, however, that the plan has been written for Lynn.

Questions for Further Reflection and Discussion

- How did the strengths and needs assessment information inform your shared goal setting and action planning?

- What sources of information, in addition to the strengths and needs assessment information, did you and your colleague use to arrive at the goal you wrote?

- From the perspective of the person who was Lynn (coachee) during the role play, what did Sirena (coach) do to support you with goal setting and action planning? What did Sirena do well? What might Sirena have done differently?

- From the perspective of the person who was Sirena (coach) during the role play, how did Lynn's actions or behaviors during the role play affect your actions or behaviors? What did Lynn do during goal setting and action planning that you expected? Did Lynn do anything you did not expect? If so, how did you respond?

- How and when might you use the Action Plan Fidelity Checklist as part of PBC implementation?

SUMMARY

PBC is a cyclical process. Informed by a practice-focused strengths and needs assessment, it begins with shared goal setting and action planning as described and illustrated in this chapter. The goal and action plan helps to identify what will be observed and how a focused observation will be conducted. What is observed is referenced to the goal specified on the action plan, progress made on action steps, and the status of goal achievement. The focused observation helps inform what occurs during reflection and feedback. What occurs during reflection and feedback connects back to informal or formal assessments of strengths and needs and to clarification and verification of the goal that has been set. The PBC cycle begins again. Once a goal is achieved, a new goal is identified and written, another action plan is developed and implemented, and the PBC cycle continues. All PBC cycles occur in the context of a collaborative partnership. The next chapter describes and illustrates the focused observation component of the PBC framework.

7

Focused Observation

Jessica K. Hardy, Ragan H. McLeod, and Mary Louise Hemmeter

FOCUSED OBSERVATION

In this chapter, we describe the focused observation component of practice-based coaching (PBC; see Figure 7.1). We clarify what makes an observation focused and why this emphasis is important for implementing PBC with fidelity. We discuss how the implementation goal and action plan guides a focused observation. Coaching processes and practices, including example coaching strategies used during focused observation, are described and illustrated using the case stories. Resources that support focused observation are provided.

FOCUSED OBSERVATION AND ITS IMPORTANCE IN PRACTICE-BASED COACHING

In PBC, a focused observation is an opportunity to gather information on the coachee's implementation of a specified set of effective practices. What makes a focused observation focused is that it is guided by the practice implementation goal specified on the action plan (Snyder et al., 2015).

> Focused observation is an opportunity to gather information on implementation of a specified set of effective practices.

During a focused observation, information is gathered on the coachee's current use of the practices, children's and others' responses to those practices, and potential opportunities or examples of how the coachee could modify, improve, or expand their use of those practices. The information is used to guide the reflection and feedback that follows the observation. A critical part of PBC is the delivery of performance-based feedback, which requires information that is anchored in the coachee's use of the identified practices (Barton et al., 2011). The context for the observation and the content of the reflection and feedback is focused on practice implementation goals and action plans. By focusing the observation and reflection and feedback on the goals and action plans, the coaching process is transparent, and it creates opportunities for the coachee to try new things, reflect on their use of practices, and receive performance-based feedback on implementation (McLeod et al., 2017).

Figure 7.1. Focused observation in the Practice-Based Coaching framework. From Snyder, P. A., Hemmeter, M. L., & Fox, L. (2015). Supporting implementation of evidence-based practices through practice-based coaching. *Topics in Early Childhood Special Education, 35*(3), 133–143. https://doi.org/10.1177/0271121415594925; reprinted by permission.

USING THE CURRENT GOAL AND ACTION PLAN TO GUIDE THE FOCUSED OBSERVATION

A focused observation in a PBC cycle is based on the current practice implementation goal and steps of the action plan. Without the goal or specific steps of an action plan to focus on, an observation is difficult to complete and is likely to lack focus (Crawford et al., 2013). The focused observation in each PBC cycle might focus on all the steps toward achieving a goal or some subset of steps. Often, goals and action plans are written so they will be achieved across 2–4 PBC cycles.

> **Key Point to Remember**
>
> Focused observation in a PBC cycle is based on the current practice implementation goal and steps of the action plan.

Sam's action plan centers on providing children with positive reminders about posted expectations and rules during centers and circle time. Sam and his coach, Kenya, agree that when Kenya conducts a focused observation, she will observe and collect data on Step 4 of Sam's action plan—Sam's use of positive reminders. Sam's other action plan steps are related to gaining knowledge of and preparing for implementing the practice. Kenya is going to do the observation live, and they have decided that the best time for Kenya to observe is during centers and circle time. They agree on a day to observe. Observations that follow this cycle might focus on Step 5, the next step in the action plan—Sam collecting and summarizing data on his use of positive reminders.

A coachee and coach might work on several practice implementation goals and action plan practices in a defined time frame (e.g., preschool year). As described in Chapter 6, these practices are usually related to an overarching set of effective practices (e.g., literacy practices, social-emotional practices, embedded instruction practices). For example, this year, Sam and Kenya are working on building Sam's skills in promoting children's social-emotional development and reducing challenging behavior. To achieve the overarching goal of having a quality classroom environment that promotes positive interactions and experiences for children and adults, Sam and Kenya have decided to focus their current goal and action plan on providing children with positive reminders about classroom expectations and rules.

Focused observations in each PBC cycle help the coachee and coach remain goal oriented, which has been identified as an important part of coaching for practice enhancement or change (Crawford et al., 2013; Grant, 2011; Snyder et al., 2015). Consider the following goal-oriented example from Maureen and Maria's classroom.

> **Key Point to Remember**
>
> Focused observations in each PBC cycle help the coachee and coach remain goal oriented.

Maureen and Maria (co-teachers) are working on a goal and action plan focused on how to use embedded instruction practices in their inclusive Head Start classroom. They meet virtually with their coach, Elley. At one of their meetings, Elley, Maureen, and Maria discuss how to record videos to allow Elley to observe and take data on their current practice goal, which is using an activity matrix to plan and implement embedded learning opportunities. The team discusses the activity matrix and how this could guide what activities they record on video. Their next video includes both small-group and free choice activities in which they implement embedded instruction with the children identified in the activity matrix. With the action plan in mind, Elley observes the specific practice implementation goal they identified.

After this successful focused observation experience, Elley reflected on one of her early coaching partnerships with another coachee—Suzette. Suzette had an action plan about asking open-ended questions to children. Elley conducted a focused observation but did not plan what types of information she needed to gather related to the current practice implementation goal and action plan. When she looked at her notes after the observation, she realized she had notes about a variety of practices and very few of the notes were focused on asking open-ended questions. She realized it was not a focused observation and recalled that when she and Suzette engaged in reflection and feedback based on her notes, Suzette appeared overwhelmed about everything Elley shared with her.

In the first example, Elley's focused observation was guided by the current practice implementation goal and action plan, which allowed her to collect information that would be useful in supporting reflection and feedback. In her reflection about past coaching experiences, Elley recognized that in the past she often collected either a random assortment of information that was too scattered to be helpful or she focused on too many practices at one time. In PBC, the current practice implementation goal and action plan should always be used to guide focused observation.

CONDUCTING A FOCUSED OBSERVATION

Careful planning for the focused observation is essential. If planning does not occur, the coachee and coach might have a difficult time interpreting the information gathered, which could negatively impact the quality of the other components of the PBC cycle. Coachees and coaches should prepare for and implement focused observations by identifying (a) the practice implementation goal or related action plan steps that will be the focus

> **Conducting a Focused Observation**
> - Identify the practice implementation goal or action plan steps that will be the focus of the observation.
> - Determine the methods for collecting and recording information.
> - Decide when and how the observation will be conducted.
> - Identify who will conduct the observation.
> - Determine what coaching strategies, in addition to observation, will be used.

of the observation; (b) methods for collecting and recording information; (c) when and how (e.g., live, review of video) the observation will be conducted; (d) who will conduct the observation; and (e) what coaching strategies, in addition to observation, will be used. What occurs during a focused observation should be always be discussed in collaboration with the coachee (McLeod et al., 2017; Snyder et al., 2015).

Type of Information to Be Collected

The information collected during a focused observation should be based on the current practice implementation goal and action plan. Before every focused observation, it is important to review the current goal and action plan. The information collected during focused observation should be used to help inform the reflection and feedback component of the coaching cycle.

Methods Used to Collect and Record Information

After reviewing the goal and action plan, consider what methods will be used to collect and record information. Focused observation data can be collected using different formats, such as written notes, numbers (e.g., number of descriptive praise statements used by the teacher during centers or length of time it takes children to complete a transition), or percentage of behaviors demonstrated. These different types of data can provide important insight into the coachee's use of the practices specified in the goal and action plan. Different types of data can be collected in the same focused observation, as in the following example.

Sirena conducted a focused observation in Lynn's toddler classroom. Lynn's current practice implementation goal and action plan include creating more opportunities to use language expansions in her classroom. Prior to the focused observation, Sirena and Lynn decided that Sirena would collect two types of data. First, she would count the number of language expansions and repetitions she heard Lynn use during the observation. Second, she would record verbatim the language expansions used by Lynn.

The data gathered during the focused observation should be aligned with the desired purpose. Purposes might include determining how often a practice is used, how fluently a practice is implemented, whether the coachee generalizes the practice across activities or routines or children, the children with whom the practice is used, or the contexts in which a practice is used.

In the first focused observation, Sirena only collected data on Lynn's use of language expansions and repetitions, but she did not identify with which children Lynn used expansions. Given this focus, Sirena's data did not provide evidence for the specific action plan step related to using the language expansions with "at least three children." Had Sirena also collected data on the children with whom Lynn used language expansions, she would have had additional information about Lynn's progress toward her goal and whether she achieved it. Having this information would have enhanced reflection and feedback. It also would have facilitated strengths and needs assessment and goal setting and action planning discussions for the next coaching cycle.

The data collection strategy used during the focused observation will depend on what type of information is appropriate based on the practice implementation goal and the goal achievement statement (Hojnoski, Gischlar, et al., 2009). If numeric data are appropriate, such as the frequency with which a behavior occurs, then a tally sheet can be used (see Figure 7.2 and Appendix IV.I). If duration of a behavior is relevant, then duration recording can be used

Tally Data Collection Form

Instructions: Write the goal that is the target of coaching ("Target goal"). Write the practice(s) related to that goal on which you plan to collect data ("Target practice"). Determine and write the frequency that is desired ("Target number"). Complete the start and stop times of the observation. During the focused observation, use the form to mark when the coachee used each practice and take notes of examples of practice implementation and missed opportunities. At the end of the focused observation, record the total number of tallies. Also calculate the total length of the observation and rate.

Target goal: _____

Start time: _____ Stop time: _____ Total length: _____

Target practice:	
Target number:	
Tally:	
Notes:	
Total number:	
Rate (Number/length):	

Figure 7.2. Tally Data Collection Form.

Duration Data Collection Form

Instructions: Write the goal that is the target of coaching ("Target goal"). Write the practice related to that goal on which you plan to collect data ("Target practice"). Determine and write the duration of the practice that is desired ("Target duration"). During the focused observation, use the form to mark the start and stop times of the target practice. At the end of the focused observation, complete the Scoring section to determine the total duration of practice use.

Target goal: _____

Target practice: _____

Target duration: _____

Start time: _____ Stop time: _____ Length: _____

Start time: _____ Stop time: _____ Length: _____

Start time: _____ Stop time: _____ Length: _____

Start time: _____ Stop time: _____ Length: _____

Scoring: Total duration = _____

Figure 7.3.   Duration Data Collection Form.

(see Figure 7.3 and Appendix IV.J). If descriptive information or specific examples are needed, then a notes form can be used (see Figure 7.4 and Appendix IV.K). If percentage of behaviors demonstrated is appropriate, a checklist can be used (see Figure 7.5 and Appendix IV.L). Multiple data collection strategies can be used in one focused observation if appropriate for the practice implementation goal, action plan step, or goal achievement statement on the current action plan. Data collection that occurs as part of focused observation might vary based on the coaching format used (e.g., expert, peer, self). Table 7.1 has additional information related to variations in data collection based on coaching formats.

There are some important considerations related to how information should be collected during focused observations. When taking notes or collecting data during a focused observation, the coach should be careful to be objective in taking notes and avoid making judgments or evaluations about the coachee's practice. A good rule is to consider that the notes would be

Practice-Based Coaching Focused Observation Notes		
Coachee(s):	**Coach:**	
Date:	**Observation Started:**	**Observation Ended:**
What was observed:	*To share with coachee(s):*	

Figure 7.4. Focused Observation Notes Form.

helpful to the coachee if they were left in the practice setting accidentally. A second consideration is that the coach should include specific examples of the coachee's implementation of the practices that are part of the goal and action plan. This will allow the coach to give the coachee examples rather than just numbers.

Sam wants specific information about how often he provides positive expectations and rule reminders. He also wants to know if he is stating the reminders positively. In addition to the data Sam plans to collect, Kenya will tally how often Sam provides positive and negative reminders. She adapts the tally data collection form shown in Figure 7.2 (and Appendix IV.I) to allow her to collect data on the frequency of positive and negative reminders and the classroom routines in which the reminders are provided (see Figure 7.6).

When and How the Focused Observation Will Be Conducted

The coachee and coach determine when and how to observe and collect the information of interest. Often, coaches observe coachees in the practice context, but livestream remote observations or video observations can also be used. As described further in Chapter 10, various types of technology can be used to obtain livestream or video of the coachee's practice implementation. Live, livestream, and video observations each have advantages and disadvantages that are listed in Table 7.2.

Percentage of Target Practices Data Collection Form

Instructions: Write the goal that is the target of coaching ("Target goal"). Write the practices related to that goal on which you plan to collect data ("Target practices"). Determine and write the percentage of practices that are desired to be present ("Target percentage present"). During the focused observation, use the checklist to mark when the coachee used the practice. Also, complete the start and stop times of the observation. At the end of the focused observation, complete the Scoring section to determine the percentage of practices present. Also, calculate the total length of the observation.

Target goal: _____

Target percentage present: _____

Start time: _____ Stop time: _____ Total length: _____

Target practices:

1.

2.

3.

4.

5.

6.

7.

8.

9.

Scoring: Total present: _____ / Total possible: _____ = _____ × 100 = _____%

Figure 7.5.   Percentage of Target Practices Data Collection Form.

Table 7.1. Coaching formats and data collection strategies

Coaching format	How data are collected
Expert	• Expert coach collects data live or via video.
Peer	• Peer coach collects data live or via video. • The peer coach and coachee should have materials to guide this process, such as an observation form that helps them complete the observation.
Self	• Coachee collects data on own use of practices, often via video. • If video is used, the self-coach watches the video to collect data for reflection and self-feedback. • The self-coach should have materials to guide this process, such as an observation form that helps them complete the observation.

Often, teachers express reluctance to be recorded on video. To address this concern, options can be provided to the coachee. For example, the coach could offer to do a live observation if the coachee does not want to be recorded on video. The coach could also suggest the coachee watch the video first and choose specific sections to share with the coach. The coaching agreement might include specific agreements related to the use of video (e.g., specific information about who will have access to the video, where the video will be stored, for how long the video will be stored). Coaches should ensure that videos are always securely stored, access is granted only to those who are involved in coaching, and a plan is in place for destroying the video after it is no longer needed. The coachee should always be consulted about storage and deletion policies and procedures. The coach could offer the coachee options about when and how they view videos—such as watching them together or watching them separately. The coach should always provide information about how and why videos will be used in PBC (e.g., focused observation, reflection and feedback).

Who Will Observe?

Focused observations can be conducted by coachees and by coaches when video recordings of practice implementation are available. Coachees who are self-coaching can conduct a focused observation using a video. Peers who are peer coaching can conduct live observations or watch livestream or video observations. Regardless of who is conducting a focused observation and how it is conducted, the current practice implementation goal and action plan should guide the focused observation.

Using Coaching Strategies During the Focused Observation

Before a focused observation occurs in the practice context, coaches and coachees identify what the coach will focus on during the observation, when and what the coach will observe, and what supports the coach will provide, when appropriate, during the focused observation. This typically happens as part of planning for the next coaching session during reflection and feedback in the current session, but it can also occur via phone, e-mail, or videoconference between the previous session and the upcoming focused observation. Coaching strategies commonly used during focused observations include modeling, side-by-side support cues, other help in the practice setting, quick problem-solving discussions, modeling, or quick environmental arrangements (see Chapter 4). The coachee and coach discuss which of these strategies are preferred and would be beneficial for the coachee. Factors to consider when determining the strategies to use are 1) coachee comfort with the strategy, 2) coach comfort/expertise with the strategy, and 3) alignment of the strategy with the goal and action plan steps.

Lynn and Sirena decide that, during the observation, it would be helpful for Sirena to provide hands-on support as needed to ensure that Lynn is able to focus on her interactions with children

Tally Data Collection Form

Instructions: Write the goal that is the target of coaching ("Target goal"). Write the practice(s) related to that goal on which you plan to collect data ("Target practice"). Determine and write the frequency desired of each practice ("Target number"). Complete the start and stop times of the observation. During the focused observation, use the form to mark when the coachee used each practice and take notes of examples of practice implementation and missed opportunities. At the end of the focused observation, write the total number of each practice. Also, calculate the total length of the observation and rate.

Target goal: *I will provide at least three positive reminders about the posted expectations and rules to either an individual child or to a group of children during center time and circle time every day.*

Start time: _____ 9:15 a.m. _____   Stop time: _____ 10:15 a.m. _____   Total length: _____ 60 min _____

Target practice	Provide positive reminders about the expectations and rules to individual children and groups of children during *centers*.	Provide positive reminders about the expectations and rules to individual children and groups of children during *circle* time.
Target number	3 At least 3:1 ratio of positive to negative	3 At least 3:1 ratio of positive to negative
Tally	Positive reminders: | | Negative reminders: | | | | |	Positive reminders: | Negative reminders: | | |
Notes	<u>Examples of positive reminders:</u> "My friends, remember to move your picture when you change centers." "Alex, remember to use your walking feet when you go to centers!" <u>Examples of negative reminders:</u> "Caleb, Emilia, and Jace, you forgot to clean up your center!" "Jess, don't run to the blocks center!"	<u>Examples of positive reminders:</u> "Friends, remember to sit with hands in lap during circle time." "Caiden, use your listening ears and looking eyes during circle time." <u>Examples of negative reminders:</u> "Jace, we don't lie on the floor during circle time." "Friends, stop yelling!"
Total number	Positive, 2; negative, 5	Positive, 1; negative, 3
Ratio	2:5	1:3

Figure 7.6.   Kenya's Tally Data Collection Form from Focused Observation of Sam.

Table 7.2. Advantages and disadvantages of live and video focused observations

Type of focused observation	Advantages	Disadvantages
Live on-site	• Coach can model practices before coachee implements. • Coach can provide verbal or gestural in-the-moment support. • Coach can see the big picture of the practice context, including children's interactions with each other or caregivers' interactions with the child.	• Reflection and feedback are based only on the coach's observation and notes, without an objective view of the practice context through video.
Live remote (e.g., livestream)	• Coach can provide verbal in the moment support using technology such as bug-in-ear.	• Coach may not see all parts of the practice context or hear everything depending on the locations of the technology (e.g., cameras, microphones). • Coaches and coachees must be comfortable using the technology. • Internet connections are required.
Video recorded	• Video is an objective view of the practice context. • Video clips can serve as video models of practice. • Video clips can provide anchors for reflection and feedback about practice opportunities or missed opportunities. • Coach and coachee can view the video together to discuss practice implementation during reflection and feedback. • Coachee can view the video independently to support reflection prior to meeting with the coach.	• Coach may not see all parts of the practice context or hear everything depending on the locations of the technology (e.g., cameras, microphones). • Coachees and coaches must be comfortable using the technology. • If videos are shared via online platforms, internet must be available. • If videos are shared via online platforms, there must be a secure site for uploading videos.

as she is practicing language expansions. For example, Sirena may help a child who is upset or may redirect children to their centers when they wander. Lynn has also asked for Sirena to model a few language expansions for her during mealtimes and free choice with a child who is not one of the three children she plans to interact with during these activities. Lynn wants to see how Sirena does this in Lynn's classroom, because although she has seen video examples of teachers using language expansions, the children in those video examples were older and had more language than her children.

Because Maureen and Maria are video recording their focused observations and meeting with Elley virtually, the strategies they use will be different from those of Lynn and Sirena. Elley cannot provide other help in the classroom. However, Elley, Maureen, and Maria have agreed that Elley will provide video examples that Maureen and Maria can view independently or together. In addition, they have decided that Elley will provide support with environmental arrangement as part of their next videoconference meeting before recording the next practice implementation video for focused observation.

As part of reflection and feedback that follows a focused observation, the types of strategies that were used during the focused observation should be discussed to determine if the strategies provided the level of support the coachee needed or if they distracted the coachee or children. This information is important for determining ongoing supports for practice implementation before the next focused observation.

Modeling during the focused observation is an opportunity not only to demonstrate the practice but also to enhance the collaborative partnership. When a coach models for a coachee, the coachee might briefly assume the role of coach by recording data on the coach's implementation of the practice and the effects on the children. The coachee might also practice providing supportive and constructive feedback to the coach, and the coach can model reflection on their use of the practice and the feedback received. This can deepen the coachee's understanding of the practice as well as the other components of PBC and their relationship to focused observation. Alternatively, if the coachee has difficulty recording data, this might signal that the coachee needs more support in understanding what the practice looks or sounds like.

An additional coaching strategy is the use of video feedback. Whether the focused observation is conducted via distance or in the practice context, video recordings of the coachee using the practice can be powerful for supporting reflection and feedback about practice implementation. If the coachee is comfortable reviewing video observations, the coach could also use video observations as part of supportive and constructive feedback or problem-solving discussions.

When supporting Lynn to use language expansions with her toddlers, Sirena recorded video while observing Lynn during free choice. Sirena then clipped two examples of Lynn using high-quality expansions of toddlers' verbalizations. Sirena also identified one clip in which Lynn had an opportunity to expand a child's language but only repeated what the child said. Lynn and Sirena watch the clips together during reflection and feedback, and these video examples served as an anchor for Sirena's supportive and constructive feedback, their collaborative reflection, updates to Lynn's current action plan, and plans for the next focused observation.

As described in Chapter 4, explicit discussions about enhancement coaching strategies are important. The Coaching Strategies Discussion Worksheet can be used to support this discussion (see Figure 7.7 and Appendix VI.U). The coach and coachee can each complete the form, identifying preferred coaching strategies. The coach and coachee would then discuss their responses to determine which strategies would be relevant to their partnership (i.e., strategies they are both comfortable with) and relevant for supporting practice implementation. The Coaching Strategies Discussion Worksheet can also be used as a reflective tool for the coach to identify which strategies they may want additional support to use as a coach. Another tool is the Preferred Coaching Strategies Checklist (Appendix VI.S), which can be used to plan which coaching strategies are used as part of focused observation and reflection and feedback (see Figure 7.8 for an example for Maureen and Maria).

SUMMARY

A well-written practice implementation goal and action plan provides the context for conducting a focused observation. In this chapter, we have described collaborative coaching processes and practices related to focused observation. These include ensuring a focus for the observation, deciding what types of information or data will be collected and the methods used to collect it, determining when and how the focused observation will occur and who will conduct them, and what coaching strategies will be used during the observation. Each of these processes is necessary for an effective focused observation. An effective focused observation results in information that is used to guide reflection and feedback and prepare for the next coaching cycle.

Coaching Strategies Discussion Worksheet

Strategy	Brief description	Comfort level					Notes
		Not at all		→		Very	
Essential Strategies							
Observation	Coach watches and listens and takes notes to share with coachee.	1	2	3	4	5	
Reflective conversation	Interaction between coach and coachee to prompt thinking and discussion about practice implementation.	1	2	3	4	5	
Performance-based feedback	Performance-based feedback is verbal or written. Supportive feedback emphasizes practice implementation strengths and positive actions. Constructive feedback includes suggestions or supports for enhancing practice implementation.	1	2	3	4	5	
Identifying or providing resources or materials	Coach or coachee identifies or provides resources or materials the coachee uses to learn about or implement practice(s) that are the focus of the goal or action plan (e.g., visual schedule, activity matrix).	1	2	3	4	5	
Goal setting	Using your strengths, needs, and priorities to identify and write practice implementation goals and action plans and to review goals and action plans as part of each coaching session.	1	2	3	4	5	
Graphic feedback	A visual display of practice implementation or a child's behavior connected to practice implementation used as part of reflection and feedback.	1	2	3	4	5	
Video feedback	A video of practice implementation that either coachee or coach records that is used as part of reflection and feedback.	1	2	3	4	5	

Figure 7.7.   Coaching Strategies Discussion Worksheet.

Figure 7.7. Continued.

Strategy	Brief description	Comfort level					Notes
		Not at all		→		Very	
Enhancement Strategies							
Side-by-side support cues	Coach supports practice implementation in the moment, verbally, with gestures, with visual cues, or through technology (e.g., bug-in-ear).	1	2	3	4	5	
Other help in practice setting	Coach provides support to coachee or children that is not directly related to goal or action plan (e.g., wiping up spilled paint, sitting on the floor beside a child at circle).	1	2	3	4	5	
Problem-solving	Coachee and coach discuss a practice implementation issue and identify options to address the issue and solutions to try out.	1	2	3	4	5	
Role play	Coachee and coach take on other roles to practice implementation (e.g., coach acts as child, coachee acts as adult).	1	2	3	4	5	
Video examples	Video examples of how another practitioner uses a practice in a similar implementation setting.	1	2	3	4	5	
Modeling	Coach demonstrates or shows how to implement a practice that is the focus of a goal or action plan.	1	2	3	4	5	
Environmental arrangements	Coach helps coachee modify or enhance practice setting or materials in setting to set occasion for practice implementation.	1	2	3	4	5	
Graphing	Coach and coachee work together to graph data the coachee or coach has collected of coachee practice implementation or child behavior.	1	2	3	4	5	

ADDITIONAL NOTES:

Preferred Coaching Strategies Checklist

Instructions: Please mark your preferred enhancement coaching strategies using the checklist below. Please feel free to add comments as well!

Coachee: __Maureen and Maria__   **Date:** __October 5__

Enhancement Coaching Strategies	I'd like to try this strategy	Notes
1. **Side-by-side support cues:** The coach supports your practice implementation in the moment, verbally, with gestures, or with visual cues, or through technology (e.g., bug-in-ear).	X	May consider bug-in-ear at a later time
2. **Other help in practice setting:** The coach provides support to you or children, which is not directly related to your goal or action plan (e.g., wiping up spilled paint, sitting on the floor beside a child at circle).	n/a	
3. **Problem solving:** An interaction between you and the coach to solve an identified practice implementation issue. Problem-solving involves four steps: 1) identify the implementation issue, 2) generate potential solutions, 3) decide on a course of action, and 4) evaluate pros and cons of the selected course of action.	X	
4. **Role play:** In a role play, you and the coach take on other roles related to practice implementation (e.g., coach acts as child, coachee acts as adult).	X	
5. **Video examples:** Video examples show how another practitioner uses a practice in a similar implementation setting.	X	
6. **Modeling:** Modeling is demonstrating or showing you how to implement a practice that is the focus of a goal or action plan.	X	Only during reflection and feedback
7. **Environmental arrangements:** The coach helps you modify or enhance your practice setting or materials in your setting to set the occasion for you to implement a practice.	X	
8. **Graphing:** You and your coach work together to graph data you or your coach has collected about your practice implementation or child behaviors.	X	
9. **Other:** *In what other ways would you want your coach to help?*		

We really would like to learn how to collect and graph data for our children's IEP goals.

Figure 7.8. Preferred Coaching Strategies Checklist: Maureen and Maria's example.

8

Reflection and Feedback

Anna Winneker, Denise Perez Binder, and Lise Fox

REFLECTION AND FEEDBACK

The third component of a practice-based coaching (PBC) cycle is reflection and feedback. Both are essential elements of a PBC cycle. Engaging in reflection and providing feedback occur in every PBC cycle.

In this chapter, we describe the importance of reflection and feedback. We offer guidance for how coaches engage in reflection and support coachees' reflections, give supportive feedback that is practice focused, and provide constructive feedback that will enhance further coachees' practice implementation. Formats and delivery methods for providing reflection and feedback are discussed and resources to support this PBC component are provided. The case stories are used to illustrate how reflection and feedback are enacted as part of every coaching cycle.

Importance of Reflection

Growing empirical evidence exists that professional development, which includes job-embedded practice opportunities such as those that occur through PBC, is associated with positive effects on practice implementation and child outcomes (Kraft et al., 2018; Kretlow & Bartholomew, 2010). As Artman-Meeker et al. (2015) noted, although consensus has not been reached on a definition for coaching, evidence is emerging around the characteristics of effective coaching. This evidence supports the use of planning (shared goal setting and action planning in PBC), observation (focused observation in PBC), actions (e.g., modeling, role play, problem solving, which are PBC strategies), and reflection and feedback. A PBC cycle is not complete without reflection and feedback.

> **Key Point to Remember**
>
> A PBC cycle is not complete without reflection and feedback.

Reflection, as a component of PBC, refers to consideration of how practices are implemented and the identification of successes, challenges, and motivators and how they connect to improvement or refinement of the practices (Snyder et al., 2015). Although many definitions for reflection exist in the

127

Figure 8.1. Reflection and feedback in the Practice-Based Coaching framework. From Snyder, P. A., Hemmeter, M. L., & Fox, L. (2015). Supporting implementation of evidence-based practices through practice-based coaching. *Topics in Early Childhood Special Education*, *35*(3), 133–143. https://doi.org/10.1177/0271121415594925; reprinted by permission.

Core Features of Reflection

- [One's] thoughts and actions
- Attentive, critical, exploratory, and iterative thinking
- Conceptual frame
- View on change
- Self

(Nguyen et al., 2014)

---

literature, consensus has not been reached on a definition. To identify a shared definition for use in practice-focused disciplines, including medicine, nursing, and other health sciences professions, Nguyen et al. (2014) conducted an exploratory thematic analysis of the 15 most cited authors publishing papers on reflection between 2008 and 2012. Based on their thematic analyses, they proposed core features of reflection. They defined reflection as ". . . the *process* of engaging the self in attentive, critical, exploratory and iterative interactions with one's thoughts and actions and their underlying conceptual frame, with a view to changing them and a view on the change itself" (p. 1176).

These authors proposed that the process of reflection can become increasingly effective, particularly when three features are added. First, conceptual frames or one's perspectives about practice are made evident. In PBC, practice perspectives are gathered through formal and informal strengths and needs assessments. Second, views on practice change are considered, which occurs in every PBC cycle as goals and action plans are discussed and as reflection and feedback occurs. Finally, the self feature involves thinking about one's actions (i.e., practice in PBC) and considering what these actions are telling oneself about one's practice. In PBC, reflection by the coachee is prompted and supported by the coach and is guided by the current goal and action plan and the focused observation. Using the model of reflection proposed by Nguyen et al. (2014), Figure 8.2 shows an example of how reflective thinking can be expanded in PBC by using features of the model.

Reflection provides the coachee with an opportunity to consider what is working well and what might need to be changed. It is used by the coachee and coach to reflect on the focused observation while considering the current goal and action plan, the coachee's practice context, and the collaborative coaching partnership.

Core features of reflection					
Context for reflection	TA	TA + ACEI	TA + ACEI + CF	TA + ACEI + CF + VC	TA + ACEI + CF + VC + S
Coachee and their implementation of practice-focused goal and action plan	Coachee and coach think about practice implementation during the focused observation.	Coachee, with support from coach, thinks about practice implementation in ways that are attentive, critical, exploratory, and iterative as part of reflection and feedback.	Coachee, with support from coach, thinks about facilitators and barriers to practice implementation while being attentive, critical, exploratory, and iterative as part of reflection and feedback.	Coachee, with support from the coach, considers facilitators and barriers to practice implementation, while being attentive, critical, exploratory, and iterative. Coachee and coach engage in problem solving to identify potential practice-focused solutions as part of reflection and feedback.	Coachee, with support from the coach, considers facilitators and barriers to practice implementation while being attentive, critical, exploratory, and iterative. Coachee and coach engage in problem solving to identify potential practice-focused solutions as part of reflection and feedback. Coachee does so to build on or modify the way they will engage in practice during the next coaching cycle.

Figure 8.2. Illustration of increasing core features of reflection as part of practice-based coaching using a five-component model. (*Source:* Adapted from Nguyen et al., 2014.) (*Key:* TA, thoughts and actions; ACEI, attentive, critical, exploratory, and iterative thinking; CF, underlying conceptual frame; VC, view on change; S, self.)

Importance of Feedback

Feedback refers to providing information to the coachee about their practice-focused performance or behavior (Cooper et al., 2007; Noell et al., 2005). Performance-based feedback has been identified as an evidence-based practice for supporting individuals to learn new behaviors, skills, or practices (Fallon et al., 2015). The use of performance-based feedback (PF) to change behavior (i.e., practices) is a fundamental principle of the science of human behavior (Crow & Snyder, 1998; Seniuk et al., 2013). PF has been used pervasively in research to improve practitioners' fidelity of implementation of evidence-based practices (Artman-Meeker et al., 2015; Fallon et al., 2015; Fox et al., 2011; Snyder et al., 2012; Solomon et al., 2012).

> **Key Point to Remember**
>
> Performance-based feedback has been identified as an evidence-based practice for supporting individuals to learn new behaviors, skills, or practices.

PF involves providing information about the fidelity of practice implementation and can also include information about relationships between coachee's practice implementation and children's development and learning (Fallon et al., 2015). In PBC, PF involves the provision of both supportive and constructive feedback (Snyder et al., 2015). It is delivered by the coach to the coachee in verbal or written format and should be direct and specific based on the coachee's goal and action plan and information gathered during the focused observation. Cusumano and Preston (2018) noted that PF should always highlight practices that were implemented accurately and fluently or that were generalized or adapted based on characteristics of the practice context and the children the

Key Point to Remember

In PBC, PF involves the provision of both supportive and constructive feedback.

coachee is supporting. These authors noted that PF should change the likelihood of a practice being used as intended. When provided as part of PBC, practitioners have reported that they find PF to be useful, acceptable, and appreciated (Shannon et al., 2015).

Relationship Between Reflection and Feedback in Practice-Based Coaching

Following the focused observation and before providing feedback to a coachee, the coach and coachee should engage in reflection. Reflection is used to carefully analyze what happened during the observation, to think about and discuss practice implementation and its relationship to the coachee's goal and action plan, and to guide the practitioner to consider next steps toward practice change. During reflection, the coach is engaged in active listening and is prompting the practitioner to reflect on their practice implementation. They are staging the reflective conversation for feedback. Reflection is critically important for the coachee. It provides the coachee with opportunities to self-assess, to examine their practice with a critical lens, and to explore options for practice modification or refinement. It also provides opportunities for the coachee to consider the impact of practice implementation on a child or family. A goal of reflection is to build the coachee's capacity to continuously self-reflect and self-evaluate their practice implementation.

Reflection helps set the stage for PF by grounding the coachee and the coach on what occurred during practice implementation and why it occurred. Reciprocal reflection and feedback exchanges over time between coachees and coaches strengthen the collaborative partnership and build the capacity of the coachee to take the lead in reflective conversations both before and after receiving PF from the coach (Shannon, Snyder, et al., 2021).

Critical Aspects of Reflection

Reflection for the coach often begins while conducting the focused observation. During the observation, the coach takes objective notes on what is occurring and is thinking about the coachee's use of the practices as they are aligned with the goal and action plan. As part of reflection, the coach considers the coachee's confidence and competence of practice implementation and the feedback that will be most reinforcing and relevant to the coachee. The coach will also be reflecting on how practice implementation facilitates children's learning or skills. For example, the coach might reflect on how the children in a classroom are responding to a coachee's use of a practice or how the practice contributes to children's engagement in learning.

> Both coachees and coaches engage in reflection.

Reflection by the coachee is facilitated by the coach and the coach's use of questions or comments. These reflective conversation starters help guide coachees to reflect on and learn to be analytical about their use of practices, be observant of their own behavior, and enhance their proficiency in identifying action plan goals and when they have achieved them. Engaging in reflection fosters self-awareness, which is essential for continued growth as a coachee. Coachees who reflect develop critical and focused insights about their practice implementation and engage in continuous improvement.

Listening as the coachee reflects, the coach learns more about the coachee's perspectives on the use of the practice, the elements of using the practice that were most salient to the coachee, and the level of awareness the coachee has about their own performance along with the responses of children to their use of practices. Reflection by the coachee helps to strengthen the coach's understanding of the practice implementation context and the coachee's perspectives about their confidence and competence. When the coachee reflects, the coach's understanding of the coachee and the context deepens. This deeper understanding allows for the coach to provide more meaningful feedback that will be effective for strengthening practice implementation.

Using Reflective Questions

In early coaching cycles, the coach often prompts reflection by asking open-ended questions to initiate reflective conversations. In later coaching cycles, coachees often initiate these conversations with support from the coach (Shannon, Snyder, et al., 2021).

To set the stage for reflection, the coach might start with an expression of gratitude linked to the focused observation (e.g., "Thanks for sending me the video. I enjoyed watching it" or "It was great to be here today and get to see your small-group activities"). The coach might follow with a comment about the goal and action plan (e.g., "I appreciated seeing how you guided the children in the problem-solving steps").

Following these types of conversation starters, the coach could prompt the coachee to reflect. This might be done using an objective question such as, "What happened when you introduced the problem-solving steps?" or "How did you introduce the problem-solving steps?" Open-ended questions that prompt reflection and support reflective conversations should elicit more than a one-word response. For example, asking, "How do you think that went?" might result in the coachee responding only with "Fine." After asking an objective question, the coach might prompt further reflection with interpretive questions (e.g., "What do you think would happen if you used visual supports when teaching the problem-solving steps?") or comparative questions (e.g., "What do you think went well with teaching the problem-solving steps?" and "What might you want to try the next time?"). Reflective questions prompt the coachee to think more deeply and analytically about their practice implementation and engage in attentive, critical, exploratory, and iterative conversations with the coach or with oneself (Nguyen et al., 2014). Table 8.1 shows example questions that might be used to facilitate reflection and support the coachee to think more critically about what occurred during the focused observation. Reflective questions can be asked as part of on-site coaching sessions or can be posed in a virtual coaching platform.

Types of Reflective Questions
• Objective
• Interpretive
• Comparative

Guiding the Reflective Conversation

Reflective conversations should be transactional. As the coachee reflects, the coach should use active listening skills, clarify and verify reflections shared by the coachee, and prompt further reflection. Paying close attention to what the coachee is sharing, engaging in nonverbal behavior (e.g., leaning in, nodding), and offering comments that support or expand on the coachee's

Table 8.1. Types of questions to facilitate reflection

Type of question	Definition	Example	Nonexample
Objective	Prompts the coachee to reflect on what happened during practice implementation	• "I noticed that you . . ." • "Tell me about what happened when . . ." • "What did you notice about the children when . . . ?"	"How did you think it went today?"
Interpretive	Encourages coachee to reflect on and form hypotheses or draw conclusions about practice implementation	• "Tell me how you felt about . . . ." • "What were your thoughts when . . . ?" • "How did the children respond when . . . ?" • "Why do you think [ ] worked?"	"Was doing (name practice) effective?"
Comparative	Assists coachee in evaluating events and interactions and comparing to other current or future alternatives	• "Would there be a different way you could . . . ?" • "How was this different from when you did . . . ?" • "What do you think went well today compared to . . . ?"	"Did this work better than how you were doing it previously?"

reflections are strategies that support reflective conversations. A primary goal of reflection in PBC is to support the coachee to think about their actions, the strategies they used, and the responses of children. Coaches are likely to encounter coachees who are eager to engage in reflection about practice implementation or coachees who might need more time and support to express their reflections. As part of the reflection process, it is important that the coach provide the coachee with time and support to reflect before sharing their perspectives about practice implementation. If the coach begins sharing their observations from the start of the conversation or becomes directive in the conversation, it can inhibit the coachee from engaging in their own reflection and sharing their ideas and perspectives. Given that reflection is a thinking process, reflective conversations help coachees and coaches use verbal or written interactions to convey their thoughts about practice implementation. Reflective conversations can occur in real time or they might take place during back-and-forth written exchanges in a virtual coaching platform.

> Given that reflection is a thinking process, reflective conversations help coachees and coaches use verbal or written interactions to convey their thoughts about practice implementation.

PERFORMANCE FEEDBACK

Through reflection, important perspectives and insights are gathered about the coachee's practice implementation and the coachee has been prompted to consider their use of the practice as identified in their goal and action plan. Reflection helps set the stage for PF, which includes having additional conversations about the quality and the consistency of practice implementation with a focus on fidelity. Although PF is directly linked to and can build upon or prompt additional reflection after it is provided, feedback serves a different purpose.

As described in Chapter 4, PF that provides both supportive and constructive feedback is an essential coaching strategy. PF provides objective information about fidelity of practice implementation and how to enhance it. PF can build on reflection when it is provided following reflective conversations or problem-solving discussions. It also can prompt additional reflection and problem solving once it is provided. PF is used specifically to increase a coachee's capacity to implement a practice, improve the use of the practice, or modify practice implementation (Sweigart et al., 2016). PF is most effective when it is descriptive, strength based, anchored in objective-focused observation data, and reciprocal. To have the most impact on practice implementation, PF should occur as immediately as possible after focused observation, particularly when both focused observation and reflection and feedback occur face to face or via livestreaming. When the focused observation is conducted using video, PF can be provided in writing by annotating the video in a video coaching platform (see Chapter 10) or as part of video review during a virtual coaching session in a videoconferencing platform. Most sources recommend PF be provided within 24 hr of a focused observation (e.g., Scheeler et al., 2004).

Features of Performance Feedback

Effective PF is focused and rooted in observation data. PF is focused when it is specific to the coachee's current goal and action plan steps. To focus the observation, it should occur at times when practices in the action plan are being implemented so the feedback that follows the observation is specific to what occurred during the observation. PF that is not connected to the practices that are the focus of PBC can weaken the effectiveness of the PF. If a coach strays too far from a focus on the current goal, action plan, and observation or the set of practices that are the focus of PBC, PF is less meaningful and is unlikely to result in forward progress toward implementation fidelity.

To plan for providing PF, the coach should review notes and data taken as part of focused observation about the current goal and action steps and then carefully plan for what feedback

Tools for Coaches in the Appendices

Appendix V.O: Providing Performance Feedback: Steps for Coaches

This is a resource that describes steps that coaches can follow to plan for the provision of performance feedback.

will be delivered and how the feedback will be delivered. Appendix V.O provides an organizational template to help coaches plan for the provision of PF.

The coach should plan to include either qualitative or quantitative data collected during the focused observation as part of PF. Data collected might be frequency counts of the use of a discrete practice, the number of children engaged in an activity when the practice is implemented, tallies of disruptive behavior, data specific to a particular child, or other types of data that are directly linked to practice implementation and the current goal and action plan. When the coach and coachee agree what data will be collected during the observation, those data should be shared as part of reflection and feedback so that the coachee has actionable information about fidelity of practice implementation and its relationship to the current goal and action plan.

Effective PF should be nonattributive. Nonattributive feedback is objective and grounded in what was seen or heard in the focused observation (e.g., "You waited 3 sec before providing an additional prompt to Kayley when she did not follow your direction the first time"). Attributive feedback includes traits, dispositions, or feelings that might not have shared meaning between the coach and coachee (e.g., "You are so patient with Kayley"). Nonattributive PF should refer to the data collected, specific practices used, or responses of children during the focused observation. It should be direct, specific, timely, and objective (Barton et al., 2011).

> **Key Point to Remember**
> Effective performance feedback should be nonattributive, focused, and grounded in the focused observation.

Two Essential Forms of Performance Feedback

PBC sessions should always include two types of performance feedback: supportive and constructive. As described in Chapter 4, supportive feedback is an essential coaching strategy.

Supportive feedback is provided during every coaching cycle as part of reflection and feedback. It is defined as the provision of positive descriptive information, verbal or written, about the coachee's actions related to practice implementation as specified on the action plan. Supportive feedback should always describe what the coachee did that supported implementation of targeted practices or outcomes of practice implementation. It provides concrete and transparent information about whether the coachee is meeting or making progress toward their current goal and action plan (Escorcia & Basler, 2019). Supportive feedback is provided in a manner that is sincere, encouraging, and motivating. The goal is to affirm the coachee's strengths and accomplishments and encourage continued efforts toward fidelity of practice implementation.

> PBC sessions should always include two types of performance feedback: supportive and constructive.

> The goal of supportive feedback is to affirm the coachee's strengths and accomplishments and motivate continued efforts toward fidelity of practice implementation.

As described in Chapter 4, constructive feedback is the provision of data-informed or performance-based suggestions or supports for enhancing the fidelity of practice implementation (Barton et al., 2011). It is also an essential coaching strategy and is provided in every coaching cycle as part of reflection and feedback. Constructive feedback helps a coachee understand how they might improve their implementation of a practice or identify missed opportunities where

Table 8.2.   Purposes, definitions, examples, and nonexamples of two types of performance feedback used in practice-based coaching

Type of feedback	Purpose	Definition	Example	Nonexample
Supportive feedback	Acknowledge coachee's efforts to implement practices related to goals and action steps and motivate future implementation.	Provision of positive descriptive information, verbal or written, about the coachee's actions related to practice implementation as specified in the goal and action plan	"Today I saw you introduce the circle-time expectations at the beginning of circle. I also counted four times that you gave positive descriptive feedback to children who were following the expectations during the activity."	"The new circle-time expectations poster looks great; it's so colorful."
Constructive feedback	Support coachee to be motivated to implement new practices, enhance current practices, or modify practice implementation.	Provision of data-informed or performance-based suggestions or supports for enhancing the fidelity of practice implementation as specified in the goal and action plan	"Today at the beginning of circle time, you told the children the expectations, but many children were not engaged. Tomorrow morning, could you use the poster with visuals when you talk about the expectations? Having the visual might help more children engage and understand your review of the expectations."	"Today at circle time, you did not review the expectations and you spent the entire activity redirecting children's off-task behavior."

a practice might be used. As noted in Chapter 4, constructive feedback is *not* telling the coachee they did something wrong (e.g., "That was not the right way to teach children expectations" or "That was an incorrect embedded instruction learning trial"). Rather, constructive feedback provides an objective description of observed practice implementation and actionable suggestions or supports for enhancing fidelity of practice implementation.

> Constructive feedback provides an objective description of observed practice implementation and actionable suggestions or supports for enhancing fidelity.

Both forms of PF are provided in a manner that is strengths based, specific, and objective. Coaches should avoid providing feedback using global statements that are not descriptive or providing feedback that is attributive or connected to qualities of the practitioner. It is also important that the provision of constructive feedback does not seem punitive or evaluative by the practitioner. Table 8.2 shows additional information about the two types of PF.

Recommendations for Providing Supportive and Constructive Feedback

Coaches should plan ahead of time what feedback they want to provide and how to provide it (e.g., verbal feedback, written feedback, graphic feedback, video feedback; see Chapter 4). For supportive feedback, the coach should give the coachee examples of practices that were seen or heard during the observation, as well as what progress was made toward an action plan step or goal. Given the purpose of constructive feedback is to provide the coachee with concrete suggestions for improving fidelity of practice implementation or to help them identify missed opportunities to utilize a specific practice, coaches want to link their suggestions to what was observed. For example, if the coach completed a formal observation of a coachee's practice implementation using a fidelity checklist for the third or fourth time, they might want to provide graphic feedback to illustrate progress. This strategy could facilitate a combination of supportive and constructive feedback (i.e., supportive feedback about progress observed over time and constructive feedback about a practice that might be the focus for the next coaching cycle if the data show it was not implemented or not implemented as intended). In initial coaching sessions, coaches might use supportive feedback more often than constructive feedback while coachees and coaches are building their collaborative partnership. Nevertheless, it is important to provide both types of feedback as part of every coaching cycle once a goal is identified and an action plan is developed.

Table 8.3. Supportive feedback conversation starters with examples and nonexamples

Supportive feedback sentence starter	Example	Nonexample
"I noticed that you did _____ (*insert specific practice*). That worked well for _____ (*indicate how you know it worked well or for whom it worked well*)."	"I noticed you used the new timer to provide an advanced cue prior to two of your transitions. That really worked well for the majority of the class."	"Great job with your transitions."
"It was great to see _____ (*insert specific practice*)."	"It was great to see you use the sentence strips posted on your walls to remind you to increase your use of positive descriptive praise."	"Good job with specific praise."
"I saw you do a lot of _____ (*insert specific practice*)."	"I saw you model your own emotions six times today and help children label their own emotions during circle time. This is a perfect example of teaching emotions to your class."	"You talked a lot about emotions during the observation today."
"You really got it when you _____ (*insert practice here*)."	"You really got it when you prompted Anna and Lily to get the solution tool kit and modeled for them how they could solve the problem they were having in the literacy center."	"So glad to see you teach problem solving."

Adapted from Hemmeter et al. (2019).

Supportive feedback should be specific enough so the coachee understands what aspects of the practice they implemented with fidelity. With constructive feedback, the feedback provided will be precise statements about how to enhance fidelity. The combination of supportive and constructive feedback is important for supporting coachees to be motivated to learn new behaviors, skills, or practices (Fallon et al., 2015).

For both types of feedback, the coach wants to consider how to frame their feedback before providing it to the coachee. Supportive feedback should be nonattributive, with the coach moving beyond general feedback. For example, instead of sharing with the coachee that they observed smooth transitions, the coach would want to cite specific examples of transitions and why they were considered smooth. For example, the coach might say, "Your transition from circle to centers was shorter, and every child knew what to do while waiting to transition." With constructive feedback, the coach should ensure that feedback is not received as evaluative but instead leads to actionable items for moving forward with fidelity of practice implementation. Tables 8.3 and 8.4 provide examples of supportive and constructive conversation starters along

Table 8.4. Constructive feedback conversation starters with examples and nonexamples

Constructive feedback sentence starter	Example	Nonexample
"I noticed that _____ (*insert what you observed*). Some strategies you might consider are . . . ."	"I noticed that two of the children had a difficult time paying attention to the story. Some strategies you might consider are offering them an individual prompt to respond to the questions, making sure they can see the illustration by showing them individually, or looking at them directly as you pose a question or offer a reflection about the book."	"Most of the children were not engaged during the story you were reading."
"One way I have observed this handled effectively is _____ (*insert strategy here*)."	"One way I have observed teachers handling this issue effectively is offering a choice of the book to read to the children. They are often more engaged when they have picked the book."	"You should try picking a different story next time."
"I noticed that _____ (*insert what you observed*). Something you might try is _____ (*insert specific idea here*)."	"I noticed that some children were still having trouble remembering the expectations at centers." "Something you might you might want to try is reviewing the expectations with the entire class before centers. Are there some children who might benefit from some individual review of the rules and expectations?"	"You did not review the expectations before centers so children did not remember them."

Adapted from Hemmeter et al. (2019).

with examples of how a coach might deliver feedback using the conversation starters. These tables also include nonexamples to compare with the examples.

Coaches should provide feedback using a strengths-based approach. Coachees should hear acknowledgment, encouragement, and affirmations about their implementation of practices. This positive feedback can help set the tone for constructive feedback. Given that PBC is a collaborative partnership and not the expert informing the coachee what to do, coaches should utilize open-ended prompts to encourage reciprocal conversations and elicit insights and ideas from coachees as feedback is provided.

Key Point to Remember

Feedback should be strengths based, with acknowledgment, encouragement, and affirmations about practice implementation.

Data-based feedback can be an important part of providing effective constructive feedback. As discussed in the previous section, the use of data-based feedback allows the coach to share information that is objective and tied directly to the practice. Data can be collected as part of the coach's observation. For example, the coach might tally how many instances of labeling emotions are seen during the focused observation. The coach would then share this information with the coachee and then use the data as a point of entry into a reflective conversation on ways to increase labeling emotions throughout the day.

As discussed previously in this chapter, the coach wants to elicit reflection from the coachee as to how well the targeted practice is working, along with ideas for ways to improve fidelity of practice implementation. Coachees and coaches should discuss what resources they might need to support fidelity of practice implementation. Resources might include materials, articles, or video examples. The coach should continue using active listening skills during reflection and feedback to ensure understanding of the coachee's perspectives and to ensure that these perspectives are incorporated into goal setting and action planning that will guide the next coaching cycle.

Methods for Providing Feedback

PF can occur during face-to-face meetings as part of reflection and feedback after focused observation. As described in Chapter 10, PF also might occur as part of videoconferencing or it might be provided in written formats (e.g., e-mail or as part of video annotations in web-based coaching platforms). PF can also be provided in the moment using bug-in-ear technology (Ottley et al., 2015; Ottley & Hanline, 2014).

The use of e-mail as a vehicle for providing PF about practice implementation has been empirically examined. Several studies have demonstrated the effectiveness of using e-mail as an efficient and effective mode for delivering PF, specifically related to increasing the implementation of positive descriptive praise (Barton et al., 2013; Di Gennaro et al., 2007; Hemmeter et al., 2011). When using e-mail to provide feedback, there are several issues to consider (Hemmeter et al., 2019). Several of these issues are also applicable when feedback is provided using video annotations. As with feedback delivered in person, the coach will want to consider what was observed and how it aligns with the goal on the action plan. Recommendations for how to structure PF when provided in an e-mail were described by Hemmeter et al. (2011). These authors suggest the message should start with a positive statement about the observation, followed by supportive feedback about practice implementation. As with face-to-face supportive feedback, the coach needs to be specific about what they observed. Constructive feedback should follow the supportive feedback. The coach should ensure that the constructive feedback describes in detail how the coachee can use this feedback (e.g., what practice implementation would look like, suggestions for when to use the practice, or words or phrases to use when implementing the practice). Within the e-mail, the coach should provide suggestions for materials or resources that would support practice implementation. This might include links to video examples, tools for use the practice context, or other resources that will support the coachee. When closing the e-mail, coaches should provide words of encouragement along with what the next steps will be for coaching. Coaches may ask the coachees to reply to the e-mail to ensure that they have read the e-mail as well as to confirm plans for the next coaching session. A template for structuring e-mail feedback that includes all of these components is provided in Appendix V.P.

> **Tools for Coaches in the Appendices**
>
> *Appendix V.P: Template for E-Mail Feedback*
>
> This is a resource that illustrates the recommended components of feedback when delivered via e-mail.

There are benefits to using e-mail to provide feedback. First, e-mail provides a coachee time to read and reflect on the feedback and the coachee can review the feedback at their convenience. By providing constructive feedback, along with resources and ideas, the coachee has time to review and reflect prior to meeting with the coach and engaging in shared goal setting and action planning for the next coaching cycle.

Before using this method of delivery, the coach wants to also consider the logistical pieces of using e-mail. First, the coach needs to consider the level of comfort the coachee has with technology. For instance, check that the coachee has regular access to e-mail and has a level of comfort in retrieving and using this platform. If the coach is planning on sending files and video via e-mail, they will want to ensure that there are no restrictions such as file type or sending large video files. For those coachees who might speak another language as their primary language, the coach should confirm the preferred modality for conveying feedback. Both parties should be equally comfortable with how feedback is provided to ensure an interpretable and useful message is being conveyed.

REVISITING THE CASE STORIES

In the sections that follow, we return to the case stories of Lynn, Maureen and Maria, and Sam to examine how the coach facilitated reflection and provided feedback.

Lynn and Sirena

Sirena prepared for her reflection and feedback discussion with Lynn by reviewing the video, reflecting on Lynn's use of expansions with multiple children, and noting the feedback she wanted to share. She wanted to provide Lynn with supportive feedback related to the frequency of her use of expansions and guide Lynn in reflecting on why expansions are important for building language. Sirena noticed that Lynn often just repeated what a child said without expanding on the child's statement, and she identified some places in the video that she could review with Lynn when providing constructive feedback.

During the session, Sirena shared the data she collected on how many times Lynn described children's experiences and the number of expansions she used. She asked Lynn to reflect on how describing children's learning experiences helps them build language. Lynn said that she thought it might give children new words for what was happening. Sirena showed Lynn a segment of the observation where Lynn expanded on Aiden's statement and then asked Lynn to reflect on what Aiden did after she provided the expansion. Lynn responded with a smile, "He repeated exactly what I said!" Sirena provided feedback on how many times Lynn had repeated without an expansion and encouraged Lynn to work on adding an expansion like she did with Aiden by saying, "It's really important to add something new to what children say so that they can learn a variety of words . . . just like you did with Aiden." Sirena suggested that they look at a couple of video clips and practice how Lynn could do that.

After reviewing and discussing the data and looking at the video clips, Lynn asked Sirena if they could look at the video again and stop it after a child said something to Lynn. She wanted to practice expanding with Sirena's support. Once they practiced a few times, Sirena suggested they

Questions for Further Reflection and Discussion

- What methods did Sirena use to provide supportive and constructive feedback?

- Why might these methods have been good choices for continuing to support Lynn's practice implementation goal?

- How did Sirena follow Lynn's lead during reflection and feedback? Why is this important for their collaborative coaching partnership?

- What connections were made at the end of the meeting to link reflection and feedback from this coaching cycle to the next coaching cycle?

- What strategies have you used effectively to connect one coaching cycle to the next?

look at Lynn's current implementation goal on her action plan and at her action plan steps. They both agreed that while Lynn was making progress, she would continue with her current goal and action plan. Lynn said she thought she needed to focus on using expansions with other children in addition to Aiden. After another week or so, she said she thought she would be ready to move on to another goal. Sirena asked Lynn if she wanted her to do the focused observation at the same time next week. Lynn asked if Sirena might come a little earlier next week so she could see some different activities that Lynn thought would be a good time to use expansions. Sirena said she could come an hour earlier and Lynn said that would work. Lynn asked Sirena if she was going to send an e-mail summarizing what they had discussed during the meeting. She said, "Those messages really help me remember what we talked about and what I am going to do this week. I have all your messages in a binder along with my action plans and I refer to them regularly. Thanks for taking time to help me stay organized!"

Maureen, Maria, and Elley

Elley prepared for her coaching session with Maureen and Maria by reviewing the video and using Appendix V.0, Providing Performance Feedback: Steps for Coaches, to make notes about guiding reflection and providing feedback. Given that Maureen's and Maria's goal focused on distributing embedded learning opportunities across activities for three of their children (Aaron, Flynn, and Liliana), Elley had agreed that she would count how many occurred for each child within and across the different activities. Elley created two graphs (Figures 8.3 and 8.4) to share with the teachers. One graph showed the number of activities with embedded learning opportunities, and the other showed how many were implemented by each teacher.

Elley began the session by acknowledging the team effort she observed with Maureen's and Maria's implementation of embedded instruction. She asked Maureen and Maria how they thought their implementation went this past week compared to previous weeks. Maria said, "I think we are using the activity matrix more to help us remember in which activities we plan to embed and to be sure we are embedding across activities." Maureen added, "Even when we get busy and can't talk directly to each other, the activity matrix is helpful to glance at and be sure we are doing it." After engaging in additional reflection about the activity matrix and how it was supporting implementation, Elley shared the graphs she had made. The graphs showed that Aaron and Liliana were provided embedded learning opportunities in different activities. Elley also pointed out that Aaron had opportunities to practice in two different activities. She shared that this was really helpful for the children to learn and generalize their skills across activities. Maureen reflected on the graph and asked if it was correct by saying, "Does this show that we did not provide any embedded learning opportunities to Flynn?" Elley responded by saying that Flynn's goal was focused on naming colors and she did not observe any opportunities to do that, but some opportunities were focused on pointing to a color. She asked the team if the priority was to name colors or identify colors by pointing or giving an item of that color. The team reflected on that question and said that they did want him to name colors and they hadn't realized that the activities were not offering those opportunities to Flynn. Maureen said, "I guess we really have not set up activities to support Flynn to get to that next level." Elley suggested that they review the video together again and identify places where opportunities could be naturally or logically created within activities for Flynn to name colors. As they watched the video, Maureen asked Elley to pause the video at snack time. Maureen said, "I remember at the workshop we saw an example of a teacher who used colored bowls and cups during snack time to create an opportunity to ask children about the colors of the bowls and cups. Maria, do you think we might be able to do that same thing during our snacks and meals?" "I don't see why not," said Maria. Elley said, "I think that's a great idea, Maureen! Given that we want to provide opportunities across

> **Questions for Further Reflection and Discussion**
> - What was different about the supportive and constructive feedback and how it occurred in this story compared to the Lynn and Sirena story?
> - Who provided the constructive feedback in this story? What does this tell you about the collaborative partnership among Maureen, Maria, and Elley?
> - How did Elley facilitate reflection about providing embedded learning opportunities for Flynn?
> - What strategies have you used successfully to facilitate reflection that supports the provision of feedback and additional reflection?

activities, what might be another time where you could provide these opportunities to Flynn? Let's watch more of the video and see if we might be able to come up with some additional ideas that are natural or logical fits for naming colors."

Sam and Kenya

As Kenya prepared for the reflection and feedback session with Sam, she reflected on the progress he has been making on his action plan goal related to expectations and rules despite some of the challenges he identified at their last meeting. By reviewing her notes from previous sessions, she

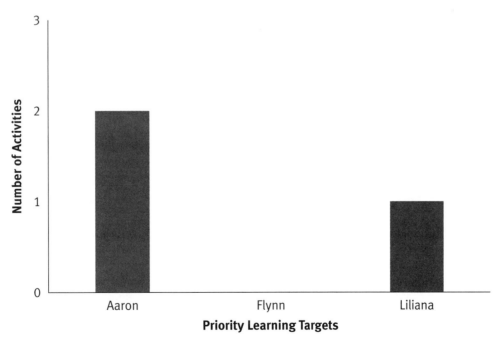

Figure 8.3. Elley's graph of the number of activities with embedded learning opportunities for Aaron, Flynn, and Liliana. (*Note:* Aaron, free choice and snack; Lilianna, small groups.)

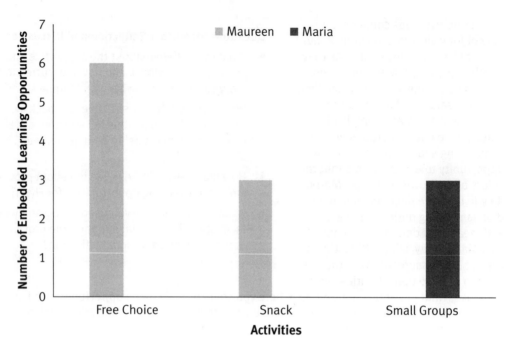

Figure 8.4. Elley's graph of how many learning opportunities were implemented by each teacher. (*Note:* Maria not observed during snack; Maureen not observed during small groups.)

realized that Sam really seems to like graphic feedback. Given that he asked Kenya for information about how often he provides positive expectations and rules reminders and in which routines or activities they are provided, she decided to graph the number of positive and negative reminders that she observed Sam using during center and circle time across her last three focused observations. It took her some time to figure out how to graph the data so that it would support both reflection and feedback during their upcoming meeting. She remembered that during coach training, the facilitators had shared some graphing templates that could be used to display different types of data. She went to the coaching website set up by the facilitators and found an example she thought would work for her. She made the graphs (Figures 8.5 and 8.6) and was proud of herself! She was excited to share it with Sam.

During their reflection and feedback meeting, Kenya showed Sam the graphs and provided supportive feedback about the progress he made increasing the number of positive reminders he gives to children during centers and circle, and she pointed out that the number of negative reminders he is providing has decreased. She gave specific examples of positive reminders she heard across three focused observations. After sharing the data and providing supportive feedback, Kenya said, "What changes have you seen in children's behavior since you have been using more positive reminders?" Sam reflected that he had more time to join children in play at centers because there are fewer instances of unsafe behavior during centers. He also shared that he was more intentional about providing positive descriptive feedback to children when they were being safe in the classroom during center time. Although he noticed these improvements during centers, Sam shared with Kenya that he was still having difficulty helping children follow rules for safe behavior during circle time. He said, "I try to use positive reminders, but then I get frustrated when they don't work with some children and I know I revert to 'Don't' or 'Stop' or 'That's not safe.'" Kenya showed the graph she made for circle time and acknowledged that there were more negative than positive reminders during circle. She asked Sam, "What do you think is working well for you during centers that you might be able to try during circle?" Sam said that the

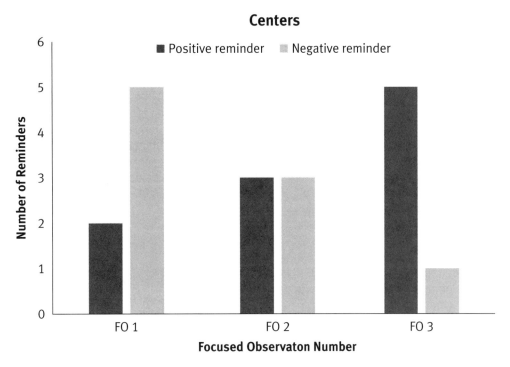

Figure 8.5. Kenya's graph of positive and negative reminders provided by Sam during centers. (*Key:* FO, focused observation.)

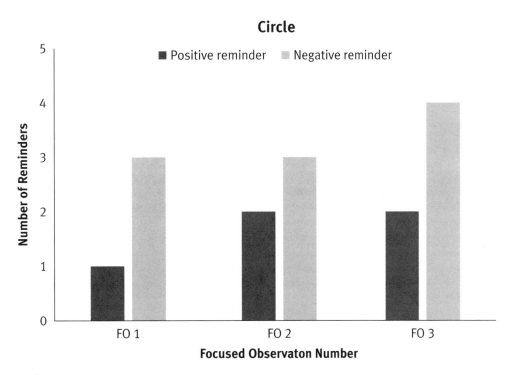

Figure 8.6. Kenya's graph of positive and negative reminders provided by Sam during circle. (*Key:* FO, focused observation.)

reminders he and Jamie posted in the center areas were very helpful but that he was having difficulty translating them to be appropriate for circle. Kenya told Sam she had some notes on the negatively phrased reminders she heard him say during her observation and asked Sam if it would be helpful to look at them and problem-solve ways they could be rephrased to be more positive. Sam said that he thought that would help give him ideas to put on reminders he could post near his circle time schedule. After engaging in the problem-solving discussion and arriving at the reminder solution, Kenya said, "Let's revisit your goal and action plan. What do you think?" Sam said, "I think we should change my goal to focus on positive reminders during circle and using my reminders. Can we also add an action step about making the reminders so I remember to do it?!" Kenya smiled and said, "Sure, an action step that reminds us to make reminders! That's a good one that I will have to remember!" They both laughed and Sam said, "I really appreciate all you are doing to support me with this stuff. It sounded so easy when I heard about it at the workshop. But, I've learned it's harder to do in the midst of everything else that goes on in my classroom every day. Your support is really helping me focus and understand how to do things in my classroom that I never would have thought about before." Kenya said, "Thanks, Sam! It helps me to know how what we are doing together and what you are doing when I'm not here is working." Sam said, "One last thing, can you video record me during the next focused observation so we can look at it during our meeting and I can practice taking data with you?" "Sure," said Kenya, I'll write myself a note about that and add another step to the action plan!"

Questions for Further Reflection and Discussion

- What was similar or different about the supportive and constructive feedback and how it occurred in this story compared to the Lynn and Sirena story? The Maureen, Maria, and Elley story?

- How did the graphs that Kenya created help facilitate reflection and feedback?

- What features of the graphs do you think helped Sam identify his strengths and needs and his revised action plan goal?

- What might Kenya have said differently at the end of the session to connect Sam's comments to the overall goals of PBC and their collaborative coaching partnership?

SUMMARY

As the third component of the PBC cycle, reflection and feedback is critical to the iterative processes of assisting coachees to gain competence and confidence with practice implementation. Reflection and feedback closes out one coaching cycle and helps sets the stage for the next cycle by supporting the clarification and verification of strengths and needs as well as revisiting shared goal setting and action planning.

9

Considerations for Implementing Practice-Based Coaching

Chelsea T. Morris, Meghan von der Embse, Jolenea B. Ferro, and Lise Fox

CONSIDERATIONS FOR IMPLEMENTING PRACTICE-BASED COACHING

In early childhood education settings, the provision of coaching is quickly becoming widely recognized as an essential component of professional development (PD) (Kraft et al., 2018; Schachter, 2015; Snyder et al., 2012). As discussed in the earlier chapters, Practice-Based Coaching (PBC) is used to help coachees implement effective practices, instructional strategies, or a new curriculum. PBC has been used to deliver PD to community early care and education providers including in Early Head Start/Head Start, public preschool program personnel, and family child care providers. In some cases, PBC is provided as an element of Quality Rating and Improvement Systems (QRIS) or as part of early intervention service provision (i.e., coaching for providers or for caregivers of children ages birth to 3). Different from a one-time workshop approach, PBC is a job-embedded PD approach focused on fidelity of practice implementation as well as program- or school-wide improvement efforts.

> PBC has been used in community early care and education, Early Head Start/Head Start, public preschool, and family child care programs. It also has been incorporated as an element of QRIS or as part of early intervention service provision with coaching for providers or for caregivers of children ages birth to 3.

In this chapter, we describe some considerations for programs and program leadership teams as they seek to offer PBC as a core component of ongoing PD to their staff. These considerations include (a) programwide implementation supports that are necessary to scale up and sustain coaching; (b) procedures used to identify and train coaches; (c) materials and training that might be used to guide coaching activities and monitor the delivery of coaching; (d) data decision-making practices to guide the allocation of coaching resources, examine fidelity of coaching, and monitor coaching outcomes; and (e) structures for guiding and supporting coaches in their roles.

PROGRAMWIDE IMPLEMENTATION

The provision of PBC in a program is often implemented by a team that has a leadership role or charge to consider how PBC can be implemented across all practitioners and sustained over time. In most programs, the installation and support of PBC is guided by a program leadership team that involves program administrators, the coach(es), and representative practitioners and consumers. The program leadership team focuses on the implementation of PBC as a core element in a broader effort for systemic change or quality improvement within the program. For example, in a program that implements the *Pyramid Model for Promoting the Social Emotional Competence for Infants and Young Children* (Fox et al., 2003; Hemmeter et al., 2006), the program leadership team makes decisions related to staff buy-in, family engagement, implementation of Pyramid Model practices, and the use of data for decision making (von der Embse et al., 2019). Decisions that the program leadership team makes in relationship to the implementation and ongoing sustainability of PBC in the program also include identifying coaches, training coaches, introducing the concept of coaching and facilitating coaching agreements with practitioners, determining the formats used for coaching, identifying who receives coaching, providing PD supports for coaches, and evaluating the implementation and outcomes of coaching.

Key Point to Remember

In most programs, the installation and support of PBC is guided by a program leadership team.

As described in Chapter 1, implementation science frameworks can be used to consider the processes or the infrastructure needed for successful installation of effective practices that will yield desired child and family outcomes. *Implementation science* refers to activities that are designed to put a defined set of practices, interventions, or activities in place (Fixsen et al., 2005). The interest in applying implementation science in early childhood programs and systems is largely an outcome of the growing interest in helping cross-sector programs in early childhood (e.g., Early Head Start/Head Start, early care and education, public pre-Kindergarten [pre-K], early intervention) implement effective practices with fidelity (Halle et al., 2013). In this way, the installation and the ability to sustain coaching programwide are critical components of implementation science. In the active implementation science frameworks, teams consider (a) the *competency drivers,* or system elements, that support the ability of personnel to implement effective practices; (b) the *organizational drivers* to develop the supports needed for the implementation of a new approach or practices, including using data for continuous improvement; and (c) the *leadership drivers* to make technical and adaptive decisions related to opportunities and challenges encountered during implementation (Fixsen et al., 2005; Fixsen et al., 2019; Halle et al., 2013).

Implementation is hypothesized to occur in stages. These stages are helpful to teams as they seek to provide programwide implementation of PBC as an ongoing PD strategy, framing their efforts as moving through exploration, initial installation, implementation, and full implementation (Fixsen et al, 2005; Fixsen et al., 2019; Metz et al., 2013; Meyers et al., 2012). Understanding that implementation is done in stages helps teams recognize that implementation occurs over time, there are activities and critical decisions that occur at incremental steps, and it might take time to achieve full implementation of PBC within the program. In Table 9.1, we provide examples of the activities and decisions of leadership teams that occur at each of these implementation stages of PBC.

Key Point to Remember

Knowing that implementation is done in stages helps teams understand that implementation occurs over time, activities and critical decisions occur at incremental steps, and it might take time to achieve full implementation of PBC within a program.

Table 9.1. Implementation stages for programwide practice-based coaching with leadership team activities and decisions

Implementation stage	Sample activities	Sample decisions
Exploration	• Identifying PBC as the approach for coaching • Examining the use of PBC by other similar programs • Identifying the content focus of PBC (e.g., specific practices, instructional strategies, new curriculum) • Identifying needed materials and resource allocations • Discussion of program practitioner interest and readiness	• Determining the contextual fit of PBC for practice improvement goals of the organization • Determining the availability of and needed materials and resources that will be used to install and sustain implementation • Determining the strengths and needs of the program to support PBC • Determining information and activities to support interest and readiness
Initial installation	• Identification of coaches • Training of coaches • Design of coaching manual or coaching protocols • Identification of strengths and needs assessment tools • Development of process for coaching assignments and coaching agreements • Design of professional development activities on a focused set of practices that coaching will enhance or extend • Identifying measures that will be used for coaching fidelity, fidelity of practice implementation, and outcomes	• Determining how coaches will be selected, trained, and supervised • Determining what strengths and needs assessment tools will be used • Determining the coaching caseload and schedule • Determining how coachees and coaches will enter into PBC agreements
Implementation	• Orientation to coach–coachee PBC meetings • Delivery of professional development in practices to coachees • Assignment of coaches to coachees • Scheduling of PBC sessions • Monitoring PBC implementation fidelity, practice implementation fidelity, and outcomes • Supervision and support of coaches • Informing families that coaching is being implemented in the program	• Determining who will receive coaching and the frequency of coaching delivery • Determining the data that will be collected from coaching and how data will be reviewed and used for decision making • Determining formats for coaching delivery and if formats might vary, when, and with whom • Determining how and when coaches will receive supervision and ongoing support • Determining how information will be shared with families and others
Full implementation	• Establishment of program policies and procedures related to PBC • Identification of fiscal resources to sustain PBC and integration of the provision of PBC into ongoing budget and organizational and leadership infrastructures • Recruitment and training of additional coaches • Finalizing systems for managing data related to provision of PBC implementation fidelity, practice implementation fidelity, and outcomes	• Using data to make decisions about how, when, and to whom coaching is provided • Introducing PBC to new personnel • Determining procedures for promoting the sustainability of practice implementation of coachees who have received PBC • Identifying and selecting new coaches • Determining factors that affect ongoing coaching delivery and outcomes • Determining innovations that might be used to increase coaching efficiency, fidelity, or outcomes

Key: PBC, practice-based coaching.

IDENTIFYING COACHES

Selection of Coaches

Given their critical role in facilitating learning and growth goals of programs and coachees, coaches must be carefully selected by program leadership teams. This is part of the initial implementation stage of PBC and requires the leadership to recruit, prepare, and retain highly qualified coaches. Coaches might be internal (e.g., practitioner leaders, existing coaches) or external candidates (e.g., recruiting/hiring individuals not currently employed by the program). In the sections that follow, the important practices, or competencies, that coaches should possess, as well as PD to acquire, improve, and sustain them are suggested. The Coaching Practices Strengths and Needs Assessment form (see Appendix II.F) can help guide

---

Tools for Teams and Coaches in the Appendices

Appendix II.F: Coaching Practices Strengths and Needs Assessment

This form is a resource in the Appendix that lists coaching practices for each part of the PBC framework. It is useful for program leadership teams and coaches to understand linkages between PBC competencies and practices.

Examples of Key Competencies for PBC Coaches

1. Advanced content knowledge, skills, and dispositions focused on effective practices relevant for the program and experiences implementing these practices

2. Fluency with the practices that are the focus of PBC

3. Ability to conduct objective observations of practice implementation and provide meaningful performance feedback

4. Knowledge and skills in data-informed decision making

5. Ability to engage in collaborative partnerships with adult learners

6. Ability to facilitate reflection and feedback with adult learners

7. Ability to support implementation of practices through lenses of equity and culturally responsive practices

---

program leader decisions related to recruiting, preparing, and retaining coaches. This form lists coaching practices for each part of the PBC framework and can help program leadership teams and coaches understand further linkages between PBC competencies and practices.

Professional Skill Competencies Important prerequisite knowledge and experiences position some individuals as more prepared to be PBC coaches. It might be beneficial for program leaders to look for individuals who have these competencies (National Center on Quality Teaching and Learning [NCQTL], 2014). In the adjacent box, we identify some of these key competencies that position some individuals as more prepared to be practice-based coaches. These competencies include advanced knowledge, skills, and dispositions in content and processes outlined by the program's organizational aims. It is important to note here that when identifying whether an individual possesses the necessary professional coaching competencies, these are different from supervision competencies. As described in Chapter 3, coaches are collaborative partners with the coachee and provide support focused on building coachee's knowledge, skills, dispositions, and practice implementation through iterative processes. Coaching is not evaluative or rooted in a coach's priorities.

Interpersonal Skill Competencies In addition to the key professional competencies, the ability to provide emotional and personal support to coachees through interpersonal skills is critical to the success of PBC implementation. The strength of the collaborative partnership between the coach and the coachee is important (Shannon, Snyder, et al., 2021). In addition, the coach should support implementation of practices through lenses of equity and culturally responsive practices (Ferro et al., 2020). Coachees receiving PBC should express that they feel valued by the program and are supported to engage in personal, as well as professional, growth. Coaches should not only demonstrate competence in professional skills important for PBC but should also show flexibility and strength in interpersonal skills to develop strong reciprocal partnerships with coachees (Borman & Feger, 2006). These skills include, but are not limited to, being trustworthy and empathetic, having effective communication skills, possessing the ability to collaborate and be open to new ideas, and promoting comfortable and engaging interactions and environments for PBC. Although content knowledge and practice fluency can be supported, interpersonal skills, which are largely based on individual attributes, might be harder to change or acquire through PD. The ability of a coach to provide emotional and personal support can help support fidelity of practice implementation, which supports coachees and leadership teams in meeting their goals (Shannon et al., 2015). A balance of professional and interpersonal skills results in a coach who is competent to and confident in providing high-quality PBC and who can cultivate collaborative partnerships and culturally responsive interactions with coachees (Ferro et al., 2020).

Additional Considerations Additional considerations for the selection of coaches include an assessment of whether the coach has the appropriate experiences to serve in a coaching role and the availability of the time needed to provide coaching. The program leadership team should identify individuals who, despite other roles they have, will be able to devote the time required for effective PBC. If programs do not have sufficient staff and must use supervisors to fill coaching roles, as described in Chapter 3, coaching must be clearly defined and separate from supervision activities (von der Embse et al., 2019). When selecting a coach, the leadership team should consider the coach's credibility from the perspective of coachees. Coaches that have related prerequisite knowledge about and experiences with the setting or the content focus of PBC (e.g., literacy practices, embedded instruction, social-emotional practices, math curriculum) increase the credibility of the coach to the coachee and the comfort of the coach in the coachee's practice setting. For example, it might be more difficult for a coachee to develop a collaborative partnership with a high school math teacher who is the coach identified to support implementation of preschool social and emotional skills. The identification of coaches might be hindered by a number of organizational or logistical barriers, so program leadership teams should carefully consider their resources and organizational capacity to support each coach and their coaching caseload.

Coach Professional Development

Once selected, coaches should receive PD in PBC, how to implement it with fidelity, and the interpersonal skills needed to support coachees. This means that coaches must receive PD that enables them to become fluent with the PBC framework and its components, coaching strategies used in PBC, how to establish and maintain collaborative coaching partnerships, and how to monitor PBC implementation fidelity. Coaches need to develop skills that include using strengths and needs assessment information to facilitate shared goal setting and action planning, gathering practice implementation data as part of focused observations, and using data to facilitate reflection and provide feedback. To develop these skills, coaches need initial and ongoing PD supports.

For coach PD, the same evidence-informed PD practices described in Chapter 2 should be used. Research has shown that adult learning is most effective when provided to small numbers of learners, in sustained and cohesive ways, with multiple exemplars, and with repeated opportunities for job-embedded practice and reflection and feedback on practice implementation (Dunst & Trivette, 2012; Dunst et al., 2010; Snyder, Denney, et al., 2011; Snyder, Hemmeter, et al., 2011). Coach PD should emphasize the importance of building and maintaining collaborative partnerships with adult learners. Collaborative partnership skills are discussed in Chapter 3 and include both coach and coachees understanding and valuing each other's input, seeing the partnership as equitable, transactional, and evolving over time.

Coach PD decisions should also be guided by organizational goals and desired outcomes. Leadership teams should deliberate and engage in reciprocal cycles of planning, implementing, and evaluating PD supports for coaches and coachees as they relate to desired proximal and distal outcomes. To facilitate these discussions, program leadership teams should use PD frameworks described in Chapter 2 and the backward mapping process (Guskey, 2014) described in Chapter 5.

Although additional research is needed to identify effective models for coach PD, several promising models and delivery formats are being implemented in various early childhood programs (e.g., Snyder et al., 2019). Evidence is emerging about the contextual fit of these models and outcomes from their implementation (e.g., Snyder, Shannon, et al., 2021). One model for coach PD has been developed by Snyder, Shannon, et al. as part of an initiative to support internal program coaches to provide workshops and PBC on embedded instruction practices to preschool teachers in California. In this model, PD for coaches uses parallel processes to those used with coachees. By *parallel processes,* we mean that coaches engage in PD focused both on the content focus of PBC and on PBC. Similar to coachees, coaches also receive PBC. They engage in strengths and needs assessments related to both PBC implementation and the practices that are the focus of PBC. With support from a lead implementation coach (LIC) within the program, or an external PBC coach who is part of a technical assistance entity, coaches set goals and develop action plans focused on their PBC implementation. They conduct focused observations of their coaching sessions, and focused observations are also conducted periodically by the LIC or external coach. They engage in self-reflection and self-evaluation of PBC implementation, and they also periodically engage in reflection and receive feedback from the LIC or external coach. Coaches participate in community-of-practice coaching calls held once a month (Snyder, Shannon, et al., 2021).

Coaches receive these PD supports, including PBC, until they demonstrate fidelity. Fidelity has been defined as at least 80% implementation of PBC practices for three coaching sessions as measured by coaching log indicators, coaching session summary forms, and an action plan fidelity checklist. Once a coach reaches fidelity, they continue to participate in monthly community-of-practice coaching calls, and they receive booster sessions once a year. Over time, coaches also can participate in trainer-of-trainer PD to become an LIC or an external PBC coach within a technical assistance entity (Snyder, Shannon, et al., 2021).

A Sample Practice-Based Coaching Workshop Agenda is provided in Appendix VI.V. It is critical to ensure that coaches are trained prior to implementation and that ongoing training and regular support ensure that effective practices and PBC processes are in place. However, training alone does not make sustainable change. The following sections highlight the additional considerations when implementing coaching that lead to more reliable and sustainable programs that implement PBC.

Tools for Leadership Teams and Coaches in the Appendices

Appendix VI.V: Sample Practice-Based Coaching Workshop Agenda

This is a resource in the Appendix that lists objectives for PBC training and an annotated outline of the scope, sequence, and duration of training.

IMPLEMENTING PRACTICE-BASED COACHING

The leadership team should determine how coaching will be delivered to coachees and how the fidelity of PBC implementation will be measured and monitored. These decisions will involve determining the coaching caseload, assigning coaches to coachees, specifying PBC procedures to follow, and determining how data on the implementation of PBC will be collected, summarized, and analyzed.

Selecting Coachees for Coaching

A program leadership team makes data-informed decisions about who receives coaching. The team might decide that all practitioners in the program will receive coaching; however, it is more likely that only some practitioners will be selected based on the program's available resources, the schedules and responsibilities of coachees, the number of coaches who are available, the coachee's strengths and needs related to the practices that are the focus of PBC, and the PD goals and desired outcomes. Some program leadership teams have used tiered PD frameworks to inform PD and coaching decisions. Using multi-tiered systems of support logic, these frameworks identify universal PD and PD supports provided to everyone in the program, targeted PD and PD supports for subgroups in a program (e.g., infant/toddler practitioners in a birth-to-5 program), and individualized PD and PD supports, including job-embedded approaches such as PBC (e.g., Thompson et al., 2012). Other teams use PD plans and select coachees to receive PBC for a specified amount of time. The questions in the adjacent box can help leadership teams and coaches make decisions about selecting coachees for coaching.

Coach Caseloads

The frequency of coaching and the amount of time coaches spend coaching each coachee and for how long vary depending on coachee's practice-focused strengths and needs. Coach caseloads (i.e., the number of coachees assigned to a coach) should be individually determined rather than based on a predetermined number. This means that coaches often have different numbers of coachees. For example, if a coach is supporting a coachee and there are many children in the classroom with persistent challenging behavior, the coachee might require more frequent coaching for a longer time because the coachee is implementing individualized behavior support practices with each child. On the other hand, coaching an experienced coachee who is fine-tuning a small set of practices might require less coaching support for a shorter time. The adjacent box provides a list of considerations that might be used when determining coaching caseloads.

Using Data to Determine Coaching Allocations Data from program or classroom assessment as well as strengths and needs assessment

---

Questions to Consider When Making Decisions About Selecting Coachees for PBC

1. Has the coachee had PD experiences that have helped them gain knowledge, skills, and dispositions to prepare them for PBC?

2. How will participation in PBC support the coachee's fidelity of practice implementation?

3. How many coachees can be selected and supported and for how long?

4. What is the organizational capacity within the program to support PBC (e.g., number of coaches, available time for coaching)?

5. What is the stage of PBC implementation (e.g., initial installation, full implementation) and what are the implications for providing PBC to coachees based on the implementation stage?

6. Is the program able to support coach/coachee schedule and responsibilities reallocations to support participation in PBC?

Determining Coaching Caseloads

1. Coaching format options (e.g., expert, reciprocal peer, self, group)

2. PBC delivery option (e.g., on-site, distance synchronous, distance asynchronous)

3. Number of coachees selected for and participating in coaching

4. Assessed strengths and needs of the coachees

5. Number and complexity of practices that are the current focus of PBC

6. Coach and coachee schedules and availability for PBC

7. Realigning or release from other duties for coachee and coach to engage in PBC

8. Number of coaches and percentages of effort available

---

tools can be used to measure fidelity of practice implementation and help inform decisions about coaching, coaching caseloads, and allocation of coaching resources. For example, coaches can use indicator and summary data from measures of practice implementation fidelity, such as the Teaching Pyramid Observation Tool (TPOT; Hemmeter et al., 2014) or the Teaching Pyramid Infant–Toddler Observation Scale (TPITOS; Bigelow et al., 2019). Examining implementation of practices aggregated and disaggregated across coachees within a classroom, program, agency, or region can assist with decisions about coaching allocations. Data from these tools can be used to determine which coachees might benefit from more intensive forms of coaching

---

Tools for Leadership Teams and Coaches in the Appendices

Appendix VI.W: Coaching Log

This is a resource that provides a coaching log and link to delete a spreadsheet that can be used to enter, summarize, and analyze the time coaches are devoting to PBC across their caseload, how coaches are spending their time, and the strategies they are using.

---

support (e.g., individual, in person) and which coachees might be more appropriate for less intensive forms of coaching support (e.g., group coaching, self-coaching).

At the program level, summary data can be used to make decisions about coaching allocations or reallocations. For example, program leaders might review data from a coaching log (sample in Appendix VI.W) to determine the time coaches are devoting to PBC across their caseload, how coaches are spending their time, and the coaching strategies they are using.

Guidance for Time Allocations and Schedules In planning for coaching caseloads, the team must consider the time available for coaching and the format used to provide coaching. In many programs, staff who provide coaching do not have full-time assignments dedicated to coaching. Although time spent coaching per coachee will ultimately vary across coachees, the following time approximations are provided (only as guidance) to programs when determining coaching schedule and caseload:

- A coach using a group coaching format will spend approximately 12–15 hr (minimum) a month for each group of 6–8 coachees, assuming that group coaching sessions are held biweekly. This time is inclusive of preparing for group meetings, facilitating biweekly group meetings, and completing occasional individual meetings with coachees or individual focused observations. In a group format, each coachee will designate approximately 2–3 hr per month to PBC.

- A coach using an individual coaching format will spend approximately 3 hr (minimum) for each coaching session per participating coachee. If coaching occurs monthly, this would be 3 hr (minimum) per month for each coachee. If coaching occurs biweekly, then it would be 6 hr (minimum) per month for each coachee. If coaching occurs every week, this would be 12 hr per month for each coachee. The 3-hr estimate per coaching session is inclusive of preparing for coaching sessions, completing focused observations, and participating in meetings with coachees for reflection and feedback and goal setting and action planning. In an individual format, each coachee will designate approximately 30–60 min per session to PBC.

Tools for Leadership Teams and Coaches in the Appendices

Appendix VII.AE: Sample Weekly Practice-Based Coaching Schedule and Appendix VII.AF: Time Management Tips for Practice-Based Coaching Coaches

These are two resources that provide a sample coaching schedule and tip sheet for coaches to assist in PBC time management.

Table 9.2 uses three example PBC implementation studies (Fettig & Artman-Meeker, 2016; Hemmeter et al., 2016; Snyder, Hemmeter, et al., 2018) to suggest the approximate time and schedule required for PBC in both group and individual coaching formats. In addition, the Sample Weekly Practice-Based Coaching Schedule and Time Management Tips for Practice-Based Coaching Coaches can be found in Appendices VII.AE and VII.AF, respectively.

When making decisions about PBC schedules, time spent on PBC implementation is an important consideration. The following box shows additional activities that not only will affect the PBC schedule but will need to be considered as coaches and leadership teams make decisions about coaching allocations and schedules, the number of coaches needed, and resources that will be needed to support PBC implementation.

Table 9.2. Approximate time allocations for group and individual practice-based coaching formats

Format	Group coaching		Individual coaching	
Ratio of coach to coachees	6:1 to 8:1		1:1	
Coach time allocation	12–15 hr per month with biweekly group coaching		2–3 hr per PBC session	
Coachee time allocation	2–3 hr per month		30–60 min per PBC session	
Activities included, with guidance for time allocation	Preparing materials for group sessions	1–2 hr per meeting	Preparing for individual session	1–2 hr per coachee
	Facilitating group PBC	90 min (minimum) per biweekly group meeting	Focused observation	15–60 min per coachee per session
	Individual meetings and/or observations	60 min per coachee per month, as needed	Debriefing meeting (i.e., reflection, feedback, action planning)	15–30 min per coachee per session

Program leaders might use a coaching assignment tracking sheet (see Figure 9.1) during the preparation stage of coaching allocation and developing a PBC schedule. Use of this type of tool can assist the team in tracking relevant decisions about coaching allocation, including which practitioners have been assigned a coach, which practitioners will be getting coaching support first, and the frequency, intensity, and duration of PBC for each coach–coachee partnership.

Alternative Coaching Delivery Methods

As program leaders plan for coaching allocations and caseloads, they should consider strategies to increase coaching efficiencies. They might consider having alternative delivery formats to expert coaching available, including reciprocal peer coaching, self-coaching, or group coaching. Technology such as videoconferenc-ing or web-based coaching platforms can be used effectively in PBC (see Chapter 10) and can help reduce time and travel needed for on-site focused observations and reflection and feedback meetings. Finally, leadership teams might consider grouping practitioners who are working on similar goals or in close geographical proximity to help reduce coach preparation time and reduce travel and meeting times.

Other PBC Time Allocation and Scheduling Considerations

- Completing and reviewing strengths and needs assessments
- Preparing for and conducting focused observations and reflection and feedback meetings
- Recording travel time and expenses
- Reviewing recorded videos
- Preparing material provision, including locating resources or developing materials or activities to support goal and action plans
- Completing documentation (e.g., coach logs, schedules, travel forms)
- Sending follow-up e-mails
- Making phone or video calls
- Recording and reviewing coaching log data
- Preparing and sharing data with other coaches and program leadership team

Coaching Manual and Materials

One way to ensure that all coaches in a program are implementing PBC with fidelity and following program guidelines for implementation is to use a coaching manual (see sample table of contents in Appendix VI.X) and consistent PBC materials. Coaching manuals are important

Practitioner	Coach	Start Date	End Date	Assigned Activity
Ciera	Alice	9/8	2/9	Monthly PBC for observation Follow-up after monthly community of practice Monthly PBC for reflection and feedback meeting Self-coaching
Christopher	Alice	9/1	1/26	Monthly PBC for observation Follow-up after monthly community of practice Monthly PBC for reflection and feedback meeting
Iris	Michael	9/1	2/20	Biweekly PBC for observation Follow-up after monthly community of practice Monthly PBC for reflection and feedback meeting

Figure 9.1. Example coaching assignment tracking sheet (individual coaching format). Adapted from von der Embse, M., Nemec, A., Vorhaus, E., Fox, L., Ferro, J., Hemmeter, M. L., & Binder, D. (2019). Program leadership team guide: Implementing practice-based coaching within the Pyramid Model. https://challengingbehavior.cbcs.usf.edu/docs/LeadershipTeam_PBC_Guide.pdf (*Key:* PBC, practice-based coaching.)

Tools for Leadership Teams and Coaches in the Appendices

Appendix VI.X: Sample Practice-Based Coaching Manual Table of Contents

This is a resource that provides a sample table of contents from a PBC manual.

---

because they help to ensure fidelity of PBC implementation and are an important and ongoing resource for coaches.

Within the coaching manual, the PBC framework is illustrated and each component is defined and illustrated. The manual should include a description of the practices that are the focus of PBC and where coaches can access additional PD resources related to these practices. The manual should include descriptions of when and how coaching sessions are delivered and the forms to be completed and data to be gathered within and across coaching cycles. Other elements include implementation documents and coaching logs, strengths and needs assessment documents, and program-specific expectations for PBC. Materials and forms included in PBC manuals have been described throughout the chapters in this book (e.g., coaching agreements, coach and coachee strengths and needs assessments, definitions of PBC strategies, shared goal-setting guidance and examples, action plans, action plan fidelity checklists, focused observation and data collection forms, reflection and feedback guidance and examples, coaching logs, coaching data entry and analysis procedures and resources).

Coaching Implementation Support

In addition to initial coach training, as described previously, decisions about "coaching the coaches" are necessary to model and monitor the strengths and needs of coaches who are facilitating PBC in a program. Coaches will benefit from opportunities to enhance their coaching skills and will need access to the same evidenced-based PD that they are promoting. Coaches often work in isolation from other coaches, and while they are included as part of the program's PD system, they are often in the role of facilitating and providing the learning and coaching opportunities for all other program staff. In programs with more than one coach, an LIC can be designated as a member of the coaching team who oversees PBC implementation and serves as the leader of the coaching team (Snyder, Shannon, et al., 2021).

When program leaders provide an opportunity for coaches to develop their skills outside of the practitioner–coach relationship, they ensure the development of a common framework of knowledge and skills about evidence-informed coaching practices/strategies, reinforce program organizational aims, and allow for critical discussion and coach collaborative learning (Shams, 2013). An additional layer of support to the PBC cycle can be envisioned, which focuses on how to prepare and build confidence in coaches to meet their responsibilities as leaders of PBC implementation.

Implementation support for coaches can focus on ensuring that there is a shared language about PBC across the program or program sites, developing interpersonal skills related to establishing a collaborative partnership with coachees, and defining methods and language for sharing data with coachees and other stakeholders, including program leadership team members. In addition, similar to expectations for coaches to facilitate reflection and provide feedback to coachees, coaches should be equipped with tools to reflect on and share feedback on their coaching practices for continuous learning. The adjacent box describes three possible

---

Helping Coaches Reflect on Coaching Knowledge, Skills, and Dispositions

Case Study Review

Once a month, coaches meet with the lead coach to share a case study about a coach–coachee partnership. The case study could focus on a successful partnership or one that is challenging. Information shared might include the context in which coaching is occurring, history and current status of the coachee's goals and action plans, the strengths and needs of the coachee, and identification of the successes or challenges of PBC implementation (e.g., challenges of meeting an action plan goal, what led to goal achievement, how to engage coachee in reflection, how to improve the provision of constructive feedback). A case study focus question (e.g., "How can I . . . ," "What are some ways to . . . ," "What can I do to practice . . .") based on the existing information is then discussed by meeting participants who generate and identify potential resources, next steps, and suggestions for PBC refinement or improvement.

Glows and Grows

On a bimonthly basis, strategically align opportunities for coaches to share the greatest successes and greatest challenges they noticed at different stages of PBC implementation.

Targeted Coaching Goals

On a monthly basis, support coaches to develop coaching goals and an action plan. Both a long-term goal and short-term goal, as well as the steps to meet the goal, will help coaches and the lead coach identify ongoing PD and resource needs of coaches (e.g., webinars, sharing of specific resources).

---

reflection practices that might help coaches enhance their PBC knowledge, skills, and dispositions; develop self-efficacy about their PBC practices; and problem-solve challenging PBC situations.

Coaching Fidelity Measures   Coaches should receive initial and ongoing PD to implement each component of the PBC framework with fidelity (NCQTL, 2014). When coaches are trained and supported to implement PBC in job-embedded environments with individualized implementation support, it is often associated with improved fidelity of practice and positive outcomes for young children (Snyder et al., 2015). Coaching fidelity measures should be used by lead coaches and program leaders, as well as coaches themselves, to guide activities and decisions about coach strengths and needs, to direct ongoing coach PD, and to monitor and sustain fidelity of PBC implementation.

Coaching fidelity measures should include both adherence and quality or competence dimensions. *Adherence* means that a coaching practice is implemented (e.g., the coach provided supportive feedback). *Quality* means that the practice was implemented competently (i.e., the coach provided supportive feedback that was descriptive and practice focused). Coaching fidelity measures often are triangulated with coaching observation data, coaching documentation (e.g., coaching logs), or other forms (e.g., action plans) to examine PBC adherence and quality. The section that follows provides more explicit guidance to ensure that PBC is being implemented with fidelity in addition to other uses of PBC data for data-based decision-making processes.

DATA USE AND DATA DECISION MAKING

PBC must be implemented with fidelity with sufficient frequency, intensity, and duration (dose), and each component of PBC must be delivered as intended across the delivery format(s) to achieve intended effects (Powell & Diamond, 2013; Snyder et al., 2015). The collection and review of data that link PBC implementation to practice change and to desired outcomes should be a continuous and ongoing process. Data-informed implementation and outcome snapshot reviews should be conducted periodically (e.g., monthly, quarterly). As part of these reviews, data are summarized and analyzed so that PBC implementation plans, which include goals and action steps, can be reviewed and updated. From the active implementation science frameworks, as described in Chapter 1, both technical and adaptive leadership and organizational drivers are needed to facilitate PBC implementation, including data systems that support decision making (Fixsen & Blase, 2008; Fixsen et al., 2019; Snyder, Shannon, et al., 2021). Data related to PBC implementation and its effects are an important part of comprehensive decision-making models that have been described in the early childhood implementation science literature (e.g., Johnson, 2017; Lloyd et al., 2013; Powell & Diamond, 2013).

Data-informed decision making about PBC requires both effort and effect data (Snyder, Hemmeter, et al., 2021). Effort data are used to address questions and inform decisions about the quantity and quality of PBC implementation (e.g., Did we do what we said we would do with PBC implementation? How well did we do what said we would do?). Effect data are used to address questions and inform decisions about quantity and quality of PBC impacts (e.g., How many coachees achieved their action plan goals? What percentage of coachees achieved their goals? How much improvement in coachees' implementation of effective practices was seen 1 year after implementation of PBC?). Using a results-based accountability framework (Friedman, 2015), Figure 9.2 shows a framework, with example data sources, that can be used to guide effort and effect data discussions about PBC (Snyder, Hemmeter, et al., 2021).

Key Point to Remember

Data-informed decision making about PBC requires both effort and effect data.

As shown in Figure 9.2, to examine whether PBC was implemented as intended, fidelity of implementation of all components of the cycle needs to occur (Snyder et al., 2015). The program leadership team has a responsibility to evaluate whether coaching is, in fact, being implemented with fidelity and whether it is effectively improving implementation of effective practices, which is the primary expected effect of coaching. The team is also responsible for examining linkages among fidelity of PBC implementation, effective practices, and desired child outcomes (see Chapter 2).

The coach is responsible for using data to inform what they are doing with coachees and to plan for future implementation. If the coach does not implement PBC with fidelity, for example, they might schedule a focused observation but fail to provide opportunities for reflection and feedback. As a result, the coachee will not receive an essential and evidence-informed ingredient of PBC. If coaches are not implementing PBC with fidelity, it is unlikely that effective practices will be used with fidelity by coachees.

Both coaches and the program leadership team should engage in data collection and data-informed decision making. In the section that follows, we describe examples of effort data that can be collected to support data-informed decision making about PBC implementation.

	Quantity	**Quality**
Was PBC implemented as intended? **Effort** →	How much, how often, or how was PBC implemented? Example data sources and data: Coaching logs • Number of sessions • Length of sessions • Duration of sessions Coaching delivery formats • Number on site • Number virtual • Number of individual sessions • Number of group sessions	How well was PBC implemented? Example data sources and data: Coaching log • Percentage of essential coaching components and strategies implemented in each coaching cycle Coach fidelity checklist • Percentage of sessions at ≥80% implementation fidelity Action Plan Fidelity Checklist • Percentage of action plans at ≥80% fidelity
Effect → **Is PBC implementation making a difference?** (for coaches, coachees, children/families)	Who changed and how much change occurred from PBC? Example data sources and data: Coaches • Number of coaches implementing PBC with fidelity Coachees • Number of practice implementation goals met • Number of action plans completed Children/Families • Number of children demonstrating learning gains • Number of families implementing effective practices with fidelity	What quality of change occurred from PBC? (knowledge, behaviors skills, attitudes, circumstances) Example data sources and data: Coaches • Percentage of coaches demonstrating improved confidence and competence as a coach Coachees • Percentage of coaches implementing effective practices with fidelity • Percentage of coaches demonstrating improved confidence to implement effective practices Children/Families • Percentage of children demonstrating desired knowledge and skills • Percentage of families demonstrating improved confidence and confidence to support child development and learning

Figure 9.2. Framework for guiding data-informed decisions about Practice-Based Coaching implementation and effects. From Snyder, P., Hemmeter, M.L., & Shannon, D. (2021). Contextual fit and practice-based coaching data-informed decision making (PBC-DIDM) [Conference poster presentation]. 2021 OSEP Leadership and Project Director's Conference, Virtual. https://osepideasthatwork.org/osep-meeting/2021-leadership-and-project-directors-conference?tab=om-agenda (*Key:* PBC, practice-based coaching.)

Implementing Practice-Based Coaching as Intended

Coaching efforts, including how much, how often, or how PBC was implemented and how well PBC was implemented, can be measured using the coaching log and action plan. The adjacent box shows the types of implementation or effort data that can be gathered from these sources.

An example of a classroom coaching log that captures select PBC implementation data quickly and efficiently is found in Appendix VI.T. The coach completes a log entry for each coaching cycle with one practitioner. This information is entered into a spreadsheet that provides a graph and table of the data for a visual display that can be used by the coach, lead coach, program

PBC Implementation or Effort Data from Coaching Logs and Action Plans

- Implementation of all coaching components during each coaching cycle (i.e., shared goals and action planning, focused observation, reflection and feedback)
- Number of cycles completed
- Coaching strategies used during observation and reflection and feedback
- Number and length of coaching sessions
- Duration of coaching sessions
- Format of coaching
- Action plan goals identified and completed
- Action plan component fidelity

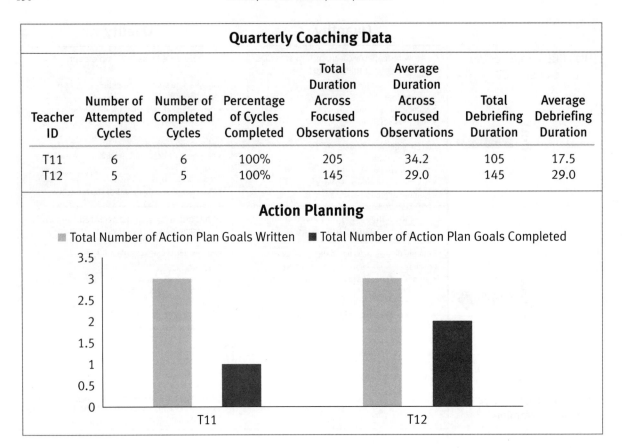

Figure 9.3. Display of classroom coaching log data.

leader, or leadership team for use in data-informed decision making. Program leadership then use data from the coaching log to do the following:

- Examine the fidelity of coaching implementation across all coaches within the program

- Evaluate policies and procedures related to coaching, including allocation of coaching resources (e.g., number of coaches, time allotted to coaching for both coaches and coachees, coaching schedules or delivery method, coach training needs)

- Examine fidelity and intensity of coaching to coachee implementation of practices

- Identify needs for additional PD for one or multiple coachees

Tools for Leadership Teams and Coaches

Appendix VI.T: Practice-Based Coaching Log

This is a resource that provides an example of a coaching log that can be used as a data source for PBC implementation.

For example, the information shown in Figure 9.3 provides a display of some data from a coaching log (i.e., coaching cycles, duration, and the number of action plan goals completed) for two teachers who are receiving PBC. Summarizing the data in a table and graph helps inform decisions about coaching implementation. In this example, one of the teachers (T11) has received more coaching cycles but has completed fewer action plan goals. In addition, the time for reflection and feedback (debrief) meetings for T11 is low in comparison to the other teacher. Analyzing and digging deeper into these data will help the program leadership team and the coach to identify what, if anything, might need to change to improve coaching implementation or outcomes.

Coaches should use implementation data from sources like the coaching log data on a more frequent basis to analyze their current coaching status and to plan next steps. Monthly data review and analysis includes each element of the coaching log to ensure that the coach consistently includes all components of the PBC cycle and completes them in a timely manner. Each element provides insight into what is working and what might need to be modified or improved. For example, the number and quality of completed action plan goals are important data elements that can help inform decisions about how coaching is affecting the implementation of practices, strategies, or curricula in the target environment.

The coach can also share data from the coaching log with each coachee to highlight accomplishments, acknowledge challenges, and identify strategic changes for future coaching. For example, the coach might share the number of action plan goals that were completed, improvements in the coachee's implementation of practices, and changes in children's skills. They might also work with the coachee to identify different strategies that might more efficiently achieve goal attainment. In addition, coaches might use data to share different strategies for developing goals and action plans so that broad goals become more focused on pivotal practices.

Although coaching implementation data at the coach and coachee levels is one important source in data-informed decision making, as shown in Figure 9.2, these data are only part of the effort and effect data that can be examined. Coaches, lead coaches, and program leadership teams who are interested in exploring relationships among fidelity of PD and PBC implementation, improved implementation of effective practices, and child or family outcomes should conduct data snapshot reviews two to three times a year and an annual review of coaching effects. The annual reviews should include data sources on coachees' fidelity of implementation of effective practices and child or family outcomes. For example, TPOT (Hemmeter et al., 2014) scores from fall and spring assessments might be used along with fall–spring measures of children's social skills. Data for coachees' fidelity of practice implementation and child outcomes should come from instruments that have been demonstrated to yield valid and reliable scores. Combined with coaching implementation data, these data will support a robust evaluation of the efforts and effects of coaching.

Look-Think-Act for Data-Based Decision Making

One useful and straightforward approach to guide the review of effort and effect data to inform data-based decisions is the Look-Think-Act Discussion Guide (see Appendix VII.AG for a sample).

Look-Think-Act was developed to provide programs and individuals

> **Tools for Leadership Teams and Coaches**
>
> *Appendix VII.AG: Look-Think-Act Discussion Guide*
>
> This resource in the Appendix provides an example of a data discussion guide framed around Look-Think-Act.

who may not know how to collect or analyze data with a how-to guide for doing so and for linking analysis to effective actions. Look-Think-Act is an effective tool to use with any type of effort or effect data, including coaching implementation data. The components and their intended purpose are as follows: 1) *Look:* examine data for trends and meaningful associations; 2) *Think:* ask questions related to the data that might help with interpretation; and 3) *Act:* identify the action plan needed to put decisions made by the team in place. It guides coaches and program leadership through an analysis of all the coaching elements in order to identify patterns. Also, it includes questions that prompt improved reflection as well as suggestions of steps that can be implemented to make informed coaching decisions.

The Look step begins with an examination of data in a factual manner and without drawing conclusions. During this part of the process, graphic display of data is an important tool for summarizing and for easier interpretation (Hojnoski, Gischlar, et al., 2009). The Think step provides questions that begin the analysis. Reflecting on each element of data leads to conclusions or identifies a need for additional information. In the Act step, actions are identified that directly link to the conclusions drawn from the data during the Think step. Actions might involve individual changes to coaching strategies or changes that are programwide, such as training for all coachees on specific practices. For example, the data presented in Figure 9.3 might lead program leadership to generate questions during the Think step, such as:

- Does the coachee who received shorter coaching sessions have enough time allocated to meet with the coach?

- Does the coach have enough time allocated to work with all coachees on their assigned caseload?

- What ideas or information does the coach have about what would make them more reliable in their implementation of PBC?

- Is the coach using a variety of coaching strategies to help practitioners meet action plan goals?

- Does more time need to be allocated to coaching?

- Does the coach need additional training on how to foster collaborative partnerships or reflection and feedback?

- Do coachees need additional PD to increase their knowledge of specific practices?

- Do program policies allocate sufficient time for coaches to work with each individual assigned to their caseloads in ways that will facilitate goal and action plan achievements?

The information generated from the Think step will then lead program leadership teams to specific action steps, such as deciding to hire additional coaches, providing classroom coverage so the coachee can meet with the coach, identifying additional resources for effective practices that the coachee and coach can use, scheduling additional coach training, or changes in schedules, caseloads, or policies to allow more dedicated time or resources for PBC.

In the Think step, coaches or lead coaches should question each element of the PBC cycle and compare differences within and across their caseload. For example, the coach might ask:

- Are incomplete coaching cycles having an effect on goal completion across and within coachees?

- What circumstances led to incomplete coaching cycles?

- Is the time spent with each practitioner affecting goal completion?

- Were a variety of coaching strategies used, and which strategies most affected practice implementation and goal completion?

- Are the coaching strategies being used with coachees who met action plan goals different from coaching strategies used with coachees that did not meet goals?

- Are there common needs for coachee practice implementation support that would benefit from specific and targeted PD?

- How much time was spent with each coachee, and did that affect action plan completion?

During the Think step, the coach might also dig deeper by reviewing additional data sources. For example, if a coachee did not meet any goals for the month, the coach might review the action plan with the coachee to ensure that the planned steps are not too small, are clear, and are appropriate for the goal. The coach might also review data from strengths and needs assessments or do short and quick practice checks to evaluate whether the coachee's current goals are appropriate. Practice checks refer to pulling out a few practices or the critical components of key practices from a larger set of practices (e.g., TPOT; Hemmeter et al., 2014) for assessing practice implementation. For example, completing an observation of classroom transitions using the Transition key practice and associated indicators on the TPOT would be a method of collecting information about goal progress and practice implementation without completing the full measure.

Sustainability of Coaching Effects

For practices to be sustainable, coachees must implement them accurately and fluently (i.e., consistently, effortlessly, and efficiently). Fluency, or competent practice, often is defined as accurate and efficient practice implementation at 80% or greater of observed opportunities. As described in Chapter 6, acquisition refers to a phase of learning in which a coachee is implementing a practice, sometimes accurately and sometimes not. Fluency involves implementing a practice accurately and efficiently. Fluency is important because it sets the occasion for generalization of practice implementation across people, settings, or times of the day and maintenance or sustainability.

Major goals of PBC are to support coachees to achieve fluency and to support generalization and sustainability of practice implementation. Achieving fluency is not linked to a specific number of coaching sessions. Instead, it is determined with reference to implementing practices at a specific criterion (e.g., 80%) over a defined period of time (e.g., 80% fidelity of practice implementation over three consecutive focused observations). Generalization of practice implementation and sustainability of practice implementation are also important to consider once fluency has been achieved. Linking practice fidelity data to child or family outcomes over time can also help inform decisions about how fluency, generalization, and maintenance should be defined and measured.

Sustainability of practice implementation by coachees might be supported through gradually reducing the dose (i.e., frequency, intensity, duration) or dose formats (e.g., group vs. individual) of coaching. In this way, programs can emphasize the importance of sustaining practice implementation after more intensive supports are removed. For example, the format of coaching might be changed from expert and individual coaching to group, peer, or self-coaching. As described previously, an important and effective approach for sustaining the effects of coaching is the collection and use of data from brief observations to full assessments of practice implementation. The adjacent box lists other strategies that will help sustain implementation after PBC on a defined set of practices ends.

Strategies to Help Sustain Practice Implementation

- Yearly assessments of practice implementation
- Periodic checks or snapshots of practice implementation
- Review of ongoing coachee efforts to improve knowledge, skills, and dispositions
- Reminders about effective practices and strategies
- Using just-in-time PD supports, including PBC, when data show practice implementation slippage
- Providing positive and descriptive feedback about practice implementation
- Incorporating practices that have been the focus of PBC into program policies, procedures, and curricula

---

ONGOING IMPLEMENTATION SUPPORTS FOR COACHES

Learning Communities to Guide and Support Coaches

As programs work toward full implementation of PBC, leadership teams and lead coaches should provide guidance and ongoing support for coaches. Careful consideration should be given to providing time and resources for coaches to engage in learning opportunities with a focus on their own professional growth and skills as a coach. To provide this level of support, the NCQTL recommends that coaches connect with a community of coaches, offering tips for sharing successes and challenges (see Top 10 Tips for Coaches in Appendix VI.Y). These types of coaching networks foster a community of collaboration among coaches. For example, in a professional learning community (PLC), PD is delivered to small groups with shared interests in a way that promotes collaboration and working together to expand knowledge and skills (Dimino et al., 2015). It is important to note that the term *PLC* is often used to describe any, and all, combinations of individuals meeting together, and the names and purposes of the groups might vary. In a review of the research literature on learning communities, the use of a PLC as a model of community learning was found to have a positive impact on continuous learning and practices (Vescio et al., 2008). These types of learning communities "operate under the assumption that the key to improved learning for students is continuous job-embedded learning for educators" (DuFour et al., 2016, p. 10), and program leadership teams and lead coaches are encouraged to provide such opportunities for supporting coaches.

Even though how and how often to establish and use a PLC model with coaches has not been extensively studied, one approach that has been identified is peer practice groups (Shams, 2013). This model of support develops coaching practices at a group level, similar to the structure and routines used during PBC group coaching. Using peer practice groups, learning communities should include a discussion protocol with a goal statement, clearly identified roles for members, and set agendas (Kosanovich & Foorman, 2016). Coach participants continue to use data to ground their group discussions and focus on effective coaching practices. The goal of a peer practice group is to provide an effective learning environment for coaches and to increase professional practices in coaching (Shams, 2013). Specific to PBC, Snyder, Shannon, et al. (2021) have applied a similar peer practice group approach with coaches involved in a project focused on embedded instruction practices. The box shows four ways the goals of a coach peer practice group can be achieved.

Peer Practice Group Activities to Strengthen PBC

1. Share resources.

2. Engage in critical discussion that can help to strengthen coaching practices.

3. Share ideas and build collaborative relationships among coaches.

4. Provide learning and skill building activities.

   a. Develop new skills.

   b. Try a new coaching technique or make a change to the coaching approach.

Establishing these collaborative learning communities requires a commitment from coaches in the same program, district, or geographical area to gather in person or virtually on a regular basis. Program leadership will need to ensure regular time allocation for the learning community to convene. Several essential components of a learning community include supportive and shared leadership, and shared values and vision (Hord, 2004). A well-established facilitator, such as a lead coach, can help build on these essentials by organizing the group, coordinating the selection of PD materials and coaching skills, and ensuring that goals of the group are met. Effective facilitators should have strong PBC content knowledge, advanced knowledge about the practices that are the focus of PBC, strong communication skills, and the ability to relate well to adult learners (Garet et al., 2001; Leithwood & Riehl, 2003). Facilitators might provide support during the peer practice group, as well as meet with coaches individually as needed. When implementing a peer practice group, it will be important that the learning community provides coaches with a safe environment where coaches can openly discuss their successes and challenges, learn new practices, and have opportunities to engage in constructive reflection and give and receive feedback.

To provide structure to a peer practice group or PLC, one recommended practice includes a five-step process for collaborative learning (Kosanovich & Foorman, 2016). This process was adapted from an inquiry-action cycle, which encourages practitioners to reflect on their current practices, explore new strategies, and consider how to apply new strategies in practice contexts (Dimino et al., 2015). Based on this process, each coaching peer practice group would include the following:

1. Discussion and debrief around a coaching component, coaching strategy, or practice

2. Defining session or group meeting goal

3. Exploration of new or refined practices and comparison to current practices

4. Experimentation or practice with newly learned knowledge or skills

5. Reflection and implementation.

The reflection component of the meeting is an integral component in the meeting. Coaches should have at least 10–15 min of the meeting to reflect on the session itself. By participat-ing in a group together, coaches can deepen their understanding of content, review coaching data, practice skills, share coaching insights, and review successes and challenges faced in coaching (Shams, 2013). An Example Coach Learning Community Meeting Agenda can be found in Appendix VI.Z.

Tools for Leadership Teams and Coaches in the Appendices

Appendix VI.Z: Coach Learning Community Meeting Agenda

This is a resource that provides an example of an agenda for a coach learning community meeting.

There might be instances in which programs cannot provide a collaborative learning approach for coaches. Coaches might work in isolation or the closest coach is beyond a distance that makes traveling to a group a reality. In these situations, program leadership teams and lead coaches might want to explore the use of virtual connections that can provide a safe space for coaches to continue to expand their knowledge base and application of coaching approaches and skills. For example, a PBC community exists through *My Peers*, a virtual learning network developed by the Office of Head Start where early childhood practitioners can exchange ideas and share resources with other colleagues across the country. The coaching learning commu-nity described by Snyder, Shannon, et al. (2021) is also conducted through a virtual learning network and uses videoconferencing and an online coaching platform. Through these or other PBC networks, coaches can elect to become members of a community committed to supporting PBC implementation, providing networking, sharing of resources, and access to ongoing PD.

SUMMARY

In this chapter, we presented key considerations for implementing and sustaining a robust PBC program. The implementation of PBC within a program is complex and requires consideration of interrelated competency, organizational, and leadership factors so that PBC can be provided in the most effective and efficient ways. Gathering effort and effect data to inform decisions about PBC implementation and outcomes is critical. The implementation science literature sug-gests it can take 4 or more years to install, reach full implementation, and sustain a robust infra-structure for PBC and the implementation of effective practices (Metz et al., 2013). Nevertheless, we are confident that an investment in a robust infrastructure for PBC will result in meaningful efforts and effects for coaches, coachees, children, and families.

10

Using Technology to Support Practice-Based Coaching Implementation

Crystal Bishop, Ragan H. McLeod, Kathleen Artman-Meeker, and Mary Louise Hemmeter

USING TECHNOLOGY TO SUPPORT PRACTICE-BASED COACHING IMPLEMENTATION

Technology can be used to support the implementation of Practice-Based Coaching (PBC) in many ways, ranging from the enhancement of essential coaching strategies of observation, reflective conversation, supportive and constructive feedback, and providing resources, to serving as the platform within which all the PBC components (i.e., strengths and needs assessment, shared goal setting and action planning, focused observation, reflection and feedback) occur. The purpose of this chapter is to describe the types of technology that can be used to support implementation of PBC and to discuss their relative benefits with respect to implementation of the essential coaching strategies discussed in Chapter 4 and coaching delivery formats described in Chapter 2. We also discuss important considerations and recommendations for using these technologies.

TYPES AND USES OF TECHNOLOGY ACROSS PRACTICE-BASED COACHING DELIVERY FORMATS

The PBC framework can be applied in a variety of delivery formats that differ by (a) who provides coaching (i.e., self, expert, peer), (b) whether coaching is provided individually or in groups, and (c) the modality through which coaching supports are provided (i.e., live, distance, synchronous, asynchronous). PBC delivery formats can also be blended to create hybrid models that optimize program resources to provide just-in-time and individualized coaching supports based on coachee strengths and needs. Figure 10.1 illustrates how Maureen and Maria, Sam, and Lynn engage in different PBC delivery formats. As can be seen from these brief examples, technology can be used to enhance or support the implementation of

> **Key Point to Remember**
>
> PBC can be implemented using a variety of delivery formats that differ by who provides coaching, whether coaching is provided individually or in groups, and the modality through which coaching supports are provided.

Sam

Sam meets with his coach, Kenya, once per week in his classroom. This week during his focused observation, Kenya is video recording Sam as he prepares children to transition to centers and as he interacts with children during centers. They watch the video during their reflection and feedback meeting. First, they work together to tally the number of positive reminders Sam provides to children about the rules and expectations for centers and the number of positive descriptive feedback statements he provides to individual children about their behavior with respect to the posted rules and expectations. Kenya provides supportive feedback to Sam for giving all children positive reminders about the rules when he reviewed them with the group before going to centers. She also notes that Sam gave positively stated reminders to three different children during centers. Sam notes that he counted seven general praise statements and two descriptive praise statements and asks to review parts of the video where he used general praise statements so he can write down some examples of descriptive praise statements he might have used instead.

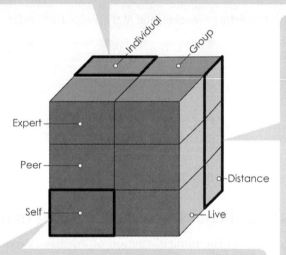

Maureen and Maria

Maureen and Maria completed 14 weeks of live coaching with Elley and are now participating in a month of distance coaching to sustain their implementation of embedded instruction practices. Together, Maureen and Maria write a shared goal and action plan focused on sustainability of embedded instruction practices, which they upload to a web-based coaching platform. They collect data on each others' implementation of embedded instruction practices and use part of their teacher planning time to review their data, provide each other with supportive and constructive feedback, and engage in reflection and feedback. In preparation for their monthly coaching session with Elley, they upload a video of themselves implementing the practices that are the focus of their action plan in a web-based coaching platform. Elley uses a commenting feature within the platform to prompt further reflection and provide supportive and constructive feedback about their use of embedded instruction. Within 1 week of uploading their video, Maureen, Maria, and Elley also have a PBC meeting via video conference.

Lynn

After completing her third action plan, Lynn and Sirena reviewed data showing Lynn's implementation of effective practices to promote children's language development. They determined that not only had Lynn increased her use of all the practices she identified as foci for her action plans, but also she was maintaining her use of practices across time. During the data review, Lynn identified a new practice she would like to work on, and she showed Sirena an action plan she had developed on her own before the session. Both Sirena and Lynn determined that Lynn would continue to enhance her use of practices to promote language development through self-coaching. Carl or Elita helps her collect video during ongoing activities one time each week. During her planning time, she reviews her video and engages in self-reflection about her progress on her action plan. She writes down areas of strength and gives herself constructive feedback identifying strategies she can use to enhance her use of the practice. Once a month, Sirena sends a text via a coaching app to get general updates about Lynn's progress and to encourage her to continue self-coaching.

Figure 10.1. Practice-Based Coaching (PBC) delivery formats and example uses of technology within and across PBC delivery formats.

PBC across delivery formats, and the types and extent to which technology is integrated can vary across formats.

This chapter focuses on the most common technologies that might be used to support the implementation of PBC, which include (a) video recordings and exemplars, (b) videoconferencing, (c) web-based coaching platforms, (d) bug-in-ear, and (e) coaching apps. Definitions of these technologies are provided in Figure 10.2. A discussion of the ways in which these technologies might be used to enhance implementation of coaching strategies or to

> Common technologies that can be used to support PBC implementation include video recordings and exemplars, videoconferencing, web-based coaching platforms, bug-in-ear, and coaching apps.

Video Recordings

The coachee is video recorded while implementing targeted practices. The coach can record video during a live observation, the coachee can self-record, or a support person (e.g., co-teacher) can record the coachee. The coachee can review the video independently or with the coach to support self-reflection or the coach can view the video to identify clips to share with the coachee to support reflection and feedback.

Video Exemplars

Video exemplars provide models of effective practices. They can be found on websites that are available publicly, in video libraries that are accessible at a cost, or in video libraries developed and maintained on-site by a program or coach. Coaches can record themselves implementing practices or use videos of other coachees as exemplars.

Video Conferencing

The coach and coachee meet in real time via web-based videoconferencing software. Videoconferencing can be used for action planning or reflection and feedback meetings. Videoconferencing can also be used in combination with bug-in-ear technology to conduct virtual, real-time focused observations.

Bug-in-Ear Technology

The coach views the classroom via videoconference using a device such as a smartphone, Wi-Fi–enabled tablet, or laptop with a webcam that is operated by the coachee. The coachee wears a small Bluetooth earbud connected wirelessly to the videoconference. This allows the coachee to hear the coach and the coach to hear and see the practice context (e.g., classroom). The coach provides real-time verbal prompts or brief supportive and constructive feedback as the coachee implements practices.

Web-Based Coaching Platforms

Web-based coaching platforms provide ways to organize and store coaching assets such as action plans, focused observation videos, or reflection and feedback notes. Coaching platforms also provide opportunities to share and comment on focused observation videos, including tagging videos at specific moments to provide reflective prompts, supportive feedback statements, or constructive feedback statements.

Coaching Apps

Coaching apps provide a platform to collect data and access resources to support coaching. Coaches collect data during focused observations to support reflection and feedback and compile data across coachees. In addition, some coaching apps include support materials for coaches, such as tips and practice checklists.

Figure 10.2. Descriptions of common technologies used to support practice-based coaching implementation.

facilitate self- and distance coaching formats follows. The chapter ends with a discussion of future frontiers regarding the use of technology to support PBC implementation.

Use of Video and Technology to Enhance Coaching Strategies

As a tool to enhance coaching strategies that are implemented as part of the focused observation or reflection and feedback components of PBC, the use of video recordings has been shown to be effective for promoting the coachees' self-reflection about their implementation of practices (e.g., Bishop et al., 2015; Wright et al., 2012). In addition, video recordings provide coaches the opportunity to enhance supportive and constructive feedback by allowing the coachee to see specific examples of their practice implementation from the focused observation (McLeod et al., 2019; Snyder, Shannon, et al., 2021). Video clips can be used to show coachees positive examples of their practice implementation and build their confidence. Although coaches routinely provide verbal or written examples of when coachees use practices effectively, video clips are a powerful tool for understanding and actualizing progress toward shared goals. In addition, video clips can provide examples of missed opportunities to use targeted practices to support continued progress toward goals.

Video exemplars are another way technology can be used to enhance coaching strategies. Video exemplars allow coachees to see others implementing practices that are the focus of their shared goals and action plans. These exemplars can serve as models or can be used to facilitate reflection about how the coachee might adapt or modify what was observed for use in their own practice. Video exemplars have been reported as particularly useful resources, given that

---

Examples of Technology and Video Options for Enhancing PBC and Coaching Strategies

- Video recordings of coachees' practice implementation
- Video exemplars of other coachees' practice implementation
- Bug-in-ear technology for immediate supportive and constructive feedback or verbal prompts

---

coachees do not always have the resources to observe other coachees' use of practice but appreciate the opportunity learn from their peers (Shannon et al., 2015).

In addition to video, bug-in-ear technology can enhance coaching strategies used during focused observation in live or distance coaching formats (Artman-Meeker et al., 2017). Bug-in-ear technology refers to a device used by a coach to observe and deliver comments to a coachee who has an earpiece receiver. This technology allows the coach to observe and provide real-time verbal prompts or immediate supportive and constructive feedback to support the coachee's implementation of practices. Providing verbal prompts via bug-in-ear technology simulates the side-by-side support cue enhancement coaching strategy that might be provided when the coach is conducting a focused observation in the practice setting (see Chapter 4). It increases opportunities for the coachee to practice skills and receive brief immediate feedback that can then be expanded as part of a reflection and feedback meeting. Overall, coachees who have used bug-in-ear technology report it to be acceptable and an asset to their learning (Ottley et al., 2015). Shaefer and Ottley conducted a systematic review of 17 intervention studies that examined the use of bug-in-ear to provide immediate feedback about instructional behaviors of preservice and in-service teachers. They concluded that there is convincing evidence that use of bug-in-ear to deliver immediate performance feedback increases the frequency and accuracy of teachers' instructional behaviors.

Use of Technology to Facilitate Self-Coaching

In self-coaching, the coachee engages independently in the PBC processes of strengths and needs assessment, goal setting and action planning, focused observation, and reflection and feedback (National Center on Quality Teaching and Learning [NCQTL], 2015; Snyder, Hemmeter, et al., 2018). As such, technology supports are often needed to ensure that coachees can conduct effective focused observations to guide their self-reflection and feedback and have adequate access to evidence-based resources so they can implement PBC with fidelity.

For example, Lynn, with support from Carl and Elita, uses a video camera to collect video of her interactions with the children in the classroom. These videos and the data collected from viewing them as part of focused observation are essential for guiding Lynn's self-reflection, identifying areas of strength for supportive feedback, and considering constructive feedback she will use to enhance her use of effective practices. In addition, now that Sirena and Lynn check in only one time per month, Lynn relies heavily on the video library Sirena has shared with her as a resource to see exemplars of other teachers implementing the practices that are the focus of her action plan.

Although self-coaching is implemented primarily by the coachee, it is also important for a self-coaching facilitator to provide regular prompts to encourage continued implementation of self-coaching (NCQTL, 2015). These contacts might not require the use of high-tech tools but are likely to involve some type of technology use. Examples of technologies that might be used by a self-coaching facilitator include coaching apps that allow secure text messaging or web-based coaching platforms in which messages and resources can be shared.

Although the components of PBC are implemented by the coachee when self-coaching is the delivery format, a self-coaching facilitator should provide occasional prompts to encourage continued implementation of PBC and ensure that resources are available to support strengths and needs assessment, goal setting and action planning, focused observation, and self-reflection and self-feedback.

Use of Technology to Support Implementation of Distance Coaching

Recent technological advances have increased the capability to implement PBC with fidelity via distance coaching formats. Videoconferencing and web-based platforms are important components of distance PBC formats because they offer features that promote active participation of both the coachee and coach as they engage virtually in strengths and needs assessment, shared goal setting and action planning, focused observation, and reflection and feedback. Although distance coaching models have been implemented without the use of these technologies (e.g., Early et al., 2017), distance PBC cannot be implemented with fidelity without some level of technological infrastructure. Any distance delivery format for PBC must ensure that methods and technologies are available for conducting data-informed strengths and needs assessment, shared goal setting and action planning, focused observations of practice implementation in the practice context, and reflection and feedback. Although it might be possible to have planning or reflection and feedback meetings via telephone or to provide written feedback, video or bug-in-ear technology is needed to facilitate the coach's completion of strengths and needs assessments as well as focused observations.

> Any distance delivery format for PBC must ensure that methods and technologies are available for conducting strengths and needs assessment, shared goals and action planning, focused observations of practice implementation, and reflection and feedback.

Advanced technologies such as web-based coaching platforms, videoconferencing, or coaching apps have the potential to increase the efficiency and the quality of PBC implementation as well as increasing access to PBC. For example, the use of these technologies allows Maureen and Maria to continue to access coaching support from Elley while freeing Elley's travel time to and from the center so other practitioners can be coached during times she would otherwise be traveling. In addition, the quality of coaching supports that can be offered from a distance are enhanced by the ability of Maureen and Maria to upload their videos and share them with Elley within 24 hr of collecting them. The use of a web-based coaching platform allows Elley to provide timely written supportive and constructive feedback and reflective prompts in advance of their videoconference. During the videoconference, Elley is able to play back video clips from the focused observation. This is particularly important given that a latency between the time the video is recorded and the time of the reflection and feedback session is likely inevitable when using a distance coaching format.

CONSIDERATIONS FOR USING TECHNOLOGY: COMBINING TECHNOLOGIES AND DELIVERY FORMATS

As is shown in Figure 10.1 and illustrated in the case of Maureen, Maria, and Elley, delivery formats can be combined to develop hybrid coaching models. The benefit of hybrid delivery formats is the ability to tailor PBC supports based on the strengths and needs of the coachee(s) and the availability of program resources to provide PBC.

> **Key Point to Remember**
>
> Decisions about the extent to which technology is integrated into PBC implementation should be informed by careful consideration of the resources and infrastructure needed to support use of the chosen technology.

Figure 10.3 illustrates the types of technology that might be used within live, self-, or distance coaching formats and the extent to which these formats rely on the use of technology to implement PBC with fidelity. Decisions about the extent to which technology is integrated into PBC implementation should be informed by careful consideration of the resources and

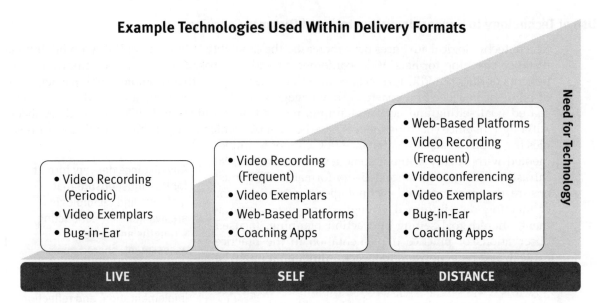

Figure 10.3. Example technologies and recommended technologies to support live, self, and distance practice-based coaching.

Four Key Considerations When Making Decisions About Technology to Support PBC Implementation

1. Costs
2. Privacy protections
3. Coach and coachee preparation
4. Coach and coachee access

infrastructure needed to support use of the chosen technology. Although many technologies offer unique features that could support implementation of PBC, it is important to consider whether there are also potential barriers to PBC implementation that might result from the use of these technologies. Four key considerations when determining whether and what types of technology to adopt to support PBC are 1) costs, 2) privacy protections, 3) coach and coachee access, and 4) coach and coachee preparation.

Costs

Technology systems vary widely in their costs. In addition to considering the list price of equipment or software (e.g., video cameras, microphones, web-based licenses or subscriptions), it is important to consider potentially hidden costs of technology. For example, most of the technologies discussed in this chapter require access for the coach and coachee to high-speed internet in order to function efficiently and properly. In addition, it might be necessary to purchase additional accessories to ensure that use of the technology strengthens PBC delivery. Accessories might include mini-tripods for video cameras, video storage devices or server space, or external microphones to enhance the quality of audio when video or bug-in-ear technologies are used. The time spent by coaches and coachees to learn about and use technology is an additional cost that is important to consider when planning for PBC implementation. Time may be needed for technology training for coaches and coachees, providing or receiving technical assistance, and uploading and downloading video. Table 10.1 provides information about relative costs for the technologies discussed in this chapter, in addition to highlighting ancillary costs that are likely to be associated with them. Before integrating technology into PBC programs, particularly those that are dependent on technology-based systems to ensure fidelity of implementation, it is recommended that these costs be researched fully to ensure that adequate financial and personnel resources are and will remain available.

Table 10.1. Direct technology costs, recommended features or settings, and additional equipment or infrastructure needed to support practice-based coaching implementation

Technology	Example equipment and platforms	Direct cost	Recommended features/ settings	Additional equipment/ infrastructure supports
Video recording devices	• Handheld camcorders • Mobile devices • Tables • Webcams • Swivl	$$–$$$$	• Video encryption • 30 FPS, MP4/h.264 codec, 4 MBPS video bitrate capability	• Camera accessories (e.g., batteries, charging dock) • Mini tripod • Wireless microphone • Media player software • Video storage device (e.g., encrypted hard drive, SD card, or USB; secure server, web-based file-sharing or coaching platform) • High-speed internet
Video conferencing	• Zoom • Skype • FaceTime • Google Meet	$–$$	• FERPA or HIPAA security • Desktop sharing • Recording capability	• Wi-Fi–enabled electronic device (e.g., computer, mobile device, tablet, phone) • Webcam • High-speed internet • Internal technology support
Bug-in-ear	• Zoom • Skype • FaceTime • Duo	$–$$	• FERPA or HIPAA security	• Portable Wi-Fi– and video-enabled electronic device (e.g., computer, mobile device, tablet) • Wireless microphone • Wireless earbuds • High-speed internet
Web-based coaching platforms	• Coaching Companion • TORSH Talent • GoReact • Iris Connect • Swivl	$$–$$$$	• FERPA or HIPAA security • ≥10 GB file upload size • Video and document sharing • Commenting and video-tagging capability • Rubric or log capability • Responsive technology support	• High-speed internet • Video-recording devices • Internal technology training • Internal and external technology support
Coaching apps	• digiCOACH	$	• FERPA or HIPAA security • Compatibility with PBC	• Electronic device (e.g., computer, mobile device, tablet) • High-speed internet • Internal and external technology support

Note: Direct costs represent the cost of the primary equipment or platform and do not include additional equipment or infrastructure supports that might be needed.

Key: $, 0–150 dollars; $$, 151–250 dollars; $$$, 251–500 dollars; $$$$, >500 dollars per user; FERPA, Family Educational Rights and Privacy Act; FPS, frames per second; HIPAA, Health Insurance Portability and Accountability Act; MP4/h.264 codec, advanced video coding; MBPS, megabits per second; PBC, practice-based coaching.

Privacy Protections

The collaborative partnership of PBC is based on coaching being a safe and secure space. Before adopting and integrating technology into PBC delivery formats, programs should assess the security of the platform and develop procedures to ensure all information collected or transferred via technology-based systems comply with relevant local, state, or federal privacy protection policies. In addition to program- or district-level policies related to privacy, many programs are also required to follow policies outlined in the Family Educational Rights and Privacy Act (FERPA, 1974) or the Health Insurance Portability and Accountability Act (HIPAA, 1996). Procedures to ensure the protection of privacy for coaches, coachees, children, and families must be developed, manualized, and taught as part of any technology-based system, regardless of the extent to which it is integrated into PBC. Preparation for implementing technology-based systems often requires program leaders to consult user manuals or technology developers to confirm compliance with privacy policies.

Strengths and Needs Assessment	Shared Goal Setting and Action Planning	Focused Observation	Reflection and Feedback
• Data shared electronically via e-mail, coaching app, or web-based platforms cannot be accessed or viewed by anyone outside the collaborative coaching partnership without the coachee's knowledge.	• Action plans cannot be accessed or viewed by anyone outside the collaborative coaching partnership without the coachee's knowledge.	• Focused observation videos are collected using encrypted video or storage devices. • Videoconferencing, web-based platforms, and coaching apps comply with local, state, or national privacy policies. • Methods for uploading or transferring focused observation data from the coachee to the coach are secure. • Storage devices or platforms for storing video data are secure.	• Reflection and feedback discussions cannot be accessed by anyone outside the collaborative coaching partnership without the coachee's knowledge. • Information about individual children or families, including video footage or data reviewed during the reflection and feedback meeting, cannot be accessed by anyone outside the program or collaborative coaching partnership.

Figure 10.4.   Requirements for ensuring privacy protections for each key practice-based coaching component.

Once the security capabilities of technology-based systems are confirmed, it is incumbent upon the program to develop and manualize procedures for ensuring that these capabilities are realized. The development of procedures for coaches and coachees to ensure privacy protections often requires program leaders to consult with members of information technology teams. Figure 10.4 shows key priorities for ensuring the security of technology-based systems. Although procedures will vary across programs and the technologies that are implemented, these priorities should be addressed by program leadership and the procedures should be clearly outlined for anyone who uses technology to support implementation of PBC.

Coach and Coachee Preparation

Training for coaches and coachees to operate technological equipment and to implement systematic procedures for using technology within PBC is essential to alleviate frustration and support sustained practice use. Formal training with opportunities for coaches and coachees to practice and receive feedback using technological equipment is recommended prior to use within the context of PBC. Although most equipment comes with a user manual, and many web-based platforms or applications include video tutorials or instructional briefs, it is important to manualize procedures for coaches and coachees within the PBC context. Manuals with concise, specific directions and screen shots illustrating how to implement technology-based procedures facilitate user confidence and competence to use technology.

Special Considerations for Preparing Coaches   Coaches are likely to be the first line of inquiry when coachees have difficulty using or accessing technology. In addition to preparation to use technology-based systems that support their coaching activities, coaches should be knowledgeable about procedures that coachees need to follow to use technology effectively. This requires additional training for coaches to understand the features of technology and procedures that coachees will use to engage in technology-based PBC systems. It also requires preparation so that coaches can provide training and technical support to coachees related to these procedures when needed.

Coach and Coachee Access

The technologies discussed in this chapter require the use of a computer, tablet, cellular phone, or other electronic device. Ensuring that both coaches and coachees have adequate access to equipment and infrastructure supports needed to use technologies effectively is a key consideration for choosing and integrating technology to support PBC implementation. Although coaching apps, web-based coaching platforms, and videoconferencing platforms can be used on a variety of devices such as desktop or laptop computers, tablets, or cellular phones, it is essential that any device used for PBC comply with privacy policies, which can prevent the use of personal devices. The extent to which the coach and coachee have access to a secure device to collect video and to upload, download, or stream video can potentially limit the feasibility of using video-based technologies such as video recordings, video exemplars, videoconferencing, and bug-in-ear.

Before purchasing technology-based implementation platforms, it is also important to consider the system requirements for using the technology. Some web-based coaching platforms might not function optimally with internet upload speeds <3 megabits per second (MBPS), because videos are uploaded to the platform and then streamed within the platform. If internet speed or stability is low, it is likely that video streaming, upload/download, and videoconferencing capabilities will be interrupted or prolonged. Some platforms or technologies might also require a particular operating system or software download to function. In cases where fidelity of implementation of key components of PBC is dependent on the function of the technology platforms within which they are implemented, it is especially important to discuss optimal system preferences and minimum system requirements with technology developers. These should be communicated to those who provide information technology support within the program to confirm adequate infrastructure is in place to support access for both the coach and the coachee based on the location from which they will be using the technology.

ADDITIONAL OPPORTUNITIES, CHALLENGES, AND RECOMMENDATIONS

In addition to the overall benefits and primary considerations already described in this chapter, additional issues should be considered with respect to use of technology in PBC. Tables 10.2–10.4 provide an overview of opportunities, challenges, and recommendations for overcoming obstacles related to the technologies discussed. In the sections that follow, we also provide experientially informed recommendations for specifications or brief descriptions of products currently available to support PBC implementation.

Video Recordings

As shown in Figure 10.3, video recordings can be used across PBC delivery formats. Although the extent to which implementation of PBC relies on video technology increases for self and distance delivery formats, the use of video recordings is an essential coaching strategy in any PBC delivery format. In order to maximize the opportunities and overcome challenges described in Table 10.2 for using video recordings to support PBC, it is important to consider (a) the video equipment used to collect video recordings; (b) software and equipment used to process, share, and store video recordings; (c) strategies to enhance video quality; and (d) strategies to increase coachee comfort while being video recorded.

Video Equipment   Programs must determine what devices will be used to collect video within practice contexts. As shown in Table 10.1, several options are available for collecting video, including mobile devices, tablets, handheld video cameras, webcams, or advanced video

Table 10.2. Opportunities and challenges using video recordings

Opportunities	Challenges	Recommendations for addressing challenges
• Objective recording of coachee's use of effective teaching practices	• Quality of data gathered from focused observation is dependent on the quality of video and audio collected	• Provide coachees and coaches with a tip sheet for collecting high-quality video (see Appendix VI.AA). • Use a mini-tripod to stabilize the recording device. • Use a portable recording device that can move with the coachee as they interact with children in the practice context. • Select equipment and specify video-recording setting to maximize video quality.
• Enhances reflective conversation, supportive feedback, and constructive feedback by allowing the coachee and coach to observe use of effective practices, missed opportunities, and effects of practice implementation on children's engagement and learning	• Difficulty using the technology including recording and sharing video	• Provide step-by-step guides for procedures that coachees and coaches are expected to follow. • Provide technology support contacts or resources for troubleshooting problems.
• Facilitates focused observation in self- and distance coaching formats	• Discomfort being video recorded and sharing video with others	• Specify procedures for who will have access to video and how video will be stored and deleted. • Ensure that the coachee retains ownership of their video. • Provide opportunities for the coachee to video record the coach as the coach models the targeted effective practices. • Identify coachees to share positive experiences with using video recording for coaching. • Use video recordings to highlight positive aspects of the coachee's use of effective teaching practices and their impacts on children's engagement and learning. • Ensure that video recordings are used to provide both supportive and constructive feedback to the coachee and never to provide only constructive feedback.

systems such as Swivl™, which is designed to follow teachers as they interact with children in the classroom. In addition to considering the costs and security of these devices, it is important to ensure that they have adequate memory storage for the size of videos that will be collected and that they capture video at a resolution that is of high enough quality to facilitate focused observation or effective reflection and feedback about the coachee's practice implementation.

Although there are numerous settings that can be selected for capturing video, we focus on three: 1) frame rate, 2) video codec, and 3) video bitrate. These are standard settings that can be adjusted on video recording devices. The recommended video settings for use to support PBC implementation are (a) a frame rate of 30 frames per second (FPS), (b) a video codec of h.264 (also referred to as MP4), and (c) a video bitrate of 4 MBPS. Before purchasing a device for capturing videos, it is important to confirm that these settings are available.

Device memory specifications will vary based on the length of the video, the frequency with which video is cleared from the device, and whether there are options to use external storage such as USB drives or SD cards. If video is used within the context of live coaching and will be collected by the coach during the focused observation, it is likely that video clips will be short in duration and will require less memory to store. However, if a coachee is collecting longer segments of video to share with their coach within a self or distance delivery format, videos will require significantly more storage space. To ensure adequate space for *temporary* storage of videos and to prevent loss of video due to inadequate storage, we recommend a minimum device (or device plus external storage) storage capability of 16 GB.

Video Processing, Sharing, and Storage   A primary consideration for selection of software to process, share, and store video recordings is the ease and capacity of video modification and uploading. Systems for processing and sharing video should be easy to navigate to avoid delays caused by barriers to user operation or access. Ideally, videos will not require processing beyond recording and uploading through an app or transferring videos from the recording device to

Table 10.3. Opportunities and challenges using video conferencing and bug-in-ear technology

Opportunities	Challenges	Recommendations for addressing challenges

• Ability to coach more coachees due to reduction in travel time and for coaches to/from face-to-face meetings
• Can be used in conjunction with bug-in-ear technology to provide in situ supports when the coach cannot be physically present during the focused observation
	• Bug-in-ear
	  ○ Potential distraction from ongoing practice context routines and activities during virtual focused observations conducted using bug-in-ear technology
		• Bug-in ear
		  ○ Use verbal cues sparingly to avoid distraction.
		  ○ Ensure that the verbal cues, supportive feedback, constructive feedback, or reflective conversation is brief.
		  ○ Provide opportunities for extended reflection and performance-based feedback during reflection and feedback meetings.

• Capability to record meetings for fidelity assessments or for future reference	• Video conferencing
	  ○ Potential limitations to coachee engagement in reflection and feedback meetings conducted via videoconference, particularly in group formats
		• Video conferencing
		  ○ Make sure that all participants have access to a webcam to ensure video capability.
		  ○ When using group formats, offer opportunities for engagement using a chat feature within the videoconferencing platform.

	○ Potential limitations for coach and coachee to jointly reference shared resources and materials during reflection and feedback meetings	○ Use a desktop-sharing feature to ensure that the coachee and coach can both view a resource that is referenced during the reflection and feedback meeting. ○ Share resources electronically via e-mail, web-based coaching platform, or secure file-sharing platform.
	• Difficulty using the technology including scheduling meetings, joining meetings, using video, audio, or desktop sharing functions	○ Provide step-by-step manuals for procedures that coachees and coaches will use to schedule and join meetings. ○ Conduct a practice observation or conference and write down video and audio settings so the coach and coachee can refer to them for future observations or conferences. ○ Provide technology support contacts or resources for troubleshooting problems.
	• Necessity for consistent internet access for coach and coachee	○ Assess Wi-Fi or hardwired internet access at sites where coach and coachee will participate in reflection and feedback meetings.

a computer where they can be uploaded to a secure viewing platform. However, it is important to consider what the expectations are for focused observation. If coaches and coachees are focused on practices that are discrete and easy to capture in short (e.g., <10 min) videos (e.g., book-reading strategies, asking open-ended questions during small-group instruction), the needed system requirements to process and share video will be different than when the focus is on foundational, comprehensive strategies (e.g., teaching and reinforcing behavior expectations, implementing a classwide group contingency, implementing embedded learning opportunities), which would require more extensive focused observations and, consequently, longer videos. Longer videos result in larger file sizes for videos, which affects the speed with which they can be uploaded to file-sharing platforms. Some platforms place a limit on file size. If video files exceed the permitted size, then software must be used to compress them, which also lowers the video quality. To avoid the need for coaches or coachees to compress videos prior to sharing them, we recommend ensuring that any file-sharing platforms that are used allow for files up to at least 10 GB.

Another consideration for using video technology to support PBC implementation is where and how long videos will be stored. For example, will video observations be deleted after goals

Table 10.4.   Opportunities and challenges using web-based coaching platforms and coaching apps

Opportunities	Challenges	Recommendations for addressing challenges
• Ability to coach more coachees due to reduction in coach travel time to/from face-to-face meetings • Central location for organizing and storing coaching activities	• When focused observation is conducted only by video and selected by the coachee, the coach may not see foundational practices or be aware of contextual factors that influence implementation of practices.	• Pair distance focused observations with on-site observations to provide a comprehensive view of the practice environment and strengths and needs.
• Consistent tools and formats across coaches and coachees in a program • Opportunity to provide timely written feedback through annotated comments and video tags	• Difficulty with using the technology, including accessing materials the coach has uploaded (e.g., action planning documents, reflection and feedback comments, resources) and uploading and sharing video	• Provide initial training to use the platform or app for coaching activities. • Provide step-by-step guides for procedures that coachees and coaches are expected to use. • Provide technology support contacts or resources for troubleshooting problems. • Use conferencing technology to guide the coachee or coach through the process of engaging with features in the platform.
	• Inability to use some coaching strategies, including modeling and in-vivo support	• Provide access to a library of video exemplars of the practices prior to implementation or during reflection and feedback. • Use commenting and tagging functions within the platform to annotate videos of coachee practice implementation with supportive and constructive feedback statements.
	• Potential for written feedback to be viewed as evaluative when taken out of context	• Limit written feedback to comments that are directly aligned with the current goal and action plan and that are the most important takeaways for the coachee. • Conduct reflection and feedback meetings via telephone or videoconference to clarify written feedback and to engage in reflective conversation.

have been achieved? At the end of the coaching year? Videos can be stored within web-based platforms such as Coaching Companion (University of Washington, 2020), TORSH Talent (Torsh Inc., 2021), GoReact (Speakworks, Inc., 2021), or Iris Connect (Iris Connect, 2020), which are described later in this chapter. Videos might also be transferred or stored in secure file-sharing platforms (e.g., Box, Sharefile, Dropbox) or on external storage devices. Most web-based coaching platforms include apps that facilitate recording, uploading, and storage of videos. If videos are stored for a time in web-based coaching or file-sharing platforms and then backed up to external storage, the long-term storage must also be considered, and procedures for any of these processes must be manualized so both coachees and coaches know what to do.

Video Quality   As noted in Table 10.2, the extent to which video recordings enhance or promote PBC is dependent on the quality of the video collected. Particularly when the full focused observation is conducted asynchronously via a review of a video recording, it is important to ensure the highest quality video possible. This includes making sure the coachee and the children with which the coachee is interacting can be seen and heard. In addition to using the video recording specifications noted previously, supplemental equipment such as a mini-tripod and a wireless microphone are recommended. Training and guidelines for collecting video are also recommended. A tip sheet for collecting video in practice contexts is provided in Appendix VI.AA.

Coachee Comfort With Video   A common challenge using video recordings is overcoming coachee discomfort with being filmed and with using technology. Typically, challenges regarding comfort using the technology can be addressed with adequate training and technical support. Coachee comfort with being video recorded is likely to develop over time, particularly as the coach continues to demonstrate that the coachee's privacy is protected and that videos are used to support the coachee's use of the effective practices they have prioritized for coaching. Strategies to increase coachees' comfort being video recorded are highlighted in Table 10.2.

> **Tools for Coaches in the Appendices**
>
> *Appendix VI.AA: Practice-Based Coaching Technology Tips*
>
> This is a resource that provides tips for coaches or coachees about collecting video for use in PBC.

Videoconferencing and Bug-in-Ear Technology

Videoconferencing is a particularly useful technology for distance coaching because it allows for synchronous, virtual coaching interactions, thus reducing travel time for coaches and potentially increasing the number of coachees they can support. Videoconferencing can also be combined with bug-in-ear technology to support the implementation of virtual focused observations that permit synchronous observation and immediate feedback opportunities when the coach cannot be physically present in the classroom (e.g., Artman-Meeker et al., 2017; Ottley & Hanline, 2014). Potential challenges to using these technologies are highlighted in Table 10.3. Suggestions for addressing these challenges, including recommendations for (a) equipment and platform features and (b) enhancing user engagement, are discussed below and summarized in Table 10.3.

Equipment and Platform Features   Multiple platforms are available to facilitate videoconferencing, including Zoom, Skype, Google G Suite's Google Meet, Adobe Connect, Cisco WebEx, and FaceTime (Edelman, 2020). Privacy is an important consideration for PBC videoconferencing. Some platforms are FERPA compliant, whereas others are HIPAA compliant (Edelman, 2020). Recommended features for these platforms vary based on which components of PBC they will be used to implement. If videoconferencing is needed only to facilitate virtual focused observations, then using bug-in-ear technology, high-quality video capability, compatibility with a portable device, and compatibility with wireless accessories (i.e., earbuds, microphones) are the features most important to consider. If videoconferencing is used to conduct PBC reflection and feedback meetings, then selecting videoconferencing platforms with additional features is recommended to ensure that all essential coaching strategies described in Chapter 4 can be implemented with fidelity. These features include desktop-sharing capability, which allows the coach and coachee to have a shared view of documents such as the action plan or resources such as electronic versions of job aids, web-based resources, or video exemplars. File sharing and whiteboard features might also be important for creating and sharing documents, graphs, or other resources. Chat and break-out room features might also be desirable if videoconferencing will be used to support groups of coachees.

Enhancing User Engagement   The use of videoconferencing and bug-in-ear coaching can present challenges related to coach and coachee engagement in coaching activities. For example, when bug-in-ear is used, there is a potential for the coach's prompts to distract the coachee from an ongoing activity if they are used too frequently. When reflection and feedback occur via videoconference, it is important for the coach to plan carefully for how they will engage the coachee. Selecting videoconferencing platforms with the features recommended in Table 10.1 will provide the coach with multiple modalities to engage coachees in reflection and feedback in ways similar to those they might experience in a face-to-face meeting.

When videoconferencing is used to support multiple coachees, it is important to ensure that all participants have opportunities to engage in reflection and feedback processes. In addition to providing verbal prompts to engage participants who might have difficulty participating in this coaching format, providing opportunities for participants to share resources via desktop sharing, to contribute using a chat function, or to engage in smaller break-out room discussions can be useful for promoting everyone's engagement. Recommendations for addressing these challenges are summarized in Table 10.3.

Web-Based Coaching Platforms and Coaching Apps

Web-based coaching platforms and coaching apps offer unique features that are useful for distance coaching or hybrid coaching formats or that might be used by coachees who are engaged in self-coaching. Common features of web-based coaching platforms and apps that support the implementation of PBC are (a) video recording and uploading through platform-specific apps, secure video, and focused observation data storage; (b) video tagging and annotation; (c) document sharing; and (d) messaging. One of the most useful features is video tagging and annotation, which allows the coach and the coachee to place a comment in a video at a specific time point at which a practice is observed or attempted. This allows the coach and coachee to communicate remotely about the coachee's implementation of practices and allows the coach to provide targeted written supportive and constructive feedback asynchronously. It also allows the coachee to draw attention to specific time points in the observation and to ask the coach for clarification about practices or to request specific feedback prior to a reflection and feedback meeting. The ability to revisit and reengage in a focused observation by watching a video with accompanying annotations addresses issues that have been identified with delayed reflection and feedback. The video and accompanying annotations put the coachee and coach back into the practice moments, which facilitates reflection and feedback and planning for the next PBC cycle. Three web-based coaching platforms that were developed for educational use and have been used to implement PBC are described in the following sections.

Coaching Companion   Coaching Companion (University of Washington, 2020) is an online coaching platform that was developed for the Office of Head Start to support Head Start grantees to facilitate implementation of PBC. Features of the Coaching Companion are directly aligned with the key components of PBC and include places to (a) upload strengths and needs assessments; (b) build action plans with goals, action steps, and support materials; (b) upload video-recorded focused observations; (c) annotate videos for reflection and feedback; and (d) upload or type reflection and feedback notes. In addition, the Coaching Companion includes a Head Start–approved resource library with video clips and documents related to effective practices in early childhood settings. The Head Start version of Coaching Companion (https://eclkc.ohs.acf.hhs.gov/professional-development/article/head-start-coaching-companion) is available for free to any early learning program. A customizable version of Coaching Companion is available for a setup fee and annual membership fee (https://www.earlyedualliance.org/coaching-companion/). This version allows a program to upload resources to a program-specific resource library, access to the University of Washington's Cultivate Learning Library, and establish communities of practice.

TORSH Talent and GoReact   TORSH Talent (Torsh, Inc., 2021) and GoReact (Speakworks, Inc., 2021) are web-based coaching platforms that were developed for use in educational settings and are available at costs that vary depending on the number of users engaging with the platform. Although not developed specifically for PBC, they offer features that are compatible with or can be customized for PBC implementation. Both platforms allow users to upload and download videos so coaches can conduct asynchronous focused observations, including the ability to tag and annotate videos to facilitate reflection and feedback. In addition, documents such as strengths and needs assessments, action plans, and resources or materials can be uploaded and shared within the platform. These platforms also allow users to construct rubrics or logs that can be used to document whether coachee and coach were observed implementing practices as intended. Rubrics or logs can be completed electronically, and data can be exported from the platform. The use of rubrics or logs can be especially useful for purposes of examining coaching implementation fidelity by coaches and program leadership teams and for examining coaching effort and coaching effect data.

Coaching Apps   Mobile apps have been increasingly available for use in educational settings. One app, digiCOACH (digiCOACH, Inc., 2021) is a mobile walkthrough system that has been used in K–12 settings to collect observational data and provide performance feedback to the teacher via e-mail. Although not currently developed for use in preschool settings, this app might be explored as a tool to support electronic feedback for teachers in schools that are using the app.

Challenges and Recommendations   In distance coaching formats, the inability of the coach to see the practice context beyond the video clips that the coachee shares can limit the coach's knowledge of the larger practice context and culture. As such, it is incumbent upon the coach to gather information from the coachee about contextual information that might impact their implementation of effective practices that are the focus of the current goal and action plan. In addition, reliance on web-based platforms to implement PBC might result in lack of opportunity for the coach to use enhancement strategies like modeling and side-by-side support if bug-in-ear technology is not available. Recommendations for addressing these challenges are summarized in Table 10.4.

A very important consideration for platforms or apps that were not developed specifically to support PBC is the extent to which they align with and promote the implementation of PBC as intended. One particular concern is the potential for coachees to interpret feedback as evaluative rather than supportive. Web-based platforms and apps initially developed for use by teachers or school principals might include tools or terminology that appears evaluative. If possible, these tools should be customized to align with PBC. If customization is not possible, we would not recommend their use with PBC. Some platforms designed for use in educational settings might also be pre-populated with practices that are intended to be the focus of observations. These should be evaluated to confirm they are effective practices that are developmentally appropriate for children birth to age 5 before they are used within the PBC implementation framework.

FUTURE FRONTIERS: VIRTUAL SIMULATIONS AND PRACTICE-BASED COACHING

Technological advances have begun to permit the use of avatars to provide opportunities to practice implementing effective practices in virtual environments (e.g., Bautista & Boone, 2015; Dalgarno et al., 2016). To date, these technologies have been used primarily with preservice teachers. The proposed benefits are that they provide opportunities to build knowledge and skills in virtual environments that can be modified by the user and that offer repeated opportunities for practice prior to applying them in real contexts. One way in which virtual simulations might be integrated with PBC is for coaches to engage in the PBC cycle with coachees as they implement practices in virtual environments and as they transition to the applied context to support the generalization and maintenance of skills from one context to another. Although virtual simulations have shown promise for supporting preservice teachers' use of teaching practices and promoting self-efficacy, these technologies continue to be developed and require additional empirical research supporting their use for coaching and for PBC.

SUMMARY

In this chapter, we described how technology can be used to support implementation of PBC. We described current technologies and future frontiers. Our perspectives are that these technologies are important supports for PBC implementation and will likely remain so as advancements in evidence-informed professional development, including coaching, continue to occur. We look forward to these new horizons for PBC!

FINAL PERSPECTIVES

PBC is an evidence-based approach for supporting fidelity of practice implementation in a variety of programs that support young children birth to age 5 and their families. Grounded in the sciences of human behavior and implementation, PBC is built on a foundation of collaborative partnerships and involves continuous cycles of practice-focused strengths and needs assessments, shared goal setting and action planning, focused observation, and reflection and feedback. Throughout the chapters in this text, we have shared the essentials of PBC from both empirical and experiential perspectives. We have provided strategies and resources to support PBC implementation efforts and the examination of its effects on coachees' practices and on the children and families who are supported by them. Technological advances have the potential to enhance the reach of PBC, provided that these technologies can further inform and continue to support fidelity of implementation of the PBC essentials.

Appendices

Appendix I

Extended Case Stories

Appendix I.A

Case Stories: Lynn

MEET LYNN

Lynn has been working at Helping Hands Childcare Center for 4 years. When Lynn began working at Helping Hands, she was attending college full time to obtain her associate's degree in early childhood education. She started as a volunteer and was hired as a part-time assistant teacher in the infant classroom within her first 3 months volunteering. She was also an assistant teacher in the 4-year-old classroom before finishing her degree. She is now a full-time lead teacher in her current classroom. Lynn has been the lead teacher in the classroom for older toddlers for 2 years. Her classroom currently has 15 children enrolled. All children attend for a full day, from 7:30 a.m. to 5:30 p.m.

Lynn has two teaching assistants. Carl is in the classroom from 7:30 a.m. to 12:00 p.m. Elita comes to the classroom from 12:00 p.m. to 5:30 p.m. Both assistants have worked at the center for less than 4 months. Lynn appreciates having Carl and Elita in the classroom. They usually help her prepare activities and clean the toys when they are in the classroom. They also help with diapering and meal preparation, which gives her more time to spend with the children.

Lynn wants to provide many opportunities for children to explore and learn. She updates the materials in the classroom based on themes every 2 weeks. She joins in children's activities as often as possible. She believes it is important to follow children's interests and to support their learning within engaging activities.

Lynn knows it is important to provide opportunities for toddlers to hear and use language and to interact regularly with adults and peers. In August, Lynn was given an opportunity to attend a local conference focused on early education and learning. Presenters were from a nearby university. Lynn attended two 90-min conference sessions. One session focused on having responsive interactions with children. The other session described strategies for creating a language-rich classroom environment. Since attending the conference, Lynn has been exploring a series of online modules focused on promoting children's language development, which was recommended to her by one of the conference presenters. Each module takes about 10–15 min to complete and includes tips for interacting with young children in ways that support their language development.

Lynn recently learned that her program will be receiving professional development (PD) from Sirena, who is a training and technical assistance specialist in a regional child care resource and referral agency. She does not know very much about what Sirena will be doing but is interested in learning more about what PD opportunities will be available.

Sirena plans to hold monthly lunch and learn sessions for teachers to learn about foundational effective practices that support children's early learning and to talk with their colleagues about how they are implementing these practices. She also plans to provide opportunities for teachers to participate in on-site practice-based coaching (PBC) or self-coaching based on the level of support needed to implement the practices as intended. Sirena was recently trained in PBC and has asked to pilot the on-site PBC coaching she and her agency leadership team are using with one or two teachers at Helping Hands. The pilot will help her refine the on-site coaching processes as well as develop a resource library and tools to support self-coaching for teachers who would benefit from self-directed professional development.

182

The center director suggested Lynn might be interested in participating in the pilot of on-site PBC, because she has been engaging independently in professional development opportunities offered outside the center. She knows Lynn has been seeking opportunities to learn more about practices that promote responsive interactions and children's language development. She suggests Sirena approach Lynn about whether she would be interested in receiving PBC to help Lynn transfer what she has learned from the conference, the online modules, and the lunch and learns to her classroom practice.

Lynn is excited about the opportunity to learn more about how she can support responsive interactions and her children's language development. She is nervous about Sirena coming to her classroom because she does not know Sirena and she does not know very much about PBC. When she spoke to Sirena on the phone, Sirena said they would work together to develop a shared goal related to practices that support responsive interactions and children's language development and an action plan to meet the goal. Lynn knows Sirena will need to observe in her classroom each week, and that they will meet after each observation to discuss her progress toward her goal. Sirena said each meeting would include opportunities for shared reflection, supportive and constructive feedback, and opportunities to receive additional resources and materials. Sirena said the information she collects in the classroom will only be used to guide reflection and feedback in their coaching sessions and other parts of PBC, but Lynn still wonders if the information Sirena collects will affect her performance evaluation, which is coming up in 2 months.

Strengths and Needs Assessment—Lynn

Lynn and Sirena had an orientation meeting where Sirena described the PBC process in more detail and shared more about how she and Lynn will collaborate to develop shared goals and action plans that are based on strengths and needs assessments that both Lynn and Sirena complete and review together. Lynn appreciated having a list of practices she could look at and use to reflect about the practices she uses to support children's language development. As she completed her strengths and needs assessment in preparation for writing her first shared goal and action plan with Sirena, Lynn focused on her strengths first. She noted that she talks to children frequently throughout the day and that she tries to respond to children's communication as quickly as possible and in a positive manner. She knows that in her busy classroom, she is not always able to respond to children right away, but she is confident about her ability to engage in responsive interactions with children. Lynn also strives to provide a language-rich environment by describing her actions and objects in the environment and listed this as a strength.

When she considered practices she needed additional support to implement, Lynn realized that although she describes her own actions frequently, she does not often describe what children do and say in the classroom. She also noted that although she would eventually like to focus on having more back-and-forth exchanges with children, she thinks it is important to focus first on building their language so they are more able to engage in back-and-forth exchanges. Lynn noted that she would like additional support to expand children's language, because she thinks this will help them learn more words. Finally, Lynn wrote down that she would like support from Sirena to use more words to describe children's experiences and feelings. Lynn thinks these practices will help her continue to build a language-rich environment for children in her classroom. Lynn's full strengths and needs assessment is in the Coachee Strengths and Needs Assessment that follows.

Strengths and Needs Assessment—Sirena

Before they met to write their first shared goal and action plan, Sirena observed in Lynn's classroom to learn more about how she was using practices to promote children's language development. Sirena observed Lynn's interactions with children for 1 hour and made sure she observed a variety of activities, including one child-directed activity, one teacher-directed activity, and one routine. When she finished her observation, Sirena completed the coach strengths and needs assessment for Lynn. She also wrote notes about what she observed so she could give Lynn initial

Coachee: __Lynn__   Coach: __Sirena__   Date: __October 15__

Coachee Strengths and Needs Assessment

Practice	How often?				Change needed?	Priority (Top 5)	Notes
	Never/ Seldom	Sometimes	Most of the time	Always			
1. I talk to children throughout the day during activities and routines.	1	2	3	(4)	No		
2. I respond positively and immediately to children's attempts to communicate.	1	2	(3)	4	No		
3. I have back-and-forth conversations or exchanges with children, appropriate for their developmental level.	1	(2)	3	4	**Yes**	5	Need to focus on modeling language for children first so they can engage in back-and-forth exchanges
4. I talk about many different things children are feeling, doing, or experiencing throughout the day.	1	(2)	3	4	**Yes**	3	
5. I use a wide range of words to describe objects, actions, and experiences throughout the day.	1	2	(3)	4	No		
6. I describe my actions as I am doing them (i.e., self-talk).	1	2	(3)	4	No		
7. I describe children's actions as they do them (i.e., parallel talk).	(1)	2	3	4	**Yes**	**2**	
8. I add more words or ideas to what children say.	(1)	2	3	4	**Yes**	**1**	
9. I ask open-ended questions to facilitate children's use of language.	1	(2)	4	4	**Yes**	4	

Key Strengths

Three strengths I have that I think support implementation of practices:

1. *I try to spend time playing with children in every center. When I visit centers, I talk about the toys children are using.*

2. *I do my best to respond to children as soon as possible. I know it is important to acknowledge when children communicate with me, even if my response is brief.*

3. *I describe what I am doing so children have opportunities to hear more language.*

Coaching Priorities

Three practices I want to prioritize for coaching:

1. *I would like to model more language by describing what children do and say in the classroom. I only do this a little bit right now.*

2. *I need ideas for how to expand children's language. I am not sure what language is most appropriate to use to expand language for children of this age.*

3. *I would like some help to make sure I use a variety of words to describe children's experiences and feelings. I already describe objects they play with but don't really describe their feelings or experiences. I think this is important for children this age.*

performance-based feedback about her strengths. Sirena's strengths and needs assessment is shown in the Coach Strengths and Needs Assessment that follows.

Sirena noted that Lynn joins children in activities, talks frequently with children, and responds to their attempts to communicate as strengths. She also noted that Lynn frequently repeats what children say when she responds to them and listed this as a strength. When she reviewed her initial observation data, Sirena saw that Lynn would benefit from support to model a wider variety of words for children. She listed two possible ways to model more diverse vocabulary for children: (a) expanding children's communication by adding a variety of new words or ideas, or (b) using more specific vocabulary to describe children's actions. Sirena also noted that Lynn did not ask any open-ended questions during her observation and listed asking open-ended questions to encourage children's language as a possible third coaching priority.

Shared Goal Setting and Action Planning

When they reviewed their strengths and needs assessments, Lynn and Sirena saw that they identified similar strengths and coaching priorities. After they reviewed their coaching priorities, Sirena asked Lynn which of the priorities they discussed was her top priority for coaching. Lynn asked if they could write a goal that focused on expanding children's language and describing children's experiences. She said she thinks these practices are complementary and working on them simultaneously will help her model language for children who are less verbal in addition to expanding language for children who are more verbal. Together, Sirena and Lynn write the following goal:

> I will expand what children say and do by describing their experiences (e.g., "You are rocking your baby gently. It looks like you really like playing with babies") or by adding at least one descriptive word to objects they name during free choice or mealtimes (e.g., The block is heavy; The cracker is crunchy). I will do this one time for at least 3 children during each free choice and mealtime every day for 2 weeks.

The action plan they write to achieve the goal is shown in the figure on Page 188.

Focused Observation

Before the first focused observation, Sirena reviews Lynn's goal and prepares her focused observation form so she can collect data related to the goal. When she reviews the goal, she decides to make a table on her focused observation form that includes places to tally (a) the number of times Lynn describes children's experiences, (b) the number of times Lynn expands children's language, and (c) the number of children with which she uses these practices. Because the goal is to use the practices during free choice and mealtimes, Lynn and Sirena have arranged for the focused observation to happen during free choice and lunch time. Sirena makes sure there is space to collect data for each activity. The table she created is shown in her focused observation notes on Page 189. Creating the table ahead of time helps Sirena perform a more focused observation. As she observes, in addition to keeping tallies in the table, Sirena also writes down examples of what Lynn says during her interactions with children.

When they developed their action plan, Lynn requested that Sirena make a video recording of her during the observation so they could watch the video together during the reflection and feedback meeting to identify opportunities when Lynn could have expanded children's language. They agreed Sirena would do this during the first focused observation for their current action plan. Sirena collects 10 min of video during free choice and lunch so she will have plenty of video to choose from to watch with Lynn during their reflection and feedback meeting.

Reflection and Feedback

After the focused observation, Sirena reviews the video she collected and writes down the times in the video she wants to share with Lynn. She also writes down reminders about what she wants to share with Lynn during the reflection and feedback meeting. Sirena's notes to herself are shown in the Focused Observation Notes.

Coachee: __Lynn__   Coach: __Sirena__   Date: __October 15__

Coach Strengths and Needs Assessment

The coachee is doing this now	Coaching priority
1—Not at all/Seldom 2—Some of the time 3—Most of the time 4—Always (or almost always)	1—Not a priority or already fluent 2—Low priority 3—Moderate priority 4—Immediate priority

Practice	The coachee is doing this now . . .				Coaching priority level			
1. Talks to children throughout the day during routines and in play	1	2	③	4	1	②	3	4
2. Responds immediately and positively to children's attempts to communicate	1	2	3	④	①	2	3	4
3. Has back-and-forth conversations or exchanges with children, appropriate for their developmental level	1	②	3	4	1	2	③	4
4. Talks about many different things children are feeling, doing, or experiencing throughout the day	1	②	3	4	1	2	③	4
5. Uses a wide range of words to describe objects, actions, and experiences throughout the day	1	②	3	4	1	2	3	④
6. Describes own actions as they do them (i.e., self-talk)	1	②	3	4	1	2	3	④
7. Describes children's actions as they do them (i.e., parallel talk)	①	2	3	4	1	2	3	④
8. Adds more words or ideas to what children say	1	②	3	4	1	2	3	④
9. Asks open-ended questions to facilitate children's use of language	①	2	3	4	1	2	③	4

Additional Notes/Comments:

Three children became upset during observation; teacher responded immediately and was able to calm or redirect each child successfully.

Teacher repeated child phrase: 10 times; Teacher expanded child phrase: 3 times

Back-and-forth exchanges: 3 observed

Questions: You want that? What do you have? What shape? Can I have a turn?

Key Strengths

Three strengths the teacher has to support implementation of these practices:

1. *You frequently talk to children during play and routine activities, and talk to children is almost always positive. In the initial observation, you visited every center and spoke with at least one child in each center. At lunch, you visited each lunch table and spoke with 8 of the 14 children in your classroom.*

2. *You respond positively to children's attempts to communicate with you. When children are upset, you respond immediately to help them calm down.*

3. *When children initiate communication with you, you frequently repeat what they say as part of your response to them. This happened 16 times during the hour I observed!*

Coaching Priorities

Three practices to consider prioritizing for coaching:

1. *Expand on children's communication by adding a variety of new words or ideas.*

2. *Provide language models to children by using more specific vocabulary to describe their actions.*

3. *Ask open-ended questions to encourage children to talk more and participate back-and-forth exchanges.*

Preferred Coaching Strategies Checklist

Instructions: Please mark your preferred enhancement coaching strategies using the checklist below. Please feel free to add comments as well!

Coachee: Lynn _____ **Date:** October 15 _____

Enhancement Coaching Strategies	I'd like to try this strategy	Notes
1. **Side-by-side support cues:** The coach supports your practice implementation in the moment, verbally, with gestures, or with visual cues, or through technology (e.g., bug-in-ear).		
2. **Other help in practice setting:** The coach provides support to you or children, which is not directly related to your goal or action plan (e.g., wiping up spilled paint, sitting on the floor beside a child at circle).	X	
3. **Problem solving:** An interaction between you and the coach to solve an identified practice implementation issue. Problem-solving involves four steps: 1) identify the implementation issue, 2) generate potential solutions, 3) decide on a course of action, and 4) evaluate pros and cons of the selected course of action.	X	
4. **Role play:** In a role play, you and the coach take on other roles related to practice implementation (e.g., coach acts as child, coachee acts as adult).	X	
5. **Video examples:** Video examples show how another practitioner uses a practice in a similar implementation setting.	X	
6. **Modeling:** Modeling is demonstrating or showing you how to implement a practice that is the focus of a goal or action plan.		
7. **Environmental arrangements:** The coach helps you modify or enhance your practice setting or materials in your setting to set the occasion for you to implement a practice.		
8. **Graphing:** You and your coach work together to graph data you or your coach has collected about your practice implementation or child behaviors.		

9. **Other:** *In what other ways would you want your coach to help?*

I like to read about things so I can really think about them before we meet or before we share them with the staff and parents.

Action Plan

Coachee(s): Lynn   **Coach:** Sirena   **Date:** October 15   **Action Plan:** #1

Implementation Goal
Goal I want to achieve: I will expand what children say and do by describing their experiences (e.g., "You are rocking your baby gently. It looks like you really like playing with babies") or by adding at least one descriptive word to objects they name during free choice or mealtimes (e.g., The block is heavy; The cracker is crunchy). I will do this one time for at least 3 children during each free choice and mealtime every day for 2 weeks.

Criterion or Goal Achievement Statement
I will know I have achieved my goal when I have collected data showing I have provided at least one expansion of three different children's actions or statements during each free choice and mealtime every day for 2 weeks.

	Steps to achieve this goal	Resources needed	Timeline
1	I will watch an online video about expansions, and I will complete the accompanying handout to practice writing expansions for child phrases. **(Learn more)**	Video web link Time to watch video (~10 min) Activity handout link Time to complete handout (~20 min)	10/22
2	My coach will record a video of me interacting with children during play (free-choice centers) and meal time. We will review the video during the reflection and feedback meeting to identify opportunities for expansion, and I will practice how I can expand what children do and say with my coach. **(Practice)**	Video camera Coach Time in meeting to watch video and role play	10/26
3	I will make an activity matrix for all classroom play and mealtimes that includes the names of three children I plan to practice expansions with during each block of time, and the matrix will have a place to mark the number of expansions I use with each child. **(Make)**	Matrix template from coach Paper/Printer Planning time (~30 min)	11/6
4	I will tally the number of expansions I use with each child on my activity matrix and review it with my coach. **(Collect and Analyze data)**	Clipboard Completed activity matrices Time to review data during meeting	11/13
5			

Review		
Review Date 1: _____ ( ) Goal achieved! ( ) Making progress, but not there yet. ( ) Modified or changed my goal.	Review Date 2: _____ ( ) Goal achieved! ( ) Making progress, but not there yet. ( ) Modified or changed my goal.	Review Date 3: _____ ( ) Goal achieved! ( ) Making progress, but not there yet. ( ) Modified or changed my goal.

Focused Observation Notes		

Coachee: Lynn		Coach: Sirena	

Date: October 26	Observation Started: 10:30 a.m.	Observation Ended: 11:30 a.m.

What was observed:

	Describe	Expand	# of children
Free choice	lll	l	ll
Lunch	l		l

Repeated child phrase—Free choice: llll llll ll
Repeated child phrase—Lunch: llll

Free Choice

10:30 a.m.—Sits with children at art table and participates in making a drawing:
  Repeat: "A duck" "Yellow paper"

  Expand: Child—"I draw." Lynn—"You're drawing a pink cloud." Child smiles—"Pink cloud."

  Describe: "You always go to art first. I think you really like to draw."

10:48—Plays restaurant at home living:
  Repeat: "Yummy pizza" "A plate" "Milk"

  Describe: "You are working together to make pizza."

10:56—Looks at books with children in library center:
  Repeat: "A cat" "He ran away!"

  Describe: "You are reading a story about a cat."

Lunch

11:12—Sits at table with children:
  Repeat: "Yummy grapes" "Yes, lunchbox" "Yes, fork"

  Describe: "It looks like you're waiting for your lunch to cool off because it's too hot!"

To share with coachee(s):

Supportive Feedback/Reflection

Describing Children's Experiences:

Feedback: You described children's experiences four times in the hour I was here today (three times in free choice and one time at lunch)! Every time, you described something the child was doing as he/she was doing it.

Some examples I heard were…

Reflection: How do you think describing children's experiences as they are having them helps build language? → Gives new words to describe their experience.

Expanding Children's Language:

Show video example @ 6:34

Reflection: What did you notice Aiden do after you expanded what he said? → Repeated words that were added in the expansion.

Constructive Feedback/Reflection

Feedback: I heard you repeat something a child said 17 times today. In addition to repeating what they say, it's really important to add something new like you did with Aiden so they can hear a variety of words. Example: Yummy pizza → This is a yummy pizza with gooey cheese.

Reflection: Play video (7:22; 9:41; 10:15) and practice expansions.

Case Stories: Maureen and Maria

MEET MAUREEN AND MARIA

Maureen and Maria co-teach in an inclusive Head Start classroom located in a rural area. Maureen is a special education teacher and Maria is the general education teacher. Maureen and Maria also work with an instructional assistant, Adam. There are 17 children in their class and 5 of those children are receiving services associated with an individualized education program (IEP). There are also six dual language learners in the classroom, and Maria is bilingual in Spanish.

Maureen has 4 years of teaching experience in a K–2 special education classroom and this is her first year in preschool and in an inclusive setting. Maria has been a Head Start teacher for 7 years and feels confident with the curriculum. She is excited to have Maureen as her new co-teacher and wants to learn more about strategies for working with young children with disabilities. This year, Maureen and Maria have elected to participate in professional development focused on embedded instruction. As part of a statewide initiative focused on supporting preschool inclusion, they will participate in a 12-hr virtual workshop series to learn about embedded instruction practices and will receive practice guides and access to a website to support their use of embedded instruction in the classroom. Four workshops are scheduled in September and January with two 3-hr workshops held on two consecutive days in each of these months. The workshops will provide foundational information about the four parts of embedded instruction, which are described in the box on the next page.

Maureen and Maria will participate in virtual practice-based coaching (PBC) with their coach, Elley. She will support them to develop shared goals and a classroom-level action plan. Maureen and Maria will video each other implementing practices on their action plan, and they will share their videos with Elley using a secure video-sharing platform. Every 2 weeks, they will meet with Elley via video conference to review their video and to engage in reflection and feedback about progress on their goals and action plans. Maureen and Maria expect that workshops and coaching will help them build on their current strengths and experiences and enhance their use of embedded instruction practices to individualize instruction for children within ongoing activities, routines, and transitions in their inclusive classroom.

Strengths and Needs Assessment—Maureen and Maria

Maureen and Maria just completed their September workshops and are looking forward to writing their first shared goal and action plan with Elley. After the first two workshops, Maureen and Maria worked together to complete a strengths and needs assessment to determine how they would like Elley to support them to use embedded instruction practices. Their completed strengths and needs assessment is shown in the Strengths and Needs Assessment figure on Page 193. When they reflected about their strengths individually and as a teaching team, a key strength they both noted is that they have several years of experience working with children with disabilities. They indicated that their collective knowledge and experience will help them make embedded instruction practices a good fit in their classroom. Although they have just begun working together, they work well as a team and are enthusiastic about using their complementary knowledge and skills to support the children in their classroom.

Four Parts of Embedded Instruction (Snyder, Hemmeter, et al., 2018)

1. What to Teach—What to teach involves identifying priority skills to teach children. These are skills children are not yet doing, but that are one or two steps ahead of what they can currently do, and that are aligned with early learning foundations and with the children's IEP or individual family support plan goals. As part of What to Teach, practitioners write priority learning targets. Each target specifies what the target skill is in ways that are observable and measurable, the conditions under which the child is expected to demonstrate the skill, when the child is expected to demonstrate the skill, and information about how the team will know the child has achieved the skill.

2. When/Where/Who to Teach—As part of When/Where/Who to Teach practitioners identify everyday activities, routines, and transitions that are natural or logical times to embed opportunities for children to practice the target skills identified in their priority learning targets and who will support embedded instruction.

3. How to Teach—How to Teach involves planning for and implementing embedded learning opportunities that support children to learn target skills within everyday activities, routines, and transitions. As part of How to Teach, practitioners use systematic instructional procedures organized as A-B-Cs (antecedents, behaviors, consequences) to help children learn target skills.

4. How to Evaluate—How to evaluate involves collecting and analyzing data about the implementation of embedded learning opportunities and children's progress toward priority learning targets. These data are used to inform decisions about embedded instruction implementation and outcomes.

When they reviewed the embedded instruction practices on the strengths and needs assessment, Maureen and Maria both indicated that they are confident about how to design high-quality activities that support embedded instruction. Although they learned about and practiced writing priority learning targets for embedded instruction in the workshop, they would like support from Elley to help them refine the targets they wrote. They do not have an embedded instruction activity matrix right now, but they are confident that they can make one for their classroom once they identify the activities that are a good fit for the embedded instruction priority learning targets they write. Since they finished the workshop, they have been practicing implementing embedded instruction learning trials in a few classroom activities. They are looking forward to sharing a few video clips of their implementation with Elley. They would like to talk more with Elley about how they can make learning trials be natural and embedded throughout the day across activities, routines, and transitions.

Strengths and Needs Assessment—Elley

Before their first coaching session, Maureen and Maria asked Adam to record video of them practicing embedded instruction with children during centers, small-group instruction, and a mealtime. They shared these videos with Elley so she could do an initial observation to inform her coach strengths and needs assessment. They also shared their classroom schedule. Elley used the notes she wrote during workshop activities she facilitated with Maureen and Maria, the video they submitted, and their classroom schedule to complete her coach strengths and needs assessment. Elley's completed strengths and needs assessment is shown in the Coach Strengths and Needs Assessment on Page 194.

During the workshop, Elley noted Maureen and Maria's ability to write short-term priority learning targets that were aligned with the curriculum as a strength. She also observed in their video that their child-directed activities included multiple opportunities for children to make choices and supported the engagement of the majority of children in the classroom. Similar to Maureen and Maria, Elley noted writing observable and measurable priority learning targets as a potential coaching priority. Given that Maureen and Maria each only embedded learning opportunities during small groups, Elley also listed developing an activity matrix and using it to guide implementation of embedded learning opportunities throughout the day as a possible coaching priority. Finally, Elley noted Maureen and Maria would benefit from support to embed learning opportunities during child-directed activities, routines, and transitions.

Preferred Coaching Strategies Checklist

Instructions: Please mark your preferred enhancement coaching strategies using the checklist below. Please feel free to add comments as well!

Coachee: _Maureen and Maria_   **Date:** _October 5_

Enhancement Coaching Strategies	I'd like to try this strategy	Notes
1. **Side-by-side support cues:** The coach supports your practice implementation in the moment, verbally, with gestures, or with visual cues, or through technology (e.g., bug-in-ear).	*x*	May consider bug-in-ear at a later time
2. **Other help in practice setting:** The coach provides support to you or children, which is not directly related to your goal or action plan (e.g., wiping up spilled paint, sitting on the floor beside a child at circle).	*n/a*	
3. **Problem solving:** An interaction between you and the coach to solve an identified practice implementation issue. Problem-solving involves four steps: 1) identify the implementation issue, 2) generate potential solutions, 3) decide on a course of action, and 4) evaluate pros and cons of the selected course of action.	*x*	
4. **Role play:** In a role play, you and the coach take on other roles related to practice implementation (e.g., coach acts as child, coachee acts as adult).	*x*	
5. **Video examples:** Video examples show how another practitioner uses a practice in a similar implementation setting.	*x*	
6. **Modeling:** Modeling is demonstrating or showing you how to implement a practice that is the focus of a goal or action plan.	*x*	Only during reflection and feedback
7. **Environmental arrangements:** The coach helps you modify or enhance your practice setting or materials in your setting to set the occasion for you to implement a practice.	*x*	
8. **Graphing:** You and your coach work together to graph data you or your coach has collected about your practice implementation or child behaviors.	*x*	
9. **Other:** *In what other ways would you want your coach to help?* We really would like to learn how to collect and graph data for our children's IEP goals.		

Strengths and Needs Assessment

Instructions: Each of the statements listed are skills needed to implement embedded instruction. Read each statement and identify how much you know about the practice, how often you use the practice, and if you would like support to use the practice. Circle one number in each column for each practice.

Coachee(s): _Maureen and Maria_   **Date:** _September 20_

Embedded Instruction Practices	How much do you know about this practice?		How often do you use this practice?		Would you like support to use this practice?	
	Just learning	Could teach others	Not often	Every day	Not right now	Very much
1. Identify and align target skills for children.	1 2 ③ 4 5		1 2 ③ 4 5		1 2 ③ 4 5	
2. Write high-quality priority learning targets (PLTs).	① 2 3 4 5		① 2 3 4 5		1 2 3 ④ 5	
3. Use high-quality activities to provide multiple and meaningful embedded learning opportunities.	1 2 3 4 ⑤		1 2 3 ④ 5		1 ② 3 4 5	
4. Develop an activity matrix to plan when and how many learning opportunities to embed within and across activities.	1 ② 3 4 5		① 2 3 4 5		1 ② 3 4 5	
5. Plan and implement embedded learning opportunities as complete learning trials.	1 2 ③ 4 5		1 2 ③ 4 5		1 2 3 ④ 5	
6. Collect and analyze data on embedded instruction implementation and child progress to inform instructional decisions.	1 2 ③ 4 5		1 2 3 ④ 5		1 2 ③ 4 5	

Strengths: List three things about your current instructional practices that you are confident about and that you believe are strengths that support your implementation of embedded instruction (e.g., We know our students' individual interests and what they like, We offer a variety of toys in each center).

Three things we are confident about and are strengths:
1. We have been working with children with disabilities for several years.
2. We know our children well and can identify their preferences or materials they find motivating.
3. Even though we just started working together, we work well together, and our combined experiences and knowledge will help us use embedded instruction in our classroom.

Priorities: List your top three priorities for embedded instruction coaching support to inform your first Action Plan goal.

Three priorities for coaching are:
1. We want to learn more about how to write priority learning targets that are observable and measurable.
2. We need some help planning how to embed learning opportunities in multiple activities throughout the day, especially during free play and meals.
3. We need to monitor children's progress on their priority learning targets so we know when to provide more support or work on something new.

Coach Strengths and Needs Assessment

Coachee(s): __Maureen and Maria__   Coach: __Elley__   Date: __October 5__   Session #: __1__

Competence and Skill Level:	Coaching Priority:
N—Needs more information **K**—Knowledge about practice but not yet acquired skill **A**—Has acquired skill **F**—Is fluent with the skill	**1**—Not a priority or already fluent **2**—Low priority **3**—Moderate priority **4**—Immediate priority

	Competence and Skill Level				Coaching Priority			
1. Identify and align target skills for children.	N	K	A	(F)	(1)	2	3	4
2. Write high-quality priority learning targets (PLTs).	(N)	K	A	F	1	2	3	(4)
3. Use high-quality activities to provide multiple and meaningful embedded learning opportunities.	N	K	(A)	F	1	(2)	3	4
4. Develop an activity matrix to plan when and how many learning opportunities to embed within and across activities.	N	(K)	A	F	1	2	3	(4)
5. Plan and implement embedded learning opportunities as complete learning trials.	N	(K)	A	F	1	2	3	(4)
6. Collect and analyze data on embedded instruction implementation and child progress to inform instructional decisions.	N	(K)	A	F	1	(2)	3	4

Key Strengths That Support Embedded Instruction

1. Priority learning targets during workshops were achievable within 2–4 weeks based on data provided related to children's current skills. They were aligned with children's IEP goals and preschool learning foundations.
2. Both Maureen and Maria joined children during daily activities and modified materials or activities based on children's interests. At least two choices were available in each activity observed, and most of the children were engaged during child-directed activities.
3. Maureen implemented four embedded learning opportunities for one child during small-group instruction. In two opportunities, the target behavior occurred. Maria implemented five learning trials for one child during small-group instruction. The target behavior occurred three times after providing additional help.

Possible Priorities for the First Shared Goal and Action Plan

1. Revise priority learning targets to include observable and measurable target behaviors.
2. Develop an activity matrix and embed learning opportunities for multiple children across more than one activity.
3. Embed learning opportunities within child-directed activities, routines, or transitions.

Focused Observation

When they finished writing their action plan in the first coaching session, and in preparation for their first focused observation, Maureen and Maria asked Elley to give them some initial feedback about whether they were embedding learning opportunities for each priority learning target in multiple activities. They said they would like some suggestions for how they could spread out their learning trials but still make sure they are providing enough embedded learning opportunities for children to practice their priority learning target skills. They would like to use this information to help them plan their first activity matrix (i.e., Action Step 2).

Action Plan

Coachee(s): _Maureen and Maria_ **Coach:** _Elley_   **Date:** _October 5_   **Action Plan:** _1_

Implementation Goal

We will practice implementing embedded learning opportunities for one priority learning target for three children in two classroom activities each day for 1 week.

Criterion or Goal Achievement Statement

We will know we have achieved this goal when we have collected data (i.e., tally marks on an activity matrix) showing we have implemented at least one embedded learning opportunity for each child's priority learning target in at least two classroom activities each day for 1 week.

	Steps to achieve this goal	Resources needed	Timeline
1	We will revise the priority learning targets we wrote during the embedded instruction workshops. Maureen will email the revised learning targets to Elley for feedback and include Maria on the email. **(Learn more)**	Learning targets Time to revise learning targets Models from the Practice Guide (p. 23) Elley's feedback	10/7 (next coaching session)
2	We will look at examples of activity matrices in the practice guide. Maria will make an activity matrix showing the planned number of opportunities for each priority learning target and activity that we can hang on the wall. Maureen will make a printable version of the activity matrix with space for tally marks. **(Learn more and Make)**	Practice Guide pp. 50, 51, 98 Time to make the matrices Printer Materials for wall matrix	10/12
3	We will practice implementing embedded learning opportunities and collecting data during classroom activities. We will take turns collecting data for each other during activities when opportunities are planned. **(Practice and Collect data)**	Paper activity matrix	10/12 and then ongoing
4	We will share and discuss our data each day at naptime and talk together about additional resources or reminders we might need to help us implement embedded learning opportunities for each priority learning target in at least two classroom activities every day. **(Talk to)**	Daily naptime meeting	10/20 (after fall break) and then ongoing
5	We will review our data with Elley at each coaching session to see if we are making progress or have met our goal. **(Summarize and Analyze data)**	Time with our coach to review data Paper activity matrices with data	10/23 and then ongoing

Review

Review Date 1: _____	Review Date 2: _____	Review Date 3: _____
( ) Goal achieved! ( ) Making progress, but not there yet. ( ) Modified or changed my goal.	( ) Goal achieved! ( ) Making progress, but not there yet. ( ) Modified or changed my goal.	( ) Goal achieved! ( ) Making progress, but not there yet. ( ) Modified or changed my goal.

In preparation for their first reflection and feedback meeting, Maureen and Maria looked at the model priority learning targets in their practice guides and revised one priority learning target they wrote for Aaron, Flynn, and Liliana during the workshops. They sent Elley their revised priority learning targets before the first focused observation (Action Step 1) so she would be able to collect data about when they embedded learning opportunities for each child's priority learning target. They agreed to send 15 min of video of them implementing embedded instruction with children during two different activities or routines. Maureen shared video of free choice and snack time. Maria shared video of free choice and small groups.

As Elley watched each video, she collected data about the number of embedded learning opportunities she observed in each activity for each child's priority learning target. She also noted whether each opportunity was provided by Maureen or Maria. When Elley reviewed her data, she noted the following:

- Aaron was provided a total of 9 embedded learning opportunities to request an object using three words across free choice (6) and snack (3).

- Liliana was provided a total of three embedded learning opportunities to count three or more objects using one-to-one correspondence during small groups.

- No embedded learning opportunities were provided for Flynn's priority learning target, which was to name colors of objects. Elley did note, however, that both Maureen and Maria embedded learning opportunities for Flynn to point to or give an object of a particular color.

- Maureen embedded six learning opportunities for Aaron during free choice and three opportunities during snack.

- Maria embedded three opportunities for Liliana during small-group instruction.

After reviewing her notes and the data she collected, Elley decided to make a graph showing the number of activities where learning opportunities were embedded for each priority learning target. The graph she made is shown below. She also makes a graph showing how many embedded learning opportunities were implemented by each teacher within each observed activity. This graph is shown on the next page.

Number of Activities Where Embedded Learning Opportunities Were Implemented for Each Priority Learning Target

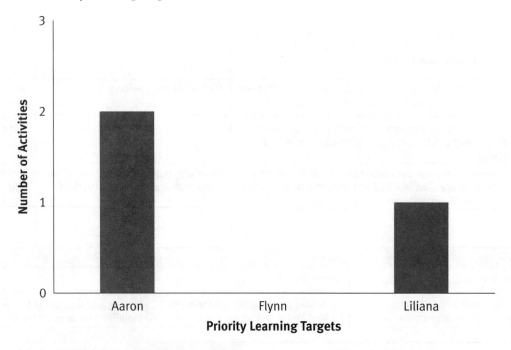

Note: Aaron = free choice and snack; Lilianna = small groups.

Number of Embedded Learning Opportunities Implemented in Each Activity

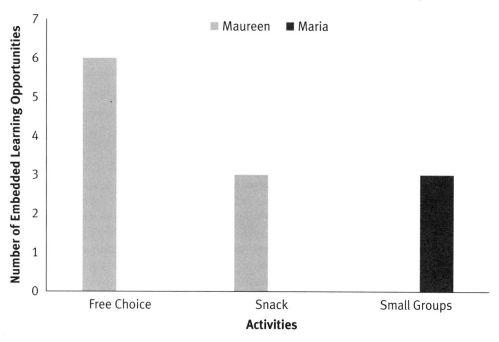

Note: Maria not observed during snack; Maureen not observed during small groups.

Reflection and Feedback

As Elley prepared for the reflection and feedback meeting, she made notes about what supportive and constructive feedback she would give, as well as prompts to facilitate reflection. Her notes to herself are provided in the following box.

Supportive Feedback

- Use Graph—Aaron and Liliana were provided embedded learning opportunities in different activities. Both Maureen and Maria provided embedded learning opportunities.

Constructive Feedback/Reflection

- Flynn's target skill is to name colors. There were no embedded learning opportunities focused on naming colors but there were three embedded learning opportunities during free choice and two embedded learning opportunities during snack that were focused on pointing to or giving an item of a particular color → Clarify whether Flynn's preferred target is to name colors or to receptively identify colors.

    If Maureen and Maria want to focus on receptive identification, support to revise priority learning target.

    If Maureen and Maria want to focus on naming colors, review video of Maria during free choice starting at 12:13. Prompt reflection about how embedded learning opportunities could have been modified to focus on naming colors rather than on receptive identification.

Case Stories: Sam

MEET SAM

It's the end of January, and Sam has been working with Kenya, his coach, since August. Sam teaches at Groveland Elementary School. He has eighteen 4-year-old children in his classroom, including two children who are dual language learners and three children with individualized education programs (IEPs). Sam has been the lead teacher in the 4 year-old class for 3 years, but this is the first year he has participated in practice-based coaching (PBC). Kenya is a program coach at Groveland. She has been working as a coach for 5 years, including 3 years as a PBC coach. Groveland's approach to professional development is to provide universal, targeted, and individualized implementation supports, including PBC, to teachers who are implementing Pyramid Model practices (Hemmeter et al., 2021). In September, Sam attended a 3-day, 16.5-hr workshop series with the other lead preschool teachers in his school. During the workshops, Sam learned about practices to promote children's social-emotional development and to prevent and address their challenging behavior. He also learned about targeted teaching practices to teach social-emotional skills and how to participate in and support the implementation of an individualized positive behavior support plan. Sam and Kenya have had on-site PBC sessions every other week since September. During their coaching sessions, Sam and Kenya reflect on Sam's progress toward the goals and action plans they have developed together to support Sam's use of Pyramid Model practices. Kenya provides supportive and constructive feedback to Sam about his practices implementation. Kenya regularly shares supplemental resources and materials related to Pyramid Model practice implementation that he can use in his classroom.

By January, Sam and Kenya completed four action plans and are getting ready to write their fifth goal and action plan. Sam's previous goals are shown in the box to the left.

To help inform professional development for preschool teachers in their school, Kenya and the professional development team at Groveland perform three observations per year in each preschool classroom using the Teaching Pyramid Observation Tool (TPOT; Hemmeter et al., 2014). In addition, all coaches keep "running TPOTs" that they regularly review with teachers as they engage in PBC sessions and cycles. The running TPOTs serve as ongoing strengths and needs assessments. Kenya conducted the first TPOT in Sam's classroom in September and the second at the beginning of January. Kenya and Sam reviewed these TPOT data and their running TPOT data since August as part of their first coaching session in January. They discussed strengths and priorities for their fifth shared goal and action plan.

> **Goal 1:** I will create and post a visual schedule at eye level for the children and review it with the children before at least four activities throughout the day.
>
> **Goal 2:** I will create five positively stated classroom rules and teach them at least two times a day during large or small group using role play and games.
>
> **Goal 3:** I will provide embedded instruction learning opportunities to children during circle time and small-group time on how to appropriately express positive and negative emotions.
>
> **Goal 4:** I will collect data on the implementation of the behavior support strategies that are part of the individualized positive behavior support plan our team developed for Nora.

Strength and Needs Assessment—Sam

In preparation for writing his fifth goal and action plan, Sam completed the Practice Implementation Checklist and updated the Preferred Coaching Strategies Checklist. On the Practice Implementation Checklist, he placed a *Y* next to practices he believes he is implementing well and that are strengths related to Pyramid Model practice implementation. On the Preferred Coaching Strategies Checklist, he indicated which enhancement strategies he wanted to try. When he discussed his strengths and needs assessment, Sam noted that he has made progress using the visual schedule to teach children the daily routines. Although it has not been the focus of an action plan, he has been more intentional about providing transition warnings to prepare children when transitions will occur and using transition strategies to ensure that all children are actively engaged in transitions.

When Sam considered coaching priorities, he noted that he still needs support teaching behavior expectations. He has been reviewing the classroom rules consistently during small and large groups, but he does not believe the children have really learned the rules yet because he frequently needs to redirect children at circle time and during centers. Sam would also like support to begin sharing information about the Pyramid Model practices with his assistant, Jamie. Jamie just joined the class when they returned from winter break, and she is not familiar with the Pyramid Model. She is interested in learning more, but unfortunately there is not coverage for her to participate in the reflection and feedback meetings with Sam and Kenya.

Strengths and Needs Assessment—Kenya

In preparation for writing their fifth goal and action plan, Kenya made a graph showing the percentage of Pyramid Model practices Sam implemented related to Schedules and Routines, Transitions, Promoting Children's Engagement, and Teaching Behavior Expectations. When reviewing the graph, Sam and Kenya celebrated the progress he had made implementing practices related to Schedules and Routines and Transitions. Sam reflected that using the visual schedule to review the daily routines had really helped children learn the schedule and routines of the day. He also said that having a visual schedule helped him communicate better when there were changes in the daily schedule or routines.

During her observation, Kenya noted that Sam needed to redirect children repeatedly who were not following behavior expectations during centers. Although he reviewed the expectations for music and movement, he ended the circle time activities early because he was concerned about children's safety. During these times, Sam became frustrated and frequently used statements such as "Stop jumping," "Don't touch your friends," and "No running in the classroom." Kenya wrote that Sam would benefit from support to provide positively stated reminders about the expectations. She also noted that another coaching priority might be to provide positive descriptive feedback to children who are following the expectations.

Shared Goal Setting and Action Planning

As they discuss their strengths and needs assessments, Sam and Kenya both agree to continue to focus on practices to teach children behavior expectations. Sam wants to focus on providing positively stated reminders to children during center time and circle time. The goal they write together is shown below:

I will provide at least three positive reminders about the posted expectations and rules to either an individual child or to a group of children during center time and circle time every day.

As they write the action steps for their action plan, Kenya and Sam identify ways that Sam can share information about teaching behavior expectations with Jamie. The action plan they write is shown on Page 202.

Practice Implementation Checklist
High Quality Environments

Practices: Pyramid Model

Name: *Sam*   **Date:** *1/12*   *Y = Yes*

Schedules & Routines

Y	Post daily schedules and routines with visual displays		Include a balance of teacher-directed and child-directed activities
Y	Review schedule and refer to it throughout the day	Y	Prepare children for changes that will occur in the regular schedule
Y	Plan both large and small group activities throughout each day		Make special preparations for individual children who may need more support to follow the routine

Classroom Design

Y	Children can easily move around the classroom	Y	Adequate number and variety of centers to maintain children's interest and support the number of children at each other (1 center for every 4 children)
Y	The learning centers have clear boundaries		
Y	No wide open spaces in the classroom where children can run		

Promoting Engagement

Y	Structure activities so that children are actively engaged almost all of the time (i.e., actively participating)		When children begin to show challenging behavior, help them become actively engaged in the activity or provide a new activity
Y	Change your activity plan when children lose interest		Comment positively and descriptively on children's engagement

Transitions

Y	Provide a while class warning prior to transitions		Provide positive and specific feedback to children who transition appropriately
Y	Develop transition games, songs, or others to ensure all children are actively engaged in the transition	Y	Provide individual prompts (e.g., verbal, visuals) to children who may have difficulty transitioning
	Specifically teach the steps and expectations for transitions		Actively engage all students in the transition even those who are waiting for their turn

Expectations & Rules

	Post behavior expectations and regularly review during large group instruction		Give specific feedback on appropriate child behavior linking back to the posted behavior expectations
	Provide instruction on posted behavior expectations to invidividual children, during play, and small group activities		Facilitate conversations with children to think about the behavior expectations and why they are important for them and the class

Preferred Coaching Strategies Checklist

Instructions: Please mark your preferred enhancement coaching strategies using the checklist below. Please feel free to add comments as well!

Coachee: _Sam_   **Date:** _September 27_

Enhancement Coaching Strategies	I'd like to try this strategy	Notes
1. **Side-by-side support cues:** The coach supports your practice implementation in the moment, verbally, with gestures, or with visual cues, or through technology (e.g., bug-in-ear).	*x*	Okay at 1/20 meeting
2. **Other help in practice setting:** The coach provides support to you or children, which is not directly related to your goal or action plan (e.g., wiping up spilled paint, sitting on the floor beside a child at circle).	*x*	Okay at 10/10 meeting
3. **Problem solving:** An interaction between you and the coach to solve an identified practice implementation issue. Problem-solving involves four steps: 1) identify the implementation issue, 2) generate potential solutions, 3) decide on a course of action, and 4) evaluate pros and cons of the selected course of action.	*x*	
4. **Role play:** In a role play, you and the coach take on other roles related to practice implementation (e.g., coach acts as child, coachee acts as adult).	*x*	
5. **Video examples:** Video examples show how another practitioner uses a practice in a similar implementation setting.	*x*	
6. **Modeling:** Modeling is demonstrating or showing you how to implement a practice that is the focus of a goal or action plan.	*x*	
7. **Environmental arrangements:** The coach helps you modify or enhance your practice setting or materials in your setting to set the occasion for you to implement a practice.	*x*	
8. **Graphing:** You and your coach work together to graph data you or your coach has collected about your practice implementation or child behaviors.		
9. **Other:** *In what other ways would you want your coach to help?* I might want to try things during the observation later.		

Essentials of Practice-Based Coaching: Supporting Effective Practices in Early Childhood by Patricia Snyder, Ph.D., Mary Louise Hemmeter, Ph.D., and Lise Fox, Ph.D. Copyright © 2022 by Paul H. Brookes Publishing Co., Inc. All rights reserved.

Action Plan

Coachee: _Sam_   **Coach:** _Kenya_   **Date:** _January 30_   **Action Plan:** _5_

Implementation Goal
Goal I want to achieve: I will provide at least 3 positive reminders about the posted expectations and rules to either an individual child or to a group of children during center time and circle time every day.

Criterion or Goal Achievement Statement
My data show I provide at least 3 positive reminders about the expectations and rules to either an individual child or a group of children in centers and during circle time (6 total) every day for 3 consecutive weeks.

	Steps to achieve this goal	Resources needed	Timeline
1	I will watch video examples of teachers providing positive reminders about classroom expectations and rules with Jamie during naptime. **(Learn more)**	Video examples from coach Time to watch videos with Jamie	Fri. 2/1
2	I will make a list of positive reminder starter phrases and post them in centers or near the circle time carpet where children typically need the most reminders (e.g., blocks, dramatic play, story time, music and movement) and share it with Jamie. **(Make)**	Construction paper Computer/printer Planning time	Wed. 2/6
3	I will share the positive reminders with Jamie and talk with her about them. **(Talk to)**	Planning time	Wed. 2/6
4	I will continue to review the center and circle expectations and rules with the children. I will give positive reminders to individual or groups of children about the expectations and rules when they are in centers and at circle. **(Practice)**	Positive reminder starter phrases	Wed. 2/20
5	I will use a rubber-band system to count how many positive reminders I provide to an individual child (blue rubber band) or to a group of children (red rubber band) during center and circle. I will summarize my rubber band data each day on a sheet of paper. I will analyze the data with Kenya during our next coaching session. **(Collect, Summarize, Analyze data)**	Blue and red rubber bands Paper Time with coach	Wed. 3/6

Review

Review Date 1: _____	Review Date 2: _____	Review Date 3: _____
( ) Goal achieved! ( ) Making progress, but not there yet. ( ) Modified or changed my goal.	( ) Goal achieved! ( ) Making progress, but not there yet. ( ) Modified or changed my goal.	( ) Goal achieved! ( ) Making progress, but not there yet. ( ) Modified or changed my goal.

Number of Reminders Provided During Centers

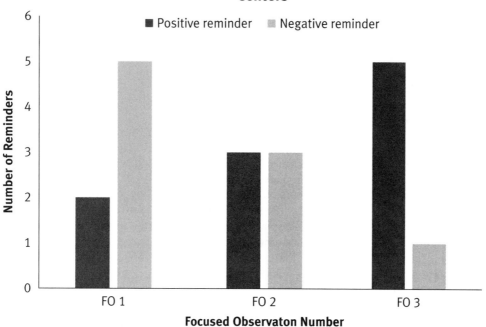

Key: FO, focused observation.

Number of Reminders Provided During Circle

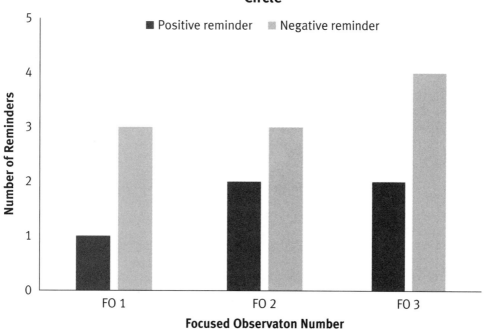

Key: FO, focused observation.

Focused Observation

During each focused observation since they wrote their action plan, Kenya has been collecting data about the number of positively stated and negatively stated reminders Sam provides in centers and in circle time. Kenya has just finished her third focused observation for this action plan, and she decided to create a graph for each activity to review with Sam during their reflection and feedback meeting (see graphs on p. 203.). She wants to use the graph to show Sam's progress toward his goal over time. Kenya also writes down examples of positive reminders she has heard Sam use in addition to negatively stated reminders.

Reflection and Feedback

During the reflection and feedback meeting, Kenya shows Sam the graph of positive and negative reminders provided about following expecations and rules during centers. She provided supportive feedback about the progress he has made increasing the number of positive reminders he gives to children during centers, and she points out that the number of negative reminders he provides has decreased. She gives examples of positive reminders she has heard and asks Sam to reflect about changes he has noticed in children's behavior since he has started using more positive reminders during centers. Sam says he has more time to join children in play at centers now because there are fewer instances of unsafe behavior during centers. He also reflects that he has been trying to be more intentional about providing positive descriptive feedback to children when they are being safe in the classroom during center time. Although he has noticed these improvements during centers, Sam says he is still having difficulty helping children follow expectations and rules for safe behavior during circle time. Kenya shows the graph she made for circle time, and acknowledges that there are more negative reminders during circle than positive reminders. She asks Sam, "What do you think is working well for you during centers that you might be able to try during circle?" Sam says that the reminders he and Jamie posted in the center areas have been very helpful but that he is having difficulty translating them to be appropriate for circle. Kenya tells Sam she has written down a couple of negatively phrased reminders she heard him say during her focused observation and asks Sam if it would be helpful to look at them and brainstorm ways to rephrase them to be more positive. Sam says he thinks that would help give him ideas for reminders he can post next to his circle time schedule. As their meeting ends, Sam says it was helpful to look at the graphs of his data and asks if Kenya would make a video recording during the next focused observation so he can practice taking data with her.

Appendix II

Strengths and Needs Assessments

Designing Your Strengths and Needs Assessment: Being Intentional About Response Options and Anchors

What are response options and anchors?

When rating scales are used to gather strengths and needs assessment information from coachees, various scale response options and anchors might be used.

Response options are what the coachee is responding to for each practice (e.g., I use this practice, I believe this practice is important for supporting child development and learning). Response options can focus on

Response options and anchors should always be strengths based and might refer to current or future practice implementation.

1. Practice use

2. Frequency/accuracy of practice use

3. Practice knowledge

4. Practice self-efficacy

5. Practice "fit" in context

6. Practice effects on child outcomes

7. Practice support

Anchors are the numerals and words or phrases aligned with the low end and high end of a scale for each response option (e.g., Not yet to Always, Strongly disagree to Strongly agree). For some items, a binary Yes or No anchor might be used.

How do you select response options and anchors?

Selection of response options is based on the type of information you want to collect. Anchors should be logical for the response option. Plan to have 3 or fewer response options for each practice. Too many response options or too many practices (i.e., more than 15) should be avoided because strengths and needs assessments need to be feasible for coachees and coaches to complete in 10–15 minutes. Strengths and needs assessment forms can gather data using one type of response option (Figure 1) or different response options (Figure 2).

Strengths and needs assessment forms can gather data about future implementation (Figure 1), current implementation response options (Figure 3), or a mix of current and future implementation (Figures 2 and 4).

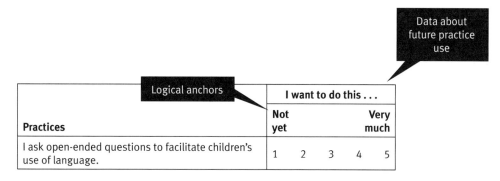

Figure 1

Practices	I want to do this . . .				
	Not yet				**Very much**
I ask open-ended questions to facilitate children's use of language.	1	2	3	4	5

Logical anchors · *Data about future practice use*

Figure 2

Practices	I know about this practice. . .					I want to do this. . .				
	Just learning				**I could teach others**	**Not yet**				**Always**
I ask open-ended questions to facilitate children's use of language.	1	2	3	4	5	1	2	3	4	5

Logical anchors · *Response options for current practice knowledge and future use data*

Figure 3

Practices	I believe this is important for children.					I am confident in my use of this practice.
	Disagree				**Agree**	
I ask open-ended questions to facilitate children's use of language	1	2	3	4	5	Yes No

Logical anchors · *Response options for current practice fit and self-efficacy*

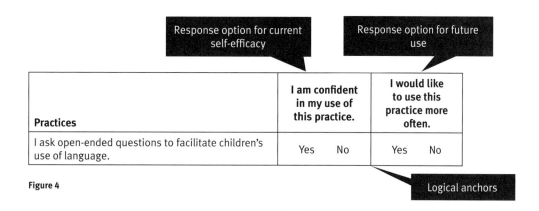

Figure 4

Practices	I am confident in my use of this practice.	I would like to use this practice more often.
I ask open-ended questions to facilitate children's use of language.	Yes No	Yes No

Response option for current self-efficacy · *Response option for future use* · *Logical anchors*

How do you identify and record coaching priorities?

There are three strategies typically used to identify and record priorities: 1) ranking, 2) discrepancy, and 3) open-ended response.

Ranking is accomplished by asking coachees to identify their top 2–5 priorities from the entire set of practices on the strengths and needs assessment by ranking them (e.g., 1 = highest priority to 5 = lowest priority).

Practice	Not yet	Seldom	Sometimes	Usually	Always	Support needed?	Priority (Rank)
I ask open-ended questions to facilitate children's use of language	1	2	3	4	5	Yes No	*1*
I add more words or ideas to what children say.	1	2	3	4	5	Yes No	

Discrepancy is accomplished by asking coachees to identify their top 2–5 priorities by calculating the difference between two response options that are related temporally (e.g., future and current) or focused on change (e.g., confidence and support needed). Once the ratings are completed for each practice on the strengths and needs assessment, compare the two columns and write the difference between them (e.g., desired use = 5, current use = 2, difference = 3). Practices with large discrepancies might be those where coaching support is targeted.

Practices	Desired use: I want to do this . . .					Current use: I am doing this now . . .					Difference between desired use and current use
	Not right now				Very much	Not Yet				Always	
I ask open-ended questions to facilitate children's use of language.	1	2	3	4	[5]	1	[2]	3	4	5	*5 – 2 = 3*

Open-ended responses are gathered by asking coachees to respond to reflective prompts about their practice implementation. This might or might not be combined with a rating scale or binary option.

A notes column or a notes box at the bottom of the strengths and needs assessment can be used with all response options. Notes can be helpful for recording questions or reflections about the practices.

Practices
1. I ask open-ended questions to facilitate children's use of language.
2. I add more words or ideas to what children say.
Of the practices listed: Which practice(s) would you like support to use more often?

Key Points to Remember:

Within practice-based coaching, both coachees and coaches complete strengths and needs assessments. These strengths and needs assessments each have the same practices. How the practices are written might be identical or they might vary in length or format based on the respondent.

Key Considerations for Strengths and Needs Assessments

Program or Practice Setting:	Date:
Practice Focus for PBC:	Age(s) of Children in Program or Practice Setting:

Instructions: Listed below are key questions to consider when constructing a formal strengths and needs assessment for use in PBC. For each indicator, check "Yes" or "Not Yet." Use the Notes column to record changes needed to enhance the strengths and needs assessment.

Key Considerations	Yes	Not Yet	Notes
1. Are the practices aligned with data-informed strengths and needs?			
2. Are the practices cohesive and limited in number (i.e., less than 15) or organized into logical or sequential groups on more than one strength and needs assessment document, if more than 15 practices are identified?			
3. Are the practices a good "fit" for the practice context?			
4. Are the practices strengths-based and positively stated?			
5. Are the practices observable and measurable?			
6. Is there practice alignment between the coachee and coach strengths and needs assessment forms?			
7. Will the design of the strengths and needs assessment form, including response options and anchors, elicit the type of information you want to obtain (e.g., use, knowledge, self-efficacy)?			
8. Will the information gathered from the strengths and needs assessment be helpful for identifying coaching priorities and PBC goals?			

THE NATIONAL CENTER ON
Quality Teaching
and Learning

PBC COACH TRAINING STRENGTHS AND NEEDS ASSESSMENT

COACHING PRACTICES STRENGTHS AND NEEDS ASSESSMENT

Coach's name _____ Date _____

Instructions: Read each statement and consider how often you use this practice. Once you have circled a number to indicate how often you use it, consider if you would like to use this practice more often. When you have done this for each practice, identify the top 5 coaching practices you would like to use more.

Coaching Practice	How Often? Never	Seldom	Sometimes	Usually	Always	Change needed?	Priority (Top 5)	Notes
COLLABORATIVE PARTNERSHIPS								
1. I maintain professionalism by being on time, organized, and prepared for each coaching session.	1	2	3	4	5	Yes No		
2. My coachees and I share an understanding of the goals and process of coaching.	1	2	3	4	5	Yes No		
3. I am clear and articulate when I communicate with coachees.	1	2	3	4	5	Yes No		
4. I model openness to learning and taking risks.	1	2	3	4	5	Yes No		
5. I foster an environment in which coachees will feel comfortable trying new things, reflecting on their practice, and receiving feedback.	1	2	3	4	5	Yes No		

Adapted from:"PBC Coach Training," by the National Center on Quality Teaching and Learning, 2015. This document was initially prepared under Grant #90HC0002 for the U.S. Department of Health and Human Services, Administration for Children and Families, Office of Head Start, by the National Center on Quality Teaching and Learning.

1

211

Coaching Practice	How Often?					Change needed?	Priority (Top 5)	Notes
	Never	Seldom	Sometimes	Usually	Always			
6. I focus on and celebrate the strengths of each coachee.	1	2	3	4	5	Yes No		
7. I seek out knowledge of the cultures and populations in the communities and programs I am working with, and I integrate this into my practice.	1	2	3	4	5	Yes No		
8. I individualize my coaching to the strengths, needs, and goals of each coachee.	1	2	3	4	5	Yes No		
9. I engage in continual self-reflection of my professional practices and how my practices influence the coachees' practice and outcomes.	1	2	3	4	5	Yes No		
SHARED GOALS AND ACTION PLANNING								
10. I work with coachees to assess and identify their strengths and areas for growth, based on strengths and needs assessment and other sources of data.	1	2	3	4	5	Yes No		
11. I support coachees in prioritizing goals for improvement/refinement of effective practices.	1	2	3	4	5	Yes No		
12. I write goals with coachees that are specific and observable and can be completed within a specified amount of time.	1	2	3	4	5	Yes No		
13. I develop action plans with coachees that provide step-by-step procedures for meeting coachees' goals.	1	2	3	4	5	Yes No		

Coaching Practice	How Often? Never / Seldom / Sometimes / Usually / Always					Change needed?	Priority (Top 5)	Notes
FOCUSED OBSERVATION								
14. During observations of coachees, I focus on specific practices related to the goal and action plan.	1	2	3	4	5	Yes No		
15. During observations of coachees, I gather data on the coachee's use of specific practices or child behaviors related to those practices.	1	2	3	4	5	Yes No		
16. I feel comfortable using support strategies (e.g., modeling practices, providing cues, role playing). I use these strategies only with the agreement of my coachees.	1	2	3	4	5	Yes No		
REFLECTION AND FEEDBACK								
17. I support coachees' ongoing reflection about progress on implementation of effective practices.	1	2	3	4	5	Yes No		
18. I provide supportive feedback to coachees about their implementation of practices.	1	2	3	4	5	Yes No		
19. I provide constructive feedback to coachees that supports refining or expanding implementation of practices.	1	2	3	4	5	Yes No		
20. I ask questions that provide information and stimulate thinking in support of the coachee's learning and goals.	1	2	3	4	5	Yes No		

Appendix III

Goal Setting and Action Planning

Action Plan Template

Coachee(s): _____ **Coach:** _____ **Date:** _____ **Action Plan:** _____

Implementation goal
Goal I (we) want to achieve:

Criterion or Goal Achievement Statement

Steps to achieve this goal		Resources needed	Timeline
1			
2			
3			
4			
5			

Review

Review Date 1: _____	Review Date 2: _____	Review Date 3: _____
( ) Goal achieved!	( ) Goal achieved!	( ) Goal achieved!
( ) Making progress, but not there yet.	( ) Making progress, but not there yet.	( ) Making progress, but not there yet.
( ) Modified or changed my goal.	( ) Modified or changed my goal.	( ) Modified or changed my goal.

Action Plan Fidelity Checklist

Action Plan Indicators	Yes	No
Implementation Goal		
1. **Practice oriented:** The goal supports the coachee to _implement_ effective practices with fidelity in context (i.e., action the coachee will do vs. making materials).		
2. **Effective practices:** The goal is directly aligned with one or more of the targeted effective practices.		
3. **Observable:** The goal describes actions or behaviors of the coachee that can be observed (i.e., such that two people could agree when the practice occurred).		
4. **Achievable:** Given the coachee's knowledge, skills, and preferences, the goal is achievable in 2–4 weeks.		
Criterion or Goal Achievement Statement		
5. **Observable:** The criterion statement includes actions or behaviors of the coachee that can be observed (i.e., two people could agree when the practice occurred).		
6. **Measurable:** The criterion statement includes a performance statement including how often _or_ how much (i.e., how many times) a practice will be implemented and for how long (i.e., number of days).		
7. **Goal focused:** The criterion or goal achievement statement is aligned with the implementation goal (i.e., includes the same practice and observable actions or behaviors stated in the implementation goal).		
Action Steps		
8. **Specific:** The action steps describe observable actions or behaviors the coachee or coach will do (e.g., Read, Watch, Make, Implement, Talk to, Analyze).		
9. **Aligned:** The action steps include key words associated with the practice and observable behaviors specified in the goal.		
10. **Logical sequence:** The action steps occur in a chronological or progressive order, which move the coachee toward accomplishing the goal by meeting the criterion or goal achievement statement specified.		
11. **Resources:** When appropriate, the specific human (i.e., who and for how long) and material resources (i.e., what and where to locate) needed to achieve each action step are specified.		
12. **Timelines:** The timelines for action steps occur within 2–4 weeks and are feasible for the coachee.		
Collaboration		
13. **Utility:** The action plan is written clearly in language the coachee can understand.		

From Embedded Instruction for Early Learning. (2018). Action plan fidelity checklist. Used with permission from the Anita Zucker Center for Excellence in Early Childhood Studies, University of Florida. https://embeddedinstruction.net/

Appendix IV

Focused Observation

Tally Data Collection Form

Instructions: Write the goal that is the target of coaching ("Target goal"). Write the practice(s) related to that goal on which you plan to collect data ("Target practice"). Determine and write the frequency that is desired ("Target number"). Complete the start and stop times of the observation. During the focused observation, use the form to mark when the coachee used each practice and take notes of examples of practice implementation and missed opportunities. At the end of the focused observation, record the total number of tallies. Also calculate the total length of the observation and rate.

Target goal: _____

Start time: _____ Stop time: _____ Total length: _____

Target practice:	
Target number:	
Tally:	
Notes:	
Total number:	
Rate (Number/length):	

Duration Data Collection Form

Instructions: Write the goal that is the target of coaching ("Target goal"). Write the practice related to that goal on which you plan to collect data ("Target practice"). Determine and write the duration of the practice that is desired ("Target duration"). During the focused observation, use the form to mark the start and stop times of the target practice. At the end of the focused observation, complete the Scoring section to determine the total duration of practice use.

Target goal: _____

Target practice: _____

Target duration: _____

Start time: _____   Stop time: _____ Length: _____

Start time: _____   Stop time: _____ Length: _____

Start time: _____   Stop time: _____ Length: _____

Start time: _____   Stop time: _____ Length: _____

Scoring: Total duration = _____

Practice-Based Coaching Focused Observation Notes

Coachee(s):	Coach:	
Date:	**Observation Started:**	**Observation Ended:**

What was observed:	*To share with coachee(s):*

Percentage of Target Practices Data Collection Form

Instructions: Write the goal that is the target of coaching ("Target goal"). Write the practices related to that goal on which you plan to collect data ("Target practices"). Determine and write the percentage of practices that are desired to be present ("Target percentage present"). During the focused observation, use the checklist to mark when the coachee used the practice. Also complete the start and stop times of the observation. At the end of the focused observation, complete the Scoring section to determine the percentage of practices present. Also calculate the total length of the observation.

Target goal: _____

Target percentage present: _____

Start time: _____ Stop time: _____ Total length: _____

Target practices:

☐ _____

☐ _____

☐ _____

☐ _____

☐ _____

☐ _____

☐ _____

☐ _____

☐ _____

Scoring: Total present _____ / Total possible _____ = _____ × 100 = _____%

Appendix V

Reflection and Feedback

Tips for Providing Supportive Feedback
Within the Practice-Based Coaching Framework

What is supportive feedback?

Supportive feedback is one form of performance-based feedback. It is the provision of positive <u>descriptive</u> information about the coachee's actions related to practice implementation as specified in the goal and action plan including:
(a) feedback about forms or materials used to implement a practice
(b) practice implementation, or
(c) use of data about practice implementation or child progress or outcomes.
Supportive feedback should emphasize strengths and positive actions of the coachee that support practice implementation. Supportive feedback is an essential strategy for each coaching session.

How is supportive feedback different from general feedback?

Supportive feedback is different from general feedback, because explicit descriptions are provided about what was observed related to practice implementation. Supportive feedback can also include statements about relationships between the coachee's observed actions and children's development and learning.

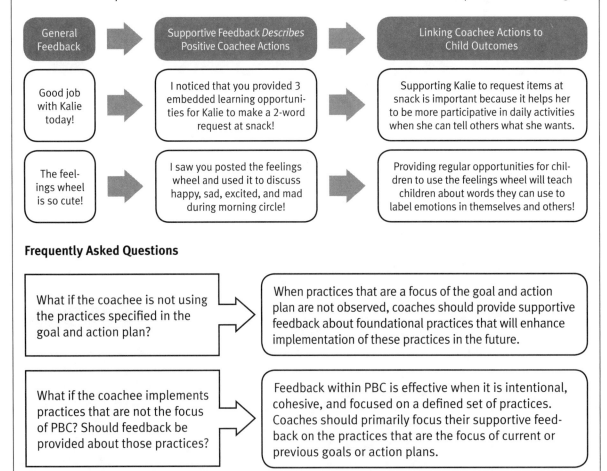

Frequently Asked Questions

What if the coachee is not using the practices specified in the goal and action plan?	When practices that are a focus of the goal and action plan are not observed, coaches should provide supportive feedback about foundational practices that will enhance implementation of these practices in the future.
What if the coachee implements practices that are not the focus of PBC? Should feedback be provided about those practices?	Feedback within PBC is effective when it is intentional, cohesive, and focused on a defined set of practices. Coaches should primarily focus their supportive feedback on the practices that are the focus of current or previous goals or action plans.

Tips for Providing Constructive Feedback
Within the Practice-Based Coaching Framework

What is constructive feedback?

Constructive feedback is one form of performance feedback. It is the provision of data-informed or performance-based suggestions or supports for enhancing the fidelity of practice implementation as specified in the goal and action plan. Constructive feedback should support the coachee to implement the practice more often, more fluently, across contexts or children, or to maintain or adapt practice implementation. Constructive feedback might be provided about resources or materials used to implement a practice; practice implementation; or the use of data related to practice implementation, child progress, or child outcomes. Constructive feedback is **_not_** telling the coachee what they did wrong.

How do you provide constructive feedback?

Constructive feedback is an essential coaching strategy for each coaching session. Constructive feedback typically includes four features when delivered as intended. Often, constructive feedback will also include the provision of resources or materials to support the coachee's enhanced practice implementation.

Feature	Example
1 Provide an *objective description* of what was observed related to a practice specified in the goal and action plan.	*Today, Jorge had 7 embedded instruction opportunities for his learning target of making 1-word requests. Two of the trials had a consequence following the correct target behavior. You or his peer gave him the object he requested.*
2 *Provide information* about the practice and how it can benefit the coachee, children, or practice context.	*When Jorge experiences a positive consequence immediately following the learning target behavior, he will be more likely to learn the behaviors you are trying to teach him.*
3 Identify *one to three suggestions or strategies* for enhancing the coachee's implementation of the practice.	*To ensure that Jorge receives embedded instruction learning trials that include a consequence, you could use the instructional plan or make a visual cue to remind you and your team to provide the consequence. Or, is there another strategy you think might help you to remember?*
4 Provide a *reflective prompt* so the coachee has an opportunity to verbally state what they will do to enhance practice implementation.	*What do you think you will do to ensure that Jorge receives a consequence?*

Constructive feedback helps a coachee reflect on and self-evaluate the use of the targeted practices.

Focus constructive feedback on the practices targeted in the goal and action plan.

Providing Performance Feedback: Steps for Coaches

Instructions: Coaches can use this resource to plan for what performance feedback they want to provide and how to provide it.

Step One: Begin with a **positive or affirmative statement** related to the focused observation and the practice(s) reflected in the goal and action plan.
> *Tip:* Open with an affirmative statement or statement of gratitude to begin the conversation.

Step Two: Use **reflective questioning** (objective, interpretive, comparative) about the focused observation.
> *Tip:* Refer to Table 8.1. "Types of questions to facilitate reflection."

Step Three: Continue the conversation with **supportive feedback** to acknowledge specific actions observed with practices. Use data-based feedback from the observation.
> *Tip:* Identify how to provide supportive feedback using Table 8.3. "Supportive feedback conversation starters with examples and nonexamples." Data should be concrete and specific and connected to the focused observation.

Step Four: Using **constructive feedback,** provide information and suggestions for enhancing fidelity of practice implementation.
> *Tip:* Identify how to begin delivering constructive feedback using Table 8.4, "Constructive feedback conversation starters with examples and nonexamples."

Step Five: Continue the conversation with the practitioner to engage in additional reflection on next steps for practice implementation. Update the goal and action plan as appropriate.
> *Tip:* Use active listening skills and follow the coachee's lead and work collaboratively to identify next steps.

Template for E-Mail Feedback

1. Provide greeting and a positive or affirming statement about the focused observation. The affirming statement might be related either to the goal and action plan or to other practices that are the focus of practice-based coaching (PBC).

Hi Sam,
I really enjoyed visiting your classroom today. Your new choices for how children can transition from activity to activity were terrific. They really made for a smooth morning and the children responded to them as well.

In this example, the affirmation is related to transition practices. Even though transition practices are not the focus of the current action plan goal, they are part of Pyramid Model practices, which **are** the focus of PBC in this example.

2. Provide supportive feedback related to the targeted practice.

It was great to see you use the sentence strips posted on your walls to remind you to increase your use of positive descriptive praise.

In this example, the current goal and action plan goal is focused on Sam's use of positive descriptive praise, which is a Pyramid Model practice.

3. Use data-based feedback to accurately describe what you observed.

You used a lot of positive descriptive feedback today. I tallied a ratio of 3:1 for positive descriptive feedback vs. general feedback. This improves every time I visit.

Supportive feedback is direct, specific, and grounded in data from the observation.

4. Provide constructive feedback related to the targeted practice(s).

I noticed that you used positive descriptive feedback frequently during centers but less during circle. Something you might try is to focus on providing positive descriptive praise in a different activity each day in the coming week. Let me know your thoughts about this suggestion and, if you try it out, how it works. We can have a follow-up discussion about other strategies the next time I see you.

Constructive feedback is direct, specific, grounded in data from the observation, and provides suggestions for enhancing fidelity of practice implementation across activities.

5. Provide resources related to implementing the constructive feedback.

Attached is a video of a teacher using positive descriptive feedback during circle time. I thought this might give some ideas about how to use positive descriptive feedback during this routine.

Provide resources and a model for practice implementation.

6. Plan for next steps of action and a response request.

I plan on being back on Wednesday, April 10, at 9 a.m. Please respond and let me know if that still works for you.

Asking for a response gives the coach information about whether the e-mail feedback is being read.

7. Closing remarks including encouragement.

I am so impressed with the Pyramid Model practices you are implementing! I look forward to our next interaction and hearing your thoughts and ideas about the positive descriptive feedback suggestion. See you soon!

Closing remarks provide encouragement and a brief reminder about the action plan goal.

Appendix VI

Practice-Based Coaching Strategies

Example Elements for Coaching Agreements

Listed below are elements that might be part of Practice-Based Coaching (PBC) agreements for coaches, coachees, and administrators. Elements are organized under the structural and process features of PBC as these relate to building rapport and maintaining and enhancing the collaborative partnership. Elements selected for inclusion on coaching agreements should be written so they are appropriate and individualized for the context in which PBC will be implemented and for the coaches and coachees who will be involved in PBC implementation.

Coach Commitments

> This section specifies commitments the coach is agreeing to as part of the collaborative partnership.

As we engage in our collaborative partnership, I commit to

Elements Related to Structural Features of the Collaborative Coaching Partnership

- Coaching frequency, intensity, duration (e.g., commit to coaching every other week for 6 weeks, commit to 1 hr of focused observation and 30 min of reflection and feedback each time)

- Timeliness and organization (e.g., be on time and prepared for session)

- Support implementation of the effective practices that are the content focus of PBC (e.g., commit to supporting knowledge about and use of effective practices)

Elements Related to Process Features of Collaborative Coaching Partnership

- Maintain confidentiality

- Learn about the coachee and their experiences, preferences, and motivations

- Engage in strengths- and support-based interactions and focus on coachee's preferences and practice goals

- Use agreed-upon coaching strategies

- Implement PBC with fidelity (e.g., commit to supporting collaborations related to strength and needs assessment, shared goals and action planning, focused observation, reflection and feedback)

- Provide additional resources and supports for practice implementation and PBC collaborations (e.g., commit to sharing resources, providing models of practice implementation)

- Other commitment(s):

Coachee Commitments

This section specifies commitments the coachee is agreeing to as part of the collaborative partnership.

As we engage in our collaborative partnership to support my implementation of [specify set of effective practices], I commit to

Elements Related to Structural Features of Collaborative Coaching Partnership

- Coaching frequency, intensity, duration (e.g., commit to coaching every other week for 6 weeks; commit to 1 hr of focused observation and 30 min of reflection and feedback each time)

- Timeliness and organization (e.g., be on time and be prepared for session)

Elements Related to Process Features of Collaborative Coaching Partnership

- Implement effective practices that are the content focus of PBC (e.g., commit to implementing specified set of practices such as Pyramid Model or embedded instruction practices)

- Work toward achievement of goals and steps specified on action plans

- Actively engage in PBC (e.g., assess strengths and needs, set goals and develop action plans, participate in focused observations of practice implementation, reflect on practice implementation and feedback received)

- Share preferences about coaching interactions and coaching strategies with coach

- Give coach ongoing feedback about how collaborative partnership is working and offering suggestions for making it more effective

- Commit to ongoing facilitated professional development and learning experiences

- Other commitment(s):

Note: In some contexts, it might be important to explicitly specify in the coaching agreement that information from PBC will not be used in performance evaluations (e.g., *When I am working with you as your coach, what I observe and what we discuss is confidential and will not be used for any purposes other than coaching. When I am working with you as a coach, my goal is to support you and not to evaluate you*).

> This section summarizes commitments and has space for signatures by coach and coachee. Coachees and coaches should retain copies of the coaching agreement and refer back to it when needed.

Coaching Agreement Signature Page

I, the coach, commit to the above and to being respectful, nonjudgmental, trustworthy, and supportive in all our coaching interactions to create a positive collaborative partnership.

_____   _____

Practice-Based Coach Signature   **Date**

I, the coachee, commit to the above and to being open to suggestions, willing to share my preferences and priorities, willing to request the supports I need, and willing to implement the practices specified in my goals and action plans to create a positive collaborative partnership.

_____   _____

Coachee Signature   **Date**

> This section specifies examples of commitments administrators or other leadership personnel might agree to in support of PBC.

Example of Commitments for Administrators

In support of the implementation of [specify practices], I commit to

- Respect the confidentiality of the collaborative coaching partnership

- Not use PBC information as part of performance evaluations

- Provide time, private space, and supports for PBC (e.g., coverage in classroom so coachee can engage in coaching sessions)

- Specify if and how coaching data will be used to inform decisions (e.g., number of coaching cycles completed; frequency, intensity, and duration of coaching as reflected in coaching logs; number of goals achieved; number of action plans written; practice implementation data; child development and learning outcomes) and with whom data will be shared

- Other commitment(s):

I, the administrator, commit to the above and agree to support implementation of PBC.

_____   _____

Administrator Signature   **Date**

Coaching Strategies Quick Reference Guide

Coaching strategy	Definition
Essential Strategies	
Used in Every Practice-Based Coaching (PBC) Cycle	
Observation	Watching, listening, and taking objective notes about the coachee's actions or behaviors related to the practice(s) specified in the goal and action plan. Observation also might involve watching, listening, and taking objective notes about the practice setting or how children respond when a coachee implements a practice(s).
Reflective conversation	Interaction between the coach and coachee to prompt thinking and discussion about practice implementation and how practice affects children or others.
Performance-based feedback	Performance-based feedback can be verbal or written. Supportive feedback emphasizes strengths and positive actions related to practice(s) implementation. Constructive feedback includes suggestions or supports for using the practices with fidelity (or as intended).
Supportive feedback	Supportive feedback is the provision of positive descriptive information about the coachee's actions related to practice implementation as specified in the goal and action plan.
Constructive feedback	Constructive feedback is the provision of data-informed or performance-based suggestions or supports for enhancing the fidelity of practice implementation as specified in the goal and action plan (i.e., more often, more fluently, across contexts or children, or maintain or adapt practice implementation).
Identifying or providing resources or materials	Identifying or providing resources or materials that help the coachee learn about or implement the practice(s) that is the focus of a goal or action plan.

Used Periodically in Cycles, When Appropriate	
Goal setting	Goal setting is a collaborative process between the coachee and coach that includes a discussion of practice-focused strengths and needs and the identification of a coaching priority. The coaching priority is recorded as the implementation goal on the action plan. Identifying and writing practice implementation goals occurs periodically. Reviewing goals and action plans occurs as part of each coaching session.
Graphic feedback	Graphic feedback is a form of performance-based feedback. It is a visual display of coachee data or child data and includes verbal or written information that is used to provide performance feedback and to analyze and communicate about coachee's practice(s) implementation.
Video feedback	Video feedback is a form of performance-based feedback. The coach records video of the coachee or the coachee shares a video they recorded in the practice context. Together or separately, the coachee and coach use the video to provide performance feedback and to analyze and communicate about coachee's practice(s) implementation.
Enhancement Strategies	
Side-by-side support cues	Side-by-side support is when the coach supports practice implementation in-the-moment verbally, with gestures, with visual cues, or through technology (e.g., bug-in-ear).
Other help in practice setting	Other help in setting is when the coach provides support to the coachee or children that is not directly related to the goal or action plan. Other help should be used to facilitate the collaborative partnership or to reduce distractions that might prevent the coachee from implementing the practice.
Problem solving	Problem solving is an interaction between the coachee and coach about solving a practice implementation issue. Problem-solving involves four steps: 1) identify the implementation issue, 2) generate potential solutions, 3) decide on a course of action, and 4) evaluate potential pros or cons of the selected course of action.
Role play	Role play is a simulated situation. In a role play, the coachee and coach take on other roles related to practice implementation (e.g., coach acts as a child, coachee acts as adult).
Video examples	Video examples show how another practitioner uses a practice in a similar implementation setting. They should be brief (e.g., 30 s to 2 min) and well aligned to the goal, action plan, or performance-based feedback.
Modeling	Modeling is demonstrating or showing the coachee how to implement a practice that is the focus of the goal or action plan.
Environmental arrangements	Environmental arrangements are when the coach helps the coachee to modify or enhance the practice setting or materials in the setting to set the occasion for the coachee to implement a practice.
Graphing	Coach and coachee work together to graph data the coachee or coach has collected for coachee or child behaviors.

Preferred Coaching Strategies Checklist

What Are Coaching Strategies?

Coaching strategies describe how the coach supports the coachee to identify and implement practices. Coaching strategies are used throughout the practice-based coaching (PBC) cycle.

Below, you will find a list of essential strategies your coach will use. On the second page, you will also find some enhancement (optional) strategies. Please review the enhancement strategies on the second page and let your coach know which strategies you would feel comfortable with them using during your coaching sessions. Strategies might look different or be enacted in different ways across different coaching delivery formats.

Observation: The coach watches and listens to practice implementation and takes notes to share with you.

Reflective conversation: Interaction between the you and your coach to prompt thinking and discussion about practice implementation and how practice affects children or others.

Performance-based feedback: Performance-based feedback is verbal or written. Supportive feedback emphasizes your practice implementation strengths and positive actions. Constructive feedback includes suggestions or supports for how you can enhance practice implementation.

Identifying or providing resources or materials: Identifying or providing resources or materials that help you learn about or implement the practice(s) that are the focus of a goal or action plan.

Goal setting: Using your strengths, needs, and priorities to identify and write practice implementation goals and action plans and to review goals and action plans as part of each coaching session.

Graphic feedback: A visual display of your practice implementation or a child's behavior connected to your practice implementation. You and your coach use the graph as part of reflection and feedback.

Video feedback: A video of your practice implementation that either you or your coach record. You and your coach use the video as part of reflection and feedback.

Preferred Coaching Strategies Checklist

Instructions: Please mark your preferred enhancement coaching strategies using the checklist below. Please feel free to add comments as well!

Coachee: _____ Date: _____

Enhancement Coaching Strategies	I'd like to try this strategy	Notes
1. **Side-by-side support cues:** The coach supports your practice implementation in the moment, verbally, with gestures, or with visual cues, or through technology (e.g., bug-in-ear).		
2. **Other help in practice setting:** The coach provides support to you or children, which is not directly related to your goal or action plan (e.g., wiping up spilled paint, sitting on the floor beside a child at circle).		
3. **Problem solving:** An interaction between you and the coach to solve an identified practice implementation issue. Problem-solving involves four steps: 1) identify the implementation issue, 2) generate potential solutions, 3) decide on a course of action, and 4) evaluate pros and cons of the selected course of action.		
4. **Role play:** In a role play, you and the coach take on other roles related to practice implementation (e.g., coach acts as child, coachee acts as adult).		
5. **Video examples:** Video examples show how another practitioner uses a practice in a similar implementation setting.		
6. **Modeling:** Modeling is demonstrating or showing you how to implement a practice that is the focus of a goal or action plan.		
7. **Environmental arrangements:** The coach helps you modify or enhance your practice setting or materials in your setting to set the occasion for you to implement a practice.		
8. **Graphing:** You and your coach work together to graph data you or your coach has collected about your practice implementation or child behaviors.		
9. **Other:** *In what other ways would you want your coach to help?*		

Practice-Based Coaching Log

Coachee(s):	**Date:**
Coach:	**Observation in minutes:**
Action plan goal:	**Meeting in minutes:**

Observation format(s): _____ In person   _____ Virtual live streaming   _____ Video

Reflection and feedback format(s):

_____ In person   _____ Phone   _____ E-mail

_____ Virtual meeting   _____ Online platform   _____ Other:

Summary notes for postobservation meeting or communication

Reflective Conversation Starters	Supportive Feedback
	I observed…
	This is important for children because…

Constructive Feedback	Resources and Materials
I observed…	
Strategies to enhance implementation:	
1.	
2.	
3.	

Focused observation indicators	Implemented	
	Yes	**No**
1. On time or reviewed the observation video by agreed-upon timeline		
2. Recorded notes about the implementation setting (e.g., location, activities or routines occurring)		
3. Collected data on coachee's goal, action plan, and practice use		
4. Reminded coachee of the plan for meeting or observation follow-up		

Postobservation meeting or communication indicators	Implemented	
	Yes	**No**
1. Opened the meeting or written correspondence with a positive greeting		
2. Asked the coachee about **goal/action plan progress**		
3. **Facilitated reflection** about the practices observed		
4. Provided **supportive feedback** about the practices observed		
5. Facilitated **constructive feedback** about the practices observed, including 1–3 strategies to address the feedback		
6. Supported coachee to reflect on the 1–3 strategies discussed as part of **constructive feedback** and to select a strategy to try out. Plans to try: _____		
7. **Recommended materials** or follow-up activities to support the goal/action plan		
8. Confirmed goal and action plan next steps/adjustments		
9. Asked the coachee how they wanted to be supported in the next observation or video review		
10. Identified when (or if) the next session would occur		
11. Invited coachee questions or comments		
12. Stated planned follow-up support (e.g., e-mail, call, send resource)		
Total		
Fidelity Percentage (Yes/Total Possible * 100)		

Essential strategies	Used	Enhancement strategies	Used
*Observation		Side-by-side support cues	
*Reflective conversation		Other help in practice setting	
*Supportive feedback		Problem solving	
*Constructive feedback		Role play	
*Identifying or providing resources and materials		Video examples	
Goal setting		Modeling	
Graphic feedback		Environmental arrangements	
Video feedback		Graphing	

Additional notes, including unexpected or unusual events:

*Used in every PBC session.

Coaching Strategies Discussion Worksheet

Strategy	Brief description	Comfort level Not at all → Very					Notes
Essential Strategies							
Observation	Coach watches and listens and takes notes to share with coachee.	1	2	3	4	5	
Reflective conversation	Interaction between coach and coachee to prompt thinking and discussion about practice implementation.	1	2	3	4	5	
Performance-based feedback	Performance-based feedback is verbal or written. Supportive feedback emphasizes practice implementation strengths and positive actions. Constructive feedback includes suggestions or supports for enhancing practice implementation.	1	2	3	4	5	
Identifying or providing resources or materials	Coach or coachee identifies or provides resources or materials the coachee uses to learn about or implement practice(s) that are the focus of the goal or action plan (e.g., visual schedule, activity matrix).	1	2	3	4	5	
Goal setting	Using coachee strengths, needs, and priorities to identify and write practice implementation goals and action plans and to review goals and action plans as part of each coaching session.	1	2	3	4	5	
Graphic feedback	A visual display of practice implementation or a child's behavior connected to practice implementation used as part of reflection and feedback.	1	2	3	4	5	
Video feedback	A video of practice implementation that either coachee or coach records that is used as part of reflection and feedback.	1	2	3	4	5	

Strategy	Brief description	Comfort level					Notes
		Not at all		→		Very	
Enhancement Strategies							
Side-by-side support cues	Coach supports practice implementation in the moment, verbally, with gestures, with visual cues, or through technology (e.g., bug-in-ear).	1	2	3	4	5	
Other help in practice setting	Coach provides support to coachee or children that is not directly related to goal or action plan (e.g., wiping up spilled paint, sitting on the floor beside a child at circle).	1	2	3	4	5	
Problem-solving	Coachee and coach discuss a practice implementation issue and identify options to address the issue and solutions to try out.	1	2	3	4	5	
Role play	Coachee and coach take on other roles related to practice implementation (e.g., coach acts as child, coachee acts as adult).	1	2	3	4	5	
Video examples	Video examples of how another practitioner uses a practice in a similar implementation setting.	1	2	3	4	5	
Modeling	Coach demonstrates or shows how to implement a practice that is the focus of a goal or action plan.	1	2	3	4	5	
Environmental arrangements	Coach helps coachee modify or enhance practice setting or materials in setting to set occasion for practice implementation.	1	2	3	4	5	
Graphing	Coach and coachee work together to graph data the coachee or coach has collected of coachee practice implementation or child behavior.	1	2	3	4	5	

ADDITIONAL NOTES:

Sample Practice-Based Coaching Workshop Agenda

Objectives

After completing practice-based coaching (PBC) workshops, coaches will be able to...

- Identify and describe the key components of PBC
- Name, define, and identify PBC essential and enhancement coaching strategies
- Describe characteristics of a collaborative coaching partnership
- Describe why strengths and needs assessments are important in PBC
- Compare and contrast different approaches for gathering strengths and needs assessment information
- Demonstrate how to work with a coachee to develop shared goals and action plans
- Conduct a focused observation based on a goal and action plan
- Facilitate reflection and provide performance feedback
- Describe and analyze different PBC formats and delivery methods
- Evaluate interpersonal skills and dispositions important for PBC implementation through lenses of equity and culturally responsive practices
- Identify and evaluate tools and resources to support PBC implementation

Initial Session(s) (one ~6-hr session or two ~3-hr sessions)

I. Introduction to PBC

    A. Defining PBC

    B. Overview of PBC Framework

    C. Effects of Quality Coaching and PBC Research

    D. Situating PBC in Professional Development: Goals of PBC

    E. Coach Competencies and Skills

II. Case Stories of PBC Implementation

    A. Introduction to Lynn and Sirena

    B. Introduction to Maureen, Maria, and Elley

    C. Introduction to Sam and Kenya

III. Collaborative Partnerships: PBC Begins Here!

   A. Characteristics of a Collaborative Partnership

   B. Building Rapport

   C. Strategies and Tools for Enhancing and Sustaining a Collaborative Partnership

   D. Application of Collaborative Partnerships in the Case Stories

IV. PBC Coaching Strategies

   A. Essential Coaching Strategies

   B. Enhancement Coaching Strategies

   C. Supporting Coachees to Identify Preferred Coaching Strategies

   D. Resources for Coaching Strategies

V. Practice-Focused Strengths and Needs Assessments

   A. Rationale for Strengths and Needs Assessments in PBC

   B. Approaches for Gathering Strengths and Needs Assessments

   C. Examples of Strengths and Needs Assessments

   D. Application of Strengths and Needs Assessments in the Case Stories

Successive Session(s) (one ~6-hr session or two ~3-hr sessions)

I. Shared Goal Setting and Action Planning

   A. Using Strengths and Needs Assessments to Inform Shared Goal Setting and Action Planning

   B. Key Features of PBC Goals

   C. Goal Writing Activity

   D. Developing Action Plans

      1. Parts of Action Plans

      2. Strategies for Writing Quality Action Plans

   E. Application Activity: Writing a Goal and Action Plan for a Case Story

   F. Resources for Goal Setting and Action Planning

II. Focused Observation

   A. What Makes an Observation Focused?

   B. How to Conduct a Focused Observation

   C. Notes and Data Collection During the Observation

   D. Application Activity: Conducting a Focused Observation Activity for a Case Story Example

   E. Resources for Focused Observations

III. Reflection and Feedback

   A. Strategies for Facilitating Reflection

   B. Examples of Reflection

   C. Application Activity: Reflection Role Play Using a Case Story Example

   D. Resources for Reflection

   E. Performance Feedback: Supportive and Constructive

      1. Key Features of Supportive Feedback

      2. Key Features of Constructive Feedback

         a) Strategies for Delivering Constructive Feedback

   F. Formats for Providing Supportive and Constructive Feedback

      1. Use of Data

      2. Graphic Feedback

      3. Video Feedback

   G. Application Activity: Performance Feedback Role Play Using a Case Story Example

   H. Resources for Performance Feedback

Successive Session (one ~4-hr session)

I. PBC Formats and Delivery Methods

   A. Menu of PBC Format and Delivery Options

   B. Finding Good Fits for Your Context

   C. Resources for Making Decisions About PBC Format and Delivery Options

II. PBC Implementation Supports

   A. Coaching Manual

   B. Coaching Log

   C. Fidelity Forms

   D. Making Data-Informed Decisions: Prepare-Look-Think-Act

   E. Resources and Materials for PBC Implementation

III. Getting Started

   A. Coaching Agreements

   B. Caseloads

   C. Scheduling Tips

   D. Resources for Coaches

IV. Ongoing Professional Development Support for Coaches

    A. Interpersonal Skills for PBC: Lenses of Equity and Culturally Responsive Practices

        1. Examples From Case Stories and Experiences

        2. Non-examples and Experiences

    B. PBC Communities of Practice

    C. Fidelity Checks

    D. PBC Booster Sessions

    E. Professional Development Resources for Coaches

V2.0 Rev. 10/03/18

NCPMI Coaching Log

Teacher ID:		Coach ID:		Program ID:
Total # of Action Plan Goals:		Cycle #:		

Activities/Strategies - check all that occurred during session(s)

Observation Strategies							Reflection and Feedback Strategies						
Dates:							Dates:						
Observed							Problem-solving discussion						
Videotaped							Reflective conversation						
Modeled							Helped with environmental arrangements						
Collected data							Role play						
Verbal support							Constructive feedback						
Side-by-side support cues							Goal setting/action planning						
Problem-solving discussion							Supportive feedback						
Reflective conversation							Resources or materials provision						
Helped with environmental arrangements							Demonstration						
Other help in the classroom							Individual child support						
Other							Other						
Total Observation Time:							Total Reflection & Feedback Time:						
Action Plan Goals Completed:							New Action Plan Goals:						
Notes:													

Use companion spreadsheet for entering data found on: https://challengingbehavior.cbcs.usf.edu/Implementation/Data/index.html

From National Center for Pyramid Model Innovations (2019). Data Decision-Making. Challenging Behavior. https://challengingbehavior.cbcs.usf.edu/Implementation/

1

Sample Practice-Based
Coaching Manual Table of Contents

Contents   **Page**

Appendix VI.Y

TOP 10 TIPS FOR COACHES

1 **Build the relationship: It will be time well spent.**

A trusting, supportive relationship will be key to the success of coaching. Take time to get to know the teacher and the classroom. This will make your coaching more relevant and more salient for the teacher. Be willing to pitch in and be an extra set of hands in the room when needed. Coaching is a partnership and the more you know and understand the classroom, the more you can support the teacher. And all of this contributes to building the supportive relationship that will be the context for your coaching.

2 **Share successes: Build on the positive.**

We all like to feel encouraged! Notice what is going well, comment on it, and then build on it. Using a strengths-based approach to coaching prevents teachers from feeling their coach is going to "fix" them. Instead, the goal is to work together to become more fluent in existing practices and learn new skills.

3 **Map it out: Use an action plan as a roadmap for your coaching journey.**

Work with the teacher to create an action plan to help guide your coaching. What practices would he or she like to work on first? What steps are needed to put the targeted practice into place? Breaking new practices into smaller steps can make the process of change less overwhelming.

4 **Provide supports: Give materials and ideas to support teacher needs.**

Sometimes offering a material such as a rules poster or a visual schedule at a coaching meeting is the jump start for getting a good strategy in place. Be sure to model what to do with the material you provide…or it may end up in a drawer instead of being used in the classroom. Avoid providing too many materials or ideas at one time, so the teacher can focus on what is most important to implement.

5 **Be transparent: Highlight coaching as part of professional development right from the start.**

It is important that teachers are prepared for coaching. Everyone involved should know the expectations and goals of coaching, before coaching begins. If coaching follows a training or workshop, discuss how the content delivered might become the focus of action plan goals. Present coaching as the "bridge" between hearing about new practices and implementing them in the classroom.

FALL 2014 V.1.1

From Embedded Instruction for Early Learning. (2018). Action plan fidelity checklist. Used with permission from the Anita Zucker Center for Excellence in Early Childhood Studies, University of Florida. https://embeddedinstruction.net/

6 Be prepared: Keep some helpful phrases handy.

Being a coach can leave you at a loss for words at times! Having a few key phrases handy can really help when you are not sure what to say next. Some tried-and-true favorites include: "Let's just give it a try," "Tell me more about…," "What can we do to make this practice easier to implement?" "How do you think circle went today?" and "What have you tried so far?"

7 Anchor it: Use data to anchor your observation and feedback.

Using data is a way to be objective when providing feedback. You can use assessments that your program is already using, such as the CLASS, ECERS, ITERS, or ELLCO; or consider collecting data on specific behaviors, such as child engagement or instances of challenging behaviors. Having something to base your coaching on gives you focus and makes feedback more objective and meaningful. Regardless of your tool, using data to provide some concrete evidence of progress can be very rewarding. It takes some getting used to, but data can be very powerful—many times teachers start asking to see more!

8 Be patient: Change takes time.

When the goal of coaching is changing teacher behaviors—it takes time. In order for meaningful change to occur and maintain, ample time is needed not just to learn a new skill, but to practice using it. Some behaviors are easier than others to change. Depending on the teacher's beliefs or years of experience, some practices may take a greater time commitment from both the coach and teacher.

9 Find the right fit: Just like teaching, coaching isn't "cookie cutter."

Know that the strategies you use, approaches you take, and the relationships you build will vary depending on the personalities involved, skills you are building, and the needs of the classroom. For example, you may have one teacher who wants the coach to mostly observe and offer suggestions, while another teacher wants the coach to do more modeling and demonstration. How you support each teacher will depend on their skills, their needs, and their preferences. This is what makes coaching difficult, but also makes it exciting!

10 Connect with a community of coaches: Share successes and challenges.

Network with other coaches to get support along the way. Being able to share "coaching highs" and work through "coaching lows" is crucial. Whether it is bouncing ideas off of each other, sharing materials, or just helping work through an issue—coaches can learn a lot from each other!

For more information, contact us at: **NCQTL@UW.EDU** or **877-731-0764**
This document was prepared under Grant #90HC0002 for the U.S. Department of Health and Human Services, Administration for Children and Families, Office of Head Start, by the National Center on Quality Teaching and Learning.

FALL 2014 V.1.1

From The National Center on Quality Teaching and Learning (NCQTL). Practice-based coaching: Top 10 Tips for Coaches [PDF file]. https://eclkc.ohs.acf.hhs.gov/sites/default/files/pdf/pbc-top-10-tips.pdf

in *Essentials of Practice-Based Coaching: Supporting Effective Practices in Early Childhood* by Patricia Snyder, Ph.D., Mary Louise Hemmeter, Ph.D., and Lise Fox, Ph.D. Copyright © 2022 by Paul H. Brookes Publishing Co., Inc. All rights reserved.

Coach Learning Community Meeting Agenda

Date:	Location:

Materials to bring to meeting:

Members:

Goals/Outcomes:

(Assign roles)

Facilitator:

Note taker:

Time keeper:

Agenda		
Topic	**Time**	**Notes**
Opening/Coaching Connections	10 min	
Reflect on Coaching Practices	15 min	
New Content/Discussion	20 min	
New Skill Practice/Didactics	15 min	
Reflection and Action Planning: What did you learn and what will you try next?	15 min	
Closing	5 min	

Group norms:

Coach Learning Community Planning Form

Reflection and feedback		
Skill I tried:	How I used the skills in coaching:	Results: Did the skill improve coaching practice and coachee implementation? What feedback did I receive from coachees?

Plan		
New skill:	Steps for implementing:	Resources needed:

Practice-Based Coaching Technology Tips

Technology can be used in many ways to support coaches' and coachees' participation in practice-based coaching.

Use of technology supports:

- Focused observation
- Data collection
- Data sharing
- Enhanced reflection and feedback
- Implementation of virtual coaching
- Sharing of resources and materials

TOOLS YOU CAN USE	TIPS
Use video to record implementation in the practice setting, collect data, and guide reflection and feedback.	• Use a device that is portable. • Put the device on a small tripod or stable surface. • Make sure the coachee's and children's faces are visible. • Make sure the materials are visible.
Use video conferencing platforms to conduct virtual focused observations or reflection and feedback meetings.	• Make sure the internet connection is stable and use a hardwire connection if possible. • Use a secure platform. • Use a platform that allows screen sharing and recording.
Use computers, tablets, or cellular phones to collect and analyze data or to participate in focused observations or reflection and feedback meetings.	• Use a password-protected and encrypted device. • Make sure the connection is stable. • Use accessories like microphones or ear buds to enhance sound.
Share video, print, and web resources during video conferences or by e-mail during or after the coaching session.	• Use screen sharing whenever possible to share resources during the session. • E-mail or text resources after the session.

Tips for Virtual Coaching

Coaching essentials	Tips for virtual coaching
Strengths and needs assessments	• Use fillable PDF forms or electronic survey formats that can be stored and shared on file sharing systems or video coaching platforms.
Shared goal setting and action planning	• Use screen sharing during a videoconference so both the coach and coachee can see the current goal and action plan. • Check or confirm any updates to the plan with the coachee. • E-mail or text the plan to ensure that the coachee has access to it.
Observation	• Watch video collected by the coachee. • Use a device like a cell phone, webcam, or tablet to watch practices as they are implemented. • Use an external microphone to enhance sound. • Use earbuds to provide side-by-side verbal support.
Reflective conversation	• Meet by videoconference or phone or use a virtual coaching platform. • Ask questions and make comments to facilitate reflection about progress toward the goal and action steps.
Performance feedback: Supportive and constructive feedback	• Meet by videoconference or phone or use a virtual coaching platform. • Give specific supportive and constructive feedback in relation to the goal and action plan. • Use screen sharing to show video or images of practices observed.
Share resources and materials	• Use screen sharing during video conferences to show resources. • Share resources electronically via e-mail, text, or virtual coaching platforms during or after the session.

Appendix VII

Practice-Based Coaching
Implementation Supports

Effective Practices Within the Practice-Based Coaching Framework

What is a practice?

A practice is a statement of observable and measurable actions or behaviors of a coachee. *Observable* means the practices can be seen or heard. *Measurable* means the practices are written in a way that two people could agree when the practice is being implemented. Practices are *written statements* because they give the coachee and coach a shared vocabulary and practice-focus for engaging in practice-based coaching (PBC).

Practice examples and non-examples

Practice non-examples	What needs to be enhanced?	Practice examples
The classroom environment is engaging.	Although you can observe the environment, two people may not agree on what *engaging* means.	• Teacher gives children choices of materials to be used in most activities. • Teacher provides opportunities for children to respond verbally and nonverbally during teacher-led activities.
Children of diverse backgrounds, experiences, and abilities are accepted and celebrated.	This statement does not describe what the teacher will say or do and therefore cannot be measured.	• Teacher communicates with children and families in their home language. • Teacher supports children to use assistive technology during daily activities. • Teacher provides materials in centers that are developmentally appropriate for all children in the classroom.

How are the practices used in PBC?

- Practices are used to inform the content of the strengths and needs assessments that lead to the development of a shared goal and action plan for coaching.

- Practices inform the coachee's actions or behaviors with children.

- Practices guide the focus of observations, the reflective conversations between the coachee and coach, and performance-based feedback provided.

*Practices help the coachee and coach **focus on a manageable set of skills** rather than on the universe of things that could be addressed by a coachee and coach.*

*Practices are effective and associated with **positive child outcomes** when implemented as intended.*

Checklist for Evaluating Effective Practices for Practice-Based Coaching

Program:				Date:			
Focus for PBC:				**Age of children:**			

Practice	Observable		Measurable		Feasible		Child outcomes	
	Yes	No	Yes	No	Yes	No	Yes	No
1.								
2.								
3.								
4.								
5.								
6.								
7.								
8.								
9.								
10.								
11.								
12.								

Note: Observable, can be seen or heard; measurable, written in a way that two people could agree when it occurs; feasible, possible for coachee to implement in practice context; child outcomes, likely to lead to desired child developmental and learning outcomes when implemented as intended (i.e., with fidelity).

Sample Weekly Practice-Based Coaching Schedule

Coaching Half-Time
1 Program; 6 Teachers

	Monday	**Tuesday**	**Wednesday**	**Thursday**	**Friday**
8:00		FO-Teacher 1	FO-Teacher 3	Team Meeting	
9:00		FO-Teacher 2	Preparation	FO-Teacher 5	
10:00		Preparation	FO-Teacher 4	FO-Teacher 6	
11:00		Preparation	Lunch	Preparation/ Material Provision	
12:00		Lunch	M-Teacher 3	Lunch	
1:00		Material Provision		M-Teacher 4	
2:00		Cover Class		M-Teacher 5	
3:00		M-Teacher 1		M-Teacher 6	
4:00		M-Teacher 2		Documentation	
5:00					

Key: FO, focused observation; M, meeting.

Sample Weekly Schedule

Coaching Full Time, Other Duties
2 Programs; 12 Teachers
Week 1

	Monday	**Tuesday**	**Wednesday**	**Thursday**	**Friday**
8:00	Admin Duties	Cover Class	Admin Duties	Preparation	M-Teacher 7
9:00		FO-Teacher 3	Material Provision	Preparation	
10:00	FO-Teacher 1	Organization/ Notes	Material Provision	FO-Teacher 6	
11:00	FO-Teacher 2	M-Teacher 2	FO-Teacher 5	FO-Teacher 7	Lunch/Travel
12:00	Lunch	Preparation	Lunch	Lunch	Leadership Team Meeting
1:00	Organization/ Notes	Lunch/Travel	M-Teacher 3	Preparation	Cover Class
2:00	Material Provision	FO-Teacher 4	Cover Class		Organization/ Notes
3:00	M-Teacher 1	Preparation	M-Teacher 5	M-Teacher 6	
4:00	Admin Duties	M-Teacher 4	Admin Duties	Admin Duties	Documentation

Key: FO, focused observation; M, meeting.

Sample Weekly Schedule

Coaching Full Time, Other Duties
2 Programs; 12 Teachers
Week 2

	Monday	**Tuesday**	**Wednesday**	**Thursday**	**Friday**
8:00	Admin Duties	Admin Meeting	Admin Duties	Admin Duties	Preparation
9:00	Preparation	FO-Teacher 9	FO-Teacher 10	Admin Duties	FO-Teacher 12
10:00	FO-Teacher 8	Organization/ Notes	Material Provision	Admin Duties	
11:00	Preparation		Material Provision	FO-Teacher 11	Material Provision
12:00	Lunch	Preparation	Lunch	Lunch	Lunch
1:00	Organization/ Notes	Lunch/Travel	M-Teacher 9	Preparation	M-Teacher 12
2:00	Material Provision			M-PTR-YC	Cover Class
3:00	M-Teacher 8	Leadership Team Meeting	M- Teacher 10	M-Teacher 11	Documentation
4:00	Admin Duties	Admin Duties	Documentation	Documentation	Documentation

Key: FO, focused observation; M, meeting; PTR-C, Prevent-Teach-Reinforce for Young Children.

Time Management Tips for Practice-Based Coaching Coaches

1. During the first coaching cycle, set aside a longer block of time, approximately 60–90 min, for initial shared goal setting and action planning. Session(s) will include a review of strengths and needs assessment data, completion of goal planning forms, and writing goals and action steps.

2. Schedule focused observations and reflection and feedback sessions with coachees ahead of time. Leave each meeting with a plan for the next observation and reflection and feedback session. Send e-mail reminders to coachees ahead of scheduled observations or meetings.

3. Block off enough time to do focused observations and be sure the focused observation aligns with the times the practice(s) specified in the action plan goal will occur. Stick to the *focus* of your observation. This will help you complete multiple focused observations in one day, if needed.

4. Adjust and balance your schedule as you get to know your coachees. Some coachees might require more time (e.g., longer reflection and feedback meetings, additional sessions for goal setting, additional focused observations). Plan observations and reflection/feedback meetings with coachees that require more support on a day in which you have additional time, or a day in which you can provide coaching supports to other coachees who might not require as much time.

5. Understand that coaching frequency (number of sessions), intensity (how many sessions you have in a specified unit of time, for example, number of sessions per week or month), duration (length of sessions), and delivery formats will vary across coachees based on fidelity of practice implementation, practice-focused strengths and needs, and time and resources available. For example, you may be coaching one coachee in a program on a weekly basis for 16, 1 hr. face-to-face sessions and another in the same program monthly for 8, 1 hr. virtual sessions. Decisions around coaching frequency, intensity, duration, and delivery formats occur through a data-based decision-making process with the coachee and with the program leadership team.

6. When using group coaching, group coachees who are working on similar practices or goals together. When doing group coaching face to face, you might group coachees who are in close geographic proximity to reduce travel time or consider use of videoconferencing or web-based coaching platforms or hybrid approaches.

7. Consider use of videoconferencing or a web-based coaching platform for focused observations and for reflection and feedback meetings to reduce travel time and reach more coachees across programs or multiple sites.

8. Schedule a consistent time to complete coaching documentation and tasks, including coaching logs, follow-up e-mails, and scheduling.

9. Keep accurate records of the time spent conducting all practice-based coaching–related activities, including planning and travel, when appropriate. If coaching face to face, schedule as many coaching sessions within the same geographic region as possible to reduce travel time.

263

Look-Think-Act Discussion Guide

Coaching Classroom Teachers

| LOOK | THINK | ACT |

Data Considerations for All:

▶ Time dedicated to coaching

▶ Coaching caseload (e.g., number of teachers being coached)

▶ Areas of focus for coaching (e.g., Pyramid-only, other curricula areas)

Look	Think	Act
What do we see?	**What are the data showing? What influences these data?**	**Consider these actions**
Look at how many complete coaching cycles are delivered by each coach. Identify how many complete coaching cycles each teacher received. Look at the number of attempted and completed coaching cylcles.	Is the delivery of coaching cycles by coaches meeting the expected target? Are all teachers receiving the targeted number of coaching cycles? Are there differences between attempted cycles and completed cycles (i.e., higher number of attempted cycles when compared to completed cycles)? Are coaches reporting resistance from teachers? Are there differences across teachers or are they limited to a few teachers?	Identify and address reasons coaches are not meeting expected coaching cycle delivery targets and/or teachers are not receiving the targeted number of cycles. Consider: ▶ coaching loads ▶ time/resources ▶ teacher/coach attendance ▶ classroom/program schedules Develop a plan for expanding coaching reach. Refer to Leadership Team Guide to Implementing Practice-Based Coaching within the Pyramid Model for considerations of coaching assignments, format, and delivery options. Revise procedures used to prepare teachers for coaching. Use handouts, online resources, teacher-coaching agreements, and so forth.
Look at the average duration of coaching observation and durations across teachers for each coach. Examine the average duration of coaching observation and durations for each teacher.	Are the average durations of coaching observation and debriefing meetings appropriate? ▶ Are teachers who spend more time with their coach making higher gains based on TPOT scores? ▶ Are teachers with more concerns on their TPOT scores (red flags) spending more time in coaching? Are there differences between teachers in duration of coaching observation and debriefing that are a concern?	Dig deeper into the data by comparing TPOT scores and average duration of coaching cycle. Determine if a goal to increase or decrease coach durations is appropriate.

From National Center for Pyramid Model Innovations (2019). Data Decision-Making. Challenging Behavior.
https://challengingbehavior.cbcs.usf.edu/Implementation/data/index.html

Look	Think	Act
What do we see?	**What are the data showing?** **What influences these data?**	**Consider these actions**
Look at the patterns of strategy use and activities across observation sessions.	What strategies are being used during observations? What strategies are not being used?	Provide coaches with additional support tools, or training for using other strategies. Allow time for coaches to network with other coaches.
Look at the patterns of strategy use and activities across debriefing sessions.	What strategies are being used during debriefing? What strategies are not being used?	Provide coaches with additional support tools, or training for using other strategies. Allow time for coaches to network with other coaches.
Identify the number of action plan goals each individual teacher is working on. Look at the percentage of action plan goals completed.	Are there differences among teachers with regards to completion of action plan goals? Do certain teachers have too few/too many action plan goals?	Partner with coaches to identify teachers who might need additional support to efficiently meet action plan goals.

ChallengingBehavior.org

The contents of this document were developed by the National Center for Pyramid Model Innovations under a grant from the Department of Education, grant # H326B170003. However, those contents do not necessarily represent the policy of the Department of Education, and you should not assume endorsement by the Federal Government. **This document is public domain and may be reproduced without permission.**

Pub. 09/18/18

References

Anita Zucker Center for Excellence in Early Childhood Studies. (2019). *Practice-based coaching* [Coach training materials]. Anita Zucker Center for Excellence in Early Childhood Studies, University of Florida.

Artman-Meeker, K., Fettig, A., Barton, E. E., Penney, A., & Zeng, S. (2015). Applying an evidence-based framework to the early childhood coaching literature. *Topics in Early Childhood Special Education, 35*(3), 183–196. https://doi.org/10.1177/0271121415595550

*Artman-Meeker, K. M., & Hemmeter, M. L. (2012). Effects of training and feedback on teachers' use of classroom preventive practices. *Topics in Early Childhood Special Education, 33*(2), 112–123. https://doi.org/10.1177/0271121412447115

*Artman-Meeker, K., Hemmeter, M. L., & Snyder, P. (2014). Effects of distance coaching on teachers' use of Pyramid Model practices: A pilot study. *Infants and Young Children, 27*(4), 325–344. https://doi.org/10.1097/IYC.0000000000000016

Artman-Meeker, K., Rosenberg, N., Badgett, N., Yang, X., & Penney, A. (2017). The effects of bug-in-ear coaching on pre-service behavior analysts' use of functional communication training. *Behavior Analysis in Practice, 10*(3), 228–241. https://doi.org/10.1007/s40617-016-0166-4

Baer, D. M., Wolf, M. M., & Risley, T. R. (1968). Some current dimensions of applied behavior analysis. *Journal of Applied Behavior Analysis, 1*(1), 91–97. https://doi.org/10.1901/jaba.1968.1-91

Ball, D. L., & Forzani, F. M. (2011). Building a common core for learning to teach and connecting professional learning to practice. *American Educator, 35*(2), 17–21, 38–39.

Bandura, A., & Locke, E. (2003). Negative self-efficacy and goal effects revisited. *Journal of Applied Psychology, 88*(1), 87–99. https://doi.org/10.1037/0021-9010.88.1.87

Barton, E. E., Kinder, K., Casey, A. M., & Artman, K. M. (2011). Finding your feedback fit: Strategies for designing and delivering performance feedback systems. *Young Exceptional Children, 14*(1), 29–46. https://doi.org/10.1177/1096250610395459

Barton, E. E., Pribble, L. & Chen, C. (2013). The use of e-mail to deliver performance-based feedback to early childhood practitioners. *Journal of Early Intervention, 35*(3), 270–297. https://doi.org/10.1177/1053815114544543

Barton, E. E., Velez, M., Pokorski, E. A., & Domingo, M. (2020). The effects of email performance-based feedback delivered to teaching teams: A systematic replication. *Journal of Early Intervention, 42*(2), 143–162. https://doi.org/10.1177/1053815119872451

Bautista, N. U., & Boone, W. J. (2015). Exploring the impact of TeachMe™ lab virtual classroom teaching simulation on early childhood education majors' self-efficacy beliefs. *Journal of Science Teacher Education, 26*(3), 237–262. https://doi.org/10.1007/s10972-014-9418-8

Bigelow, K. M., Carta, J. J., Irvin, D. W., & Hemmeter, M. L. (2019). *Teaching Pyramid Infant–Toddler Observation Scale (TPITOS) for Infant–Toddler Classrooms manual, research edition.* Paul H. Brookes Publishing Co.

Bigelow, K. M., Walker, D., Jia, F., Irvin, D., & Turcotte, A. (2020). Text messaging as an enhancement to home visiting. Building parents' capacity to improve child language-learning environments, *Early Childhood Research Quarterly, 51*(2), 416–429. https://doi.org/10.1016/j.ecresq.2019.12.010

Bishop, C. Kinder, K., & Shannon, D. (2019). "Lights…Camera…Action Plan!" presentation at the National Training Institute, St. Petersburg, FL. Retrieved from https://tft-ca.embeddedinstruction.net/wp-content/uploads/2020/07/Lights-Camera-Action-4.28.19.pdf

Bishop, C. D., Shannon, D., & Snyder, P. (2018, October 23–26). *Constructing a coaching roadmap: Tips for collaborative goal setting and action planning* [Pre-conference workshop]. International Division for Early Childhood Conference. Orlando, FL. https://ca.embeddedinstruction.net

*Bishop, C. D., Snyder, P., & Crow, R. (2015). Impact of video self-monitoring with graduated training on implementation of embedded instruction learning trials. *Topics in Early Childhood Special Education, 35*(3), 170–182. https://doi.org/10.1177/0271121415594797

Borman, J., & Feger, S. (2006). *Instructional coaching: Key themes from the literature.* Brown University, The Education Alliance. https://www.brown.edu/academics/education-alliance/publications/instructional-coaching-key-themes-literature

Brock, M. E., & Carter, E. W. (2017). A meta-analysis of educator training to improve implementation of interventions for students with disabilities. *Remedial and Special Education, 38*(3), 131–144.

California Department of Education. (2010). *California preschool curricular frameworks.* https://www.cde.ca.gov/sp/cd/re/psframework.asp

California Department of Education. (2015). *Desired Results Developmental Profile.* https://desiredresults.us

California Department of Education and First 5 California. (2011). *California early childhood educator competencies.* California Department of Education. https://www.cde.ca.gov/sp/cd/re/documents/ececompetencies2011.pdf

*Conroy, M. A., Sutherland, K. S., Algina, J., Ladwig, C., Werch, B., Martinez, J., Jessee, G., & Gyure, M. (2019). Outcomes of the BEST in CLASS intervention on teachers' use of effective practices, self-efficacy, and classroom quality. *School Psychology Review, 48*(1), 31–45. https://doi.org/10.17105/SPR-2018-0003.V48-1

*Conroy, M. A., Sutherland, K. S., Algina, J., Werch, B., & Ladwig, C. (2018). Prevention and treatment of problem behaviors in young children: Clinical implications from a randomized controlled trial of BEST in CLASS. *AERA Open, 4*(1), 1–16. https://doi.org/10.1177/2332858417750376

*Conroy, M. A., Sutherland, K. S., Algina, J., Wilson, R., Martinez, J., & Whalon, K. (2015). Measuring teacher implementation of the BEST in CLASS intervention program and corollary child outcomes. *Journal of Emotional and Behavioral Disorders, 23,* 144–155. https://doi.org/10.1177/1063426614532949

Cooper, J. O., Heron, T. E., & Heward, W. L. (2007). *Applied behavior analysis* (2nd ed.). Merrill/Prentice Hall.

Council for Exceptional Children, Division for Early Childhood. (2017). *Initial specialty set: Early childhood special education/early intervention.* https://www.deccecpersonnelstandards.org

Crawford, A. D., Zucker, T. A., Williams, J. M., Bhavsar, V., & Landry, S. (2013). Initial validation of the prekindergarten classroom observation tool and goal setting system for data-based coaching. *School Psychology Quarterly, 28*(4), 277–300. https://doi.org/10.1037/spq0000033

Crow, R. (2017). *Nudge and boost for better living: Insights from behavioral sciences you can use everyday.* CreateSpace.

Crow, R., & Snyder, P. (1998). Organizational behavior management in early intervention: Status and implications for research and development. *Journal of Organizational and Behavior Management, 18*(2–3), 131–156. https://doi.org/10.1300/J075v18n02_07

Cusumano, D., & Preston, D. (2018, May). *Practice profile for coaching for AI hub module 1.7.* National Implementation Research Network. https://nirn.fpg.unc.edu/resources/coaching-practice-profile-0

Dalgarno, B., Gregory, S., Reiners, T., & Knox, C. (2016). Practising teaching using virtual classroom role plays. *Australian Journal of Teacher Education, 41*(1), 126–154. http://dx.doi.org/10.14221/ajte.2016v41n1.8

David, S., Clutterbuck, D., & Megginson, D. (2016). *Beyond goals: Effective strategies for coaching and mentoring.* Routledge.

DiGennaro, F. D., Martens, B. K., & Kleinmann, A. E. (2007). A comparison of performance feedback procedures on teachers' treatment implementation integrity and students' inappropriate behavior in special education classrooms. *Journal of Applied Behavior Analysis, 40*(3), 447–461. https://doi.org/10.1901/jaba.2007.40-447

digiCOACH, Inc. (2017). *digiCOACH.* http://www.digicoach.com/

Dimino, J. A., Taylor, M., & Morris, J. (2015). *Professional learning communities facilitator's guide for the What Works Clearinghouse practice guide: Teaching academic content and literacy to English learners in elementary and middle school* (REL 2015–105). U.S. Department of Education, Institute of Education Sciences, National Center for Education Evaluation and Regional Assistance, Regional Educational Laboratory Southwest. https://ies.ed.gov/ncee/edlabs/regions/southwest/pdf/REL_2015105.pdf

Division for Early Childhood. (2014). *DEC recommended practices in early intervention/early childhood special education 2014.* http://www.dec-sped.org/recommendedpractices

DuFour, R., DuFour, R., Eaker, R., Many, T. W., & Mattos, M. (2016). *Learning by doing: A handbook for professional learning communities at work* (3rd ed.). Solution Tree Press.

Dunst, C. J., & Trivette, C. M. (2012). Moderators of the effectiveness of adult learning method practices. *Journal of Social Sciences, 8*(2), 143–148. https://doi.org/10.3844/jssp.2012.143.148

Dunst, C. J., Trivette, C. M., & Hamby, D. W. (2010). Meta-analysis of the effectiveness of four adult learning methods and strategies. *International Journal of Continuing Education and Lifelong Learning, 3*(1), 91–112.

Durlak, J. A., & DuPre, E. P. (2008). Implementation matters: A review of research on the influence of implementation on program outcomes and the factors affecting implementation. *American Journal of Community Psychology, 41*(3–4), 327–350. https://doi.org/10.1007/1046400891650

Early Childhood Learning and Knowledge Center. (n.d.). *Professional development: Practice-based coaching.* https://eclkc.ohs.acf.hhs.gov/professional-development/article/practice-based-coaching-pbc

Early, D. M., Maxwell, K. L., Ponder, B. D., & Pan, Y. (2017). Improving teacher–child interactions: A randomized controlled trial of Making the Most of Classroom Interactions and My Teaching Partner professional development models. *Early Childhood Research Quarterly, 38*(1), 57–70. https://doi.org/10.1016/j.ecresq.2016.08.005

Eccles, M. P., Armstrong, D., Baker, R., Cleary, K., Davies, H., Davies, S., Glasziou, P., Ilott, I., Kinmonth, A., Leng, G., Logan, S., Marteau, T., Michie, S., Rogers, H., Rycroft-Malone, J., & Sibbald, B. (2009). An implementation research agenda. *Implementation Science, 4*, 18–25. https://doi.org/10.1186/1748-5908-4-18

Edelman, L. (2020, April). *Planning for the use of video conferencing for early intervention home visits during the COVID-19 pandemic*. https://ectacenter.org/~pdfs/topics/disaster/Planning_for_the_Use_of_Video _Conferencing_in_EI_during_COVID-19_Pandemic.pdf

Embedded Instruction for Early Learning. (2016). *Self-coaching orientation* [PowerPoint slides]. Anita Zucker Center for Excellence in Early Childhood Studies, University of Florida. http://embeddedinstruction.net

Embedded Instruction for Early Learning. (2018). *Example Action Plan*. Used with permission from the Anita Zucker Center for Excellence in Early Childhood Studies, University of Florida. https://embedded instruction.net/

Embedded Instruction for Early Learning. (2018). *Action plan fidelity checklist*. Used with permission from the Anita Zucker Center for Excellence in Early Childhood Studies, University of Florida. https://embedded instruction.net/

Escorcia, J., & Basler, S. (2019, May 22). *Reflection and feedback: Strategies for success*. https://eclkc.ohs.acf.hhs .gov/professional-development/article/coaching-corner-series

Fallon, L. M., Collier-Meek, M. A., Maggin, D. M., Sanetti, L. M., & Johnson, A. H. (2015). Is performance feedback for educators an evidence-based practice? A systematic review and evaluation based on single-case research. *Exceptional Children, 81*(2), 227–246. https://doi.org/10.1177/0014402914551738

Family Educational Rights and Privacy Act (FERPA) of 1974, PL 93-380, 20 U.S.C., §§ 1232g *et seq.* (1974). https://www2.ed.gov/policy/gen/guid/fpco/ferpa/index.html

Ferro, J., Fox, L., Binder, D., & von der Embse, M. (2020). *Equity coaching guide*. National Center on Pyramid Model Innovations. https://challengingbehavior.cbcs.usf.edu/docs/Equity-Coaching-Guide.pdf

Fettig, A., & Artman-Meeker, K. (2016). Group coaching on pre-school teachers' implementation of Pyramid Model strategies: A program description. *Topics in Early Childhood Special Education, 36*(3), 147–158.

Fixsen, D., & Blase, K. (2008). *The National Implementation Research Network*. University of North Carolina at Chapel Hill, Frank Porter Graham Child Development Institute. https://nirn.fpg.unc.edu/national -implementation-research-network

Fixsen, D. L., & Blase, K. A. (2008). Effective applications of innovations. Paper presented at the OASAS Meetings, New York State.

Fixsen, D. L., Blase, K. A., & VanDyke, M. K. (2019). *Implementation practice and science*. Chapel Hill, NC: Active Implementation Research Network.

Fixsen, D. L., Naoom, S. F., Blase, K. A., Friedman, R. M., & Wallace, F. (2005). *Implementation research: A synthesis of the literature*. University of South Florida, Louis de la Parte Florida Mental Health Institute, The National Implementation Research Network (FMHI Publication #231). https://nirn.fpg.unc.edu /sites/nirn.fpg.unc.edu/files/resources/NIRN-MonographFull-01-2005.pdf

Fox, L. (2017, April). *Supporting practitioners in their implementation of recommended practices: Using practice-based coaching*. http://ectacenter.org/~calls/2017/learninglab-supporting.asp

Fox, L., Dunlap, G., Hemmeter, M. L., Joseph, G. E., & Strain, P. S. (2003). The Teaching Pyramid: A model for supporting social competence and preventing challenging behavior in young children. *Young Children, 58*(4), 48–53. https://www.jstor.org/stable/42728957

*Fox, L., Hemmeter, M. L., Snyder, P., Binder, D. P., & Clarke, S. (2011). Coaching early childhood special educators to implement a comprehensive model for promoting young children's social competence. *Topics in Early Childhood Special Education, 31*(3), 178–192. https://doi.org/10.1177/0271121411404440

Fox, L., Veguilla, M., & Perez Binder, D. (2014). *Data decision-making and program-wide implementation of the Pyramid Model: Roadmap to effective intervention practices #7*. University of South Florida, Technical Assistance Center on Social Emotional Intervention for Young Children. https://files.eric.ed.gov/fulltext /ED577844.pdf

Frates, E. P., Moore, M. A., Lopez, C. N., & McMahon, G. T. (2011). Coaching for behavior change in physiatry. *American Journal of Physical Medicine & Rehabilitation, 90*(12), 1074–1082. https://doi.org/10.1097 /PHM.0b013e31822dea9a

Friedman, M. (2015). *Trying hard is not good enough: How to produce measurable improvements for customers and communities* (10th anniv. ed.). Parse Publishing.

Gallegos, A. M. (1979). Some critical issues for inservice education. *Journal of Teacher Education, 30*(1), 23. https://doi.org/10.1177/002248717903000110

Garet, M. S., Porter, A. C., Desimone, L., Birman, B. F., & Yoon, K. S. (2001). What makes professional development effective? Results from a national sample of teachers. *American Educational Research Journal, 38*(4), 915–945. https://doi.org/10.3102/00028312038004915

Gentile, A. (2006, April). *Professional development to support student achievement* [PowerPoint slides]. U.S. Department of Education. https://www2.ed.gov/admins/tchrqual/learn/nclbsummit/gentile/gentile.pdf

Grant, A. M. (2006). An integrative goal-focused approach to executive coaching. In D. Stober & A. M. Grant (Eds.), *Evidence based coaching handbook* (pp. 153–192). Wiley.

Grant, A. M. (2011). An integrated model of goal-focused coaching: An evidence-based framework for teaching and practice. *International Coaching Psychology Review, 7,* 146–165. https://www.beckforsland .com/wp-content/uploads/2016/06/Restoring-meaning-and-wholeness-—-the-role-for-coaching-after-a -trauma.pdf#page=8

*Greenwood, C. R., Abbott, M., Beecher, C., Atwater, J., & Petersen, S. (2017). Development, validation, and evaluation of Literacy 3D: A package supporting tier 1 preschool literacy instruction implementation and intervention. *Topics in Early Childhood Special Education, 37*(1), 29–41. https://doi.org /10.1177/0271121416652103

Gregory, J. B., Beck, J. W., & Carr, A. E. (2011). Goals, feedback, and self-regulation: Control theory as a natural framework for executive coaching. *Consulting Psychology Journal: Practice and Research, 63*(1), 26–38. https://doi.org/10.1037/a0023398

Griffiths, K. (2005). Personal coaching: A model for effective learning. *Journal of Learning Design, 1,* 55–65. https://doi.org/10.5204/jld.v1i2.17

Guskey, T. R. (2014). Measuring the effectiveness of educators' professional development. In K. L. Bauserman, & L. Martin (Eds.), *Handbook of professional development in education: Successful models and practices, PK–12* (pp. 447–466). Guilford Press.

Halle, T., Metz, A., & Martinez-Beck, I. (2013). *Applying implementation science in early childhood programs and systems.* Paul H. Brookes Publishing Co.

Haring, N. G., Lovitt, T. C., Eaton, M. D., & Hensen, C. L. (1978). *The fourth R: Research in the classroom.* Merrill.

Harris, B. M. (1980). *Improving staff performance through inservice education.* Allyn & Bacon.

Head Start National Center on Early Development, Teaching, and Learning, (2021). Program Leaders' Guide to Practice-Based Coaching, https://eclkc.ohs.acf.hhs.gov/document/program-leaders-guide -practice-based-coaching

Head Start National Center for Quality Teaching and Learning. (2014). Leadership academy: Applying practice-based coaching [PowerPoint slides].

Head Start/ECLKC: Early Childhood Learning and Knowledge Center. (n.d.). *Professional development: Practice-based coaching.* https://eclkc.ohs.acf.hhs.gov/professional-development/article/practice -based-coaching-pbc

Health Insurance Portability and Accountability Act (HIPAA) of 1996, PL 104-191, 42 U.S.C. §§ 201 *et seq* (1996).

Hemmeter, M. L., Fox, L., & Snyder, P. (2013). A tiered model for promoting social-emotional competence and addressing challenging behavior. In V. Buysse & E. Peisner-Feinberg (Eds.), *Handbook of response to intervention in early childhood* (pp. 85–101). Paul H. Brookes Publishing Co.

Hemmeter, M. L., Fox, L., & Snyder, P. (2014). *Teaching Pyramid Observation Tool (TPOT™) for preschool classrooms manual: Research edition.* Paul H. Brookes Publishing Co.

*Hemmeter, M.L., Fox, L., Snyder, P., Algina, J., Hardy, J.K., Bishop, C., & Veguilla, M. (2021). Corollary child outcomes from the Pyramid Model professional development intervention efficacy trial. *Early Childhood Research Quarterly, 54*(1), 204-218. https://doi.org/10.1016/j.ecresq.2020.08.004

Hemmeter, M. L., Hardy, J. K., & Basler, S. (2019, July). *Coaching conversations: Using constructive and supportive feedback to build practitioners' confidence and competence.* https://challengingbehavior.cbcs.usf.edu /Training/Webinar/archive/2019/07-10/2019-07-10_Coaching-Conversations.html

*Hemmeter, M. L., Hardy, J. K., Schnitz, A., Adams, J. M., & Kinder, K. A. (2015). Effects of training and coaching with performance feedback on teachers' use of Pyramid Model practices. *Topics in Early Childhood Special Education, 35*(3), 144–156. https://doi.org/10.1177/0271121415594924

Hemmeter, M. L., Ostrosky, M., & Fox, L. (2006). Social and emotional foundations for early learning: A conceptual model for intervention. *School Psychology Review, 35*(4), 583–601.

Hemmeter, M. L., Ostrosky, M., & Fox, L. (Eds.). (2021). *Unpacking the Pyramid Model: A practical guide for preschool teachers.* Paul H. Brookes Publishing Co.

Hemmeter, M. L., Snyder, P., & Fox, L. (2018). Using the Teaching Pyramid Observation Tool (TPOT) to support implementation of social-emotional teaching practices. *School Mental Health, 10,* 202–213. https:// doi.org/10.1007/s12310-017-9239-y

*Hemmeter, M. L., Snyder, P. A., Fox, L., & Algina, J. (2016). Evaluating the implementation of the Pyramid Model for promoting social-emotional competence in early childhood classrooms. *Topics in Early Childhood Special Education, 36*(3), 133–146. https://doi.org/10.1177/0271121416653386

*Hemmeter, M. L., Snyder, P., Kinder, K., & Artman, K. (2011). Impact of performance feedback delivered via electronic mail on preschool teachers' use of descriptive praise. *Early Childhood Research Quarterly, 26*(1), 96–109. https://doi.org/10.1016/j.ecresq.2010.05.004

Hojnoski, R. L., Caskie, G. I., Gischlar, K. L., Key, J. M., Barry, A., & Hughes, C. L. (2009). Data display preference, acceptability, and accuracy among urban Head Start teachers. *Journal of Early Intervention, 32*(1), 38–53. https://doi.org/10.1177/1053815109355982

Hojnoski, R. L., Gischlar, K. L., & Missall, K. N. (2009). Improving child outcomes with data-based decision making: Collect data. *Young Exceptional Children, 12*(3), 32–44. https://doi.org/10.1177/1096250609333025

Hord, S. (2004). *Learning together, leading together: Changing schools through professional learning communities.* Teachers College Press & NSDC.

Horner, R., Blitz, C., & Ross, S. W. (2014, September). The importance of contextual fit when implementing evidence-based interventions. *ASPE Issue Brief.* Office of Assistant Secretary for Planning and Evaluation, Office of Human Services Policy, US Department of Health and Human Services. https://aspe.hhs.gov/system/files/pdf/77066/ib_Contextual.pdf

Howes, C., Hamre, B. K., & Pianta, R. C. (2012). *Effective early childhood professional development: Improving teacher practice and child outcomes.* Paul H. Brookes Publishing Co.

*Hsieh, W. Y, Hemmeter, M. L., McCollum, J. A., & Ostrosky, M. M. (2009). Using coaching to increase preschool teachers' use of emergent teaching strategies. *Early Childhood Research Quarterly, 24*(3), 229–247. https://doi.org/10.1016/j.ecresq.2009.03.007

Institute of Medicine and National Research Council. (2015). *Transforming the workforce for children birth through age 8: A unifying foundation.* National Academies Press. https://doi.org/10.17226/19401

Intervention Central. (n.d.). *The instructional hierarchy: Linking stages of learning to effective instructional techniques.* https://www.interventioncentral.org/academic-interventions/general-academic/instructional-hierarchy-linking-stages-learning-effective-in

IrisConnect. (2020). https://www.irisconnect.com/us/

Jablon, J., Dombro, A. L., & Johnsen, S. (2016). *Coaching with powerful interactions: A guide for partnering with early childhood teachers.* National Association for the Education of Young Children.

Johnson, L. D. (2017). Scaling the Pyramid Model across complex systems providing early care for preschoolers: Exploring how models for decision making may enhance implementation science. *Early Education and Development, 28*(7), 822–838. https://doi.org/10.1080/10409289.2017.1286205

Johnson, L. D., Wehby, J. H., Symons, F. J., Moore, T. C., Maggin, D. M., & Sutherland, K. S. (2014). An analysis of preference relative to teacher implementation of intervention. *The Journal of Special Education, 48*(3), 214–224. https://doi.org/10.1177/0022466913475872

Johnson, S. R., Pas, E. T., & Bradshaw, C. P. (2016). Understanding and measuring coach–teacher alliance: A glimpse inside the "black box." *Prevention Science, 17*(4), 439–449. https://doi.org/10.1007/s11121-016-0633-8

Johnson, S. R., Pas, E. T., Bradshaw, C. P., & Ialongo, N. S. (2018). Promoting teachers' implementation of classroom-based prevention programming through coaching: The mediating role of the coach–teacher relationship. *Administration and Policy in Mental Health, 45*(3), 404–416. https://doi.org/10.1007/s10488-017-0832-z

Joyce, B., & Showers, B. (2002). *Student achievement through staff development* (3rd ed.). Association for Supervision and Curriculum Development.

Jung, L. A. (2007). Writing SMART objectives and strategies that fit the routine. *Exceptional Children, 39*(4), 54–58. https://doi.org/10.1177/004005990703900406

Kelly, B., & Perkins, D. F. (Eds.). (2014). *Handbook of implementation science for psychology in education.* Cambridge University Press.

Knight, J. (1999, April). *Partnership learning: Putting conversation at the heart of professional development* [Paper presentation]. American Educational Research Association, Montreal, Canada. https://www.instructionalcoaching.com/Research/Partnership-Learning/Partnership-Learning-AERA1999.pdf

Knight, J. (2007). *Instructional coaching: A partnership approach to improving instruction.* National Staff Development Council & Corwin Press.

Knight, J. (2009). What can we do about teacher resistance? *Phi Delta Kappan, 90*(7), 508–513. https://doi.org/10.1177/003172170909000711

Kosanovich, M., & Foorman, B. (2016). *Professional learning communities facilitator's guide for the What Works Clearinghouse practice guide: Foundational skills to support reading for understanding in kindergarten through 3rd grade* (REL 2016-227). U.S. Department of Education, Institute of Education Sciences, National Center for Education Evaluation and Regional Assistance, Regional Educational Laboratory Southeast. https://ies.ed.gov/pubsearch/pubsinfo.asp?pubid=REL2016227

Kraft, M. A., Blazar, D., & Hogan, D. (2018). The effect of teacher coaching on instruction and achievement: A meta-analysis of the causal evidence. *Review of Educational Research, 88*(4), 547–588. https://doi.org/10.3102/0034654318759268

Kretlow, A. G., & Bartholomew, C. C. (2010). Using coaching to improve the fidelity of evidence-based practices: A review of studies. *Teacher Education and Special Education, 33*(4), 279–299. https://doi.org/10.1177/0888406410371643

Kubina, R. M., Kostewicz, D. E., & Lin, F. Y. (2009). The taxonomy of learning and behavioral fluency. *Journal of Precision Teaching and Celeration, 25*(1), 17–28. https://celeration.org/wp-content/uploads/2020/05/2009_JPTC_V25.01_03.pdf

Kunemund, R.L., Kennedy, M.J., Carlisle, L.M., VanUitert, V.J., & McDonald, S.D. (2021). A multi-media option for delivering feedback and professional development to teachers. *Journal of Special Education Technology.* Advance online publication. https://doi.org/10.1177/01626434211004121

La Paro, K. M., Pianta, R. C., & Hamre, B. K. (2011). *Classroom Assessment Scoring System (CLASS™): Toddler manual.* Paul H. Brookes Publishing Co.

Leithwood, K. A., & Riehl, C. (2003). *What we know about successful school leadership.* National College for School Leadership. http://olms.cte.jhu.edu/olms2/data/ck/file/What_we_know_about_School Leadership.pdf

Lloyd, C. M., & Modlin, E. L. (2012, February). *Coaching as a key component in teachers' professional development: Improving classroom practices in Head Start settings.* OPRE Report 2012-4. Office of Planning Research and Evaluation, Administration for Children and Families, U.S. Department of Health and Human Services. https://www.acf.hhs.gov/opre/resource/coaching-as-a-key-component-in-teachers-professional -development

Lloyd, C. M., Supplee, L. H., & Mattera, S. K. (2013). An eye to efficient and effective fidelity measurement for both research and practice. In T. Halle, A. Metz, & I. Martinez-Beck (Eds.), *Applying implementation science in early childhood programs and systems* (pp. 139–155). Paul H. Brookes Publishing Co.

Lorio, C., Woods, J. C., & Snyder, P. (2021). An exploration of reflective conversations in early intervention caregiver coaching sessions. *Journal of Early Intervention.* Advance online publication. https://doi .org/10.1177/1053815121992132

Martin, G., & Hrycaiko, D. (1983). Effective behavioral coaching: What's it all about? *Journal of Sport and Exercise Physiology, 5*(1), 8–20.

McCollum, J. A., & Catlett, C. (1997). Designing effective personnel preparation for early intervention: The-oretical frameworks. In P. J. Winton, J. A. McCollum, & C. Catlett (Eds.), *Reforming personnel preparation in early intervention: Issues, models, and practical strategies* (pp. 105–125). Paul H. Brookes Publishing Co.

*McCollum, J. A., Hemmeter, M. L., & Hsieh, W. Y. (2011). Coaching teachers for emergent literacy instruc-tion using performance-based feedback. *Topics in Early Childhood Special Education, 33*(1), 28–37. https:// doi.org/10.1177/0271121411431003

McLaughlin, T., Denney, M. K., Snyder, P., & Welsh, J. L. (2012). Behavior support interventions imple-mented by families of young children: Examination of contextual fit. *Journal of Positive Behavior Interven-tions, 14*(2), 87–97. https://doi.org/10.1177/1098300711411305

McLeod, R., Artman-Meeker, K., & Hardy, J. K. (2017). Preparing yourself for coaching: Partnering for suc-cess. *Young Children, 72*(3), 75–81. https://www.jstor.org/stable/90013689

McLeod, R. H., Kim, S., & Resua, K. A. (2019). The effects of coaching with video and email feedback on preservice teachers' use of recommended practices. *Topics in Early Childhood Special Education, 38*(4), 192–203. https://doi.org/10.1177/0271121418763531

Metz, A., Halle, T., Bartley, L., & Blasberg, A. (2013). The key components of successful implementation. In T. Halle, A. Metz, & I. Martinez-Beck (Eds.), *Applying implementation science in early childhood programs and systems* (pp. 21–42). Paul H. Brookes Publishing Co.

Meyers, D. C., Durlak, J. A., & Wandersman, A. (2012). The quality implementation framework: A synthe-sis of critical steps in the implementation process. *American Journal of Community Psychology, 50*(3–4), 462–480. https://doi.org/10.1007/s10464-012-9522-x

Nagro, S. A., DeBettencourt, L. U., Rosenberg, M. S., Carran, D. T., & Weiss, M. P. (2017). The effects of guided video analysis on teacher candidates' reflective ability and instructional skills. *Teacher Education and Special Education, 40*(1), 7–25. https://doi.org/10.1177/0888406416680469

National Association for the Education of Young Children. (2020). *Professional standards and competencies for early childhood educators.* https://www.naeyc.org/resources/position-statements/professional-standards -competencies

National Association for the Education of Young Children (2020). *Professional Standards and Competencies for Early Childhood Educators.* NAEYC. Retrieved from https://www.naeyc.org/resources/position-state-ments/professional-standards-competencies

National Association for the Education of Young Children and the National Association of Child Care Resource and Referral Agencies. (2012). *Early childhood education professional development: Training and tech-nical assistance glossary.* NAEYC. https://www.naeyc.org/sites/default/files/globally-shared/downloads /PDFs/our-work/public-policy-advocacy/glossarytraining_ta.pdf

National Center for Pyramid Model Innovations (2018). Coaching. Challenging Behavior. https://challeng-ingbehavior.cbcs.usf.edu/Implementation/coach.html

National Center for Pyramid Model Innovations. (2020). *Pyramid Model: Implementing evidence-based promo-tion, prevention, and intervention practices in early care and education programs.* https://childcareta.acf.hhs .gov/sites/default/files/public/ncpmi_resource_guide_final_508_compliant.pdf

National Center for Systemic Improvement. (2014). *Effective coaching: Improving teacher practice and outcomes for all learners.* https://www.air.org/sites/default/files/NCSI_Effective-Coaching-Brief-508.pdf

National Center on Quality Teaching and Learning. (2014). *Program leaders' guide to practice-based coaching.* https://eclkc.ohs.acf.hhs.gov/document/program-leaders-guide-practice-based-coaching

National Center on Quality Teaching and Learning. (2015). *Practice-based coaching: Self-coaching.* U.S. Dept. of Health and Human Services, Administration on Children and Families, Office of Head Start, National Center on Quality Teaching and Learning. https://eclkc.ohs.acf.hhs.gov/sites/default/files/pdf/pbc-brief -self-coaching.pdf

National Center on Quality Teaching and Learning. (2020). *Practice-based coaching: Collaborative coaching partnerships*. https://eclkc.ohs.acf.hhs.gov/professional-development/article/practice-based-coaching-pbc

The National Center on Quality Teaching and Learning (NCQTL). (2021). Practice-based coaching: Top 10 Tips for Coaches [PDF file]. https://eclkc.ohs.acf.hhs.gov/sites/default/files/pdf/pbc-top-10-tips.pdf

National Professional Development Center on Inclusion. (2008). *What do we mean by professional development in the early childhood field?* FPG Child Development Institute, University of North Carolina. https://fpg.unc.edu/sites/fpg.unc.edu/files/resource-files/NPDCI_ProfessionalDevelopmentInEC_03-04-08.pdf

National Research Council. (2000). *How people learn: Brain, mind, experience, and school: Expanded edition*. National Academies Press. https://doi.org/10.17226/9853

National Research Council. (2015). *Transforming the workforce for children birth through age 8: A unifying foundation*. National Academies Press. https://www.nap.edu/catalog/19401/transforming-the-workforce-for-children-birth-through-age-8-a

Nguyen, Q. D., Fernandez, N., Karsenti, T., & Charlin, B. (2014). What is reflection? A conceptual analysis of major definitions and a proposal of a five-component model. *Medical Education, 48*(12), 1176–1189. https://doi.org/10.1111/medu.12583

Noell, G. H., Witt, J. C., Slider, N. J., Connell, J. E., Gatti, S. L., Williams, K. L., et al. (2005). Treatment implementation following behavioral consultation in schools: A comparison of three follow-up strategies. *School Psychology Review, 34*(1), 87–106.

O'Keefe, B. (2017, December). *Primetime for coaching: Instructional coaching in early childhood education.* Bellwether Education Partners. https://bellwethereducation.org/sites/default/files/Bellwether_ECECoaching_GHS_Final.pdf

Odom, S. L. (2009). The tie that binds: Evidence-based practice, implementation science, and outcomes for children. *Topics in Early Childhood Special Education, 29*(1), 53–61. https://doi.org/10.1177/0271121408329171

Office of Head Start. (2015). *Head Start early learning outcomes framework ages birth to five*. U.S. Department of Health and Human Services, Administration on Children and Families. https://eclkc.ohs.acf.hhs.gov/sites/default/files/pdf/elof-ohs-framework.pdf

Ottley, J. R., Coogle, C. G., & Rahn, N. L. (2015). The social validity of bug-in-ear coaching: Findings from two studies implemented in inclusive early childhood environments. *Journal of Early Childhood Teacher Education, 36*(4), 342–361. https://doi.org/10.1080/10901027.2015.1100146

Ottley, J. R., & Hanline, M. F. (2014). Bug-in-ear coaching: Impacts on early childhood educators' practices and associations with toddlers' expressive communication. *Journal of Early Intervention, 36*(2), 90–110. https://doi.org/10.1177/1053815114563614

Peterson, S. M. (2013). Readiness to change: Effective implementation processes for meeting people where they are. In T. Halle, A. Metz, & I. Martinez-Beck (Eds.), *Applying implementation science in early childhood programs and systems* (pp. 43–64). Paul H. Brookes Publishing Co.

Pierce, J. D. (2015). *Teacher–coach alliance as a critical component of coaching: Effects of feedback and analysis on teacher practice* [Unpublished doctoral dissertation]. University of Washington.

Powell, D. R., & Diamond, K. E. (2013). Studying the implementation of coaching-based professional development. In T. Halle, A. Metz, & I. Martinez-Beck (Eds.), *Applying implementation science in early childhood programs and systems* (pp. 97–116). Paul H. Brookes Publishing Co.

Rush, D. D., & Shelden, M. L. (2020). *The early childhood coaching handbook* (2nd ed.). Paul H. Brookes Publishing Co.

Sanetti, L. M. H., Collier-Meek, M. A., Long, A. C., Byron, J., & Kratochwill, T. R. (2015). Increasing teacher treatment integrity of behavior support plans through consultation and implementation planning. *Journal of School Psychology, 53*(3), 209–229. https://doi.org/10.1016/j.jsp.2015.03.002

Schachter, R. E. (2015). An analytic study of the professional development research in early childhood education. *Early Education and Development, 26*(8), 1057–1085. https://doi.org/10.1080/10409289.2015.1009335

Scheeler, M. C., Ruhl, K. L., & McAfee, J. K. (2004). Providing performance feedback to teachers: A review. *Teacher Education and Special Education, 27*(4), 396–407. https://doi.org/10.1177/088840640402700407

Seniuk, H. A., Witts, B. N., Williams, W. L., & Ghezzi, P. M. (2013). Behavioral coaching. *The Behavior Analyst, 36*(1), 167–172. https://doi.org/10.1007/bf03392301

Shaefer, J. M., & Ottley, J. R. (2018). Bug-in-ear as an evidence-based practice for professional development. *Journal of Special Education Technology, 33*(4), 247–258. https://doi.org/10.1177/0162643418766870

Shams, M. (2013). Communities of coaching practice: Developing a new approach. *International Coaching Psychology Review, 8*(2), 89–91.

Shannon, D., Bishop, C., Snyder, P., & Jaramillo, J. (2019). Developing a collaborative partnership to enhance teaming using a practice-based coaching framework. In P. J. Winton, C. Guillen, & A. Schnitz (Eds.), *Teaming and collaboration: Building and sustaining partnerships: DEC recommended practice monograph series No. 6* (pp. 39–53). Division for Early Childhood.

Shannon, D., Snyder, P., Hemmeter, M. L. & McLean, M. (2021). Exploring coach–teacher interactions within a practice-based coaching partnership. *Topics in Early Childhood Special Education, 40*(4), 229-240. https://doi.org/10.1177/0271121420910799

Shannon, D., Snyder, P., & McLaughlin, T. (2015). Preschool teachers' insights about web-based self-coaching versus on-site expert coaching. *Professional Development in Education, 41*(2), 290–309. https://doi.org /10.1080/19415257.2014.986819

Sheridan, S. M., Edwards, C. P., Marvin, C. A., & Knoche, L. L. (2009). Professional development in early childhood programs: Process issues and research needs. *Early Education and Development, 20*(3), 377–401. https://doi.org/10.1080/10409280802582795

Smith, M. W., Brady, J. P., & Anastasopoulos, L. (2008). *Early Language and Literacy Classroom Observation Tool, Pre-K (ELLCO Pre-K).* Paul H. Brookes Publishing Co.

Snyder, P. (2006). Best available research evidence: Impact on research in early childhood. In V. Buysse & P. W. Wesley (Eds.), *Evidence-based practice in the early childhood field* (pp. 35–70). Zero to Three.

Snyder, P. (2014). NCQTL Front Parch Series. Available at https://eclkc.ohs.acf.hhs.gov/video/supporting-quality-teaching-learning-conversation-about-professional-development.

Snyder, P. (2015). *A conversation about professional development.* Head Start Front Porch Broadcast Series. Head Start Early Childhood Learning and Knowledge Center. https://eclkc.ohs.acf.hhs.gov/school-readiness/article/front-porch-broadcast-series

Snyder, P., & Ayankoya, B. (2015). Revising the Division for Early Childhood recommended practices: When, who, and how. In A. Santos (Ed.), *DEC recommended practices monograph series No. 1: Enhancing services and supports for young children with disabilities and their families* (pp. 11–24). Division for Early Childhood.

Snyder, P., Bishop, C., & McLaughlin, T. (2017). Frameworks for guiding program focus and practices in early intervention. In J. M. Kauffman, D. P. Hallahan, and P. C. Pullen (Series Eds.) & M. Conroy (Section Ed.), *Handbook of special education: Section XII Early identification and intervention in exceptionality* (2nd ed., pp. 865–881). Routledge.

Snyder, P., Crowe, C., Hemmeter, M. L., Sandall, S., McLean, M., Crow, R., & Embedded Instruction for Early Learning Project. (2009). *EIOS: Embedded Instruction for Early Learning Observation System* [Unpublished instrument - manual and training videos]. University of Florida.

Snyder, P., Denney, M., Pasia, C., & Rakap, S., & Crowe, C. (2011). Professional development in early childhood intervention: Emerging issues and promising approaches. In C. Groark (Series Ed.) & L. Kaczmarek (Vol. Ed.), *Early childhood intervention: Shaping the future for children with special needs and their families: Vol. 3. Emerging trends in research and practice* (pp. 169–204). Praeger/ABC-CLIO.

Snyder, P., Hemmeter, M.L., Algina, J., Bishop, C., McLean, M., & Reichow, B. (2021). *Effects of professional development for embedded instruction on children's learning outcomes.* [Manuscript in preparation].

*Snyder, P., Hemmeter, M. L., Algina, J., Bishop, C., Shannon, D., & McLean, M. (2021). *Professional development effects on preschool teachers' implementation of embedded instruction practices.* [Manuscript in preparation].

Snyder, P. A., Hemmeter, M. L., & Fox, L. (2015). Supporting implementation of evidence-based practices through practice-based coaching. *Topics in Early Childhood Special Education, 35*(3), 133–143. https:/doi.org/10.1177/0271121415594925

Snyder, P., Hemmeter, M. L., & McLaughlin, T. (2011). Professional development in early childhood intervention: Where we stand on the 25th anniversary of P.L. 99-457. *Journal of Early Intervention, 33*(4), 357–370. https://doi.org/10.1177/1053815111428336

*Snyder, P., Hemmeter, M. L., McLean, M., Sandall, S., McLaughlin, T., & Algina, J. (2018). Effects of professional development on preschool teachers' use of embedded instruction practices. *Exceptional Children, 84*(2), 213–232. https://doi.org/10.1177/0014402917735512

Snyder, P., Hemmeter, M. L., & Shannon, D. (2021, July 19–22). *Contextual fit and practice-based coaching data-informed decision making (PBC-DIDM)* [Conference poster presentation]. 2021 OSEP Leadership and Project Director's Conference, Virtual. https://osepideasthatwork.org/osep-meeting/2021-leadership -and-project-directors-conference?tab=om-agenda

Snyder, P., Hemmeter, M. L., Meeker, K. A., Kinder, K., Pasia, C., & McLaughlin, T. (2012). Characterizing key features of the early childhood professional development literature. *Infants & Young Children, 25*(3), 188–212. https://doi.org/10.1097/IYC.0b013e31825a1ebf

Snyder, P., McLaughlin, T., Sandall, S., McLean, M., Hemmeter, M. L., Crow, R., & Scott, C., & Embedded Instruction for Early Learning Project. (2009). *LTRS: Learning Target Rating Scale: Manual.* [Unpublished instrument]. University of Florida, Gainesville.

Snyder, P., & McWilliam, P. J. (2003). Using the case method of instruction effectively in early intervention personnel preparation. *Infants and Young Children, 16*(4), 284–295. https://doi.org/10.1097/00001163 -200310000-00003

Snyder, P., Shannon, D., & Bishop, C., & McLean, M. (2021). *A model for coach professional development: Implementation and effects.* [Manuscript in preparation]. Anita Zucker Center for Excellence in Early Childhood Studies, University of Florida.

Snyder, P., Shannon, D., & McLean, M. (2019). *Embedded instruction California coach training* [PowerPoint slides and coach manual]. Anita Zucker Center for Excellence in Early Childhood Studies, University of Florida.

Snyder, P., & Wolfe, B. (2008). The big three process components in early childhood professional development: Needs assessment, follow-up, and evaluation. In P. Winton, J. McCollum, & C. Catlett (Eds.), *Practical approaches to early childhood professional development: Evidence, strategies, and resources* (pp. 13–51). Zero to Three.

Snyder, P., Woods, J., Reichow, B., Clark, C., & Romano, M. (2018, May). *Early Steps professional development: Supporting Part C providers to coach caregivers to enhance social-emotional outcomes for children with or at risk for disabilities* [Unpublished professional development workshop and coaching series]. University of Florida and Florida State University.

Solomon, B. G., Klein, S. A., & Plitylo, B. C. (2012). Effects of performance feedback on teachers' treatment integrity: A meta-analysis of single-case literature. *School Psychology Review, 41*(2), 160–175.

Speakworks, Inc. (2018). GoReact. https://get.goreact.com/

Stober, D. R., & Grant, A. M. (2006a). *Evidence based coaching handbook: Putting best practices to work for your clients.* Wiley.

Stober, D. R., & Grant, A. M. (2006b). Toward a contextual approach to coaching models. In D. R. Stober & A. M. Grant (Eds.), *Evidence based coaching handbook: Putting best practices to work for your clients* (pp. 355–365). Wiley.

Sutherland, K. S., Conroy, M. A., McLeod, B. D., Algina, J., & Wu, E. (2018). Teacher competence of delivery of BEST in CLASS as a mediator of treatment effects. *School Mental Health, 10,* 214–225. https://doi.org/10.1007/s12310-017-9224-5

Sweigart, C. A., Collins, L. W., Evanovich, L. L., & Cook, S. C. (2016). An evaluation of the evidence base for performance feedback to improve teacher praise using CEC's quality indicators. *Education and Treatment of Children, 39*(4), 419–444. https://doi.org/10.1353/etc.2016.0019

Teaching Pyramid Research Project. (2012). *The Teaching Pyramid teacher implementation guide—Guide 2: High quality environments* (2nd ed.) [Teacher implementation guide]. Teaching Pyramid Research Project: University of South Florida, University of Florida, & Vanderbilt University.

Thompson, M. T., Marchant, M., Anderson, D., Prater, M. A., & Gibb, G. (2012). Effects of tiered training on general educators' use of specific praise. *Education and Treatment of Children, 35*(4), 521–546. https://scholarsarchive.byu.edu/cgi/viewcontent.cgi?article=3070&context=facpub

Torsh, Inc. (2020). *Torsh: The most comprehensive platform for all your professional learning needs.* https://www.torsh.co/

Training and Professional Development, 45 C.F.R. § 1302.92 (2016). https://eclkc.ohs.acf.hhs.gov/policy/45-cfr-chap-xiii/1302-92-training-professional-development

Trivette, C. M., Dunst, C. J., Hamby, D. W., & O'Herin, C. E. (2009, March). Characteristics and consequences of adult learning methods and strategies. *Practical Evaluation Reports, 2*(1), 1–32. https://files.eric.ed.gov/fulltext/ED565253.pdf

University of Washington. (2020). *Coaching Companion overview.* College of Education, University of Washington. https://www.earlyedualliance.org/coaching-companion/

Vescio, V., Ross, D., & Adams, A. (2008). A review of research on the impact of professional learning communities on teaching practice and student learning. *Teaching and Teacher Education, 24*(1), 80–91. https://doi.org/10.1016/j.tate.2007.01.004

von der Embse, M., Nemec, A., Vorhaus, E., Fox, L., Ferro, J., Hemmeter, M. L., & Binder, D. (2019). *Program leadership team guide: Implementing practice-based coaching within the Pyramid Model.* https://challengingbehavior.cbcs.usf.edu/docs/LeadershipTeam_PBC_Guide.pdf

Wehby, J. H., Maggin, D. M., Partin, T. C. M., & Robertson, R. (2012). The impact of working alliance, social validity, and teacher burnout on implementation fidelity of the good behavior game. *School Mental Health, 4*(1), 22–33. https://doi.org/10.1007/s12310-011-9067-4

Whitehurst, G. (n.d.). *Dialogic reading: An effective way to read aloud to young children.* Reading Rockets. https://www.readingrockets.org/article/dialogic-reading-effective-way-read-aloud-young-children

Winton, P. J., McCollum, J. A., & Catlett, C. (Eds.). (2007). *Practice approaches to early childhood professional development: Evidence, strategies, and resources.* Zero to Three.

Winton, P. J., Snyder, P., & Goffin, S. (2016). Beyond the status quo: Rethinking professional development for early childhood teachers. In L. Couse & S. Recchia (Eds.), *Handbook of early childhood teacher education* (pp. 54–68). Routledge.

Wolf, M. M. (1978). Social validity: The case for subjective measurement or how applied behavior analysis is finding its heart. *Journal of Applied Behavior Analysis, 11*(2), 203–214. https://doi.org/10.1901/jaba.1978.11-203

Woods, J., Snyder, P. A., & Salisbury, C. (2018). Embedded practices and intervention with caregivers (EPIC): Linking instruction and family capacity-building recommended practices. In P. A. Snyder & M. L. Hemmeter (Eds.), *Instruction: Effective strategies to support engagement, learning, and outcomes: DEC Recommended Practices Monograph Series* (No. 4, pp. 145-158). Division for Early Childhood.

Wright, M. R., Ellis, D. N., & Baxter, A. (2012). The effect of immediate or delayed video-based self-evaluation on Head Start teaches' use of praise. *Journal of Research in Childhood Education, 26*(2), 187–198. https://doi.org/10.1080/02568543.2012.657745

Zaslow, M., Tout, K., Halle, T., Whittaker, J. V., & Lavelle, B. (2010). *Toward the identification of features of effective professional development for early childhood educators: Literature review.* U.S. Department of Education. https://www2.ed.gov/rschstat/eval/professional-development/literature-review.pdf

*References with asterisks in the reference list reflect reports found in Table 1.3. See also Chapter 1.

Index

Tables and figures are indicated by *f* and *t*, respectively.